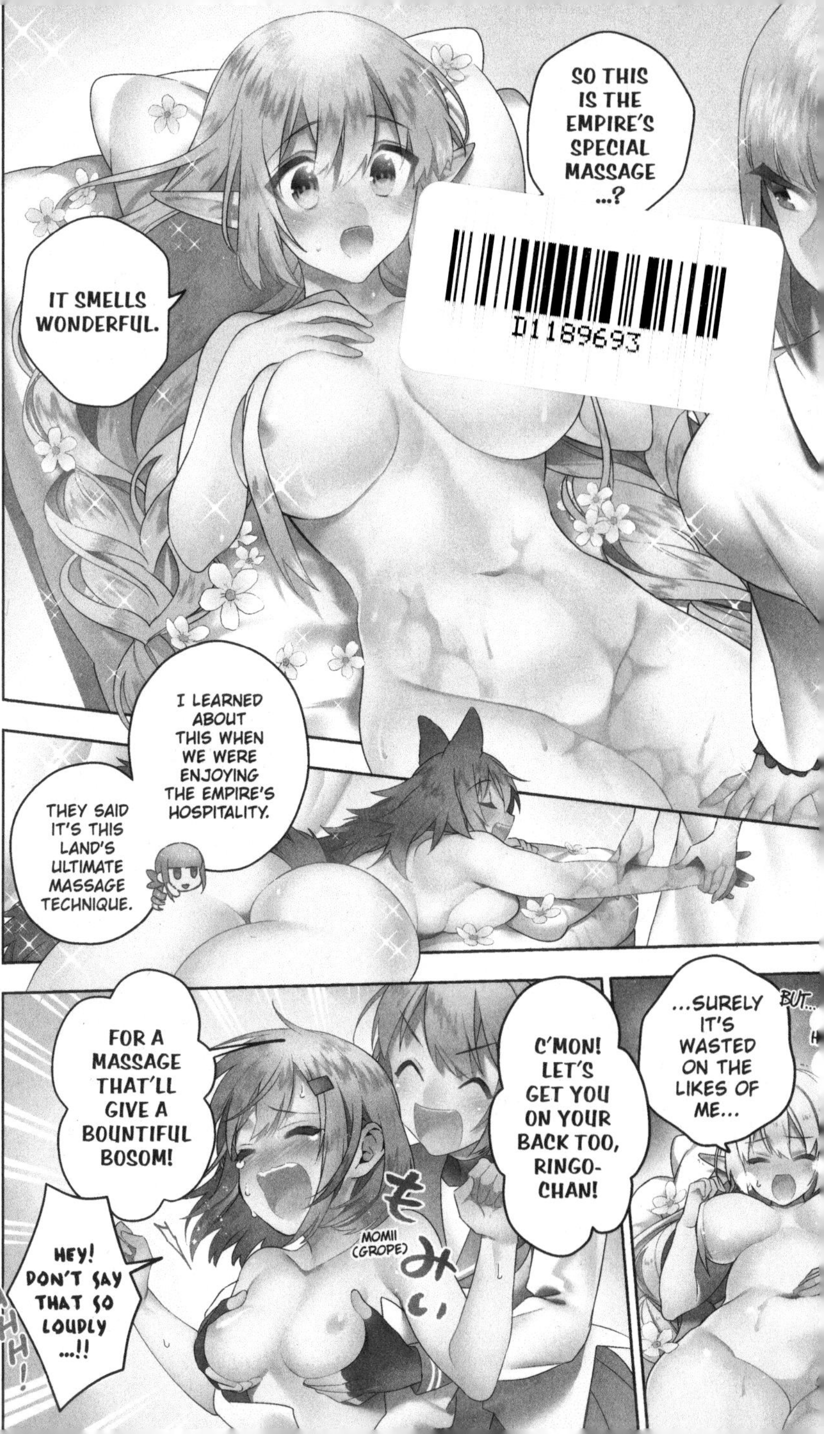
SO THIS IS THE EMPIRE'S SPECIAL MASSAGE ...?
IT SMELLS WONDERFUL.
I LEARNED ABOUT THIS WHEN WE WERE ENJOYING THE EMPIRE'S HOSPITALITY.
THEY SAID IT'S THIS LAND'S ULTIMATE MASSAGE TECHNIQUE.
BUT...
...SURELY IT'S WASTED ON THE LIKES OF ME...
C'MON! LET'S GET YOU ON YOUR BACK TOO, RINGO-CHAN!
FOR A MASSAGE THAT'LL GIVE A BOUNTIFUL BOSOM!
もみ
MOMII (GROPE)
HEY! DON'T SAY THAT SO LOUDLY ...!!
AHH!

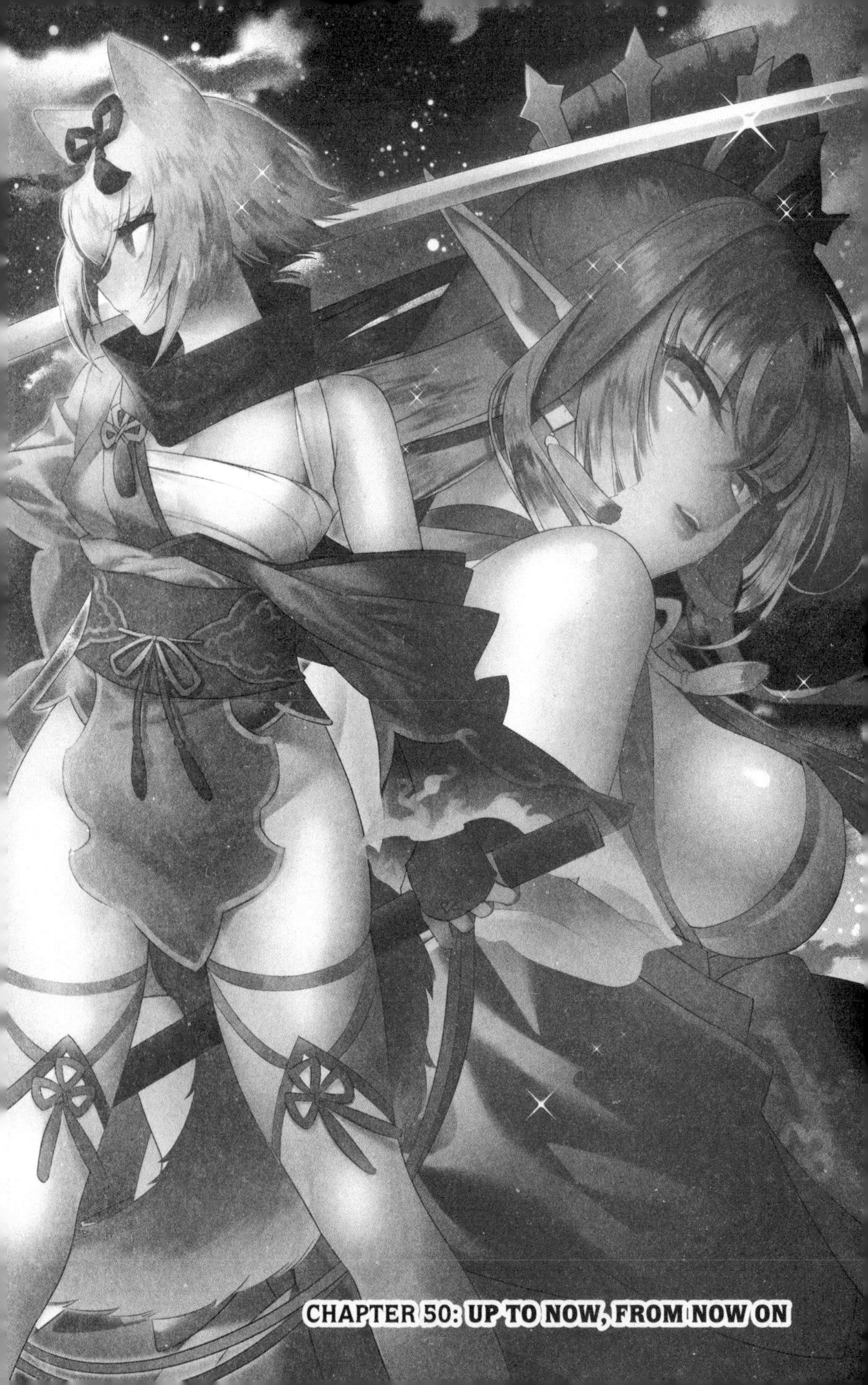

CHAPTER 50: UP TO NOW, FROM NOW ON

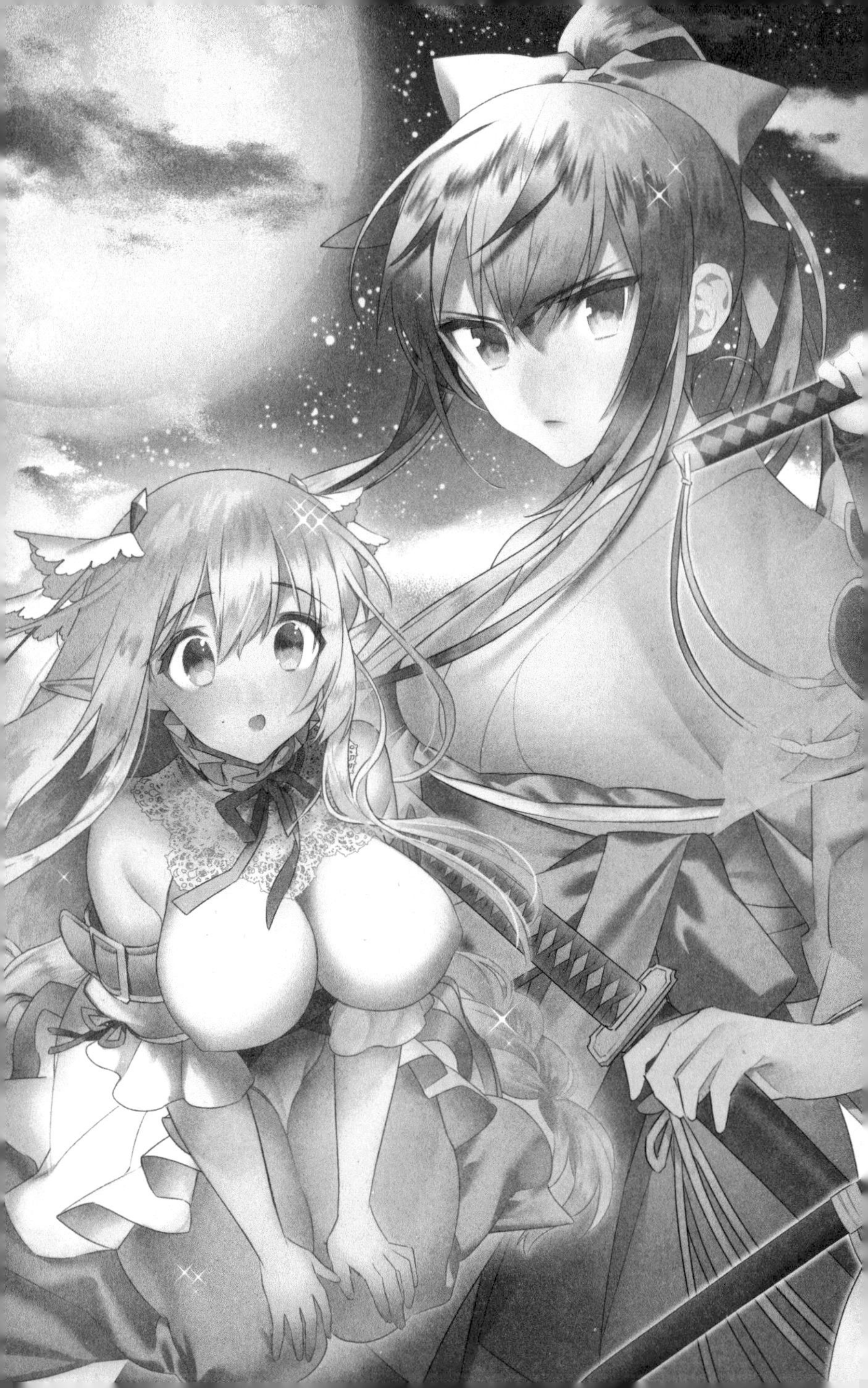

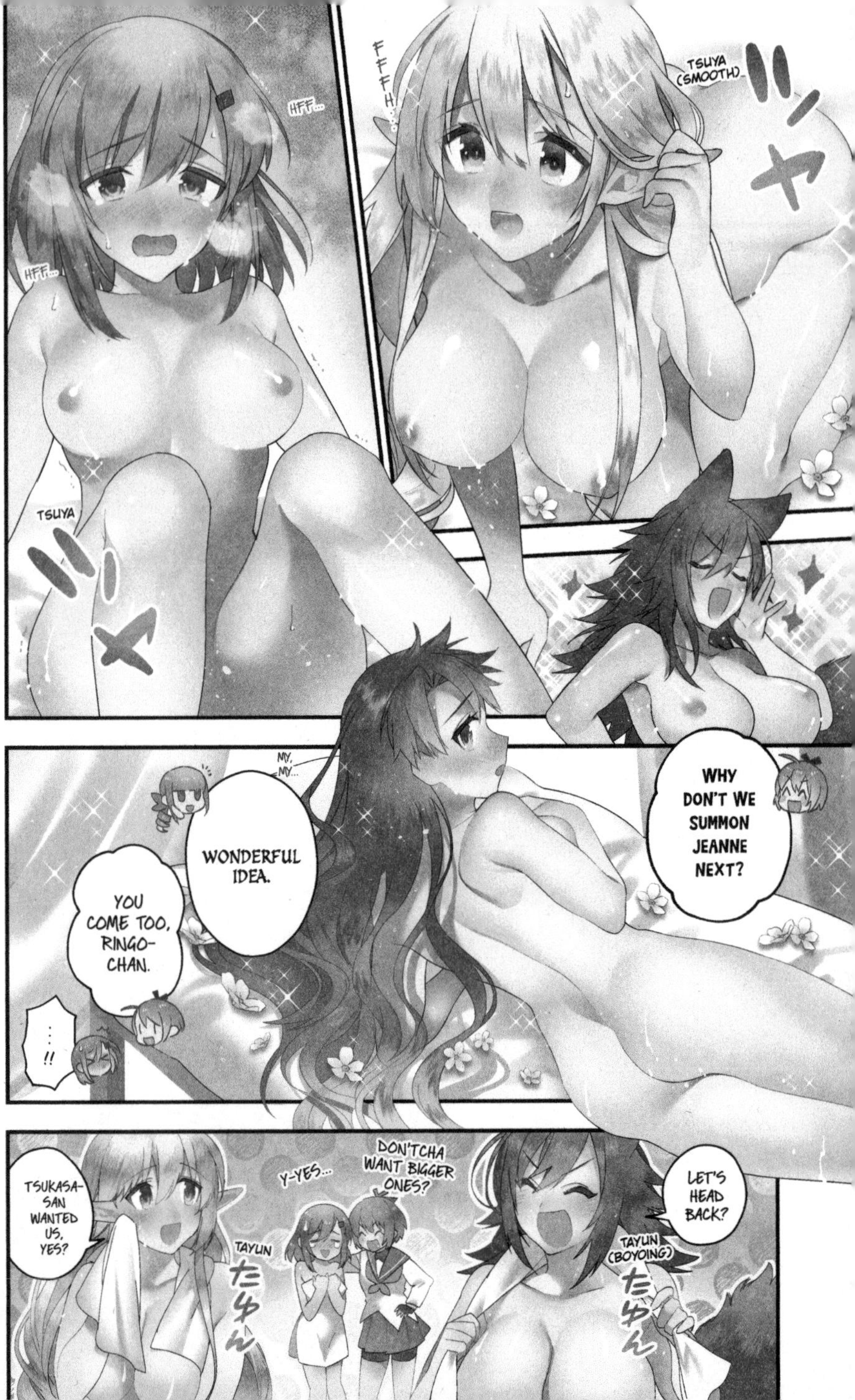

TSUYA (SMOOTH)
FFFH...
HFF...
HFF...
TSUYA
WHY DON'T WE SUMMON JEANNE NEXT?
MY, MY...
WONDERFUL IDEA.
YOU COME TOO, RINGO-CHAN.
...!!
LET'S HEAD BACK?
TAYUN (BOYOING)
たゆん
DON'TCHA WANT BIGGER ONES?
Y-YES...
TAYUN
たゆん
TSUKASA-SAN WANTED US, YES?

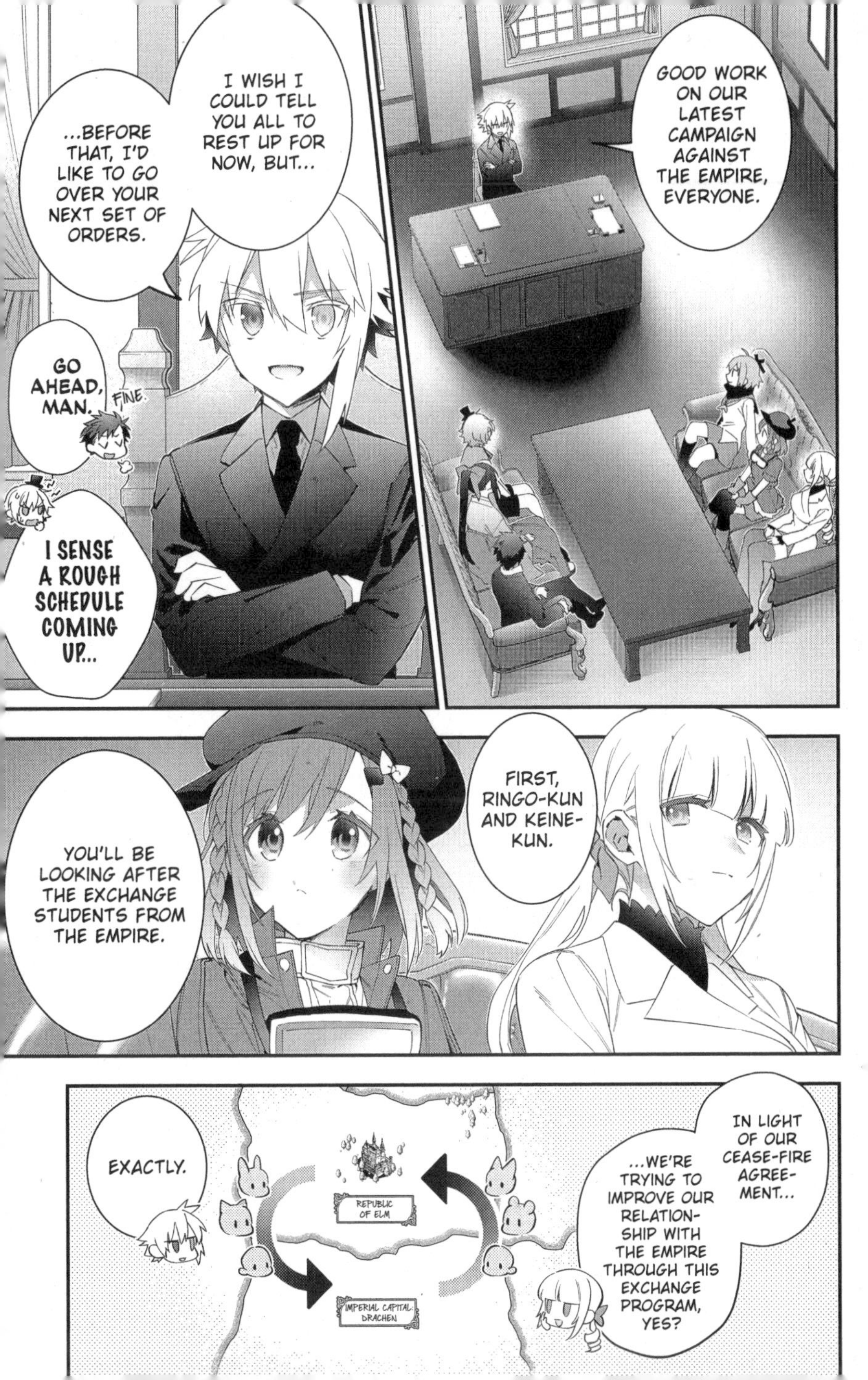
GOOD WORK ON OUR LATEST CAMPAIGN AGAINST THE EMPIRE, EVERYONE.
I WISH I COULD TELL YOU ALL TO REST UP FOR NOW, BUT...
...BEFORE THAT, I'D LIKE TO GO OVER YOUR NEXT SET OF ORDERS.
GO AHEAD, MAN.
FINE.
I SENSE A ROUGH SCHEDULE COMING UP...
FIRST, RINGO-KUN AND KEINE-KUN.
YOU'LL BE LOOKING AFTER THE EXCHANGE STUDENTS FROM THE EMPIRE.
IN LIGHT OF OUR CEASE-FIRE AGREE-MENT...
...WE'RE TRYING TO IMPROVE OUR RELATION-SHIP WITH THE EMPIRE THROUGH THIS EXCHANGE PROGRAM, YES?
REPUBLIC OF ELM
IMPERIAL CAPITAL DRACHEN
EXACTLY.

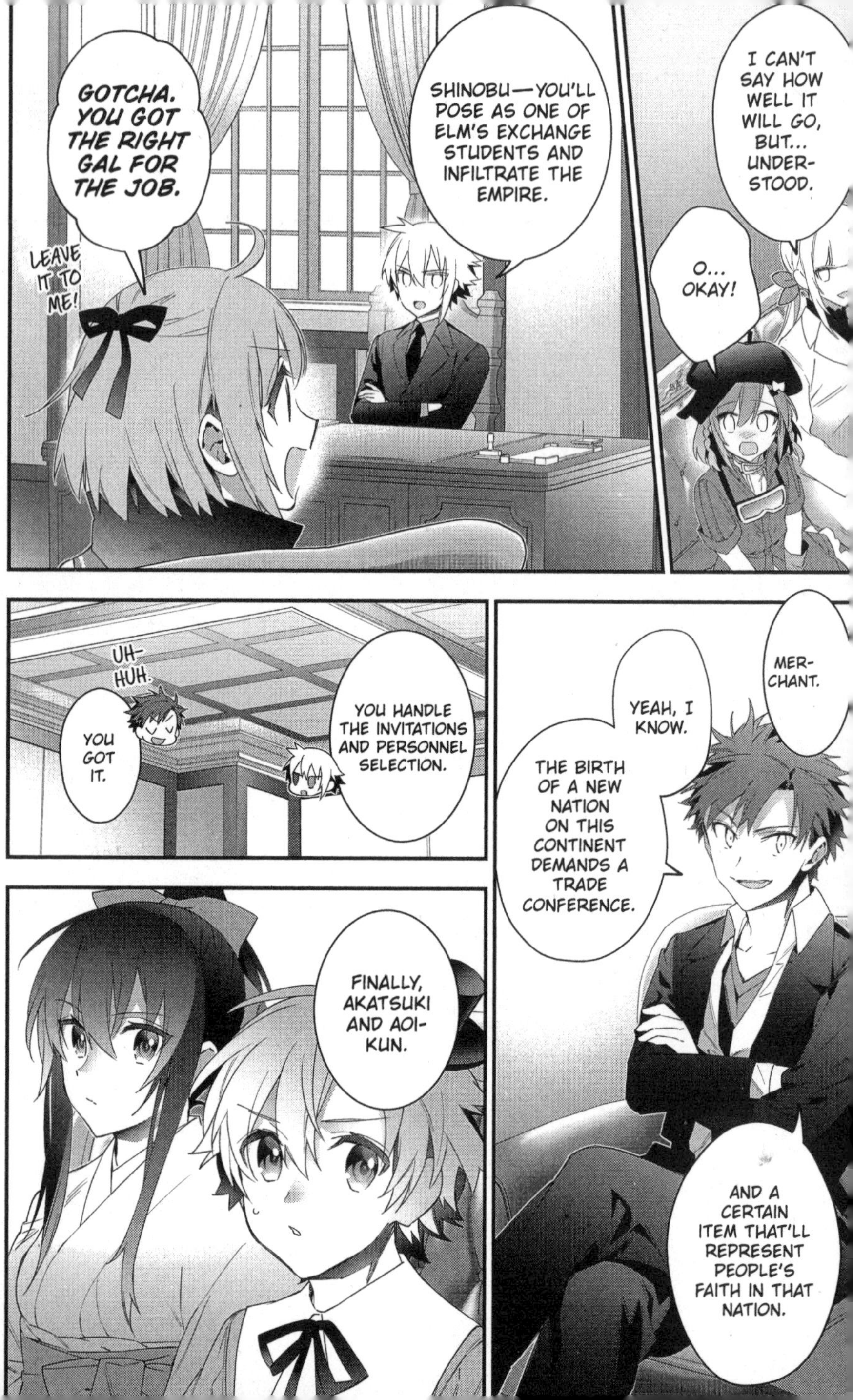
I CAN'T SAY HOW WELL IT WILL GO, BUT... UNDER-STOOD.
O... OKAY!
SHINOBU—YOU'LL POSE AS ONE OF ELM'S EXCHANGE STUDENTS AND INFILTRATE THE EMPIRE.
GOTCHA. YOU GOT THE RIGHT GAL FOR THE JOB.
LEAVE IT TO ME!
MER-CHANT.
YEAH, I KNOW.
THE BIRTH OF A NEW NATION ON THIS CONTINENT DEMANDS A TRADE CONFERENCE.
AND A CERTAIN ITEM THAT'LL REPRESENT PEOPLE'S FAITH IN THAT NATION.
YOU HANDLE THE INVITATIONS AND PERSONNEL SELECTION.
UH-HUH.
YOU GOT IT.
FINALLY, AKATSUKI AND AOI-KUN.

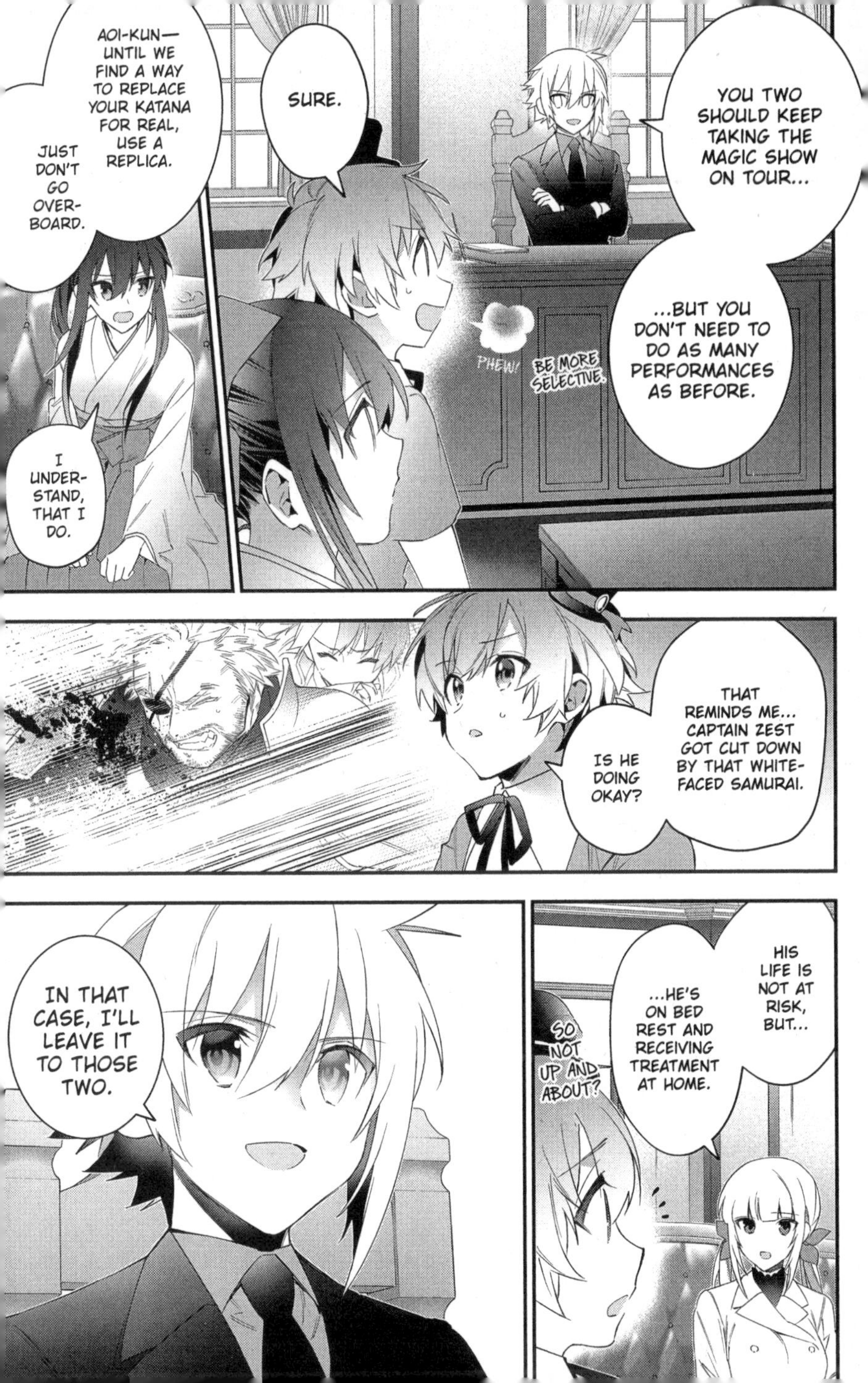
YOU TWO SHOULD KEEP TAKING THE MAGIC SHOW ON TOUR...
...BUT YOU DON'T NEED TO DO AS MANY PERFORMANCES AS BEFORE.
BE MORE SELECTIVE.
PHEW!
SURE.
AOI-KUN—UNTIL WE FIND A WAY TO REPLACE YOUR KATANA FOR REAL, USE A REPLICA.
JUST DON'T GO OVER-BOARD.
I UNDER-STAND, THAT I DO.
THAT REMINDS ME... CAPTAIN ZEST GOT CUT DOWN BY THAT WHITE-FACED SAMURAI.
IS HE DOING OKAY?
HIS LIFE IS NOT AT RISK, BUT...
...HE'S ON BED REST AND RECEIVING TREATMENT AT HOME.
SO NOT UP AND ABOUT?
IN THAT CASE, I'LL LEAVE IT TO THOSE TWO.

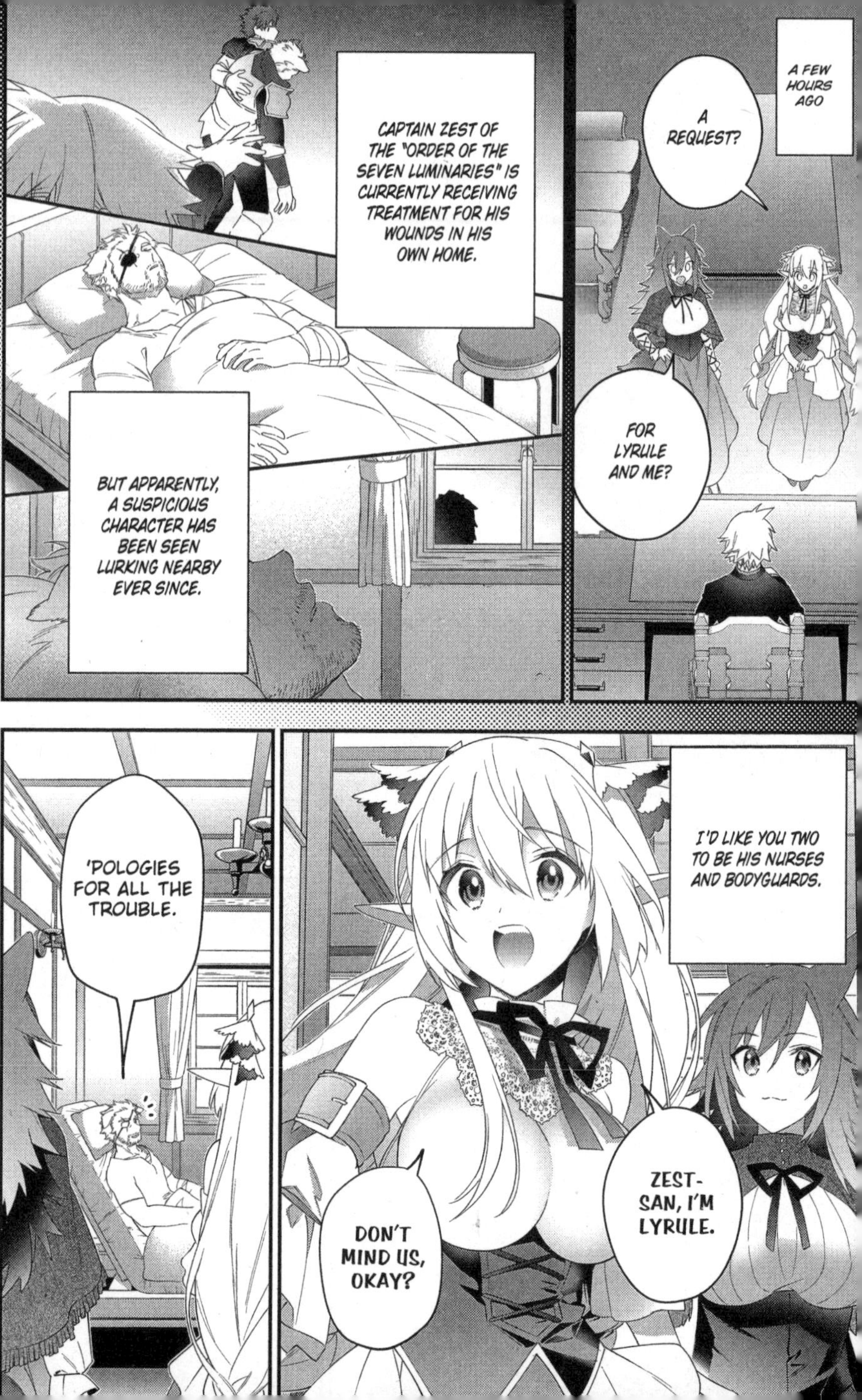
A FEW HOURS AGO
A REQUEST?
FOR LYRULE AND ME?
CAPTAIN ZEST OF THE "ORDER OF THE SEVEN LUMINARIES" IS CURRENTLY RECEIVING TREATMENT FOR HIS WOUNDS IN HIS OWN HOME.
BUT APPARENTLY, A SUSPICIOUS CHARACTER HAS BEEN SEEN LURKING NEARBY EVER SINCE.
I'D LIKE YOU TWO TO BE HIS NURSES AND BODYGUARDS.
ZEST-SAN, I'M LYRULE.
DON'T MIND US, OKAY?
'POLOGIES FOR ALL THE TROUBLE.

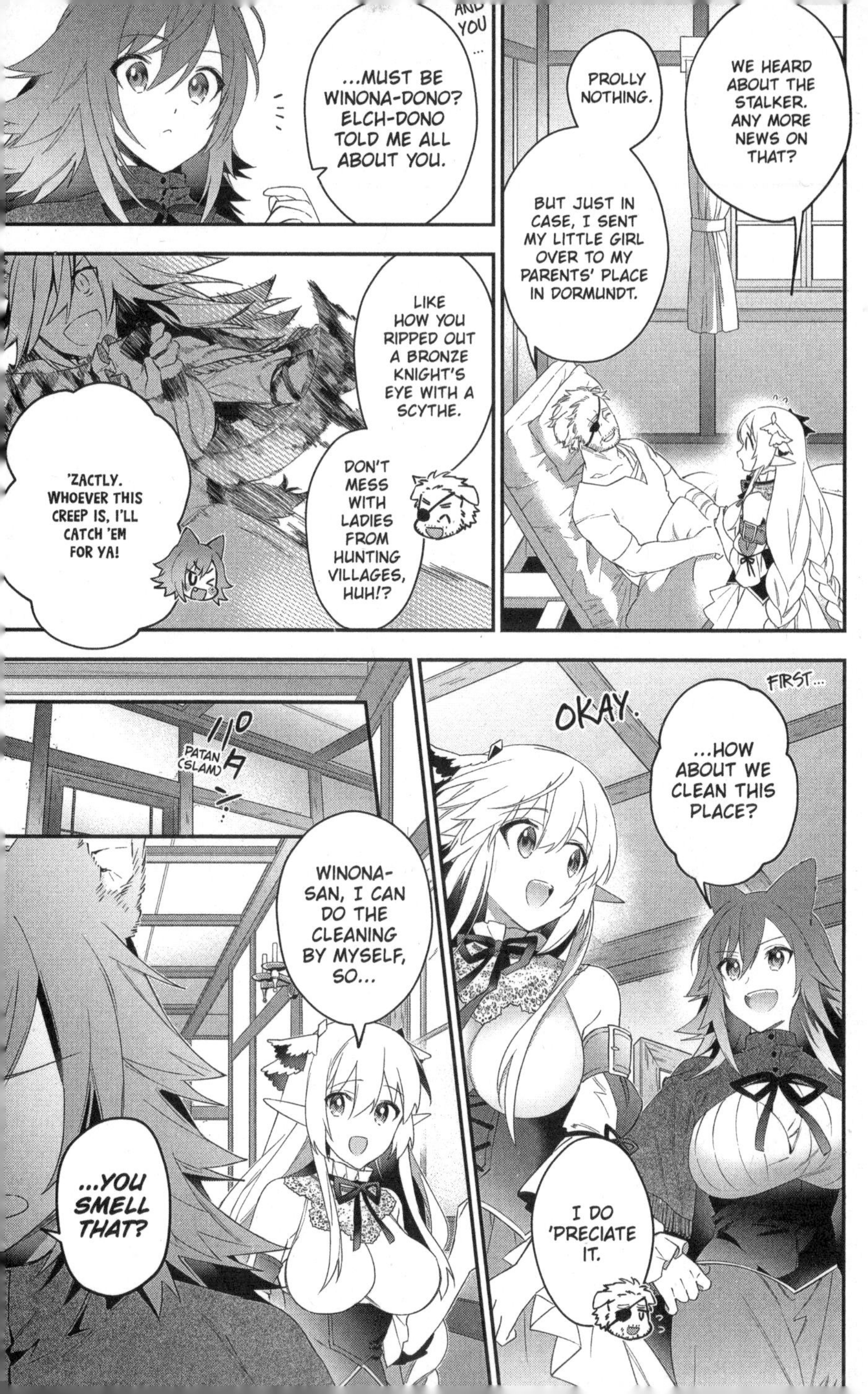
WE HEARD ABOUT THE STALKER. ANY MORE NEWS ON THAT?
PROLLY NOTHING.
BUT JUST IN CASE, I SENT MY LITTLE GIRL OVER TO MY PARENTS' PLACE IN DORMUNDT.
AND YOU...
...MUST BE WINONA-DONO? ELCH-DONO TOLD ME ALL ABOUT YOU.
LIKE HOW YOU RIPPED OUT A BRONZE KNIGHT'S EYE WITH A SCYTHE.
DON'T MESS WITH LADIES FROM HUNTING VILLAGES, HUH!?
'ZACTLY. WHOEVER THIS CREEP IS, I'LL CATCH 'EM FOR YA!
FIRST...
...HOW ABOUT WE CLEAN THIS PLACE?
OKAY.
I DO 'PRECIATE IT.
PATAN (SLAM)
WINONA-SAN, I CAN DO THE CLEANING BY MYSELF, SO...
...YOU SMELL THAT?

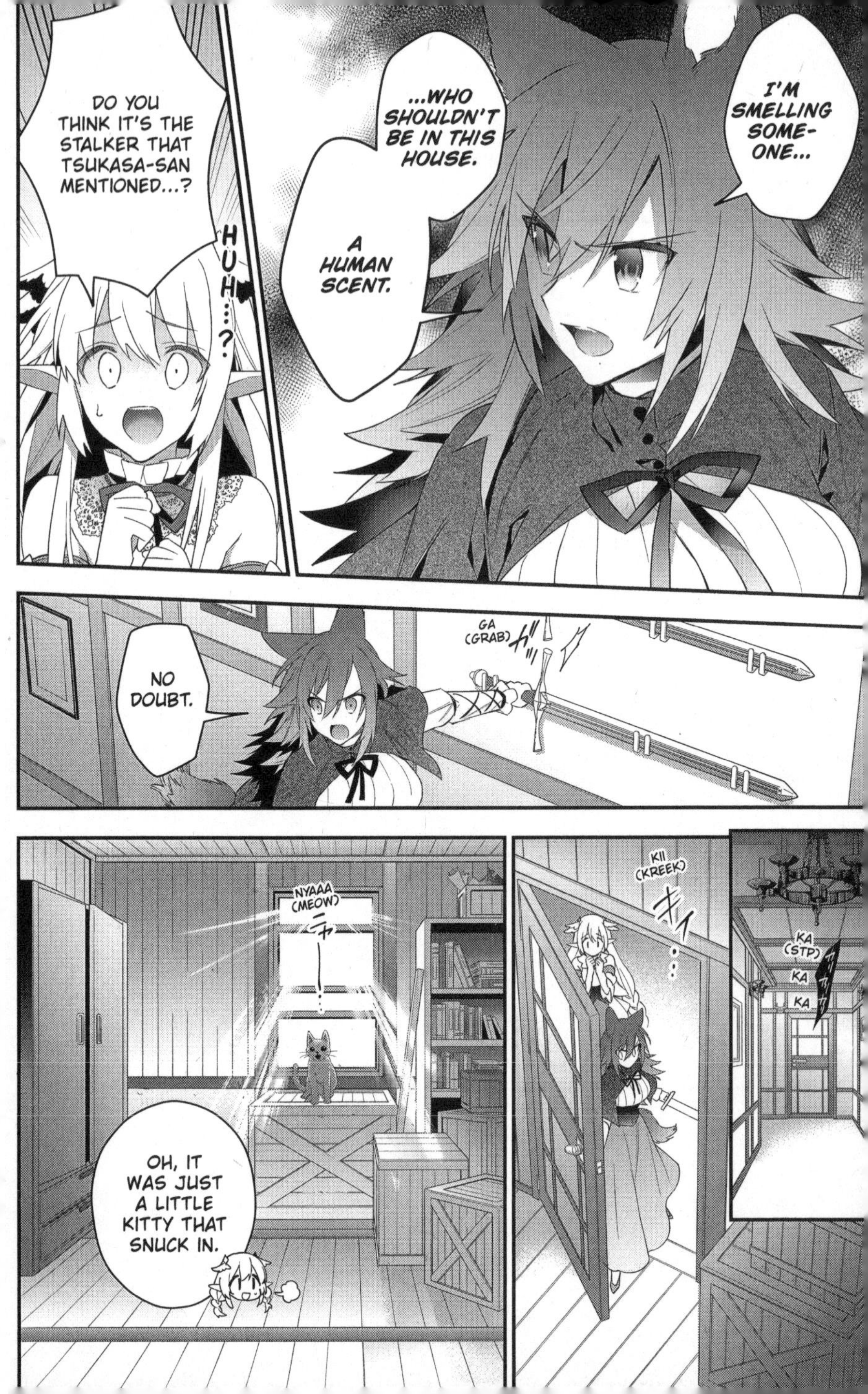
I'M SMELLING SOME-ONE...
...WHO SHOULDN'T BE IN THIS HOUSE.
A HUMAN SCENT.
DO YOU THINK IT'S THE STALKER THAT TSUKASA-SAN MENTIONED...?
HUH...?
GA (GRAB)
NO DOUBT.
KA (STP) KA KA
KII (KREEK)
NYAAA (MEOW)
OH, IT WAS JUST A LITTLE KITTY THAT SNUCK IN.

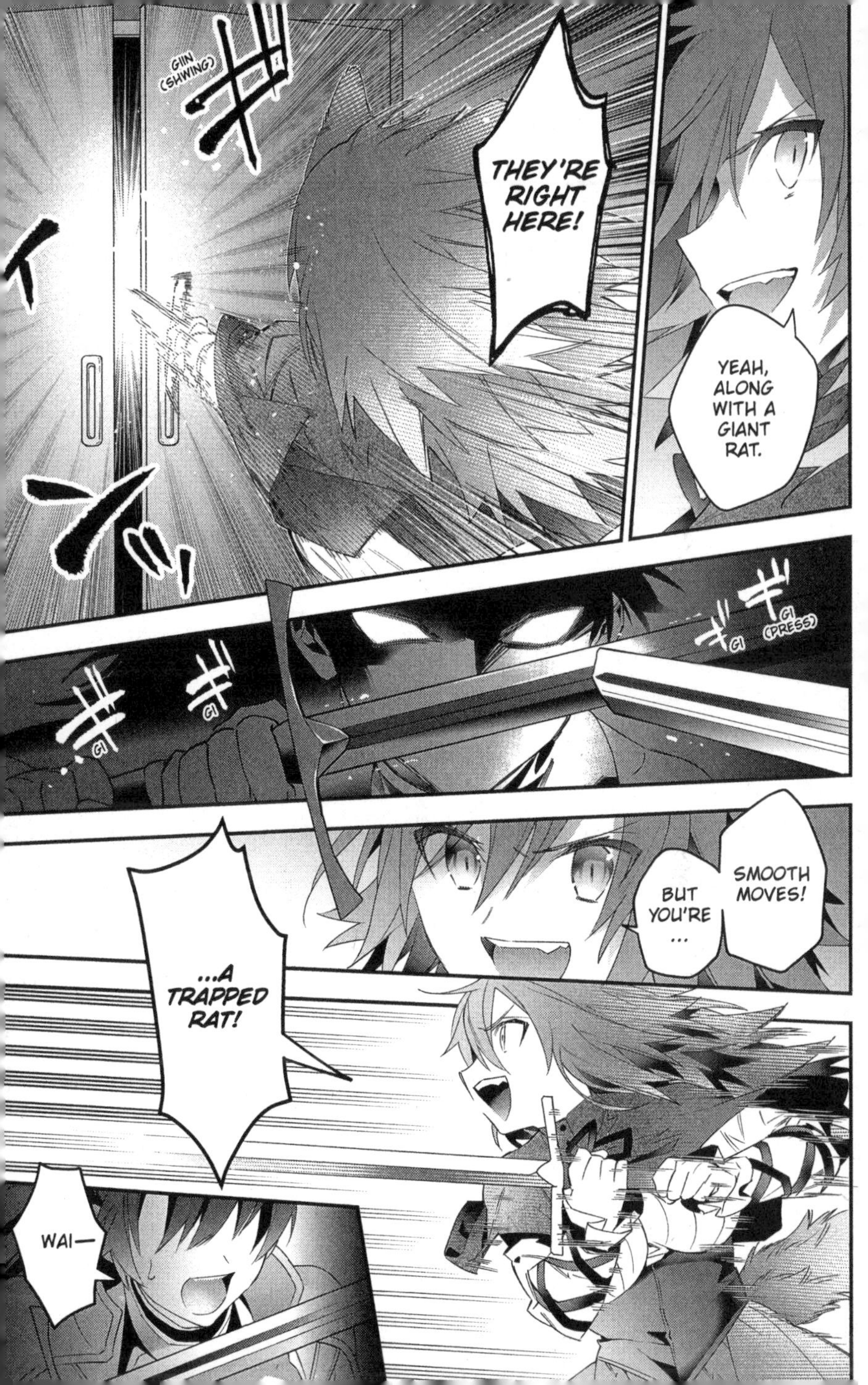
YEAH, ALONG WITH A GIANT RAT.
GIIN (SHWING)
THEY'RE RIGHT HERE!
GI (PRESS)
GI
GI
GI
SMOOTH MOVES!
BUT YOU'RE ...
...A TRAPPED RAT!
WAI—

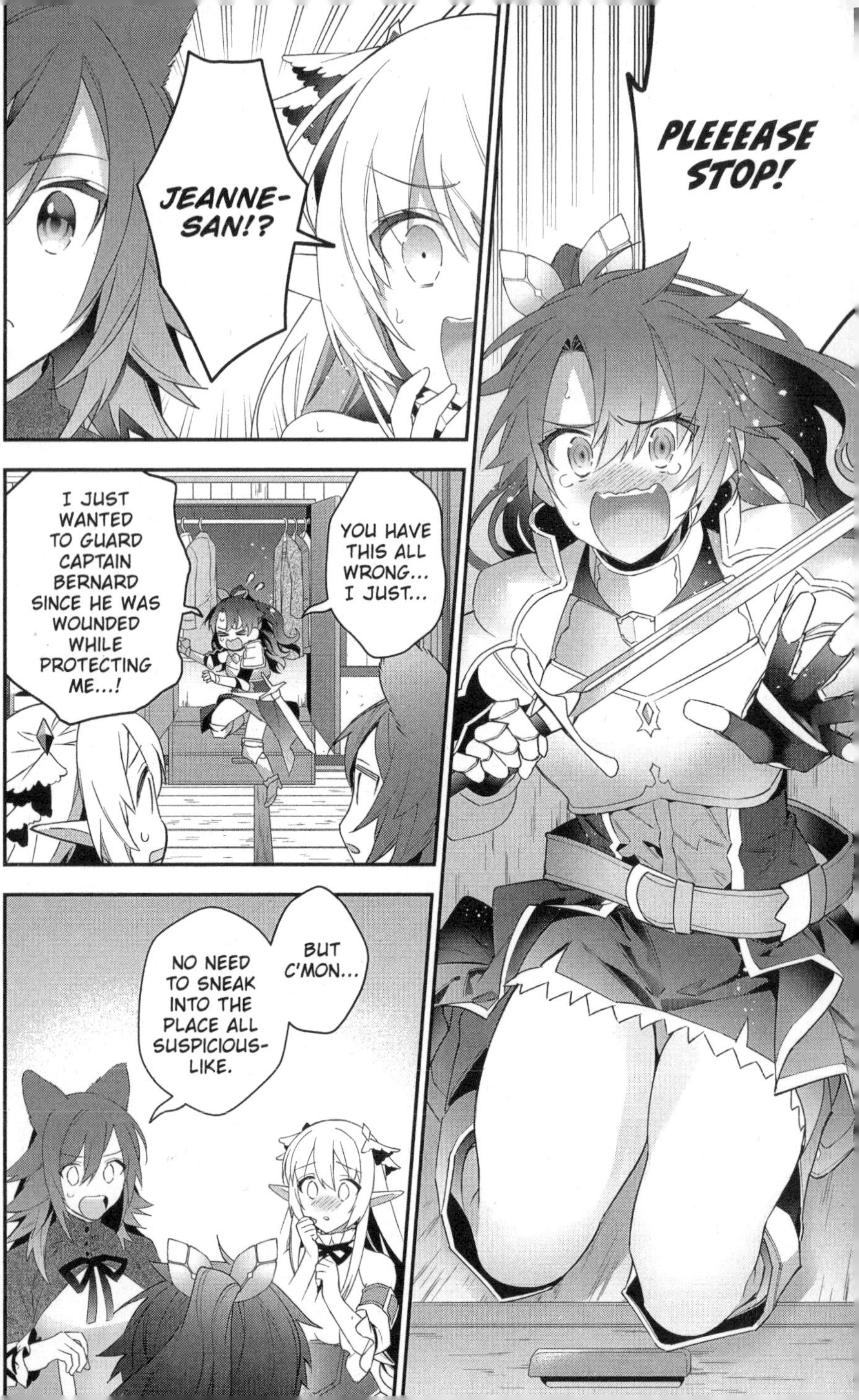
PLEEEASE STOP!
JEANNE-SAN!?
YOU HAVE THIS ALL WRONG... I JUST...
I JUST WANTED TO GUARD CAPTAIN BERNARD SINCE HE WAS WOUNDED WHILE PROTECTING ME...!
BUT C'MON...
NO NEED TO SNEAK INTO THE PLACE ALL SUSPICIOUS-LIKE.

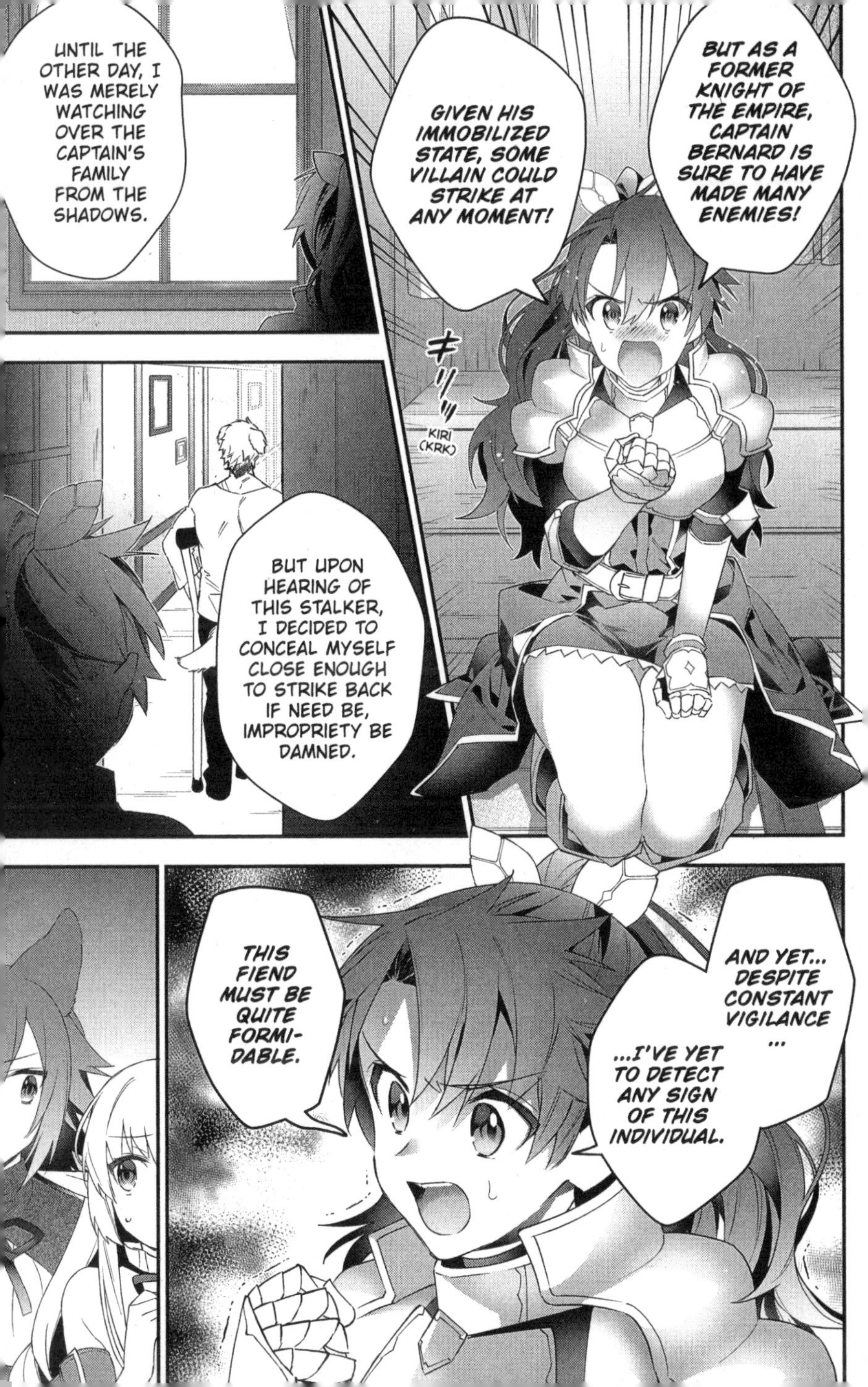
BUT AS A FORMER KNIGHT OF THE EMPIRE, CAPTAIN BERNARD IS SURE TO HAVE MADE MANY ENEMIES!
GIVEN HIS IMMOBILIZED STATE, SOME VILLAIN COULD STRIKE AT ANY MOMENT!
キリッ
KIRI (KRK)
UNTIL THE OTHER DAY, I WAS MERELY WATCHING OVER THE CAPTAIN'S FAMILY FROM THE SHADOWS.
BUT UPON HEARING OF THIS STALKER, I DECIDED TO CONCEAL MYSELF CLOSE ENOUGH TO STRIKE BACK IF NEED BE, IMPROPRIETY BE DAMNED.
AND YET... DESPITE CONSTANT VIGILANCE ...
...I'VE YET TO DETECT ANY SIGN OF THIS INDIVIDUAL.
THIS FIEND MUST BE QUITE FORMI-DABLE.

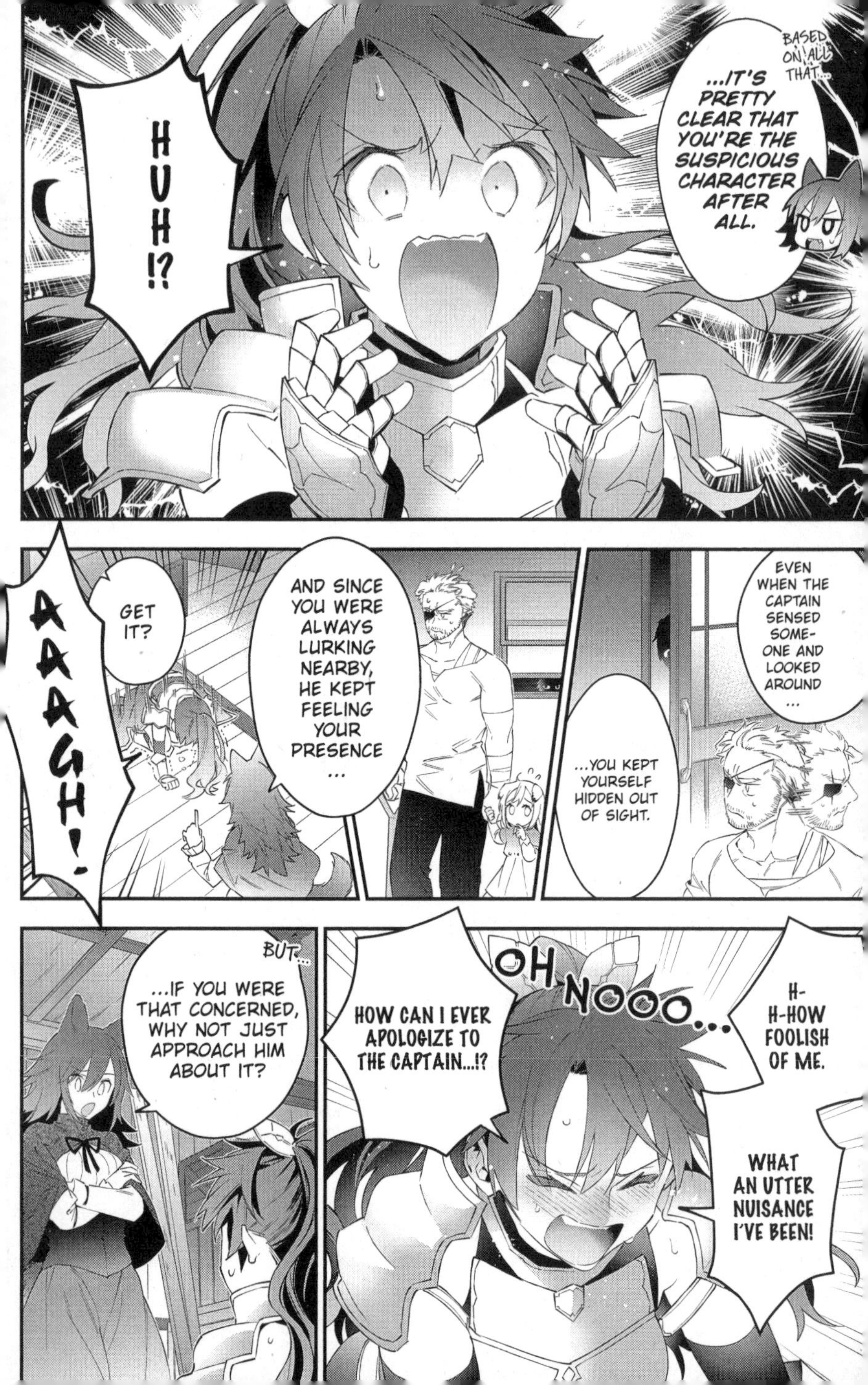
BASED ON ALL THAT...
...IT'S PRETTY CLEAR THAT YOU'RE THE SUSPICIOUS CHARACTER AFTER ALL.
HUH!?
EVEN WHEN THE CAPTAIN SENSED SOME-ONE AND LOOKED AROUND...
...YOU KEPT YOURSELF HIDDEN OUT OF SIGHT.
AND SINCE YOU WERE ALWAYS LURKING NEARBY, HE KEPT FEELING YOUR PRESENCE...
GET IT?
AAAGH!
H- H-HOW FOOLISH OF ME.
WHAT AN UTTER NUISANCE I'VE BEEN!
OH NOOO...
HOW CAN I EVER APOLOGIZE TO THE CAPTAIN...!?
BUT...
...IF YOU WERE THAT CONCERNED, WHY NOT JUST APPROACH HIM ABOUT IT?

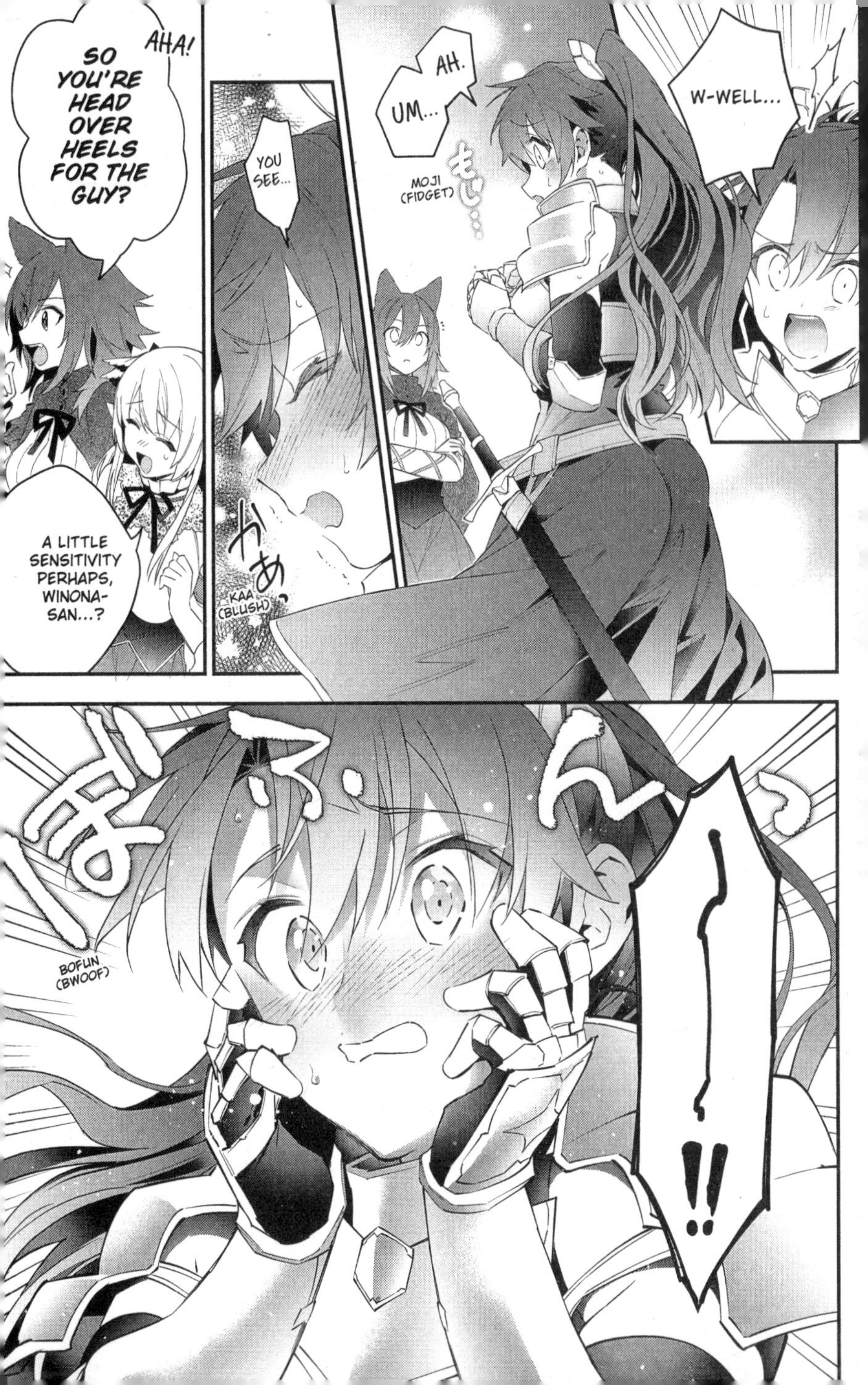
W-WELL...
AH.
UM...
もじ・・・
MOJI (FIDGET)
YOU SEE...
かあ、
KAA (BLUSH)
AHA!
SO YOU'RE HEAD OVER HEELS FOR THE GUY?
A LITTLE SENSITIVITY PERHAPS, WINONA-SAN...?
ぼふん
BOFUN (BWOOF)
!!

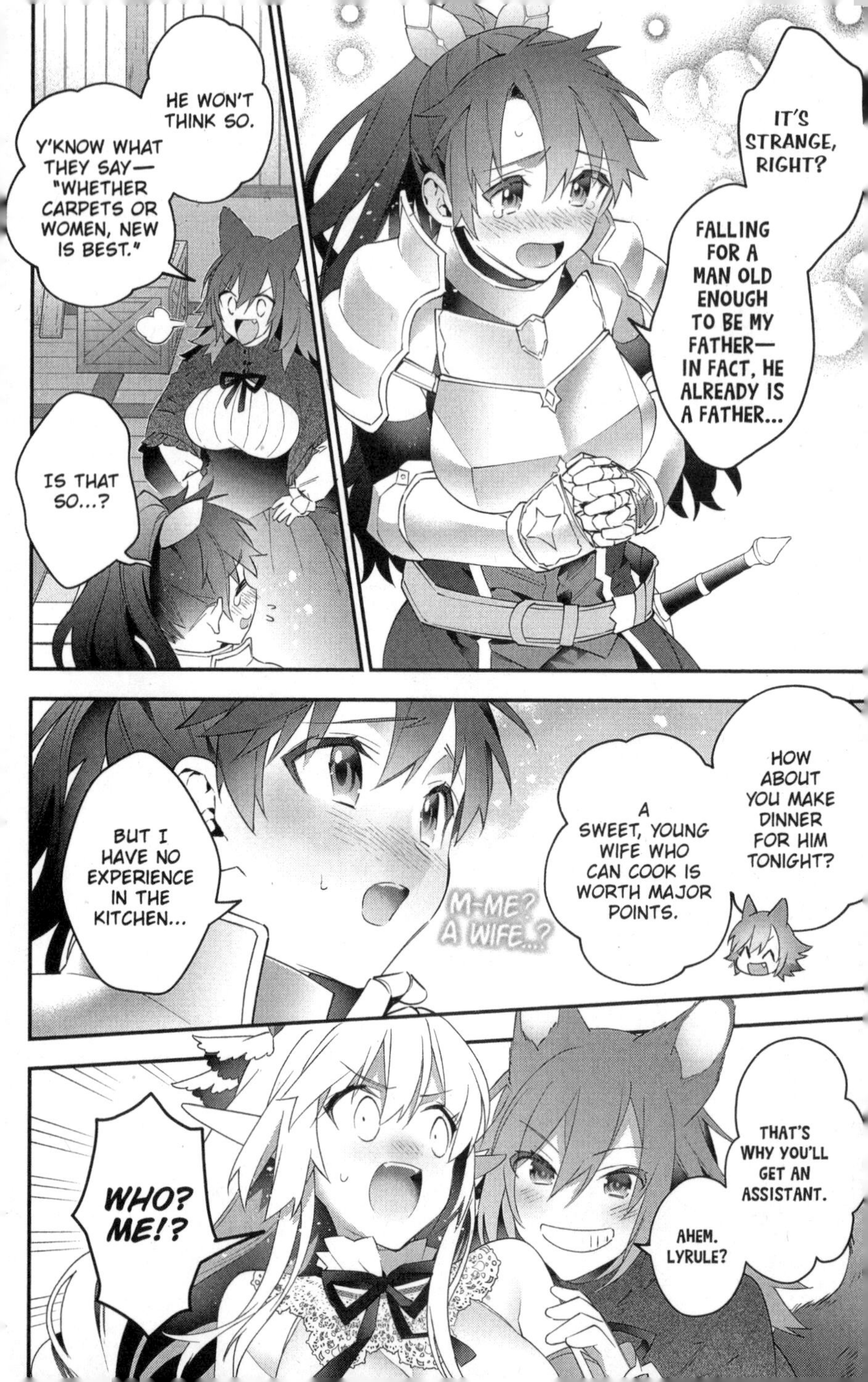
IT'S STRANGE, RIGHT?
FALLING FOR A MAN OLD ENOUGH TO BE MY FATHER— IN FACT, HE ALREADY IS A FATHER...
HE WON'T THINK SO.
Y'KNOW WHAT THEY SAY— "WHETHER CARPETS OR WOMEN, NEW IS BEST."
IS THAT SO...?
HOW ABOUT YOU MAKE DINNER FOR HIM TONIGHT?
A SWEET, YOUNG WIFE WHO CAN COOK IS WORTH MAJOR POINTS.
M-ME? A WIFE...?
BUT I HAVE NO EXPERIENCE IN THE KITCHEN...
THAT'S WHY YOU'LL GET AN ASSISTANT.
AHEM. LYRULE?
WHO? ME!?

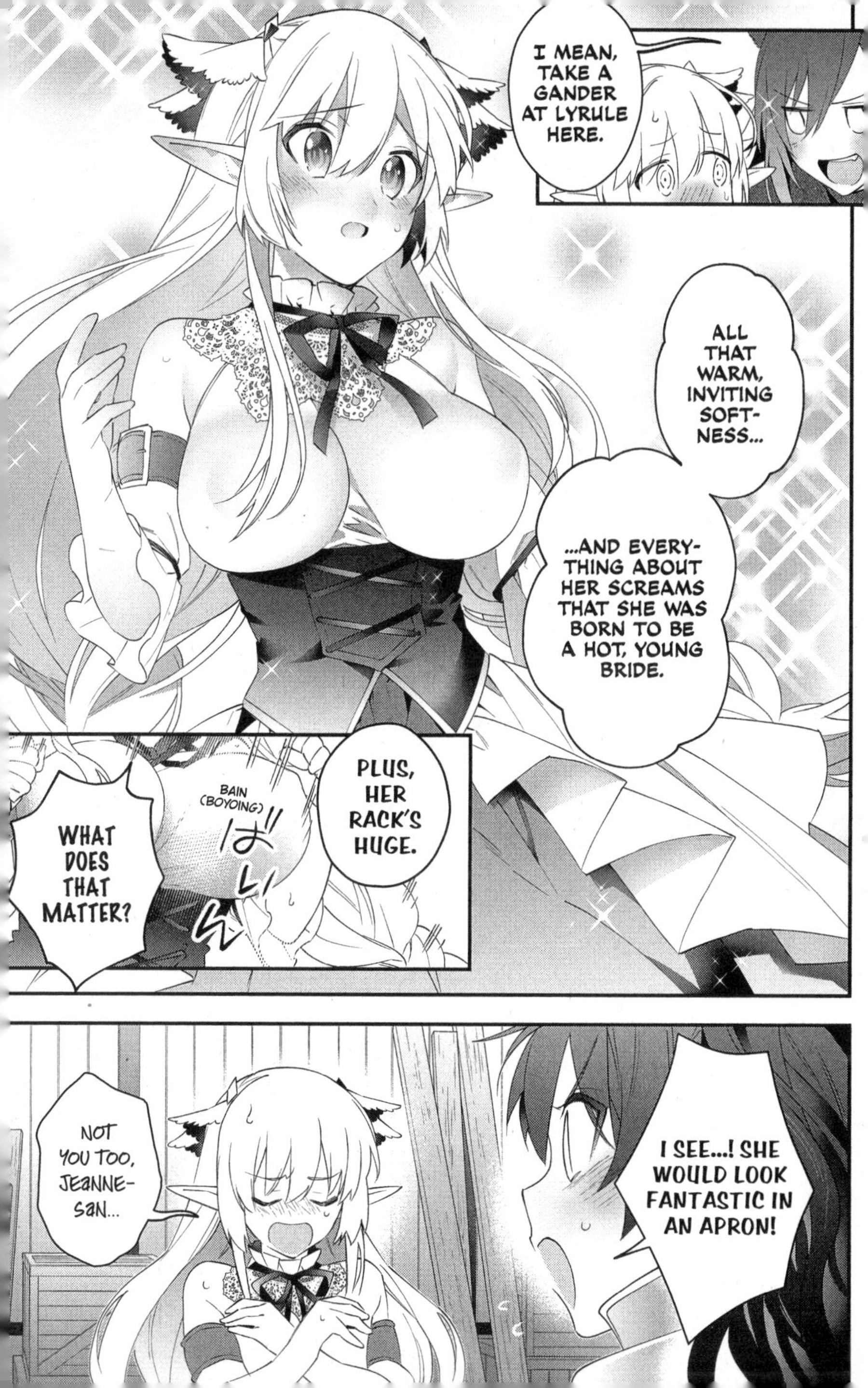
I MEAN, TAKE A GANDER AT LYRULE HERE.
ALL THAT WARM, INVITING SOFTNESS...
...AND EVERYTHING ABOUT HER SCREAMS THAT SHE WAS BORN TO BE A HOT, YOUNG BRIDE.
PLUS, HER RACK'S HUGE.
BAIN (BOYOING)
WHAT DOES THAT MATTER?
I SEE...! SHE WOULD LOOK FANTASTIC IN AN APRON!
NOT YOU TOO, JEANNE-SAN...

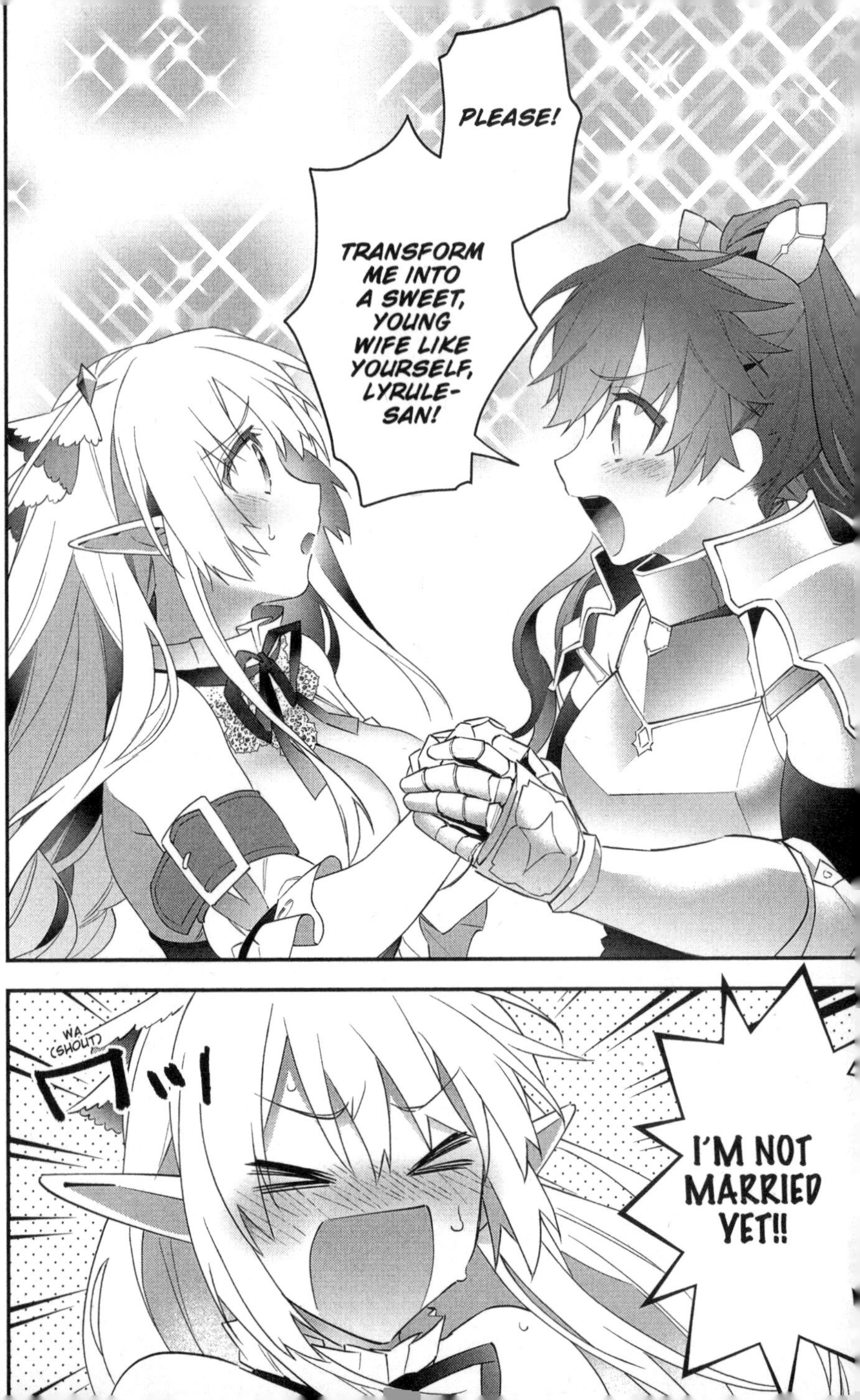
PLEASE!
TRANSFORM ME INTO A SWEET, YOUNG WIFE LIKE YOURSELF, LYRULE-SAN!
I'M NOT MARRIED YET!!
WA (SHOUT)

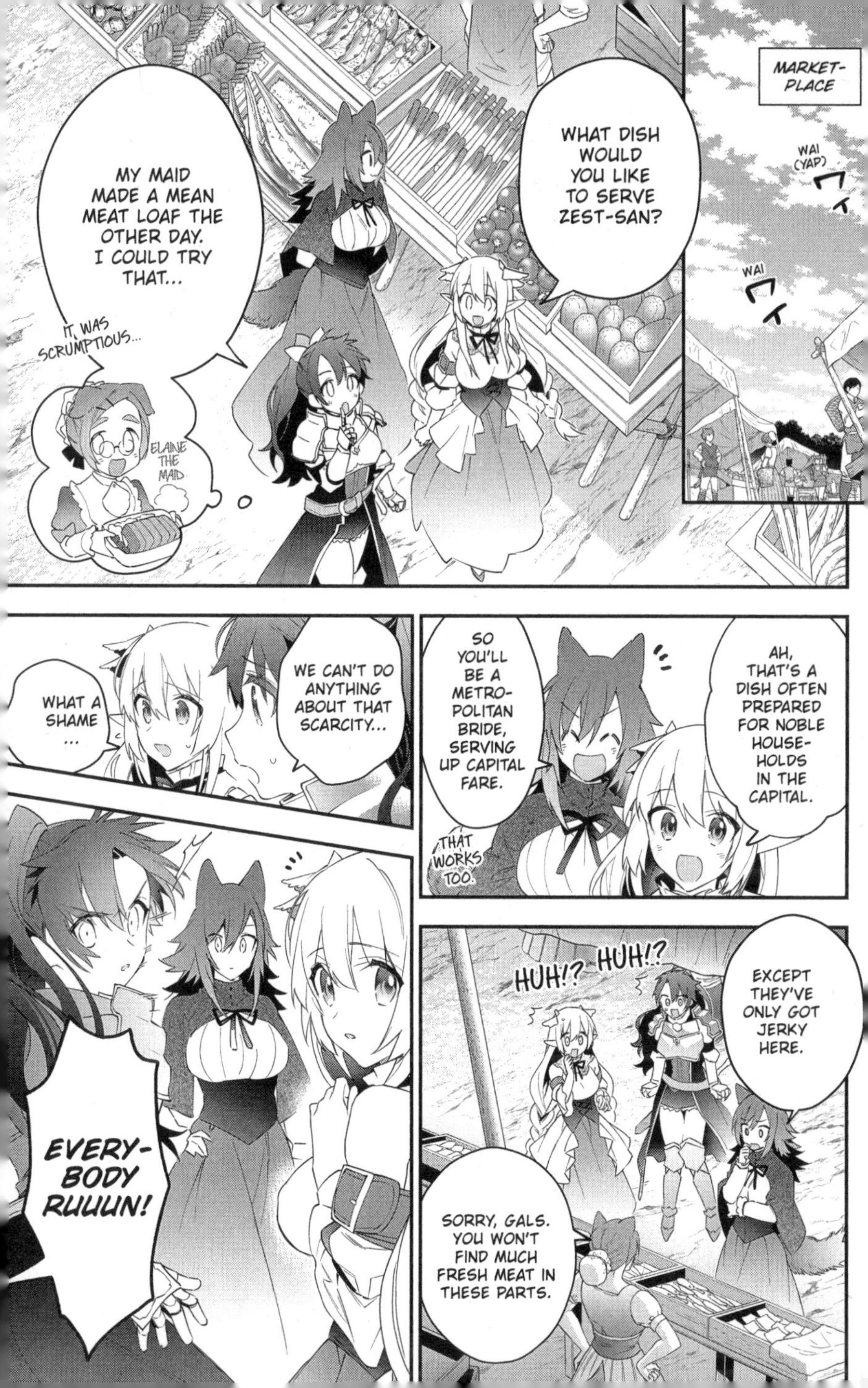
MARKET-PLACE
WAI (YAP)
WAI
WHAT DISH WOULD YOU LIKE TO SERVE ZEST-SAN?
MY MAID MADE A MEAN MEAT LOAF THE OTHER DAY. I COULD TRY THAT...
IT WAS SCRUMPTIOUS...
ELAINE THE MAID
AH, THAT'S A DISH OFTEN PREPARED FOR NOBLE HOUSE-HOLDS IN THE CAPITAL.
SO YOU'LL BE A METRO-POLITAN BRIDE, SERVING UP CAPITAL FARE.
THAT WORKS TOO.
EXCEPT THEY'VE ONLY GOT JERKY HERE.
HUH!? HUH!?
SORRY, GALS. YOU WON'T FIND MUCH FRESH MEAT IN THESE PARTS.
WE CAN'T DO ANYTHING ABOUT THAT SCARCITY...
WHAT A SHAME...
EVERY-BODY RUUUN!

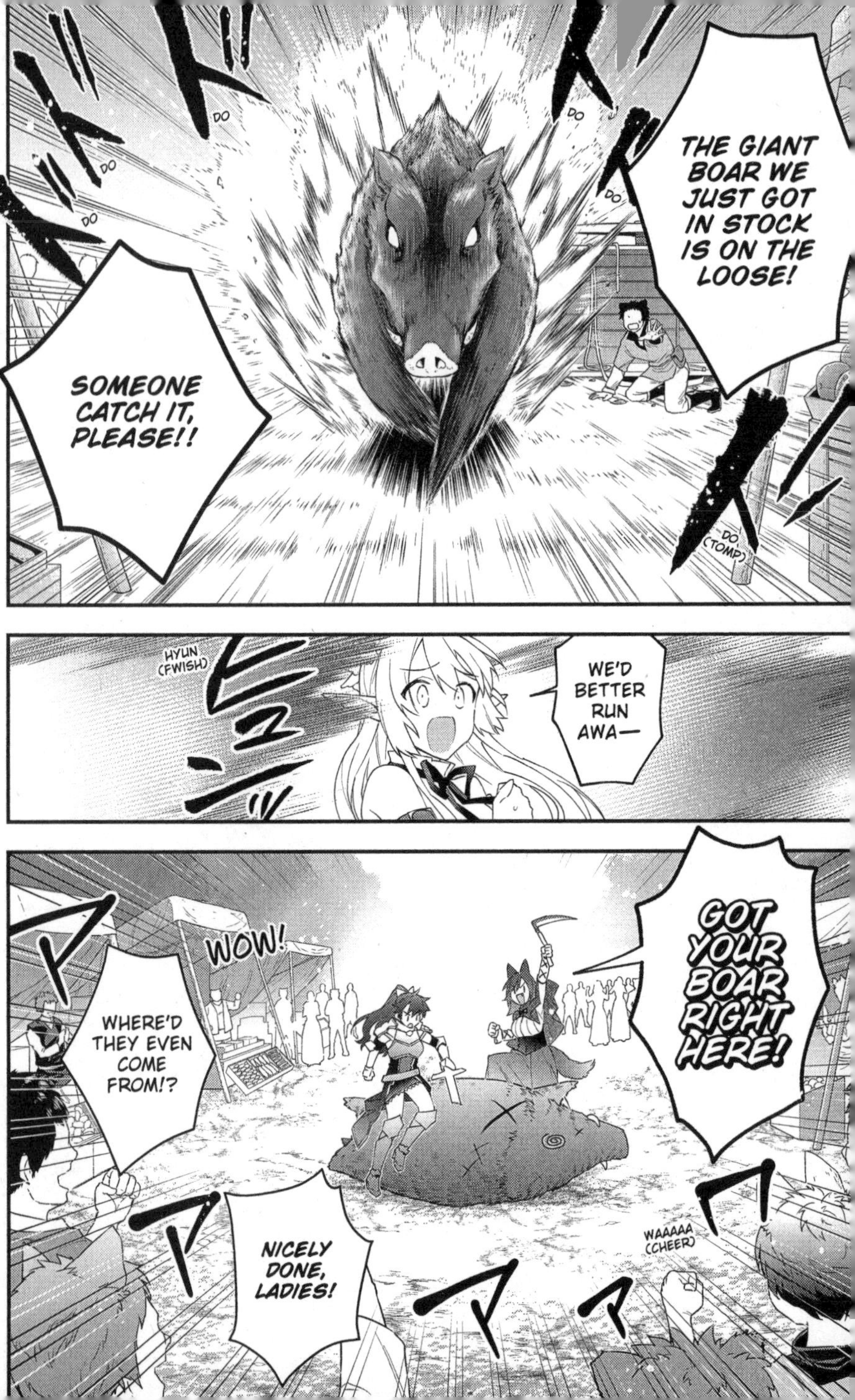
DO
DO
DO
DO
DO
THE GIANT BOAR WE JUST GOT IN STOCK IS ON THE LOOSE!
SOMEONE CATCH IT, PLEASE!!
DO (TOMP)
WE'D BETTER RUN AWA—
HYUN (FWISH)
GOT YOUR BOAR RIGHT HERE!
WOW!
WHERE'D THEY EVEN COME FROM!?
WAAAAA (CHEER)
NICELY DONE, LADIES!

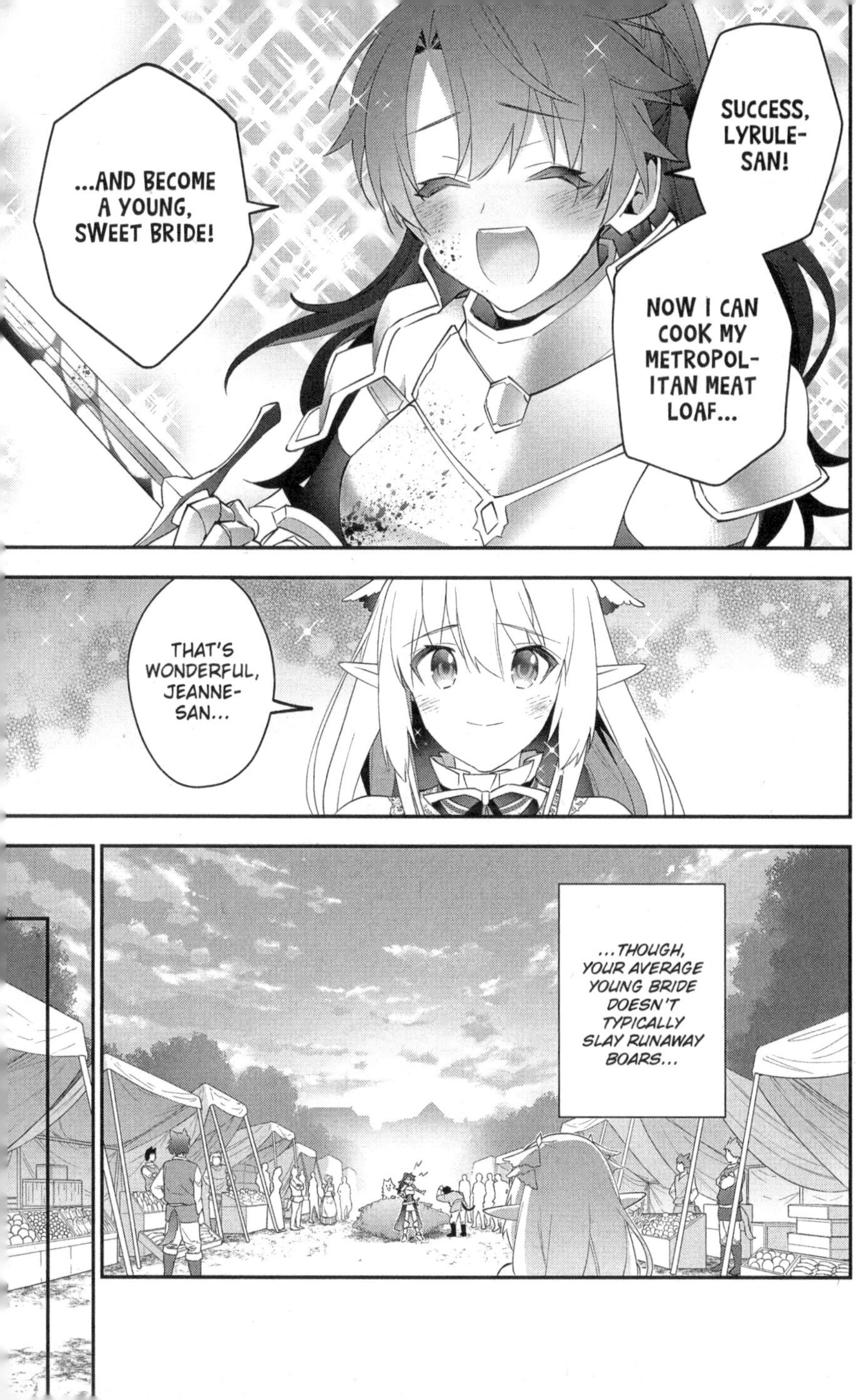
SUCCESS, LYRULE-SAN!
NOW I CAN COOK MY METROPOLITAN MEAT LOAF...
...AND BECOME A YOUNG, SWEET BRIDE!
THAT'S WONDERFUL, JEANNE-SAN...
...THOUGH, YOUR AVERAGE YOUNG BRIDE DOESN'T TYPICALLY SLAY RUNAWAY BOARS...

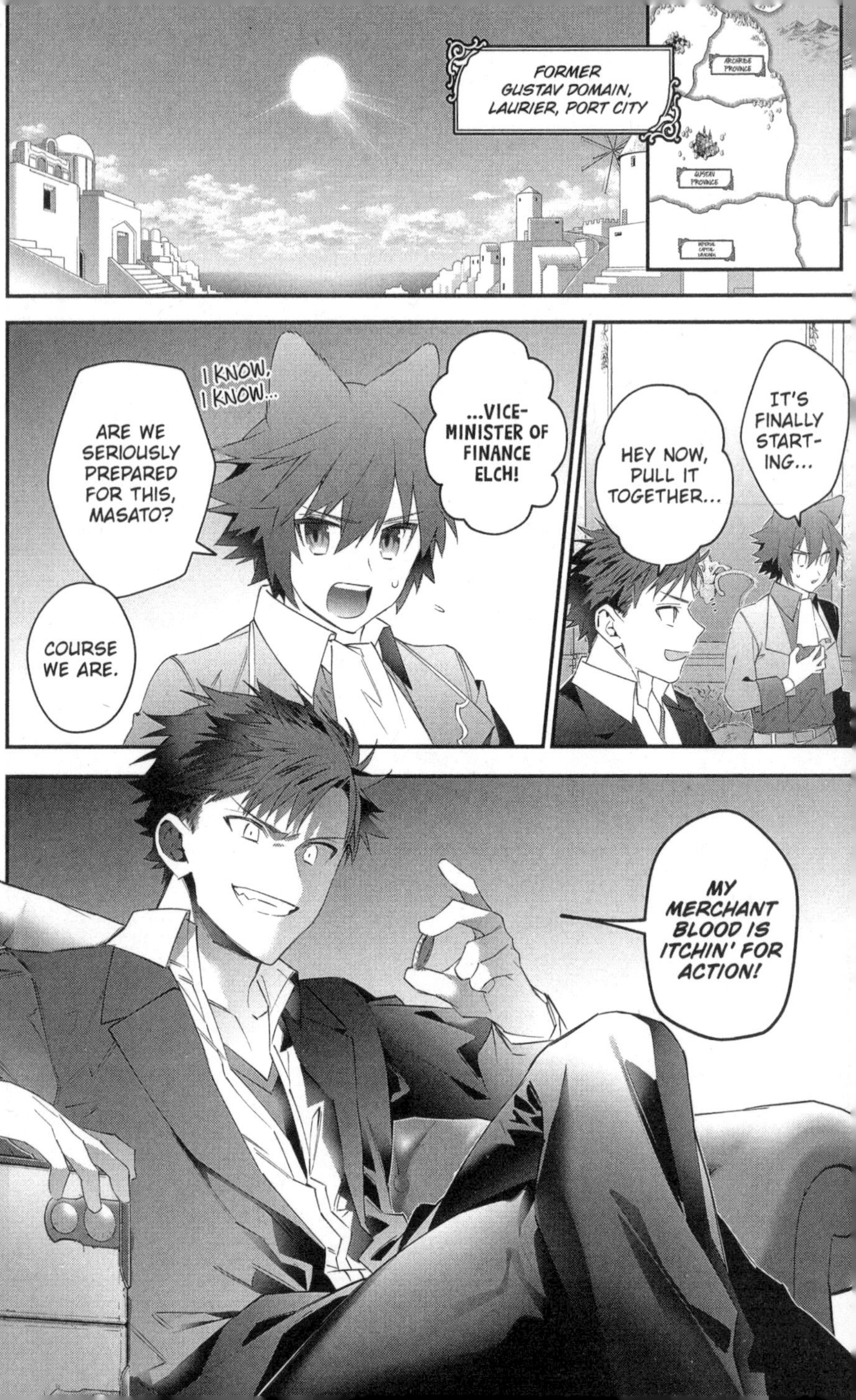
ARCHRIDE PROVINCE
GUSTAV PROVINCE
IMPERIAL CAPITAL DRACHEN
FORMER GUSTAV DOMAIN, LAURIER, PORT CITY
IT'S FINALLY STARTING...
HEY NOW, PULL IT TOGETHER...
...VICE-MINISTER OF FINANCE ELCH!
I KNOW, I KNOW...
ARE WE SERIOUSLY PREPARED FOR THIS, MASATO?
COURSE WE ARE.
MY MERCHANT BLOOD IS ITCHIN' FOR ACTION!

HIGH SCHOOL
PRODIGIES HAVE
IT EASY EVEN IN
ANOTHER
WORLD!

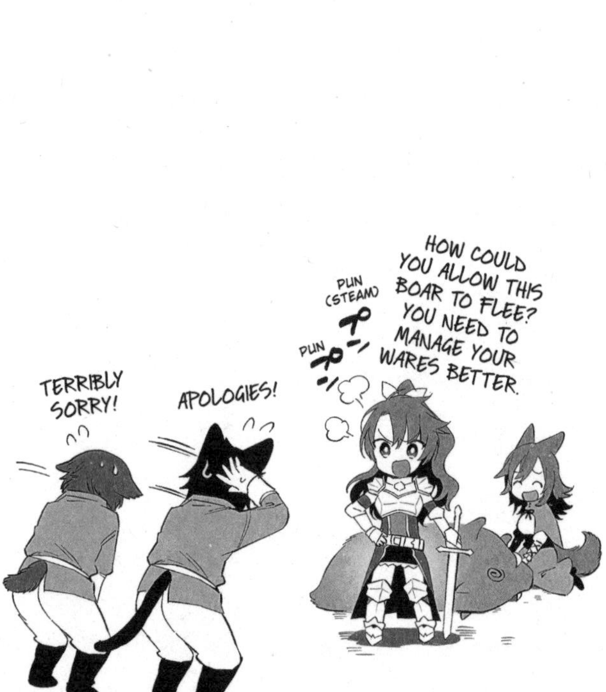
HOW COULD YOU ALLOW THIS BOAR TO FLEE? YOU NEED TO MANAGE YOUR WARES BETTER.
PUN (STEAM)
PUN
APOLOGIES!
TERRIBLY SORRY!

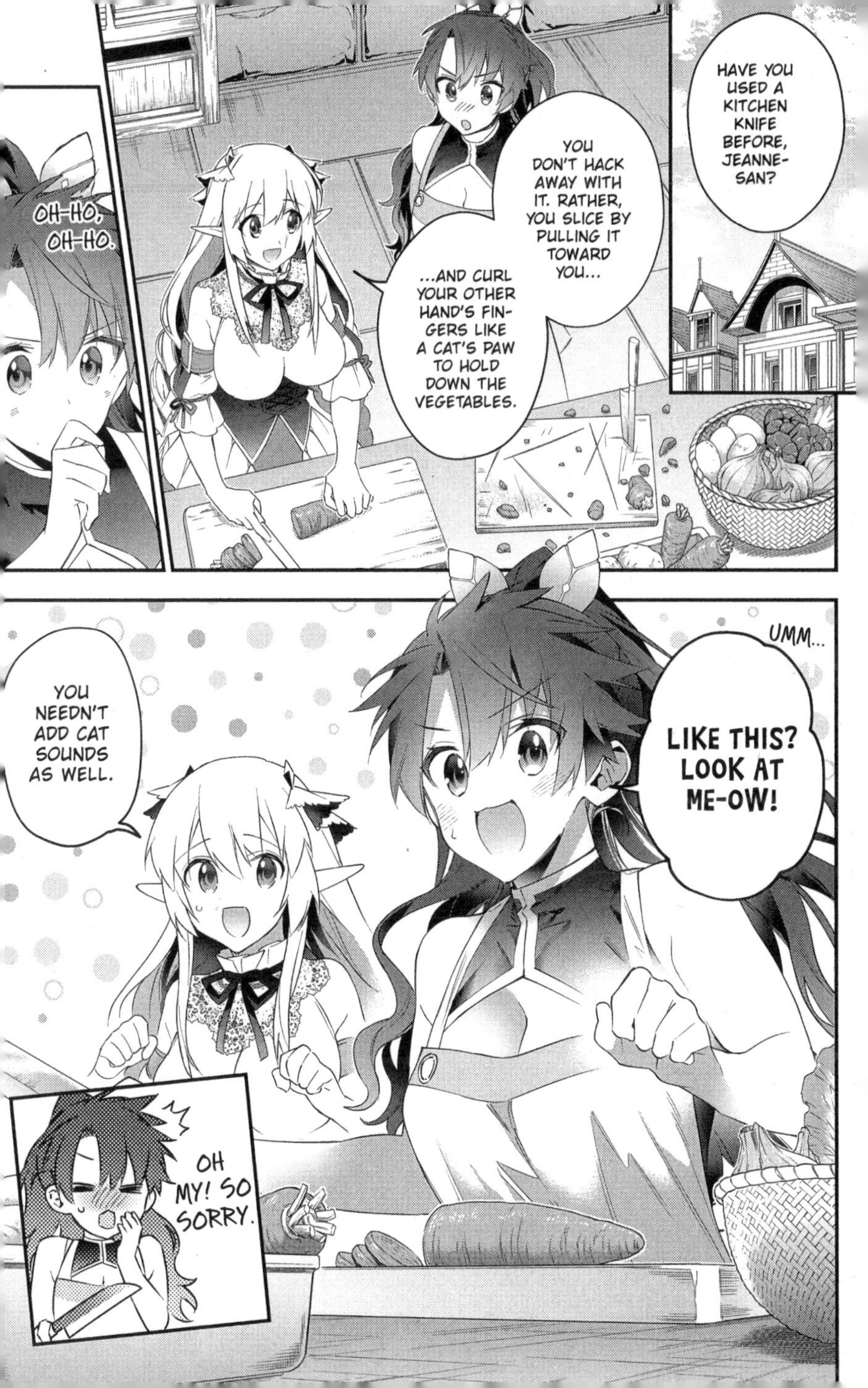
HAVE YOU USED A KITCHEN KNIFE BEFORE, JEANNE-SAN?
YOU DON'T HACK AWAY WITH IT. RATHER, YOU SLICE BY PULLING IT TOWARD YOU...
...AND CURL YOUR OTHER HAND'S FIN-GERS LIKE A CAT'S PAW TO HOLD DOWN THE VEGETABLES.
OH-HO, OH-HO.
UMM...
LIKE THIS? LOOK AT ME-OW!
YOU NEEDN'T ADD CAT SOUNDS AS WELL.
OH MY! SO SORRY.

CHAPTER 51: WOMEN'S RESOLVE

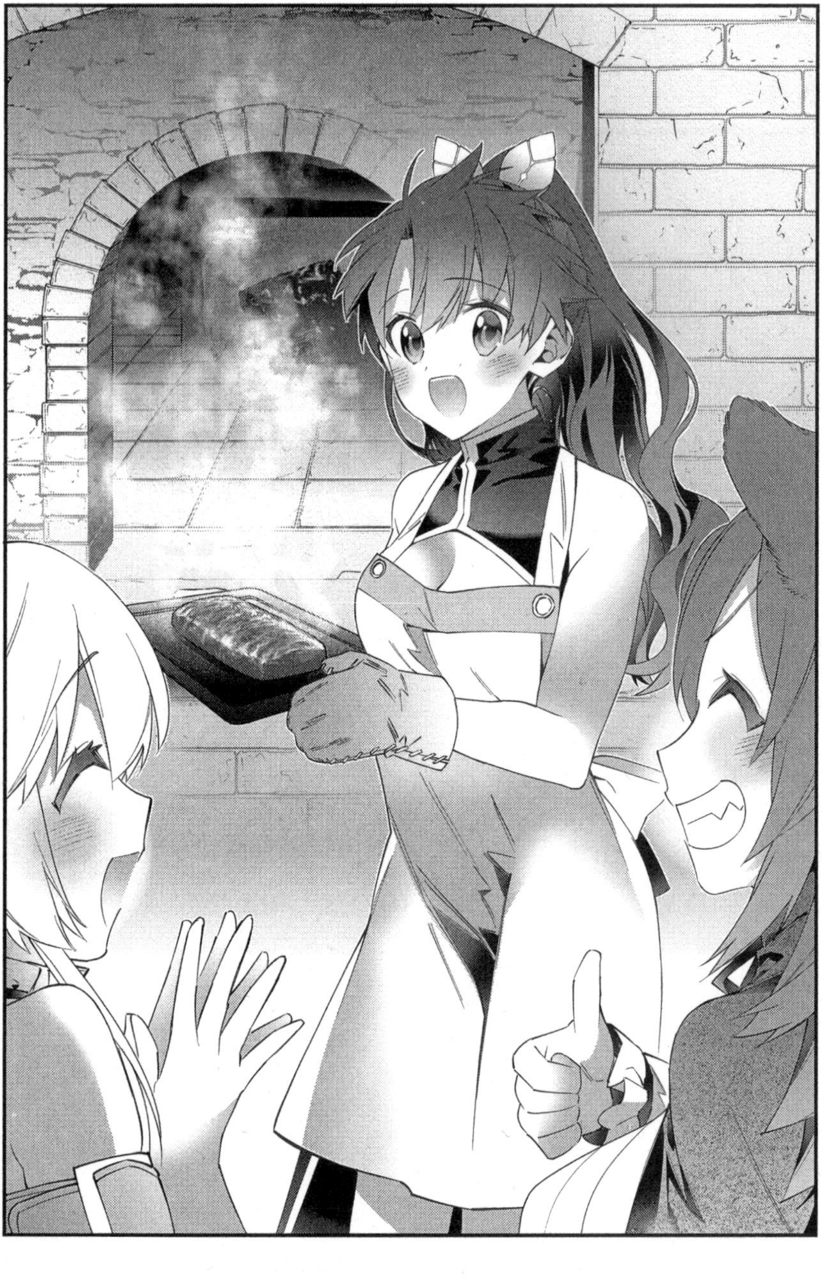

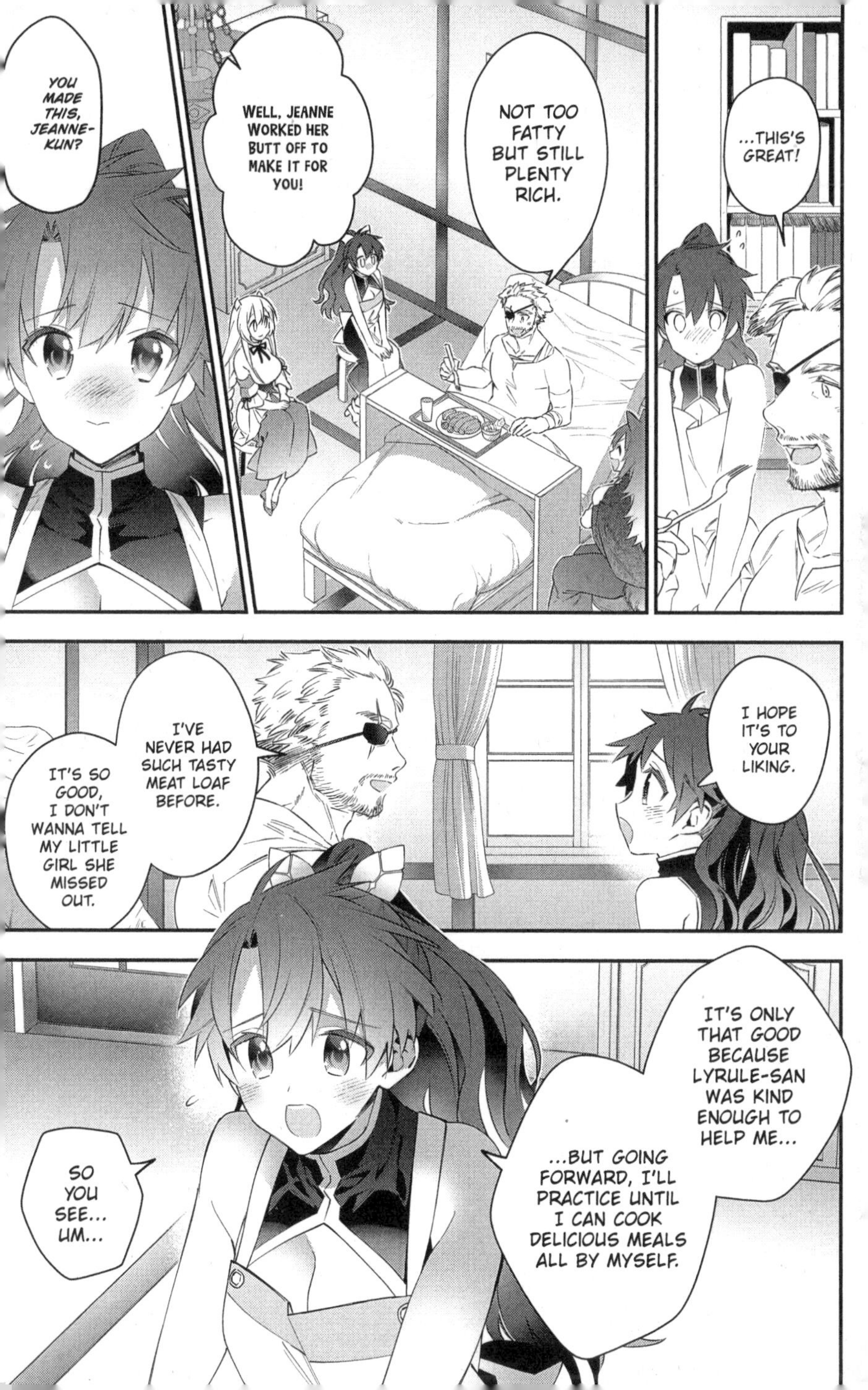
...THIS'S GREAT!
NOT TOO FATTY BUT STILL PLENTY RICH.
WELL, JEANNE WORKED HER BUTT OFF TO MAKE IT FOR YOU!
YOU MADE THIS, JEANNE-KUN?
I HOPE IT'S TO YOUR LIKING.
I'VE NEVER HAD SUCH TASTY MEAT LOAF BEFORE.
IT'S SO GOOD, I DON'T WANNA TELL MY LITTLE GIRL SHE MISSED OUT.
IT'S ONLY THAT GOOD BECAUSE LYRULE-SAN WAS KIND ENOUGH TO HELP ME...
...BUT GOING FORWARD, I'LL PRACTICE UNTIL I CAN COOK DELICIOUS MEALS ALL BY MYSELF.
SO YOU SEE... UM...

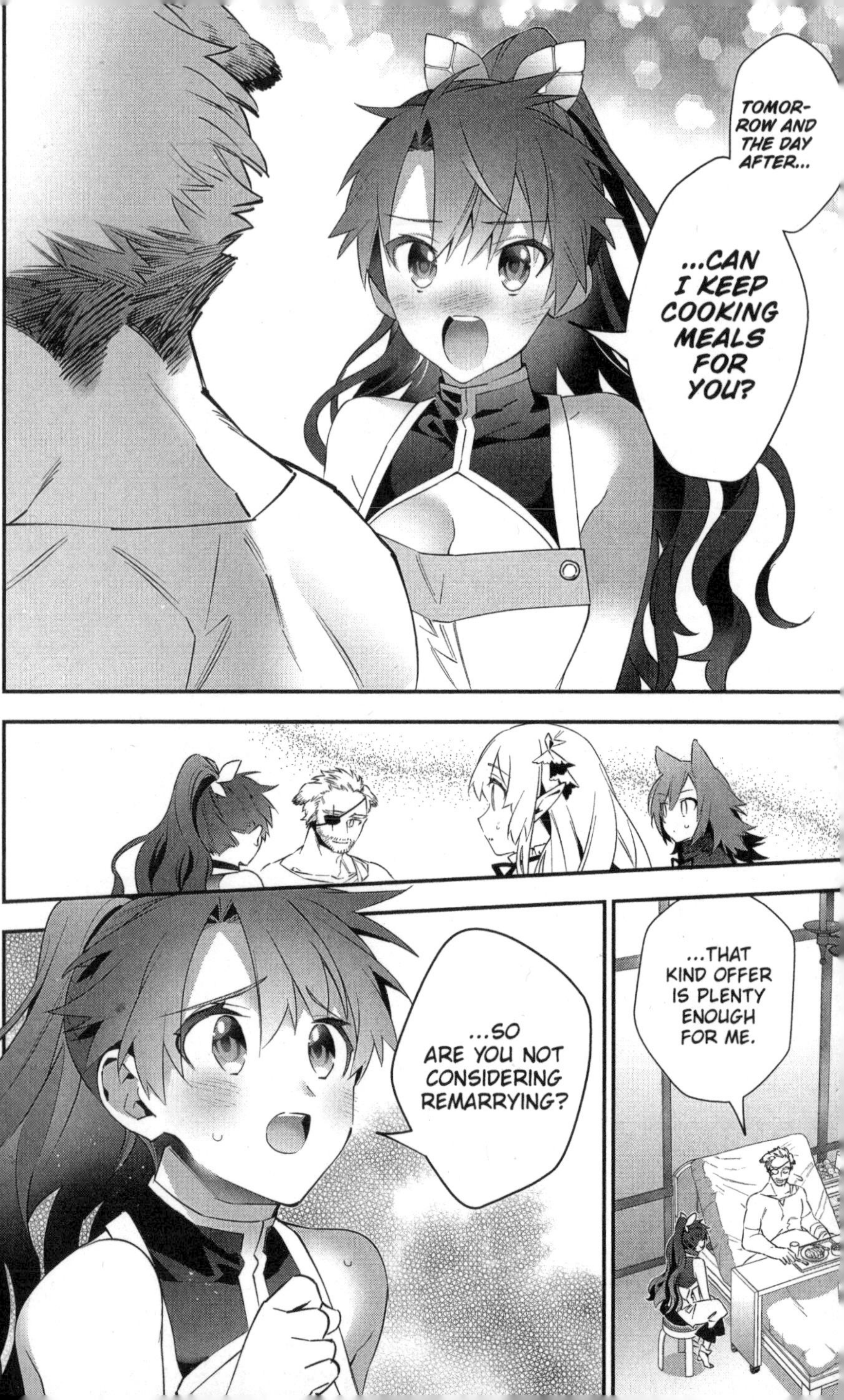
TOMORROW AND THE DAY AFTER...
...CAN I KEEP COOKING MEALS FOR YOU?
...THAT KIND OFFER IS PLENTY ENOUGH FOR ME.
...SO ARE YOU NOT CONSIDERING REMARRYING?

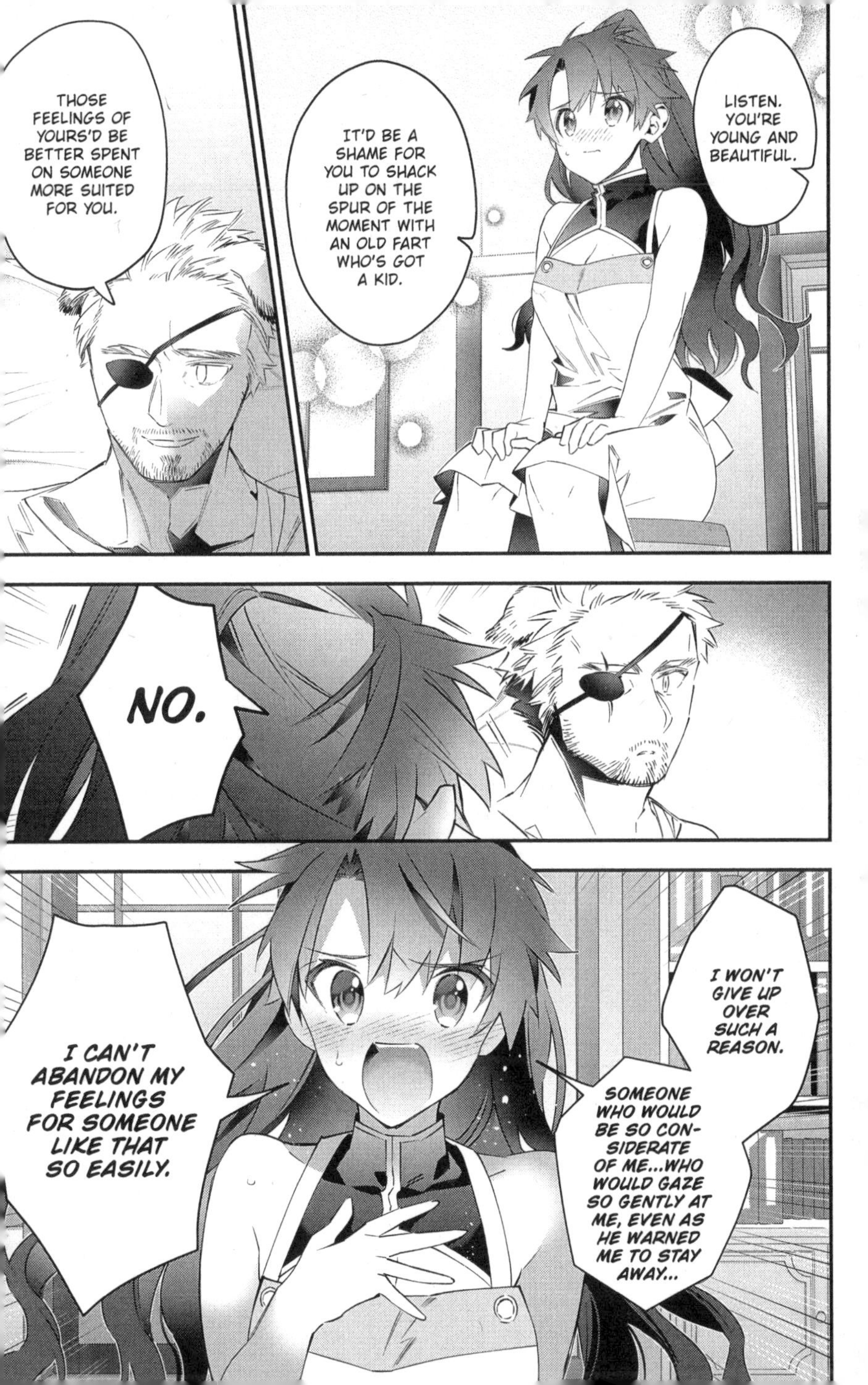
LISTEN. YOU'RE YOUNG AND BEAUTIFUL.
IT'D BE A SHAME FOR YOU TO SHACK UP ON THE SPUR OF THE MOMENT WITH AN OLD FART WHO'S GOT A KID.
THOSE FEELINGS OF YOURS'D BE BETTER SPENT ON SOMEONE MORE SUITED FOR YOU.
NO.
I WON'T GIVE UP OVER SUCH A REASON.
SOMEONE WHO WOULD BE SO CON-SIDERATE OF ME...WHO WOULD GAZE SO GENTLY AT ME, EVEN AS HE WARNED ME TO STAY AWAY...
I CAN'T ABANDON MY FEELINGS FOR SOMEONE LIKE THAT SO EASILY.

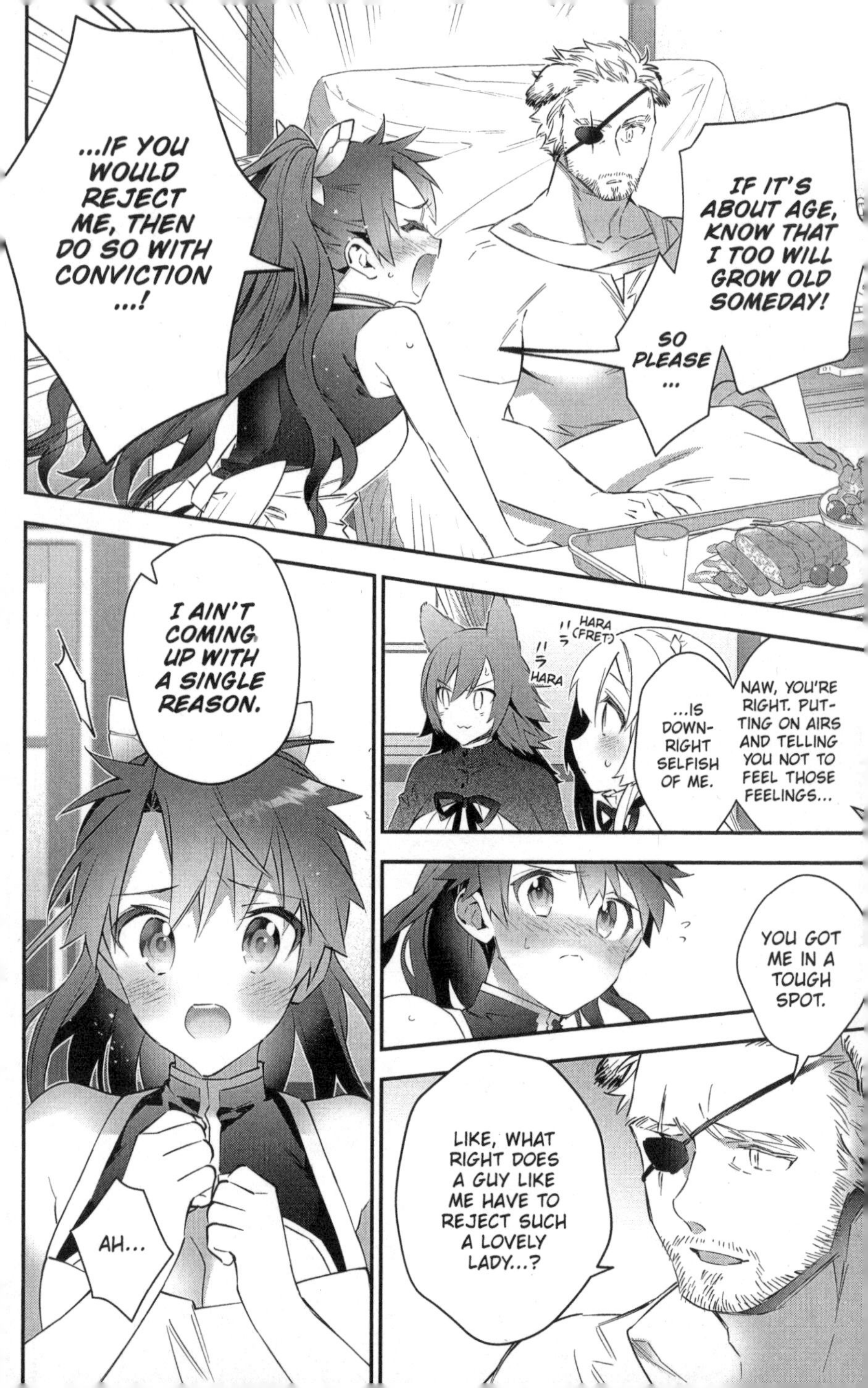
IF IT'S ABOUT AGE, KNOW THAT I TOO WILL GROW OLD SOMEDAY!
SO PLEASE ...
...IF YOU WOULD REJECT ME, THEN DO SO WITH CONVICTION ...!
HARA HARA (FRET)
NAW, YOU'RE RIGHT. PUTTING ON AIRS AND TELLING YOU NOT TO FEEL THOSE FEELINGS...
...IS DOWNRIGHT SELFISH OF ME.
YOU GOT ME IN A TOUGH SPOT.
LIKE, WHAT RIGHT DOES A GUY LIKE ME HAVE TO REJECT SUCH A LOVELY LADY...?
I AIN'T COMING UP WITH A SINGLE REASON.
AH...

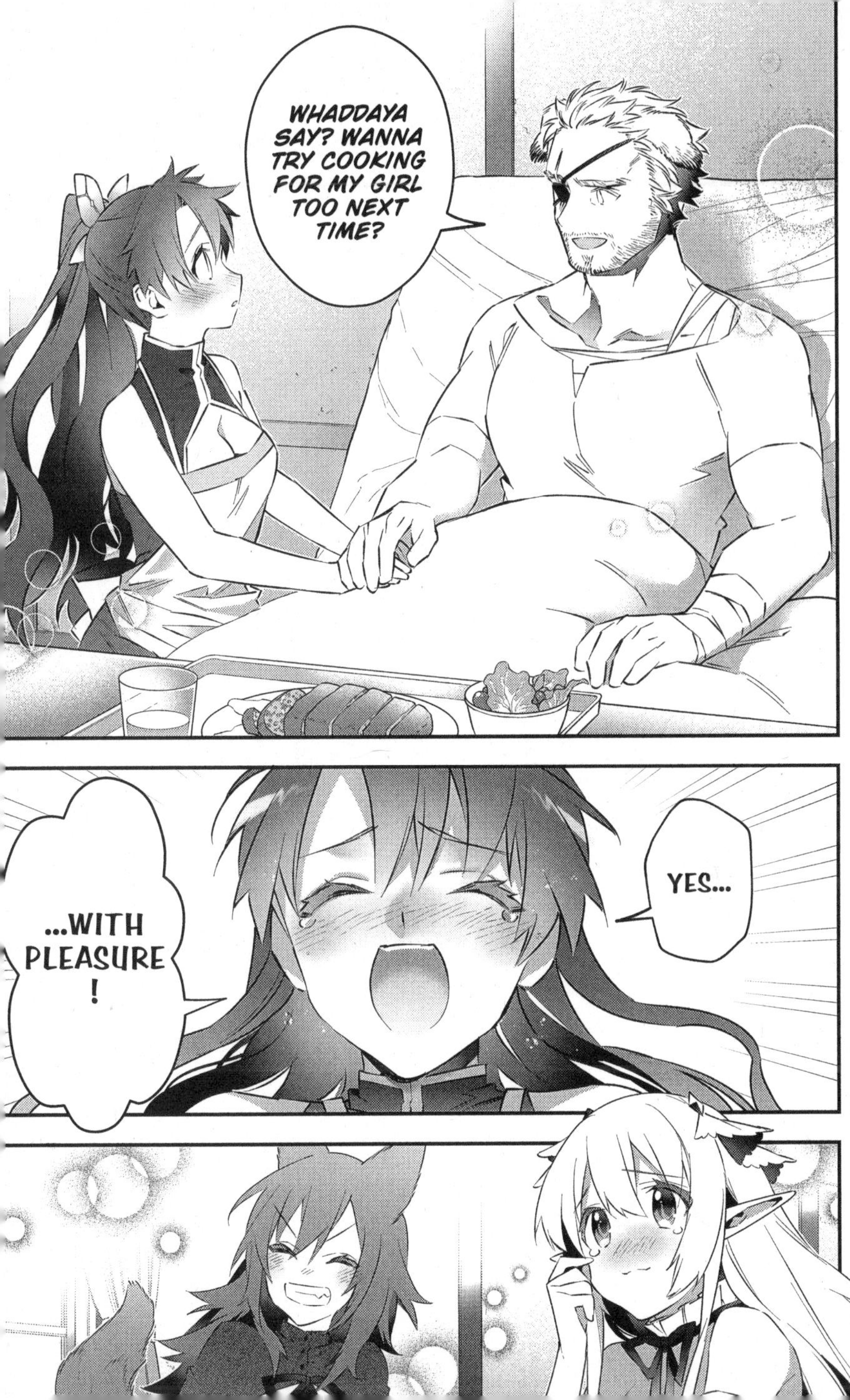
WHADDAYA SAY? WANNA TRY COOKING FOR MY GIRL TOO NEXT TIME?
YES...
...WITH PLEASURE!

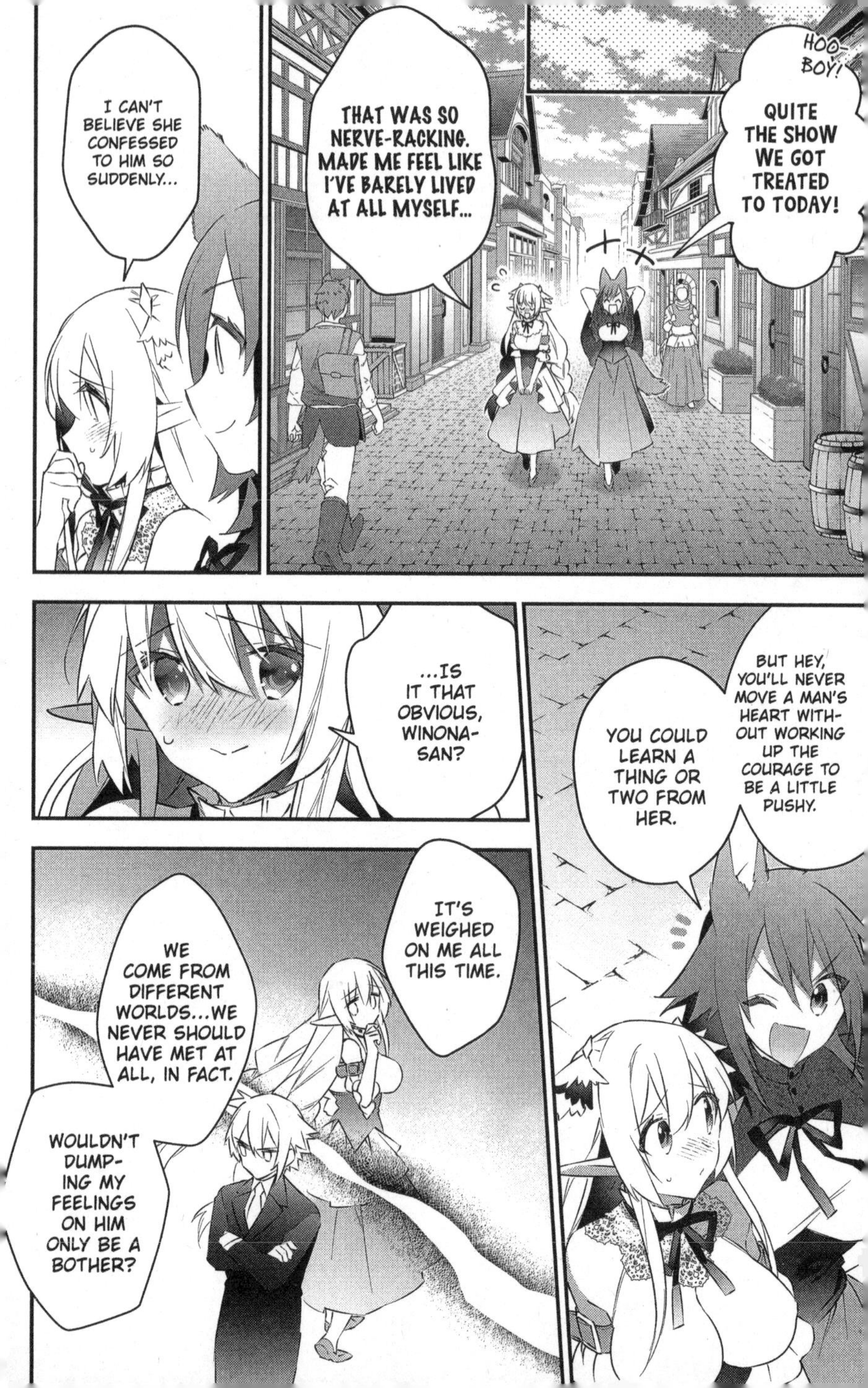
HOO-BOY!
QUITE THE SHOW WE GOT TREATED TO TODAY!
THAT WAS SO NERVE-RACKING. MADE ME FEEL LIKE I'VE BARELY LIVED AT ALL MYSELF...
I CAN'T BELIEVE SHE CONFESSED TO HIM SO SUDDENLY...
BUT HEY, YOU'LL NEVER MOVE A MAN'S HEART WITH-OUT WORKING UP THE COURAGE TO BE A LITTLE PUSHY.
YOU COULD LEARN A THING OR TWO FROM HER.
...IS IT THAT OBVIOUS, WINONA-SAN?
IT'S WEIGHED ON ME ALL THIS TIME.
WE COME FROM DIFFERENT WORLDS...WE NEVER SHOULD HAVE MET AT ALL, IN FACT.
WOULDN'T DUMP-ING MY FEELINGS ON HIM ONLY BE A BOTHER?

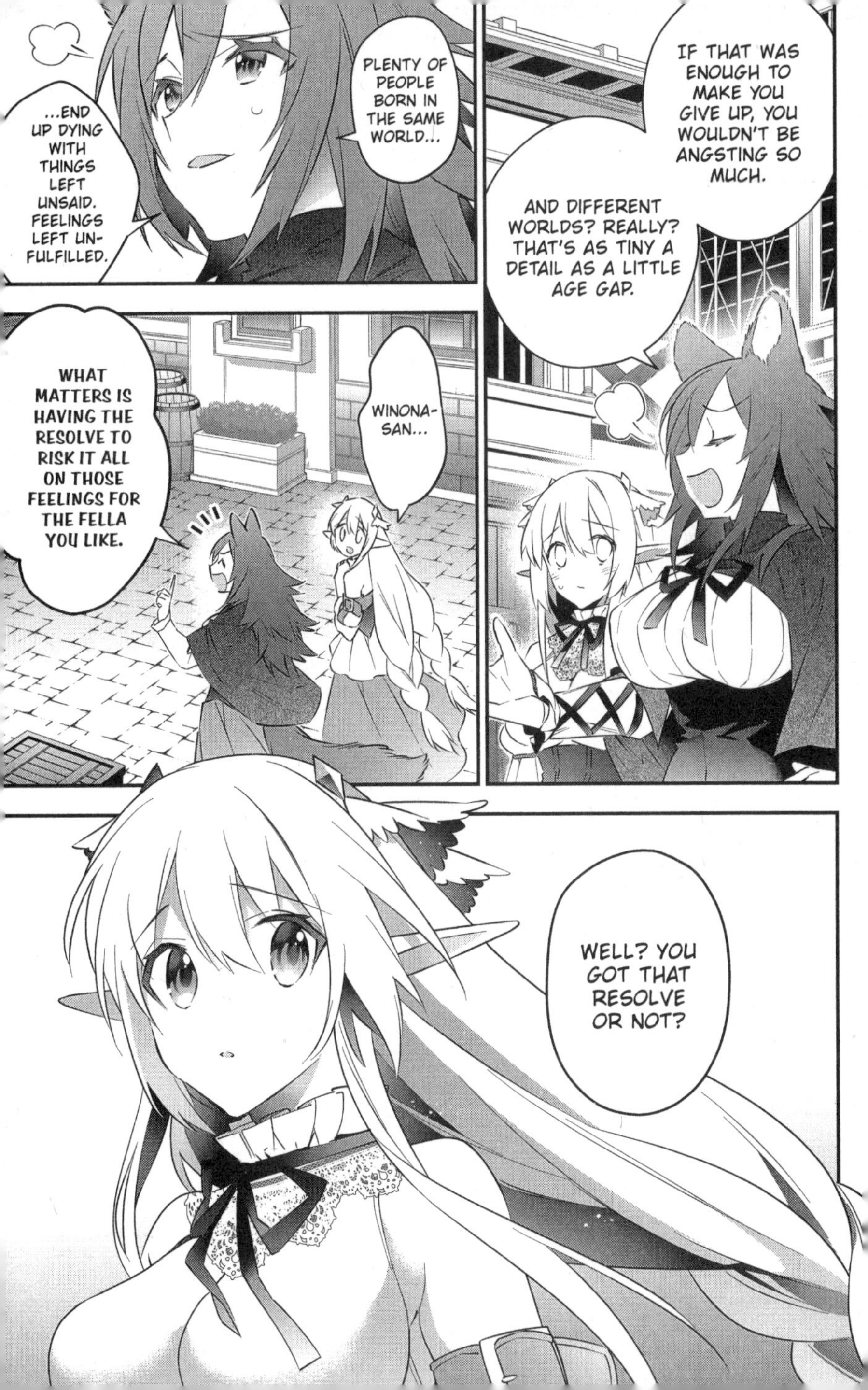
IF THAT WAS ENOUGH TO MAKE YOU GIVE UP, YOU WOULDN'T BE ANGSTING SO MUCH.
AND DIFFERENT WORLDS? REALLY? THAT'S AS TINY A DETAIL AS A LITTLE AGE GAP.
PLENTY OF PEOPLE BORN IN THE SAME WORLD...
...END UP DYING WITH THINGS LEFT UNSAID. FEELINGS LEFT UN-FULFILLED.
WINONA-SAN...
WHAT MATTERS IS HAVING THE RESOLVE TO RISK IT ALL ON THOSE FEELINGS FOR THE FELLA YOU LIKE.
WELL? YOU GOT THAT RESOLVE OR NOT?

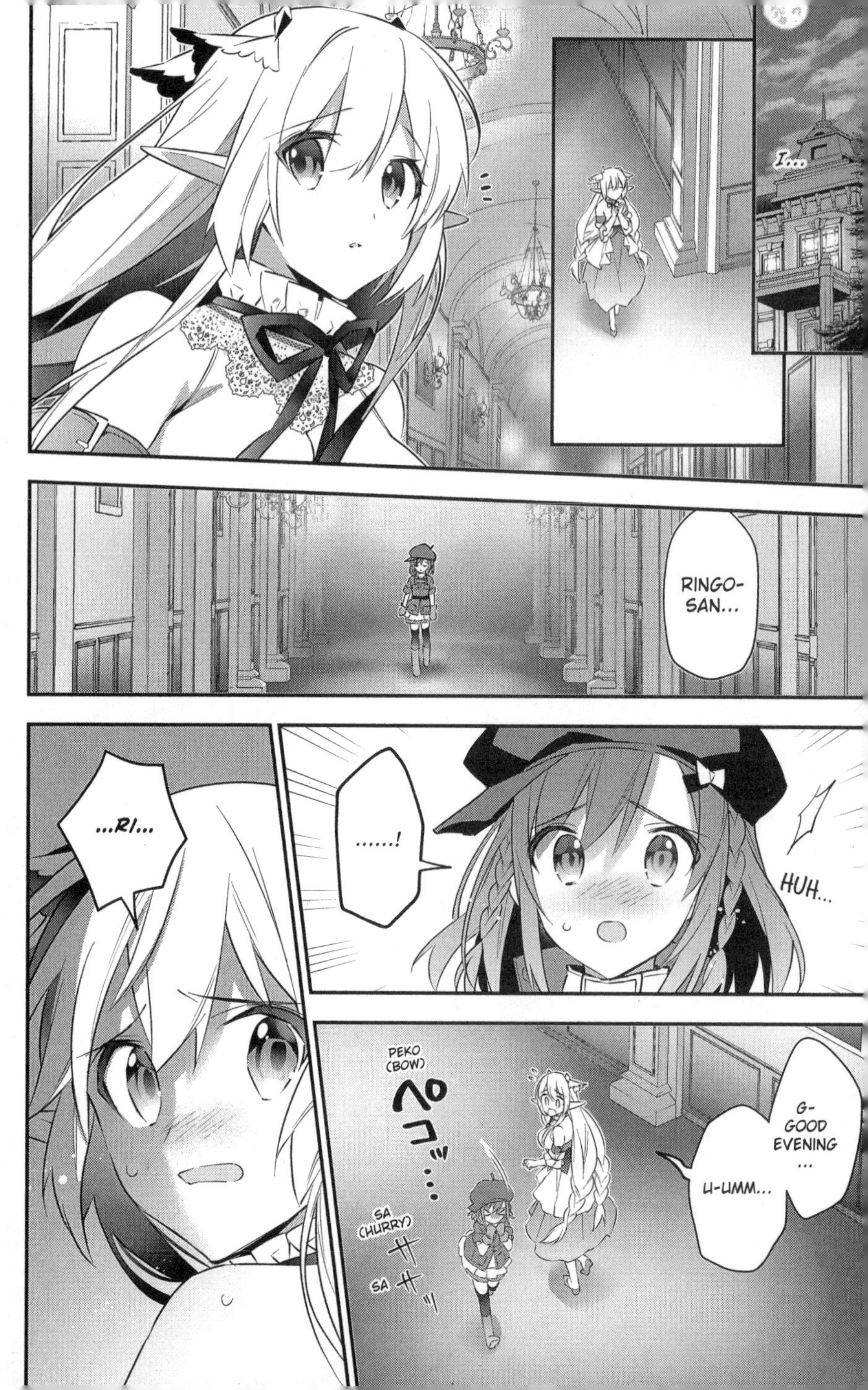

I...
RINGO-SAN...
HUH...
......!
G-GOOD EVENING ...
U-UMM...
PEKO (BOW)
ペコッ...
SA (HURRY)
サ
SA
サッ
...RI...

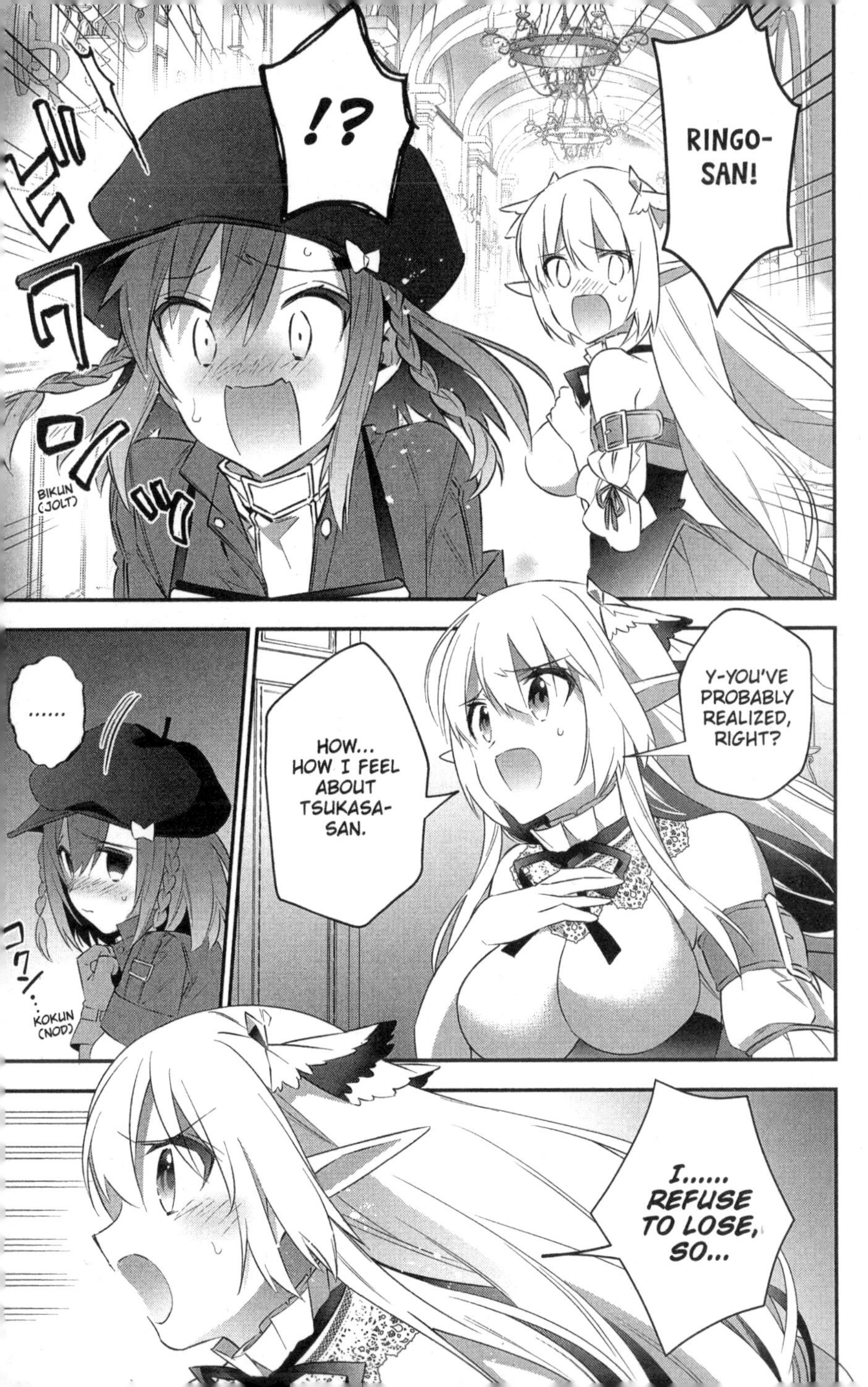
RINGO-SAN!
!?
BIKUN (JOLT)
Y-YOU'VE PROBABLY REALIZED, RIGHT?
HOW... HOW I FEEL ABOUT TSUKASA-SAN.
......
KOKUN (NOD)
I...... REFUSE TO LOSE, SO...

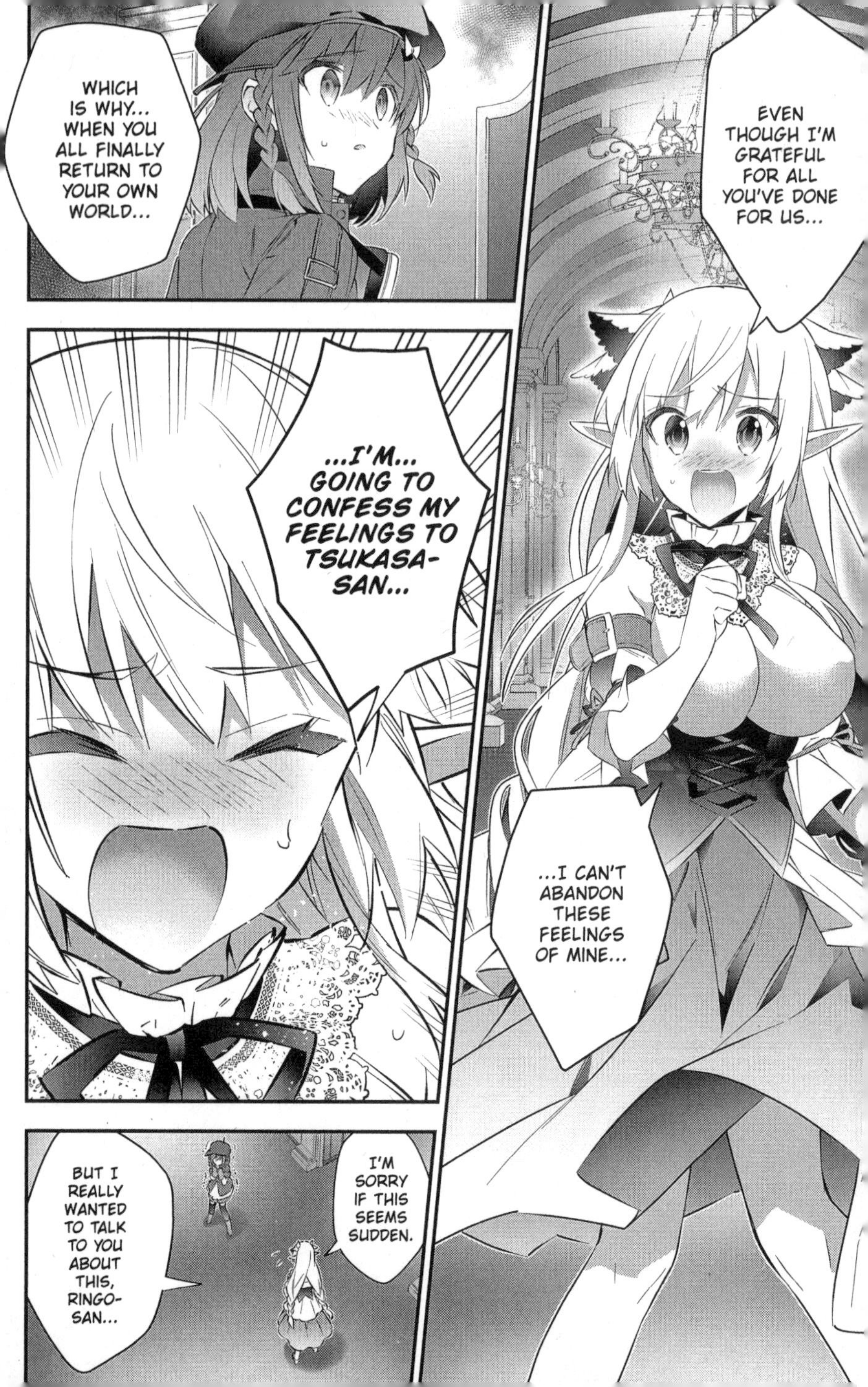
EVEN THOUGH I'M GRATEFUL FOR ALL YOU'VE DONE FOR US...
...I CAN'T ABANDON THESE FEELINGS OF MINE...
WHICH IS WHY... WHEN YOU ALL FINALLY RETURN TO YOUR OWN WORLD...
...I'M... GOING TO CONFESS MY FEELINGS TO TSUKASA-SAN...
I'M SORRY IF THIS SEEMS SUDDEN.
BUT I REALLY WANTED TO TALK TO YOU ABOUT THIS, RINGO-SAN...

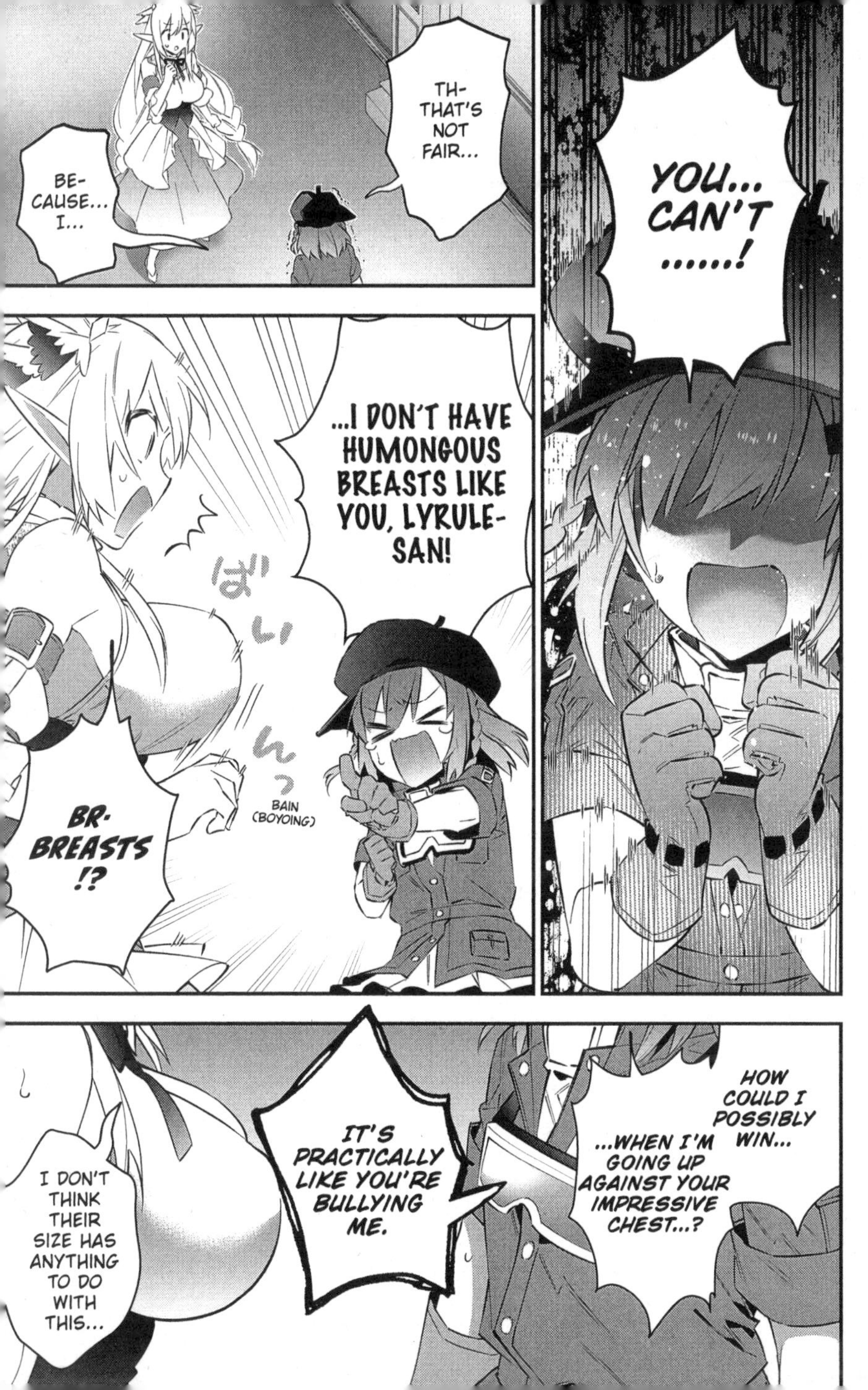
YOU... CAN'T ......!
TH-THAT'S NOT FAIR...
BE-CAUSE... I...
...I DON'T HAVE HUMONGOUS BREASTS LIKE YOU, LYRULE-SAN!
ばいんっ
BAIN (BOYOING)
BR-BREASTS !?
HOW COULD I POSSIBLY WIN...
...WHEN I'M GOING UP AGAINST YOUR IMPRESSIVE CHEST...?
IT'S PRACTICALLY LIKE YOU'RE BULLYING ME.
I DON'T THINK THEIR SIZE HAS ANYTHING TO DO WITH THIS...

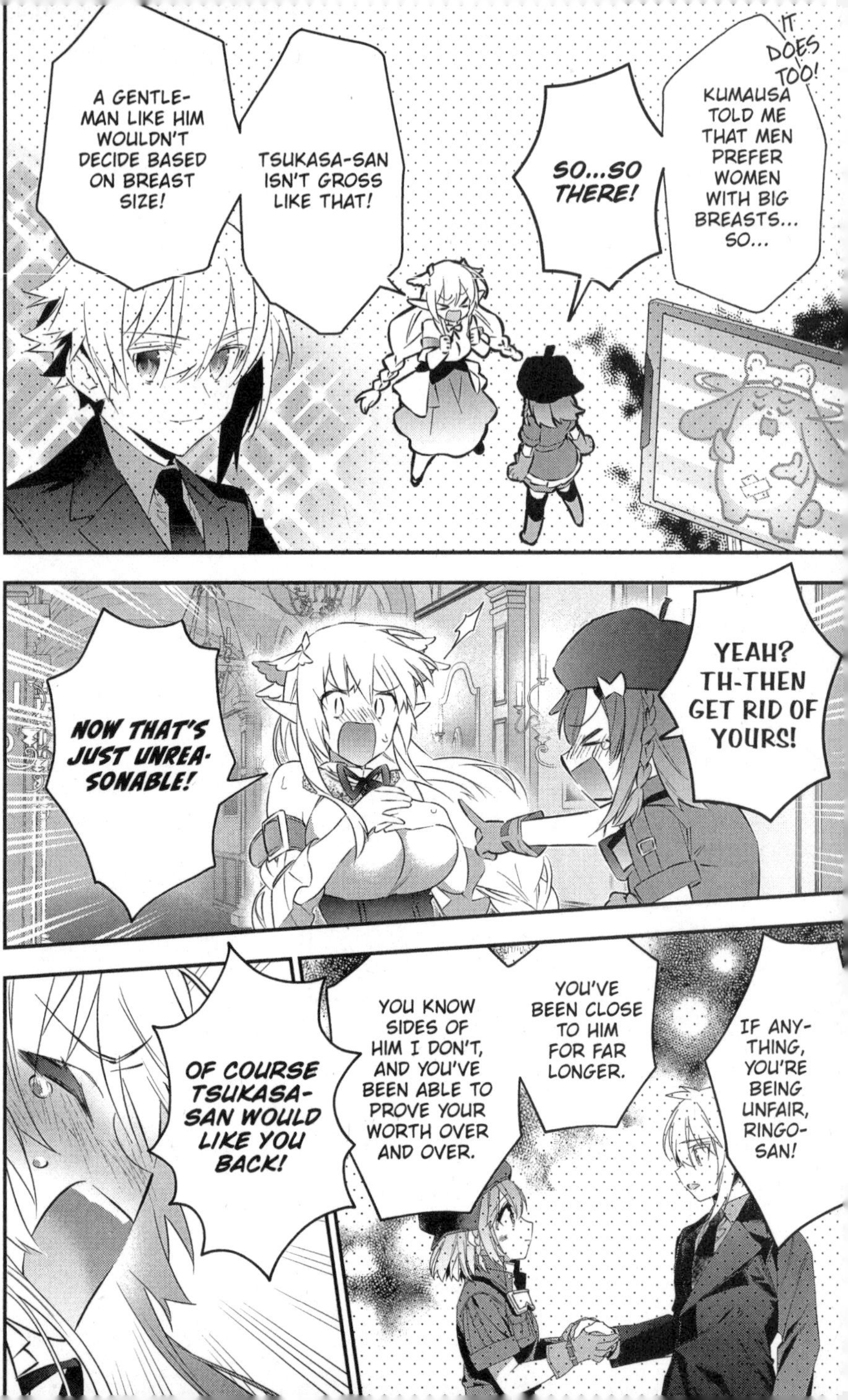
IT DOES TOO!
KUMAUSA TOLD ME THAT MEN PREFER WOMEN WITH BIG BREASTS... SO...
SO...SO THERE!
TSUKASA-SAN ISN'T GROSS LIKE THAT!
A GENTLEMAN LIKE HIM WOULDN'T DECIDE BASED ON BREAST SIZE!
YEAH? TH-THEN GET RID OF YOURS!
NOW THAT'S JUST UNREASONABLE!
IF ANYTHING, YOU'RE BEING UNFAIR, RINGO-SAN!
YOU'VE BEEN CLOSE TO HIM FOR FAR LONGER.
YOU KNOW SIDES OF HIM I DON'T, AND YOU'VE BEEN ABLE TO PROVE YOUR WORTH OVER AND OVER.
OF COURSE TSUKASA-SAN WOULD LIKE YOU BACK!

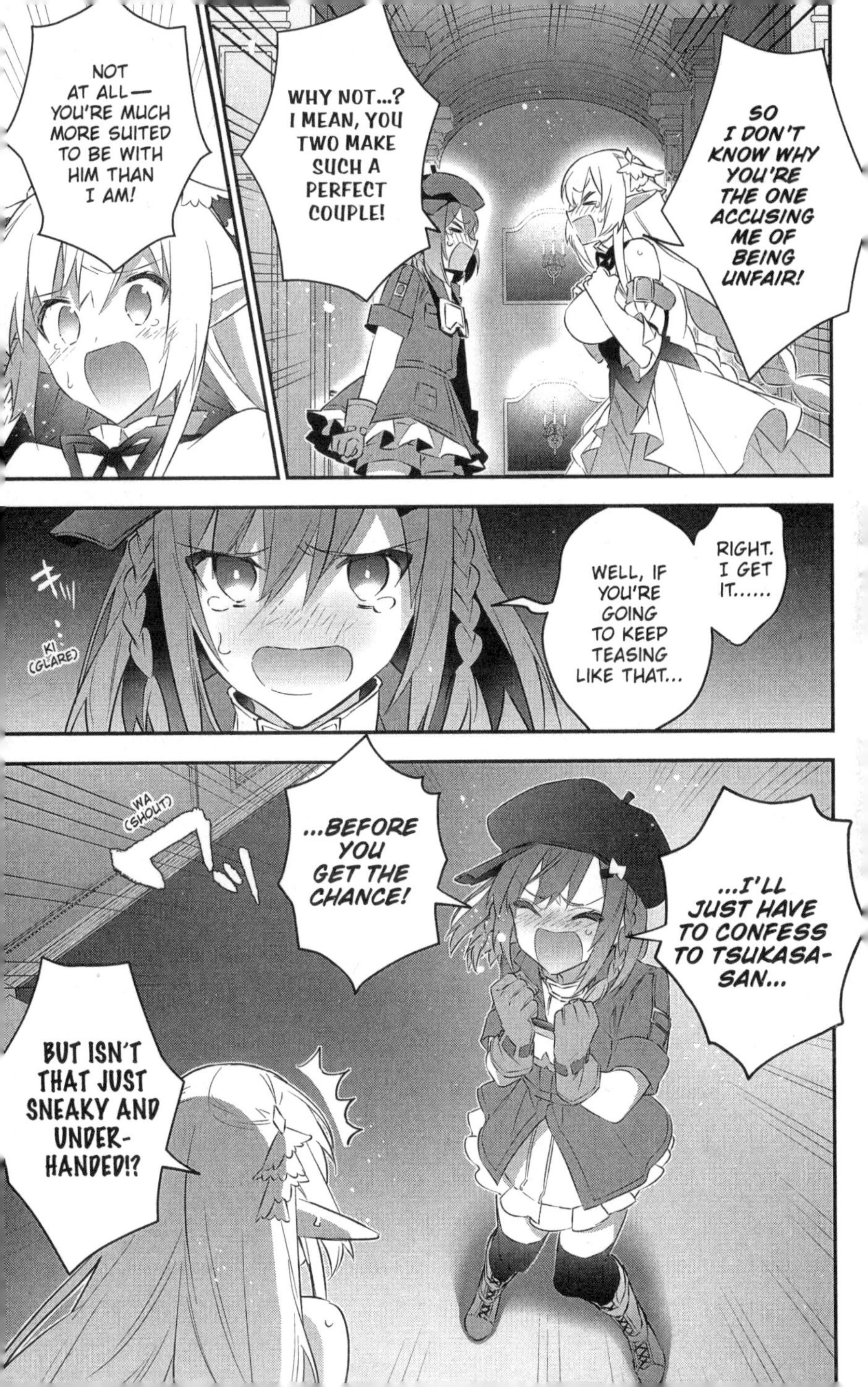
SO I DON'T KNOW WHY YOU'RE THE ONE ACCUSING ME OF BEING UNFAIR!
WHY NOT...? I MEAN, YOU TWO MAKE SUCH A PERFECT COUPLE!
NOT AT ALL— YOU'RE MUCH MORE SUITED TO BE WITH HIM THAN I AM!
RIGHT. I GET IT......
WELL, IF YOU'RE GOING TO KEEP TEASING LIKE THAT...
KI (GLARE)
...I'LL JUST HAVE TO CONFESS TO TSUKASA-SAN...
...BEFORE YOU GET THE CHANCE!
WA (SHOUT)
BUT ISN'T THAT JUST SNEAKY AND UNDER-HANDED!?

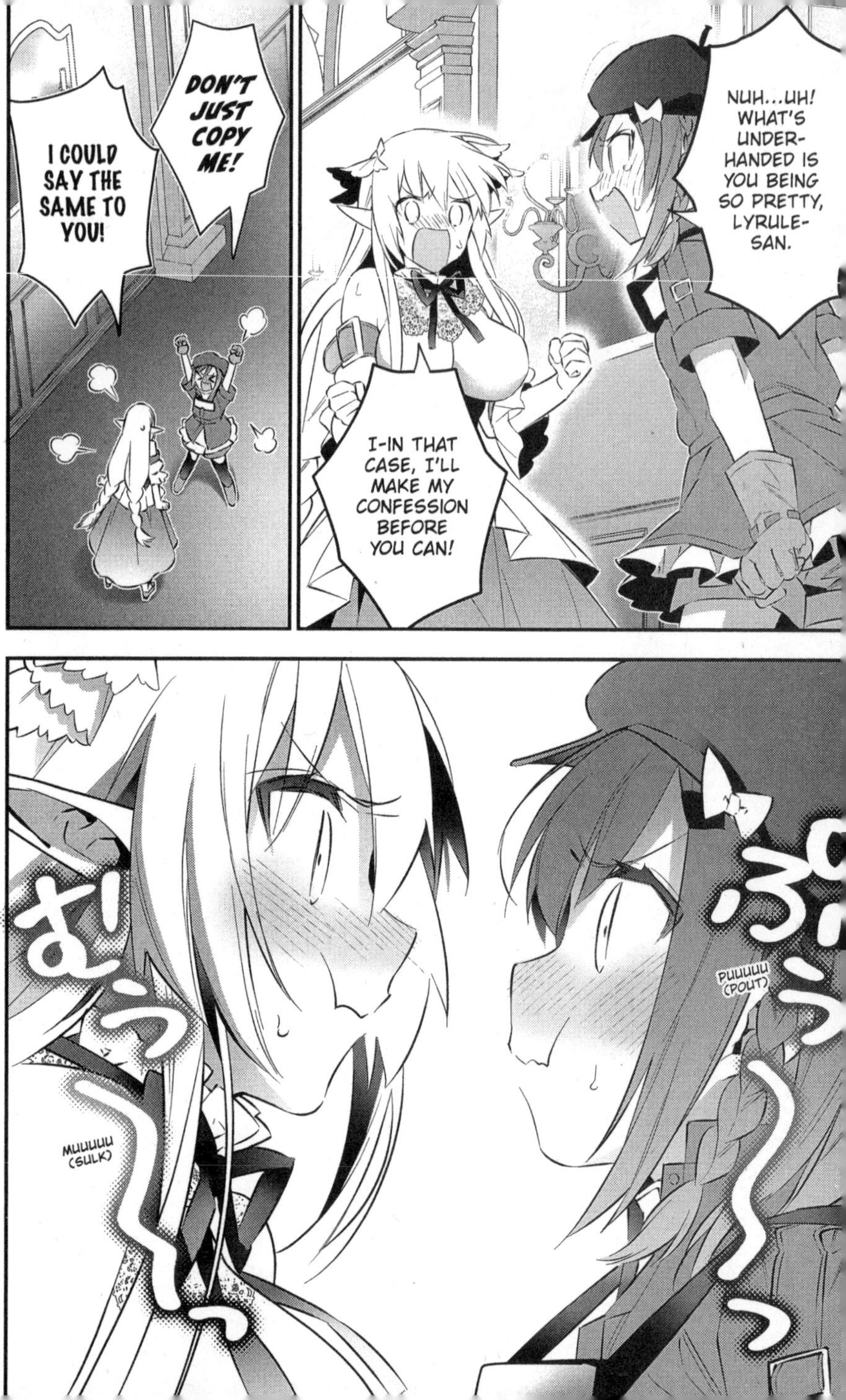

NUH...UH! WHAT'S UNDER-HANDED IS YOU BEING SO PRETTY, LYRULE-SAN.
I-IN THAT CASE, I'LL MAKE MY CONFESSION BEFORE YOU CAN!
DON'T JUST COPY ME!
I COULD SAY THE SAME TO YOU!
ぷう〜っ
PUUUUU (POUT)
むう〜っ
MUUUUU (SULK)

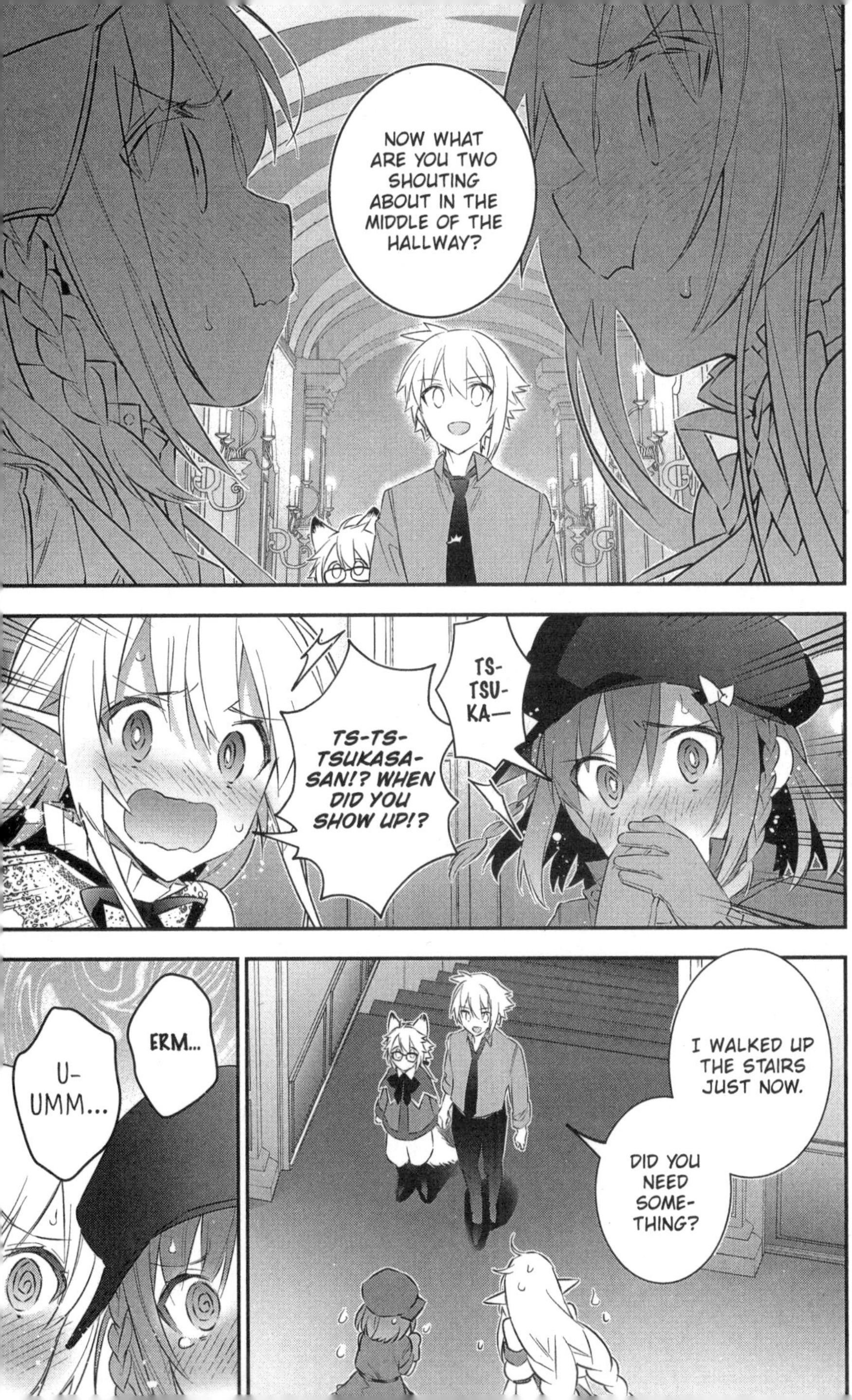
NOW WHAT ARE YOU TWO SHOUTING ABOUT IN THE MIDDLE OF THE HALLWAY?
TS-TSU-KA—
TS-TS-TSUKASA-SAN!? WHEN DID YOU SHOW UP!?
I WALKED UP THE STAIRS JUST NOW.
DID YOU NEED SOME-THING?
ERM...
U-UMM...

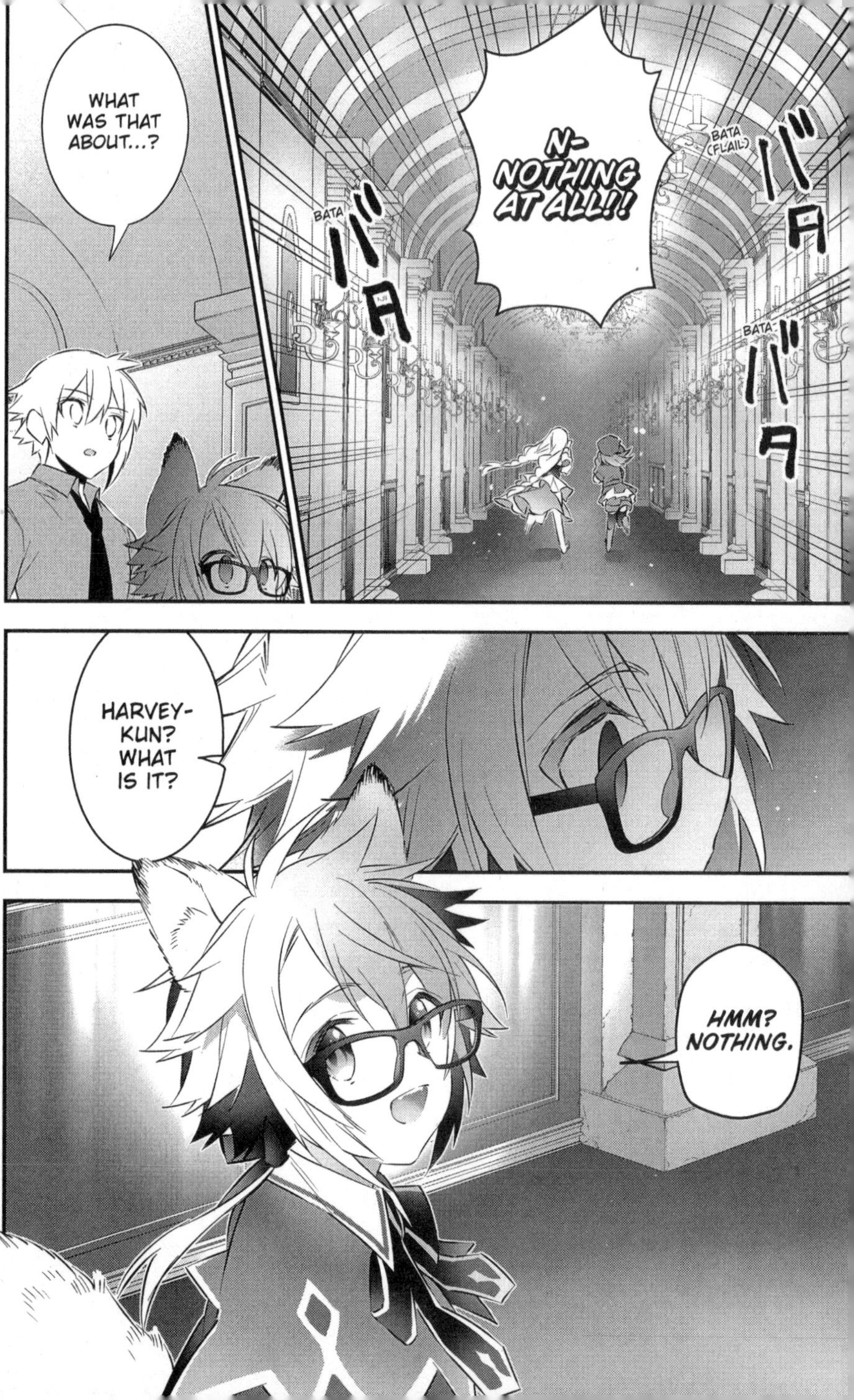
N-NOTHING AT ALL!!
BATA (FLAIL)
バタ
BATA-
バタバタ
BATA
バタ
WHAT WAS THAT ABOUT...?
HARVEY-KUN? WHAT IS IT?
HMM? NOTHING.

HIGH SCHOOL
PRODIGIES HAVE
IT EASY EVEN IN
ANOTHER
WORLD!

CHARACTER FILE 24

Nio Harvey

The cease-fire treaty with the Freyjagard Empire came with a provision for an exchange program, and Harvey is one such student. He has come to the Republic of Elm in order to learn about government as Tsukasa's aide.

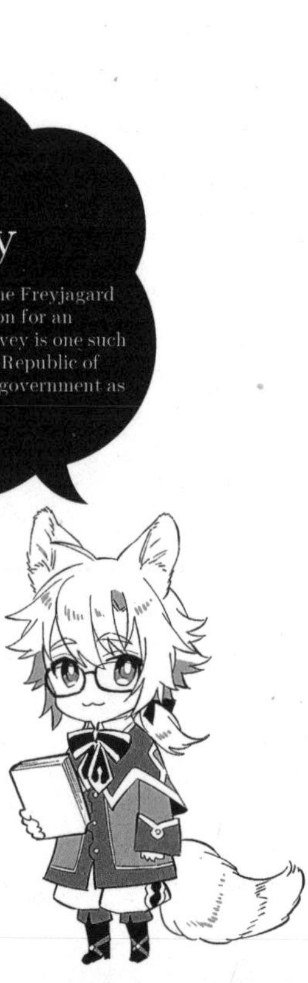

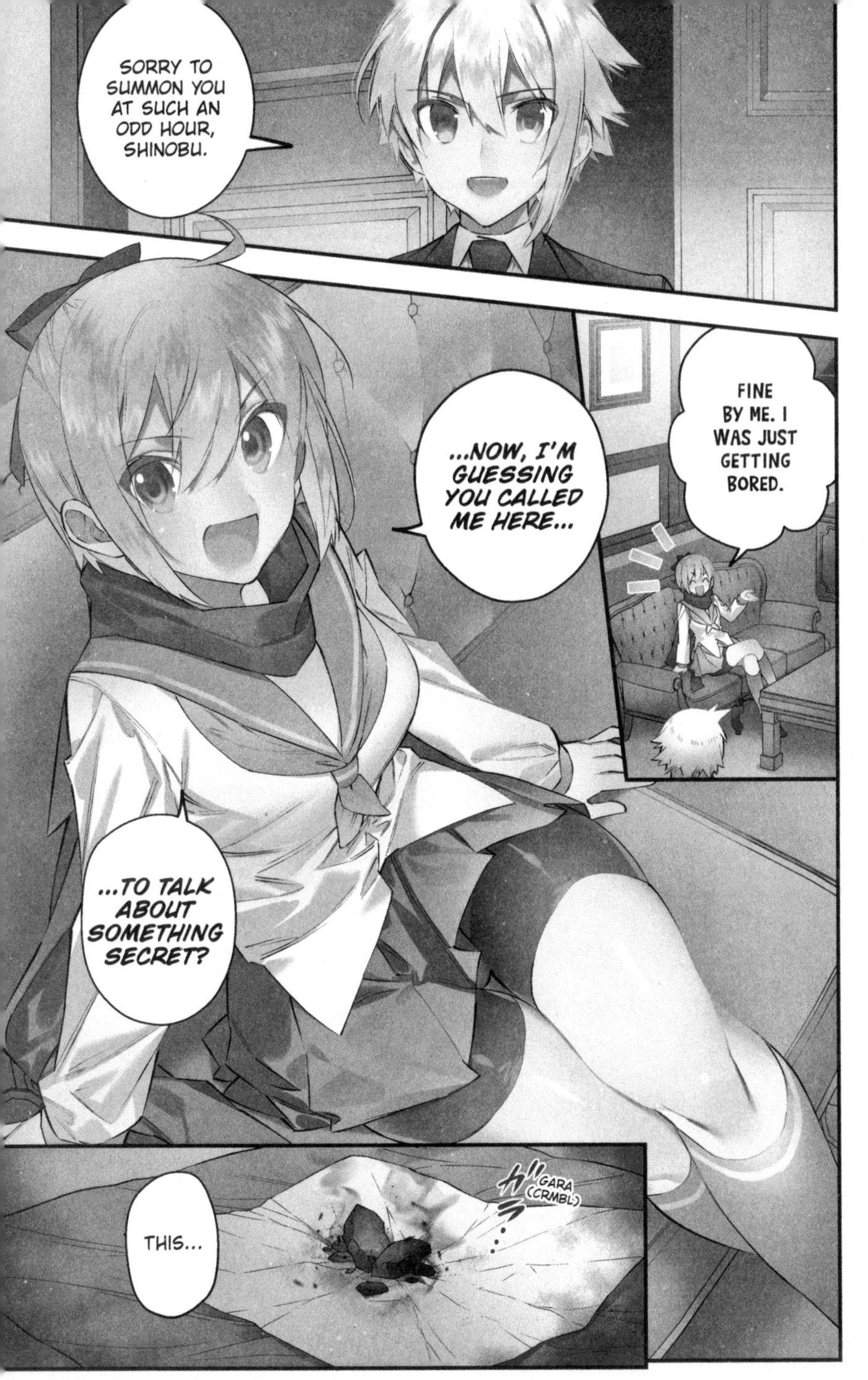
SORRY TO SUMMON YOU AT SUCH AN ODD HOUR, SHINOBU.
FINE BY ME. I WAS JUST GETTING BORED.
...NOW, I'M GUESSING YOU CALLED ME HERE...
...TO TALK ABOUT SOMETHING SECRET?
GARA (CRMBL)
THIS...

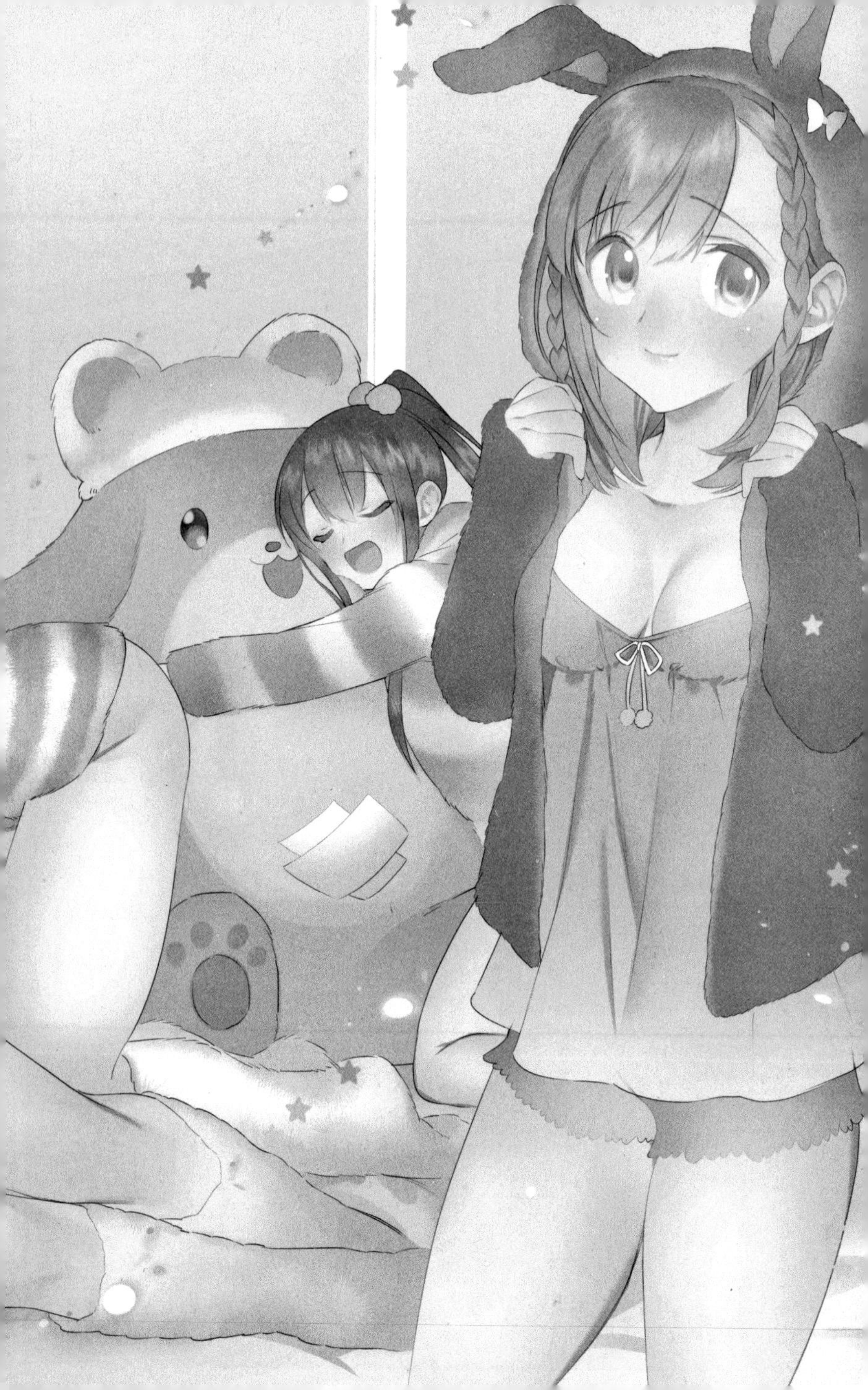

CHAPTER 52: EVOLUTION AND TRANSFORMATION

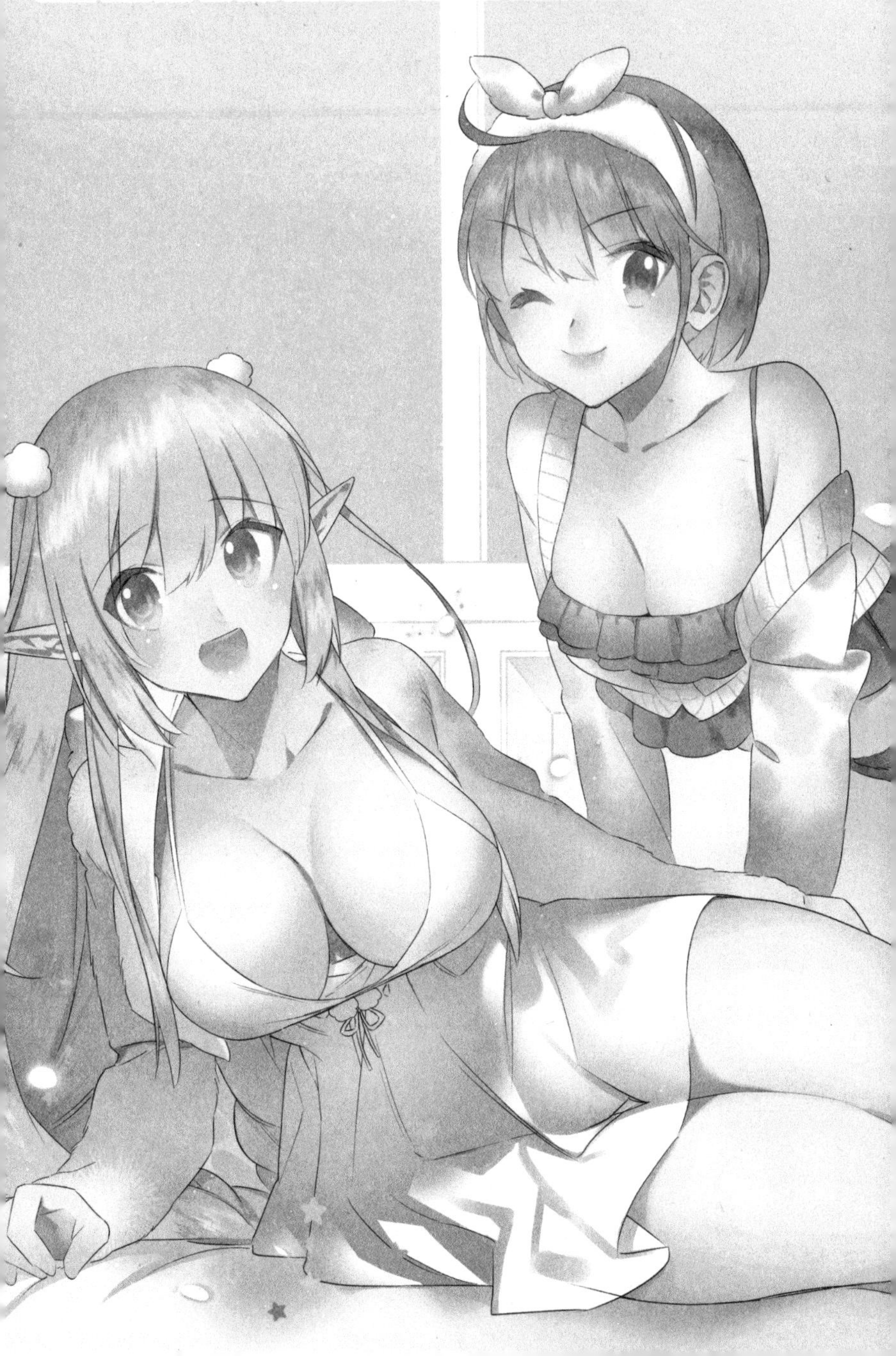

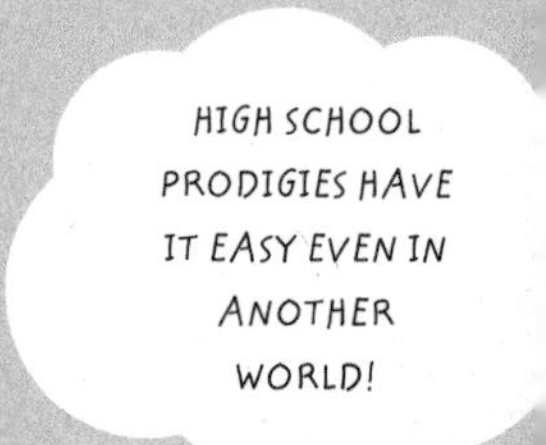
HIGH SCHOOL PRODIGIES HAVE IT EASY EVEN IN ANOTHER WORLD!

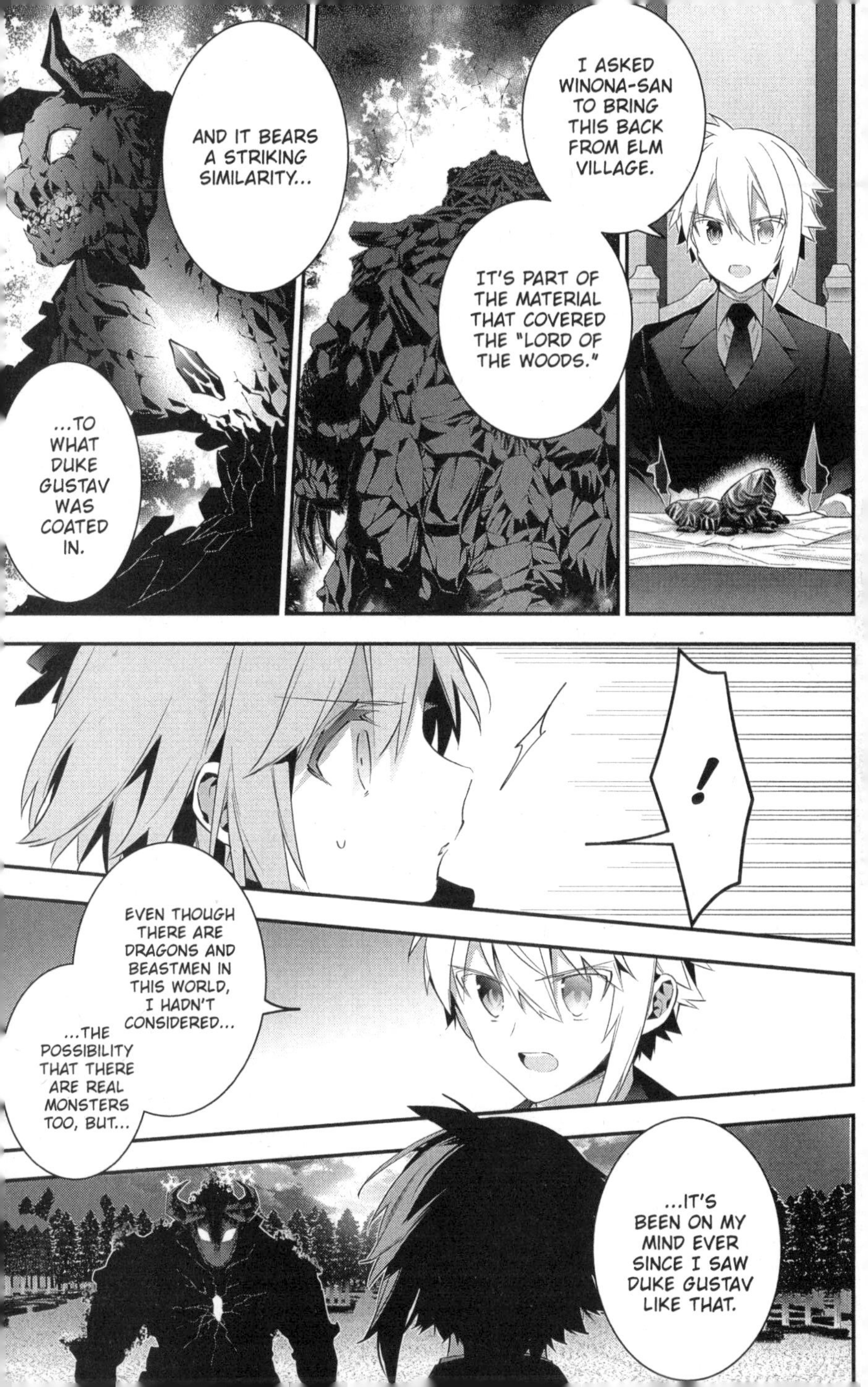
I ASKED WINONA-SAN TO BRING THIS BACK FROM ELM VILLAGE.
IT'S PART OF THE MATERIAL THAT COVERED THE "LORD OF THE WOODS."
AND IT BEARS A STRIKING SIMILARITY...
...TO WHAT DUKE GUSTAV WAS COATED IN.
!
EVEN THOUGH THERE ARE DRAGONS AND BEASTMEN IN THIS WORLD, I HADN'T CONSIDERED...
...THE POSSIBILITY THAT THERE ARE REAL MONSTERS TOO, BUT...
...IT'S BEEN ON MY MIND EVER SINCE I SAW DUKE GUSTAV LIKE THAT.

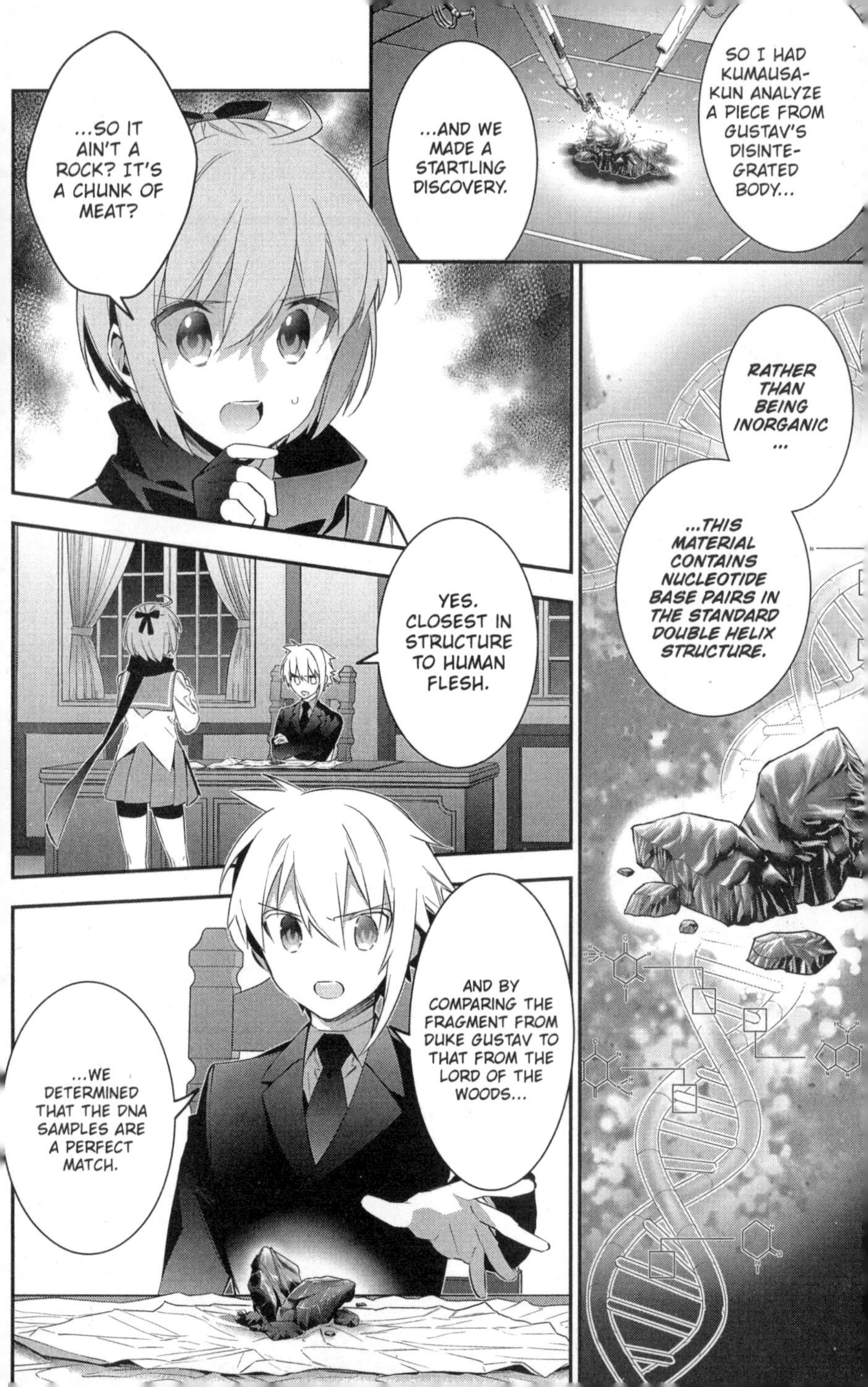
SO I HAD KUMAUSA-KUN ANALYZE A PIECE FROM GUSTAV'S DISINTE-GRATED BODY...
...AND WE MADE A STARTLING DISCOVERY.
RATHER THAN BEING INORGANIC...
...THIS MATERIAL CONTAINS NUCLEOTIDE BASE PAIRS IN THE STANDARD DOUBLE HELIX STRUCTURE.
...SO IT AIN'T A ROCK? IT'S A CHUNK OF MEAT?
YES. CLOSEST IN STRUCTURE TO HUMAN FLESH.
AND BY COMPARING THE FRAGMENT FROM DUKE GUSTAV TO THAT FROM THE LORD OF THE WOODS...
...WE DETERMINED THAT THE DNA SAMPLES ARE A PERFECT MATCH.

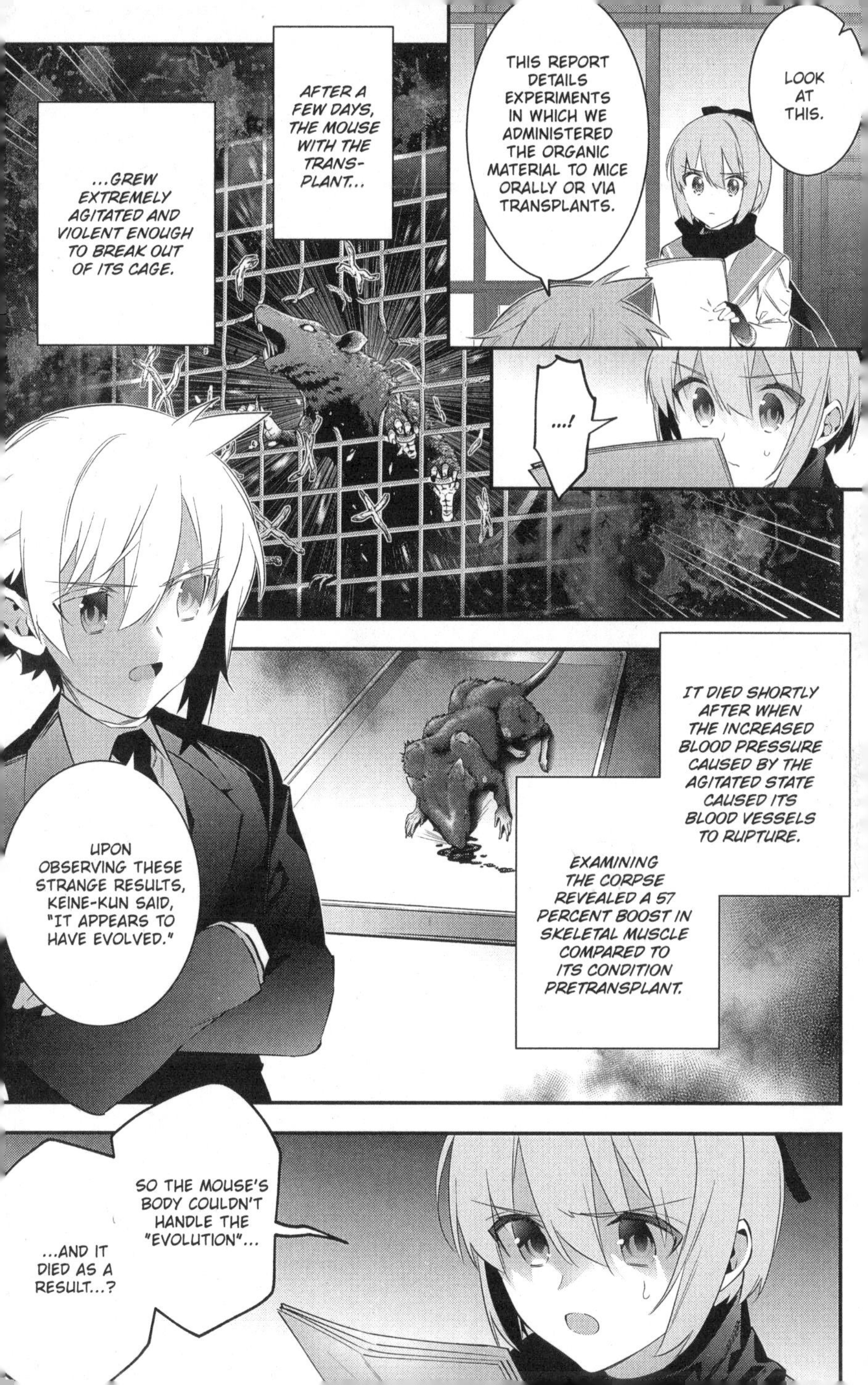
LOOK AT THIS.
THIS REPORT DETAILS EXPERIMENTS IN WHICH WE ADMINISTERED THE ORGANIC MATERIAL TO MICE ORALLY OR VIA TRANSPLANTS.
...!
AFTER A FEW DAYS, THE MOUSE WITH THE TRANS-PLANT...
...GREW EXTREMELY AGITATED AND VIOLENT ENOUGH TO BREAK OUT OF ITS CAGE.
IT DIED SHORTLY AFTER WHEN THE INCREASED BLOOD PRESSURE CAUSED BY THE AGITATED STATE CAUSED ITS BLOOD VESSELS TO RUPTURE.
EXAMINING THE CORPSE REVEALED A 57 PERCENT BOOST IN SKELETAL MUSCLE COMPARED TO ITS CONDITION PRETRANSPLANT.
UPON OBSERVING THESE STRANGE RESULTS, KEINE-KUN SAID, "IT APPEARS TO HAVE EVOLVED."
SO THE MOUSE'S BODY COULDN'T HANDLE THE "EVOLUTION"...
...AND IT DIED AS A RESULT...?

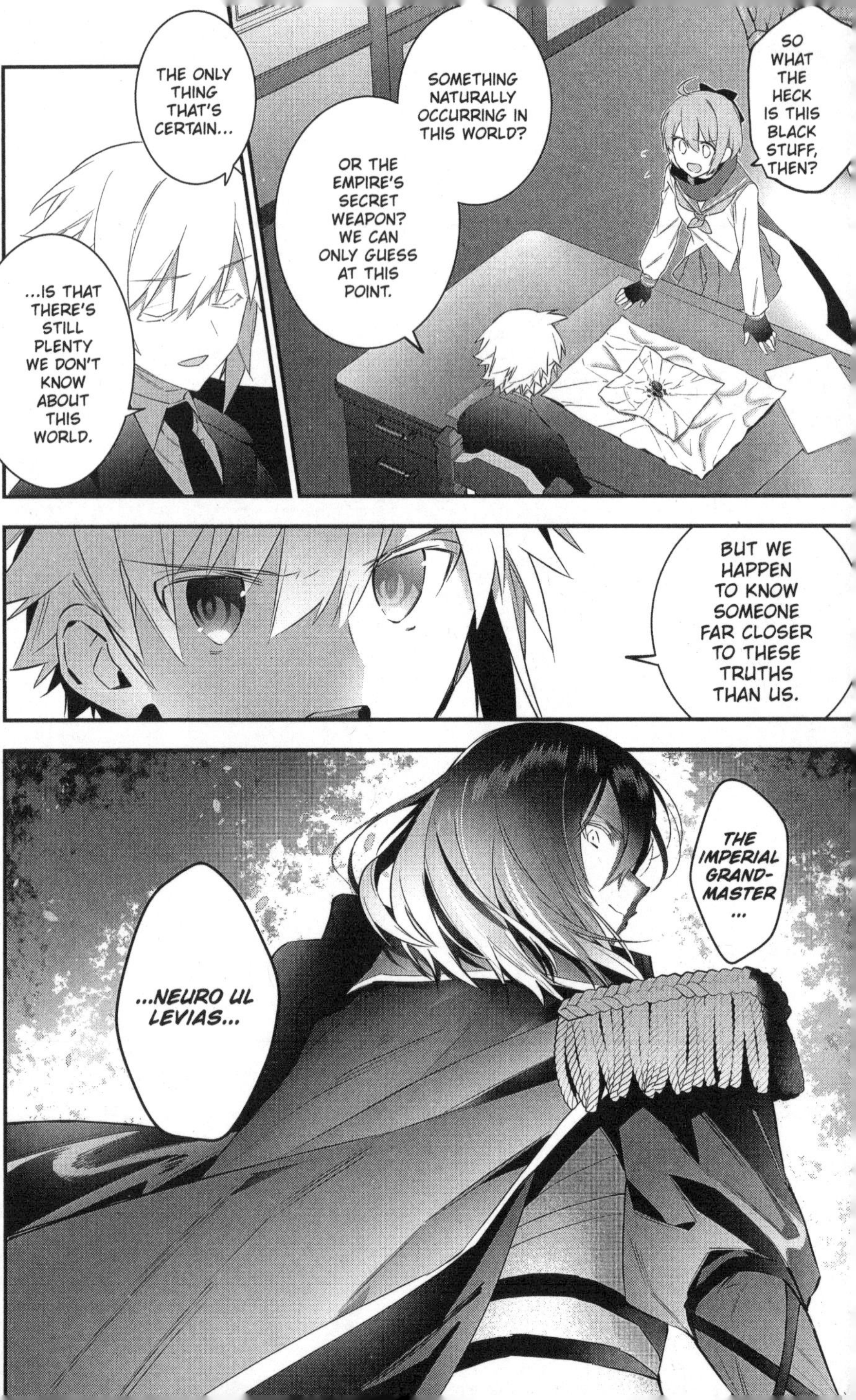
SO WHAT THE HECK IS THIS BLACK STUFF, THEN?
SOMETHING NATURALLY OCCURRING IN THIS WORLD?
OR THE EMPIRE'S SECRET WEAPON? WE CAN ONLY GUESS AT THIS POINT.
THE ONLY THING THAT'S CERTAIN...
...IS THAT THERE'S STILL PLENTY WE DON'T KNOW ABOUT THIS WORLD.
BUT WE HAPPEN TO KNOW SOMEONE FAR CLOSER TO THESE TRUTHS THAN US.
THE IMPERIAL GRAND-MASTER...
...NEURO UL LEVIAS...

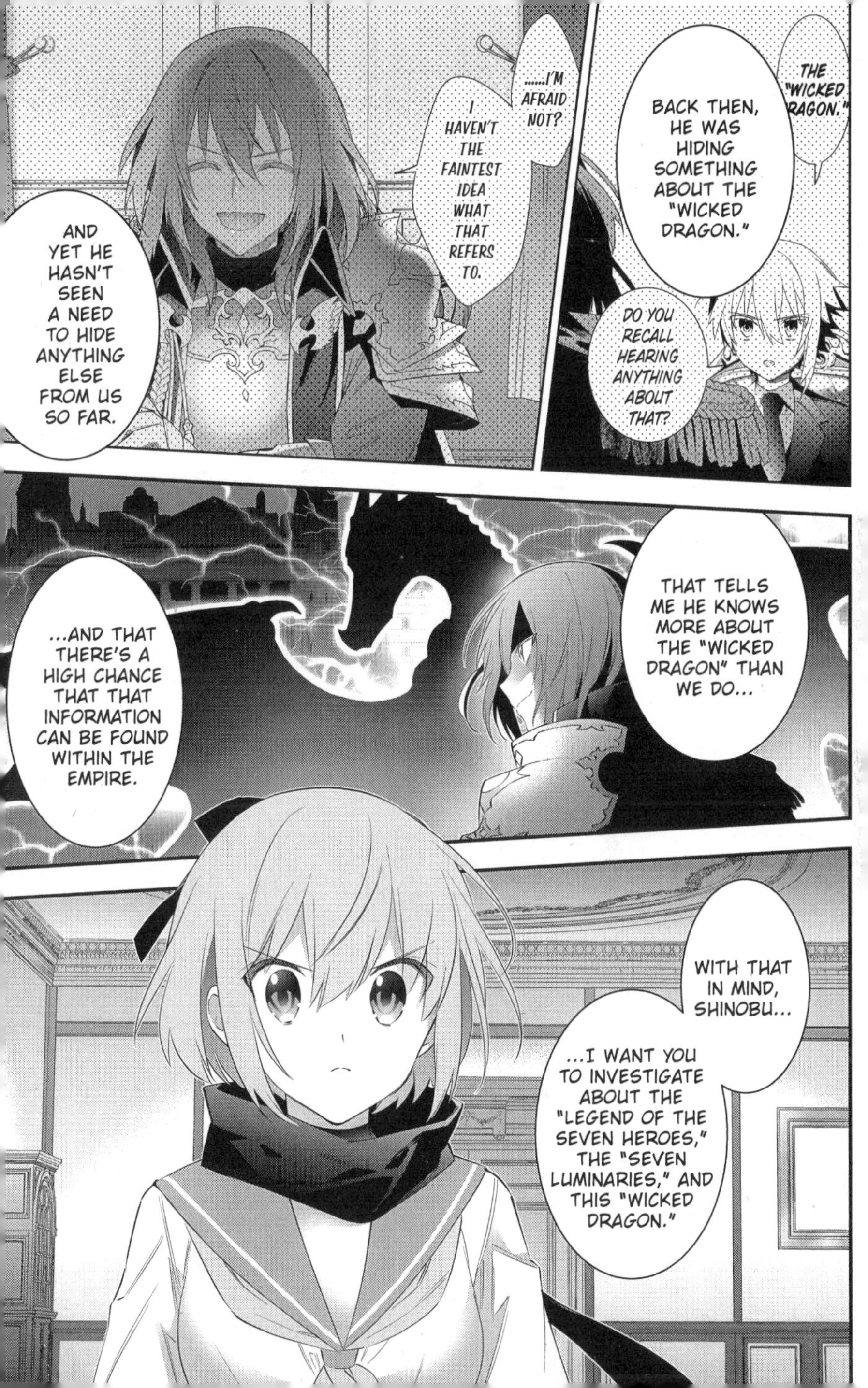
THE "WICKED DRAGON."
BACK THEN, HE WAS HIDING SOMETHING ABOUT THE "WICKED DRAGON."
DO YOU RECALL HEARING ANYTHING ABOUT THAT?
......I'M AFRAID NOT?
I HAVEN'T THE FAINTEST IDEA WHAT THAT REFERS TO.
AND YET HE HASN'T SEEN A NEED TO HIDE ANYTHING ELSE FROM US SO FAR.
THAT TELLS ME HE KNOWS MORE ABOUT THE "WICKED DRAGON" THAN WE DO...
...AND THAT THERE'S A HIGH CHANCE THAT THAT INFORMATION CAN BE FOUND WITHIN THE EMPIRE.
WITH THAT IN MIND, SHINOBU...
...I WANT YOU TO INVESTIGATE ABOUT THE "LEGEND OF THE SEVEN HEROES," THE "SEVEN LUMINARIES," AND THIS "WICKED DRAGON."

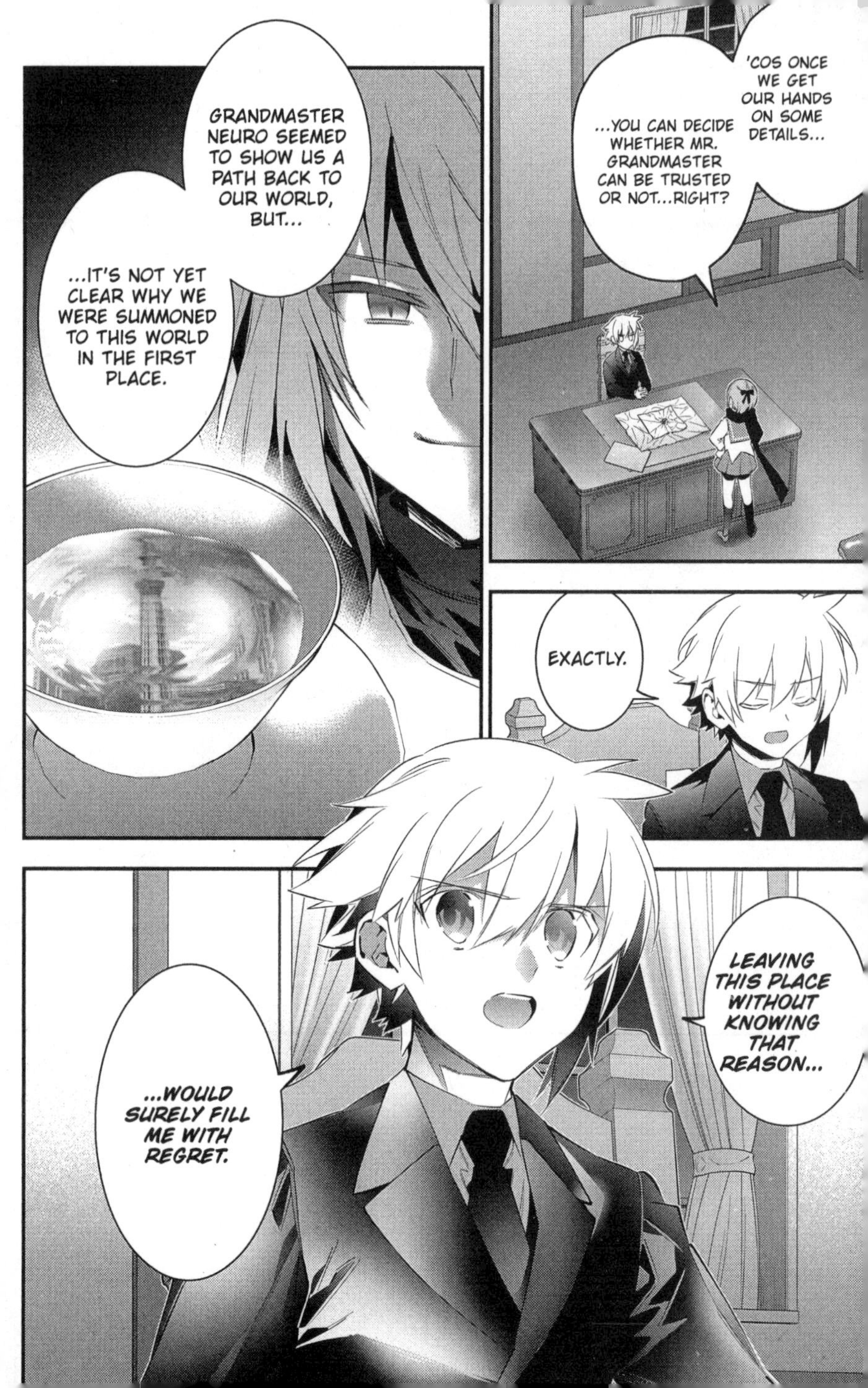
'COS ONCE WE GET OUR HANDS ON SOME DETAILS...
...YOU CAN DECIDE WHETHER MR. GRANDMASTER CAN BE TRUSTED OR NOT...RIGHT?
EXACTLY.
GRANDMASTER NEURO SEEMED TO SHOW US A PATH BACK TO OUR WORLD, BUT...
...IT'S NOT YET CLEAR WHY WE WERE SUMMONED TO THIS WORLD IN THE FIRST PLACE.
LEAVING THIS PLACE WITHOUT KNOWING THAT REASON...
...WOULD SURELY FILL ME WITH REGRET.

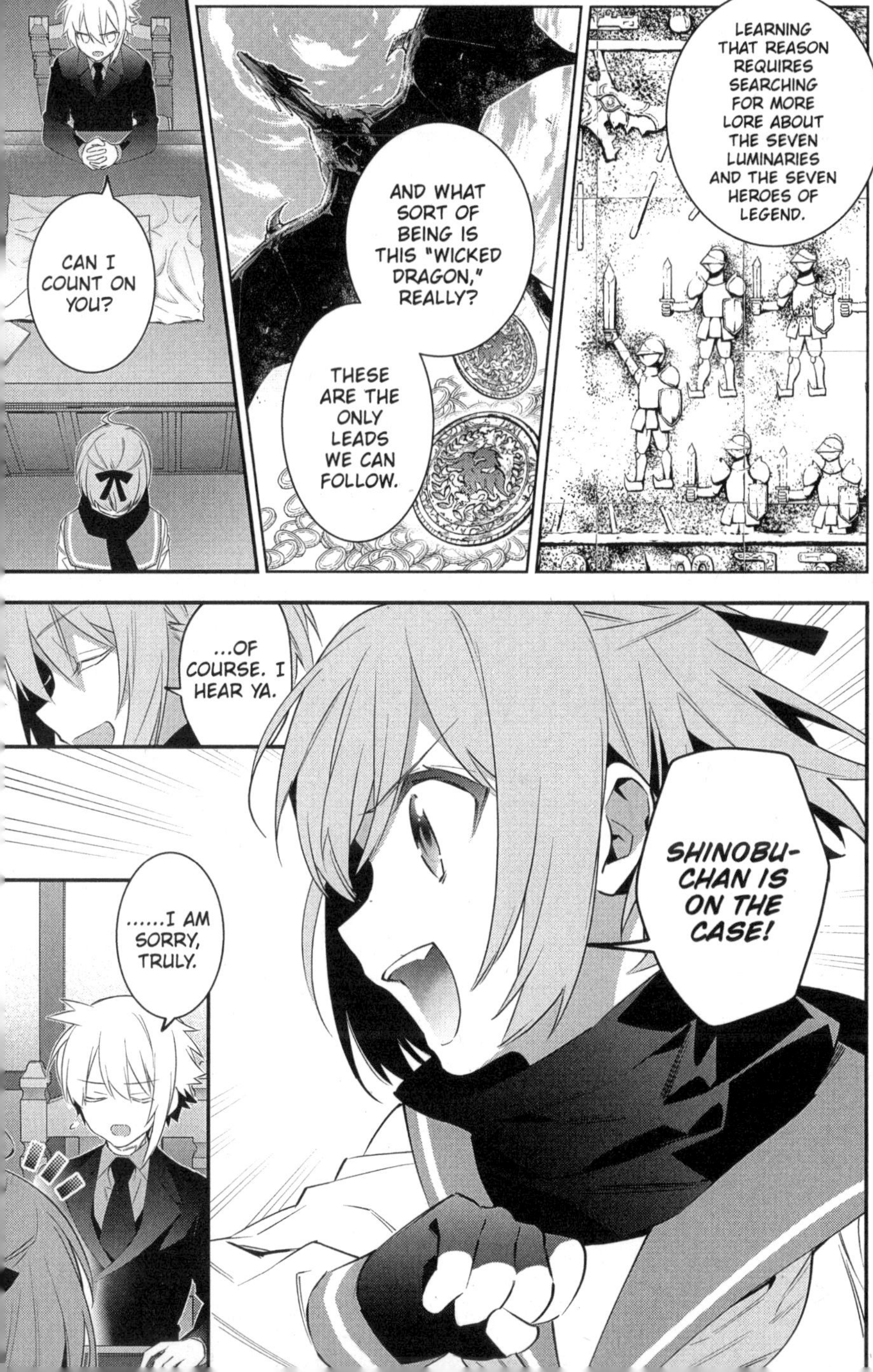
LEARNING THAT REASON REQUIRES SEARCHING FOR MORE LORE ABOUT THE SEVEN LUMINARIES AND THE SEVEN HEROES OF LEGEND.
AND WHAT SORT OF BEING IS THIS "WICKED DRAGON," REALLY?
THESE ARE THE ONLY LEADS WE CAN FOLLOW.
CAN I COUNT ON YOU?
...OF COURSE. I HEAR YA.
SHINOBU-CHAN IS ON THE CASE!
......I AM SORRY, TRULY.

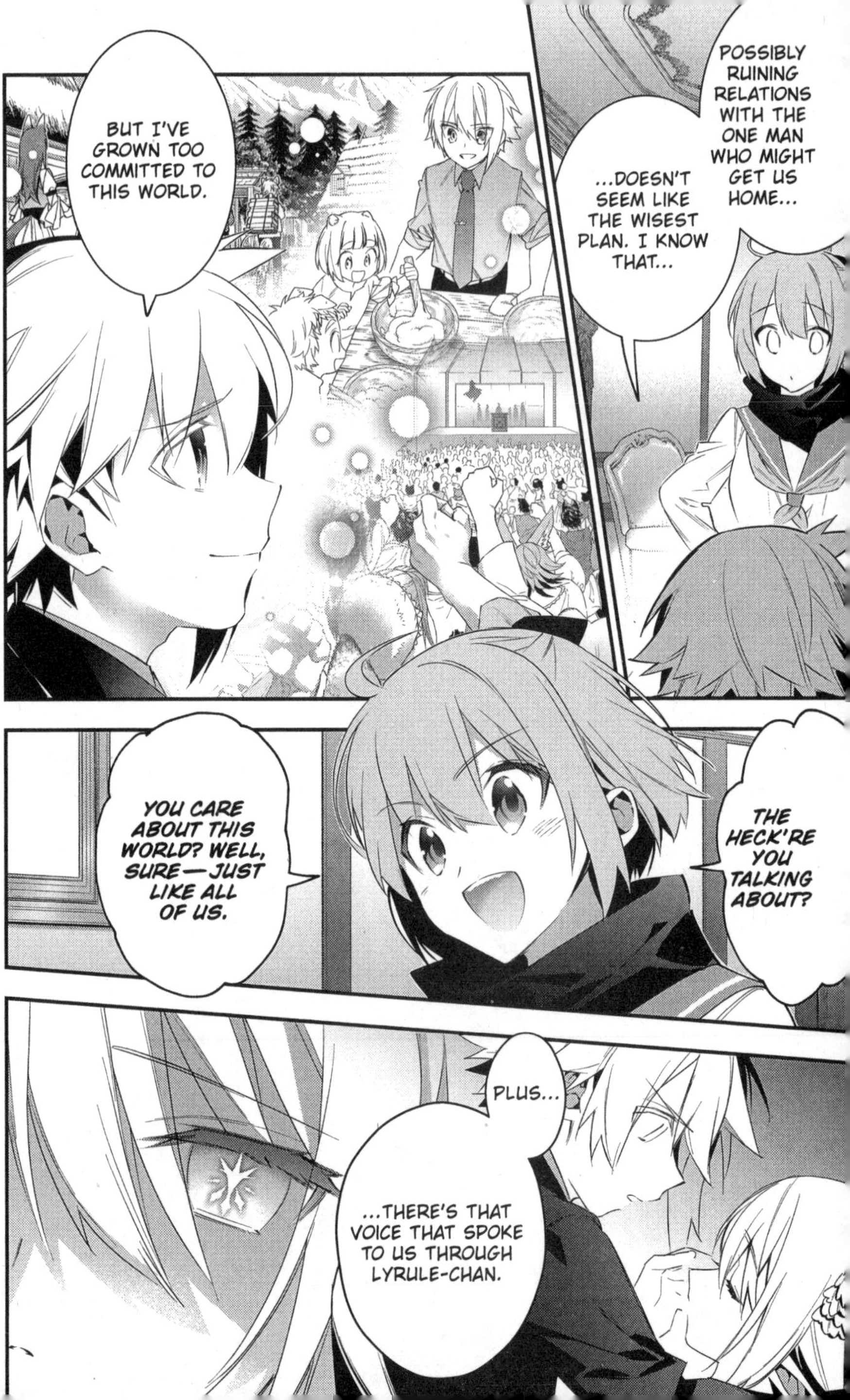
POSSIBLY RUINING RELATIONS WITH THE ONE MAN WHO MIGHT GET US HOME...
...DOESN'T SEEM LIKE THE WISEST PLAN. I KNOW THAT...
BUT I'VE GROWN TOO COMMITTED TO THIS WORLD.
THE HECK'RE YOU TALKING ABOUT?
YOU CARE ABOUT THIS WORLD? WELL, SURE—JUST LIKE ALL OF US.
PLUS...
...THERE'S THAT VOICE THAT SPOKE TO US THROUGH LYRULE-CHAN.

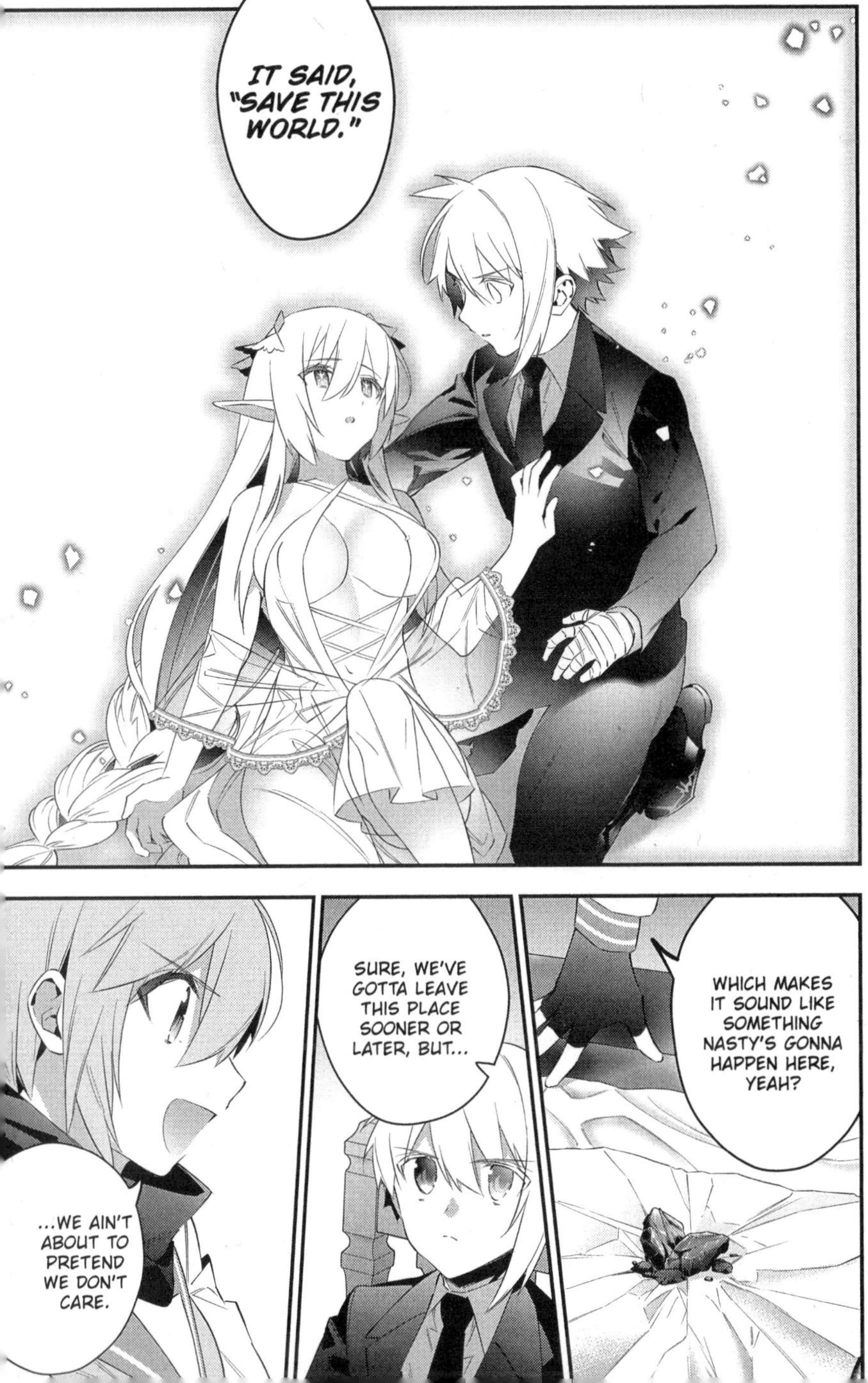
IT SAID, "SAVE THIS WORLD."
WHICH MAKES IT SOUND LIKE SOMETHING NASTY'S GONNA HAPPEN HERE, YEAH?
SURE, WE'VE GOTTA LEAVE THIS PLACE SOONER OR LATER, BUT...
...WE AIN'T ABOUT TO PRETEND WE DON'T CARE.

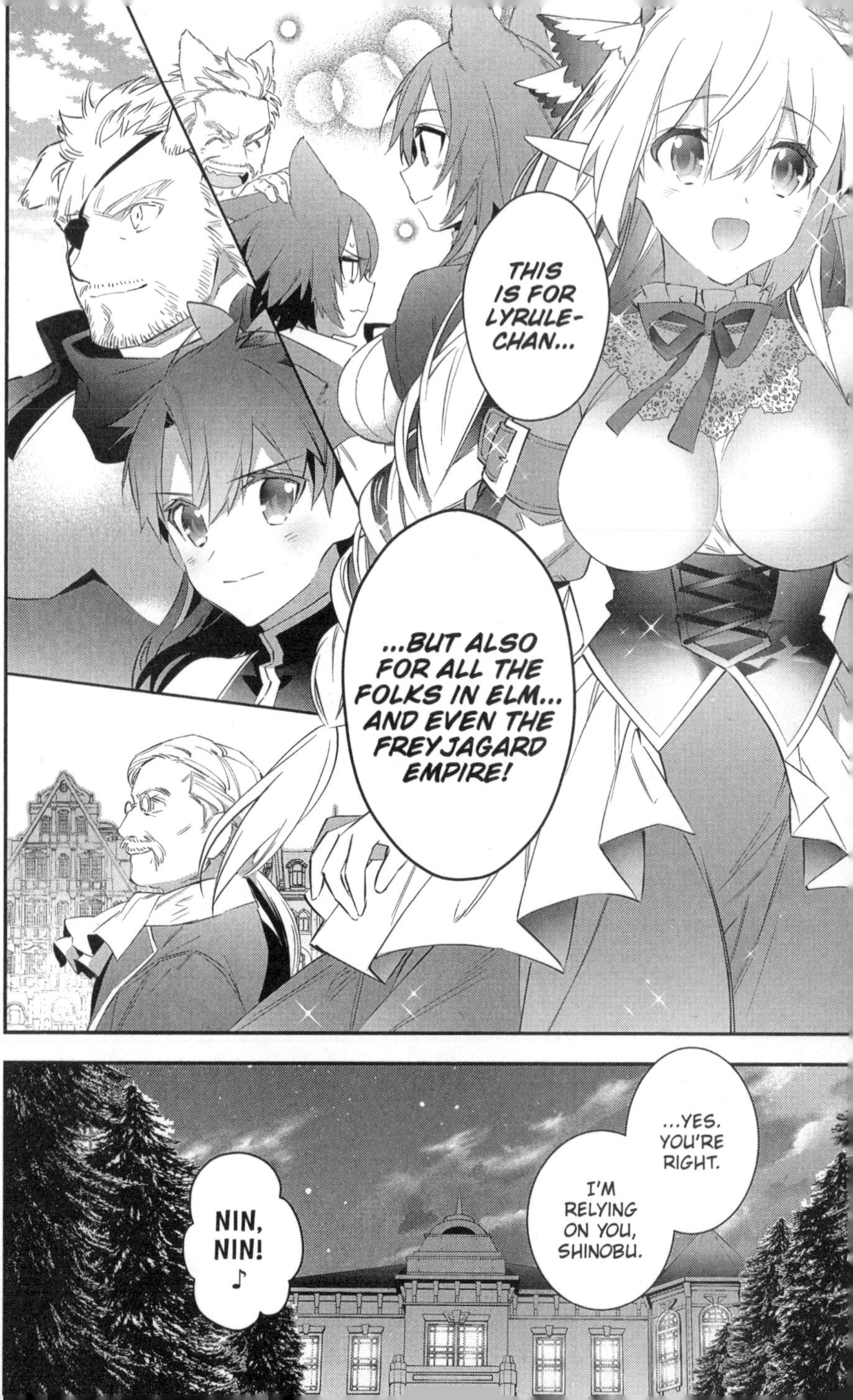
THIS IS FOR LYRULE-CHAN...
...BUT ALSO FOR ALL THE FOLKS IN ELM... AND EVEN THE FREYJAGARD EMPIRE!
...YES. YOU'RE RIGHT.
I'M RELYING ON YOU, SHINOBU.
NIN, NIN! ♪

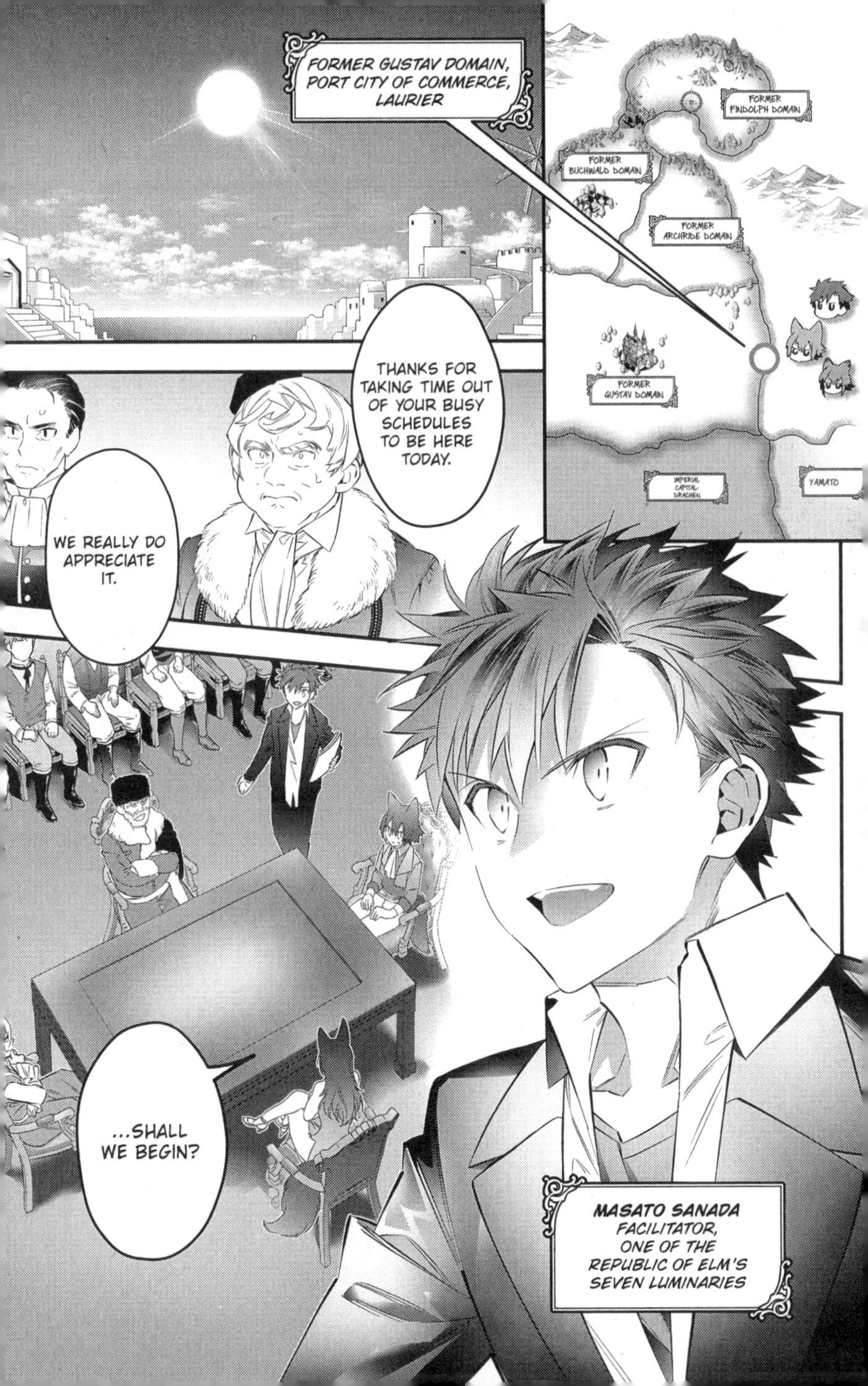
FORMER FINDOLPH DOMAIN
FORMER BUCHWALD DOMAIN
FORMER ARCHRIDE DOMAIN
FORMER GUSTAV DOMAIN
IMPERIAL CAPITAL DRACHEN
YAMATO
FORMER GUSTAV DOMAIN, PORT CITY OF COMMERCE, LAURIER
THANKS FOR TAKING TIME OUT OF YOUR BUSY SCHEDULES TO BE HERE TODAY.
WE REALLY DO APPRECIATE IT.
MASATO SANADA FACILITATOR, ONE OF THE REPUBLIC OF ELM'S SEVEN LUMINARIES
...SHALL WE BEGIN?

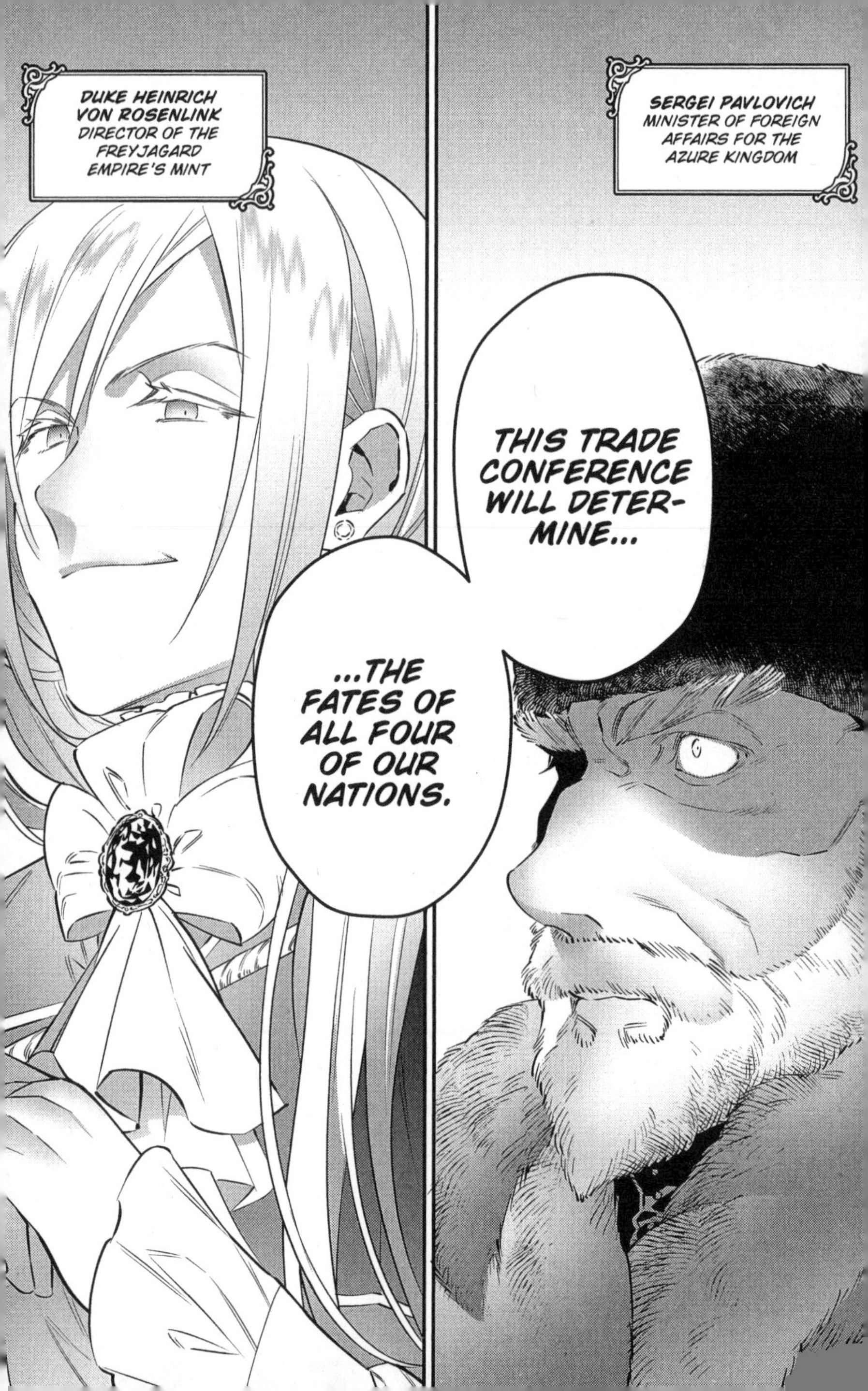
SERGEI PAVLOVICH MINISTER OF FOREIGN AFFAIRS FOR THE AZURE KINGDOM
THIS TRADE CONFERENCE WILL DETER-MINE...
...THE FATES OF ALL FOUR OF OUR NATIONS.
DUKE HEINRICH VON ROSENLINK DIRECTOR OF THE FREYJAGARD EMPIRE'S MINT

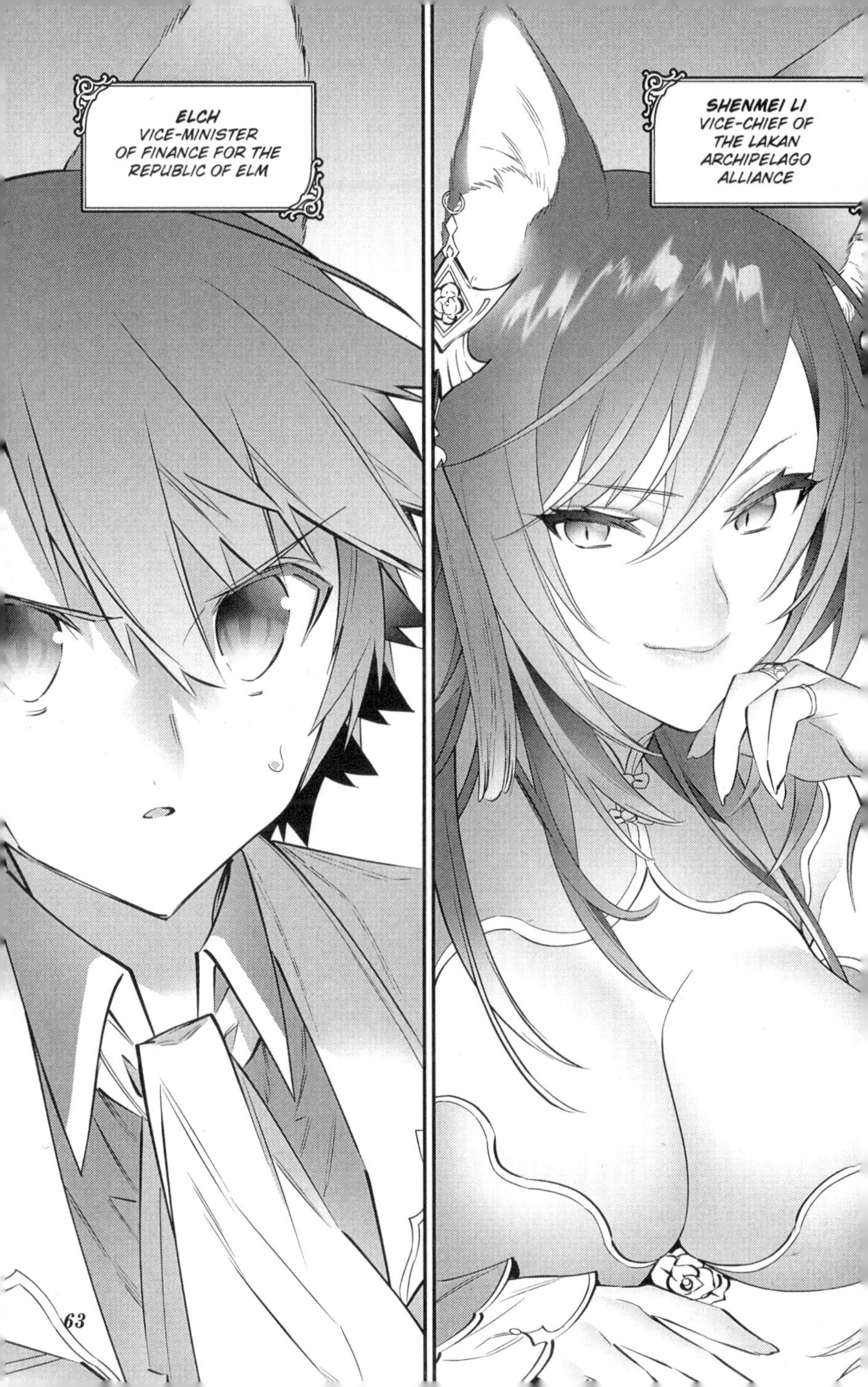
SHENMEI LI
VICE-CHIEF OF THE LAKAN ARCHIPELAGO ALLIANCE
ELCH
VICE-MINISTER OF FINANCE FOR THE REPUBLIC OF ELM

CHARACTER FILE 25

Elch

Winona's son and the grandson of Ulgar (the head of Elm Village). He and Roo are learning about economics from Masato.

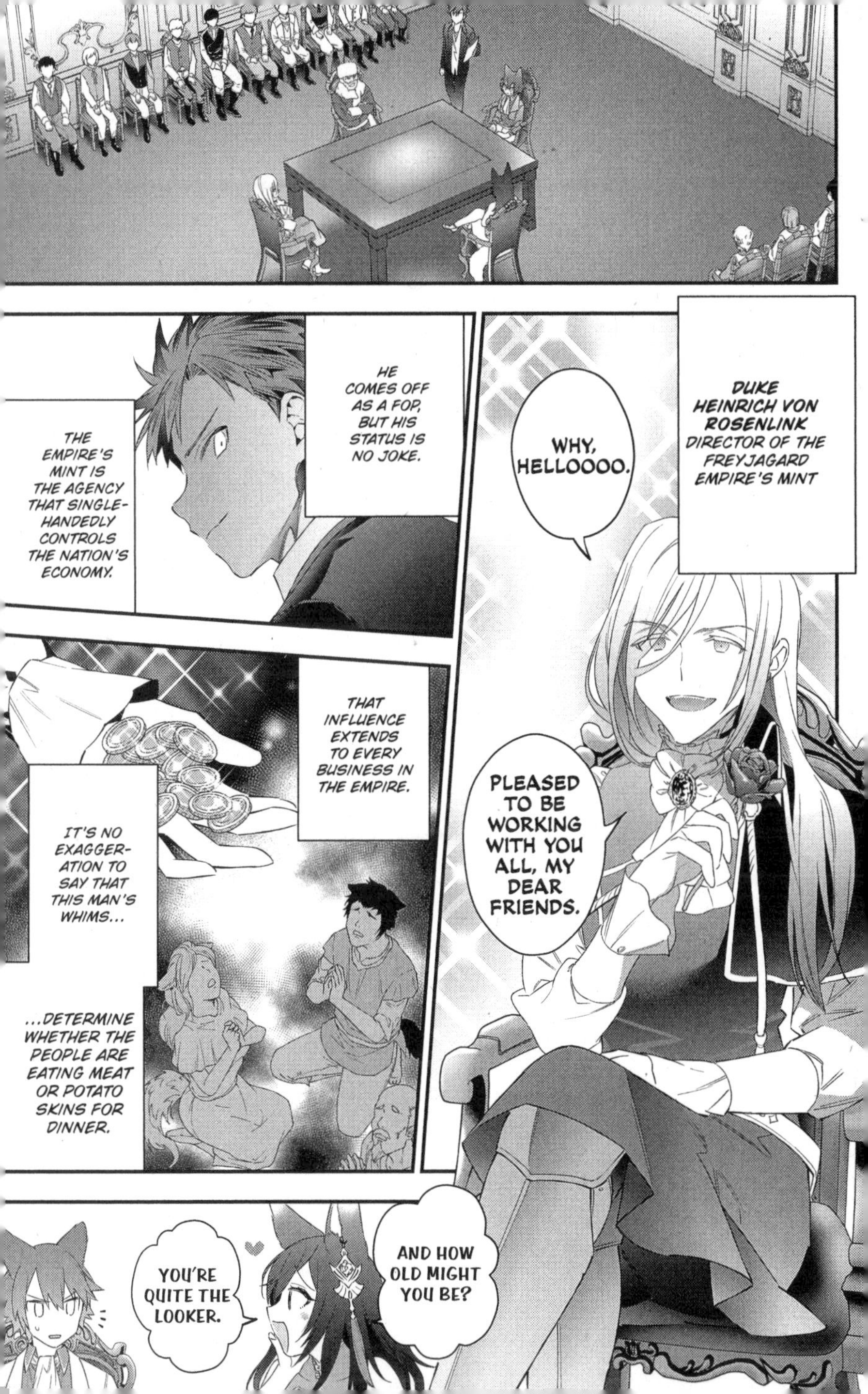
DUKE HEINRICH VON ROSENLINK
DIRECTOR OF THE FREYJAGARD EMPIRE'S MINT
WHY, HELLOOOO.
PLEASED TO BE WORKING WITH YOU ALL, MY DEAR FRIENDS.
HE COMES OFF AS A FOP, BUT HIS STATUS IS NO JOKE.
THE EMPIRE'S MINT IS THE AGENCY THAT SINGLE-HANDEDLY CONTROLS THE NATION'S ECONOMY.
THAT INFLUENCE EXTENDS TO EVERY BUSINESS IN THE EMPIRE.
IT'S NO EXAGGER-ATION TO SAY THAT THIS MAN'S WHIMS...
...DETERMINE WHETHER THE PEOPLE ARE EATING MEAT OR POTATO SKINS FOR DINNER.
AND HOW OLD MIGHT YOU BE?
YOU'RE QUITE THE LOOKER.

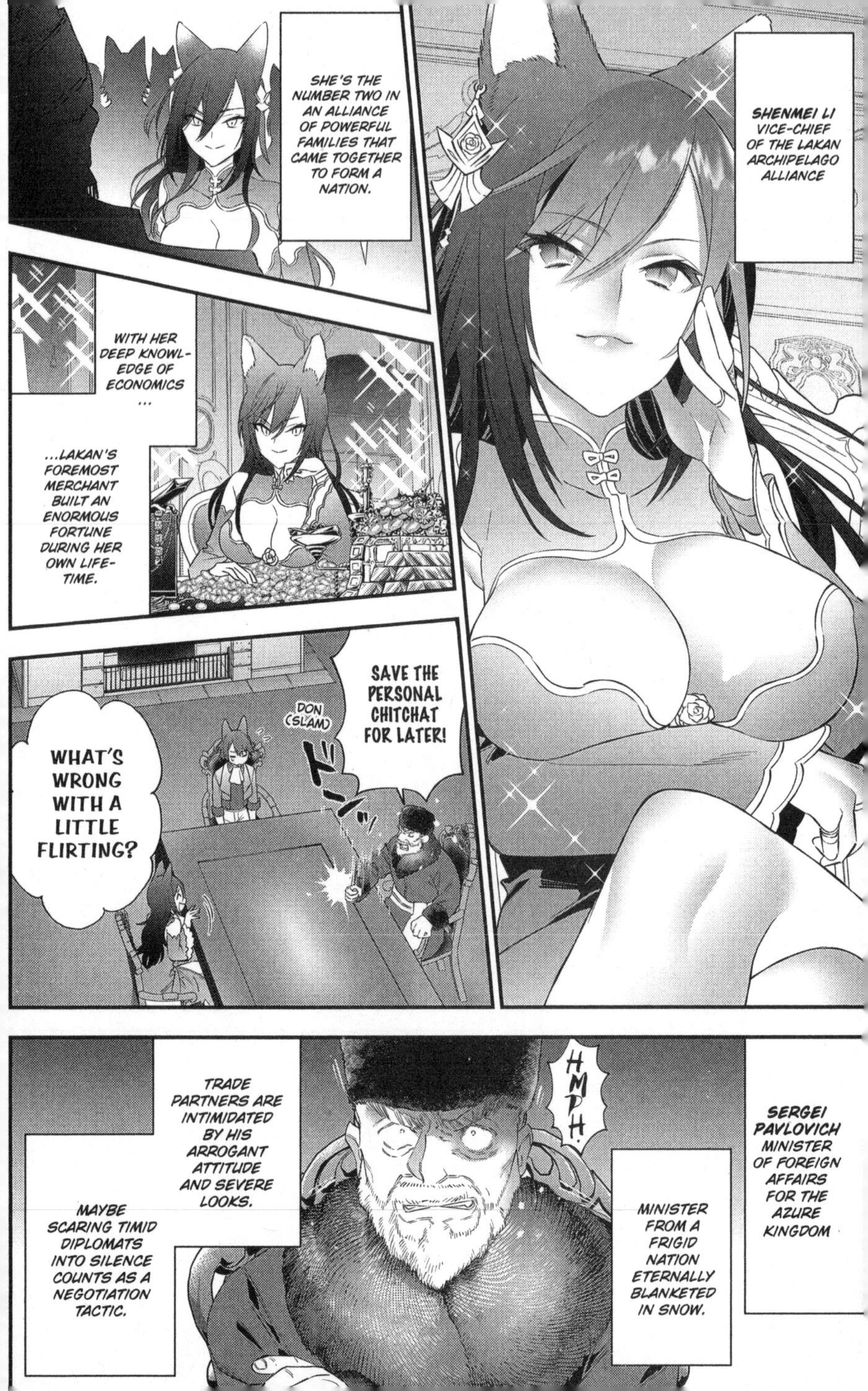
SHENMEI LI
VICE-CHIEF OF THE LAKAN ARCHIPELAGO ALLIANCE
SHE'S THE NUMBER TWO IN AN ALLIANCE OF POWERFUL FAMILIES THAT CAME TOGETHER TO FORM A NATION.
WITH HER DEEP KNOWL-EDGE OF ECONOMICS ...
...LAKAN'S FOREMOST MERCHANT BUILT AN ENORMOUS FORTUNE DURING HER OWN LIFE-TIME.
SAVE THE PERSONAL CHITCHAT FOR LATER!
DON (SLAM)
WHAT'S WRONG WITH A LITTLE FLIRTING?
SERGEI PAVLOVICH
MINISTER OF FOREIGN AFFAIRS FOR THE AZURE KINGDOM
MINISTER FROM A FRIGID NATION ETERNALLY BLANKETED IN SNOW.
HMPH.
TRADE PARTNERS ARE INTIMIDATED BY HIS ARROGANT ATTITUDE AND SEVERE LOOKS.
MAYBE SCARING TIMID DIPLOMATS INTO SILENCE COUNTS AS A NEGOTIATION TACTIC.

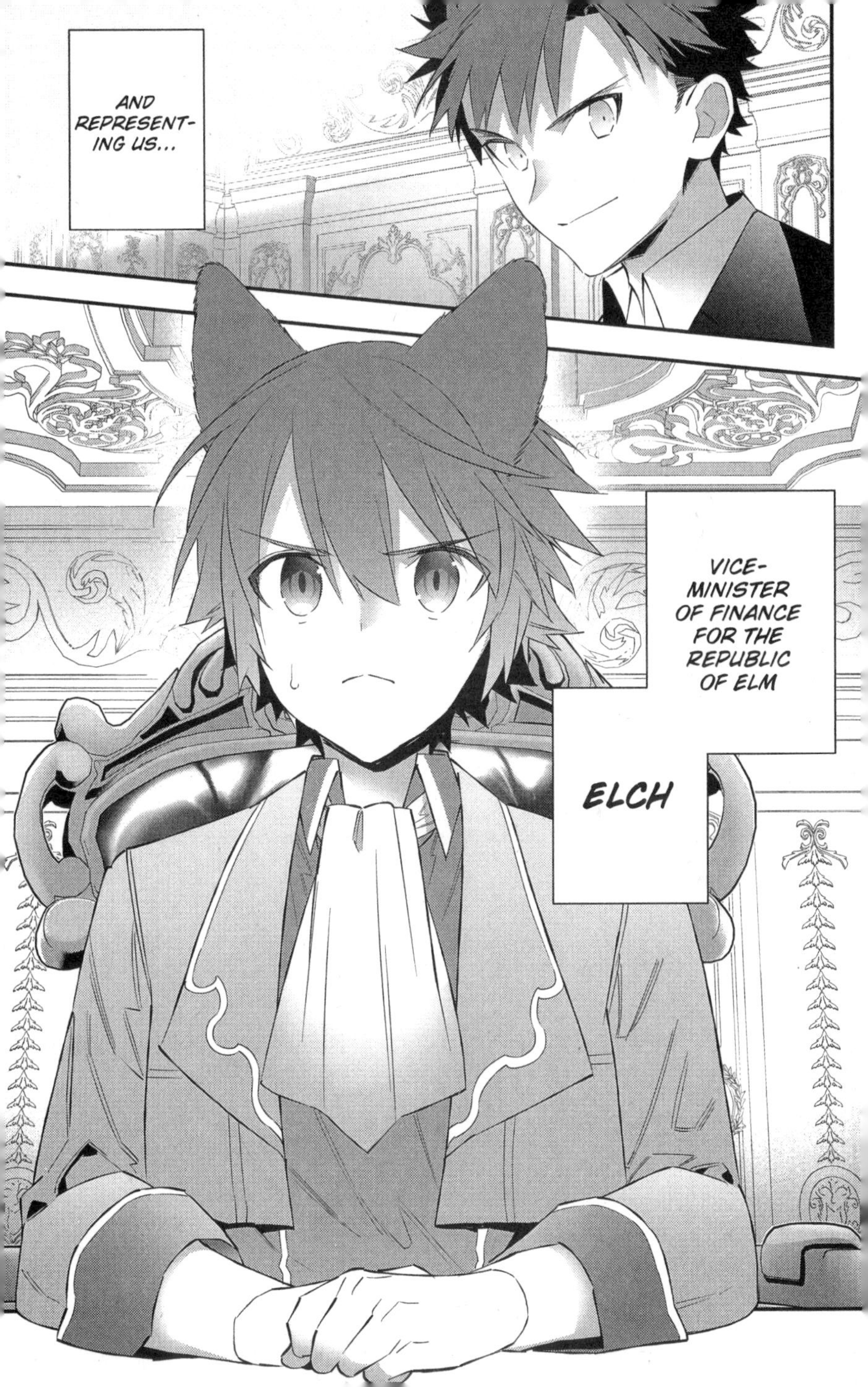
AND REPRESENT-ING US...
VICE-MINISTER OF FINANCE FOR THE REPUBLIC OF ELM
ELCH

CHAPTER 53:
THE PRODIGY BUSINESSMAN AND THE TRADE CONFERENCE

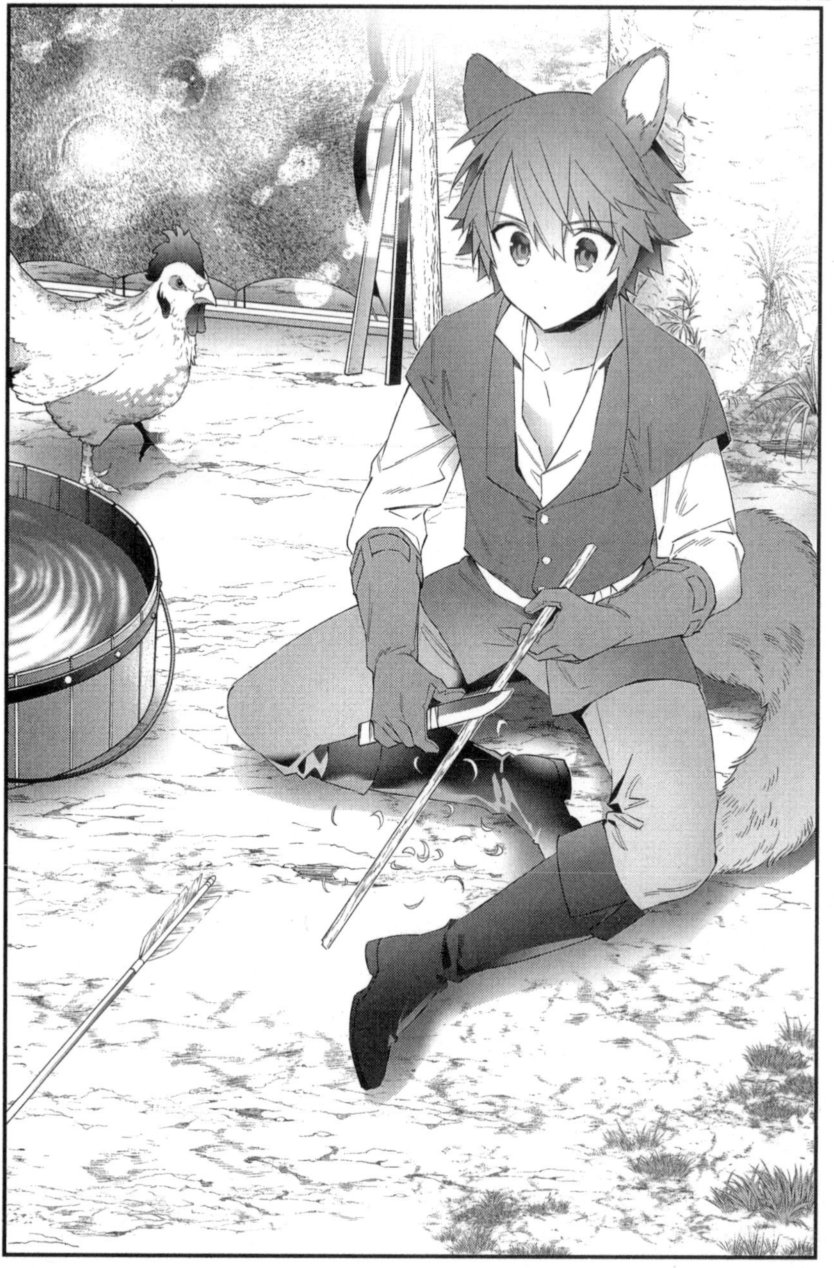

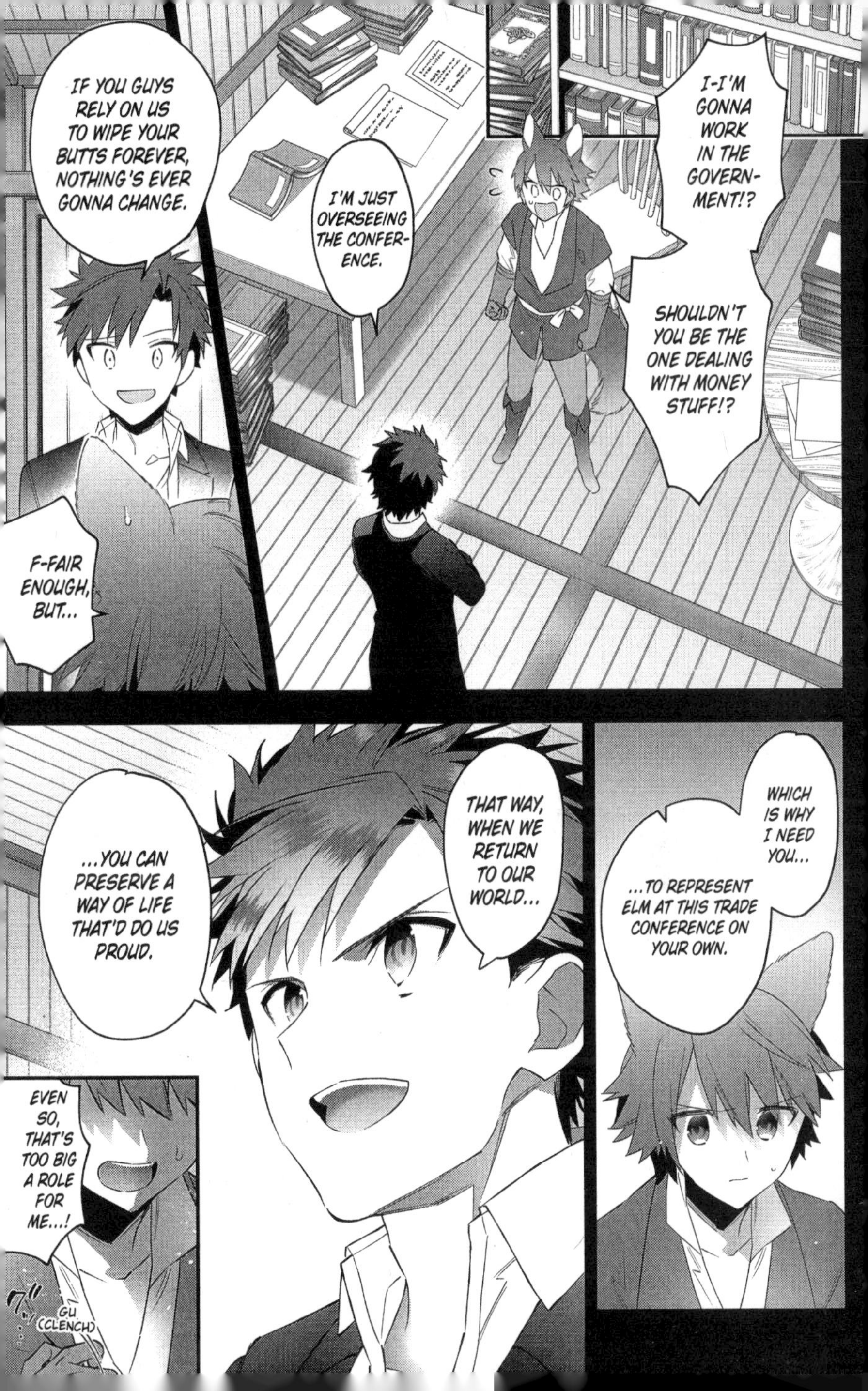
I-I'M GONNA WORK IN THE GOVERNMENT!?
SHOULDN'T YOU BE THE ONE DEALING WITH MONEY STUFF!?
I'M JUST OVERSEEING THE CONFERENCE.
IF YOU GUYS RELY ON US TO WIPE YOUR BUTTS FOREVER, NOTHING'S EVER GONNA CHANGE.
F-FAIR ENOUGH, BUT...
WHICH IS WHY I NEED YOU...
...TO REPRESENT ELM AT THIS TRADE CONFERENCE ON YOUR OWN.
THAT WAY, WHEN WE RETURN TO OUR WORLD...
...YOU CAN PRESERVE A WAY OF LIFE THAT'D DO US PROUD.
EVEN SO, THAT'S TOO BIG A ROLE FOR ME...!
GU (CLENCH)

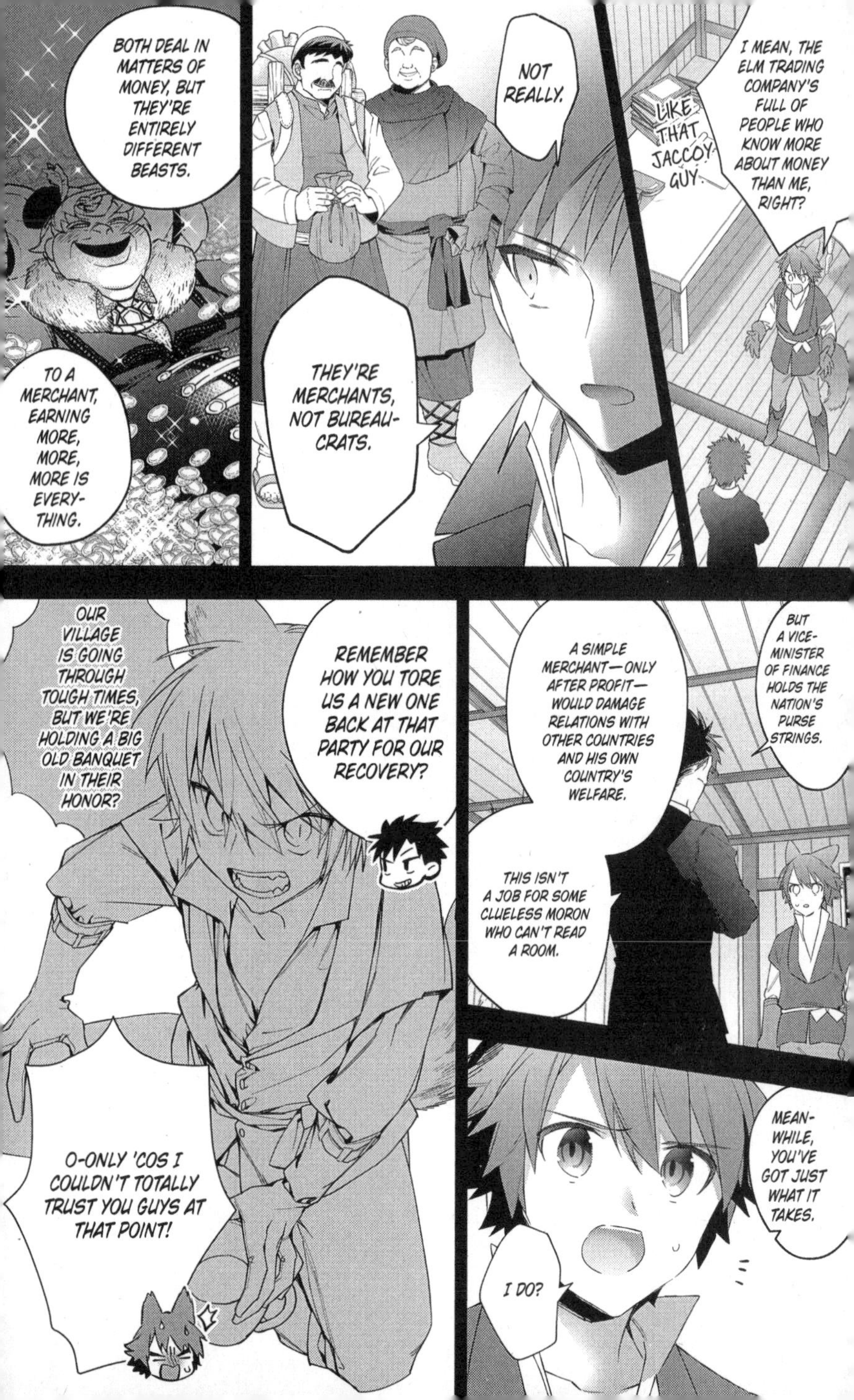
I MEAN, THE ELM TRADING COMPANY'S FULL OF PEOPLE WHO KNOW MORE ABOUT MONEY THAN ME, RIGHT?
LIKE THAT JACCOY GUY.
NOT REALLY.
THEY'RE MERCHANTS, NOT BUREAU-CRATS.
BOTH DEAL IN MATTERS OF MONEY, BUT THEY'RE ENTIRELY DIFFERENT BEASTS.
TO A MERCHANT, EARNING MORE, MORE, MORE IS EVERY-THING.
BUT A VICE-MINISTER OF FINANCE HOLDS THE NATION'S PURSE STRINGS.
A SIMPLE MERCHANT—ONLY AFTER PROFIT—WOULD DAMAGE RELATIONS WITH OTHER COUNTRIES AND HIS OWN COUNTRY'S WELFARE.
THIS ISN'T A JOB FOR SOME CLUELESS MORON WHO CAN'T READ A ROOM.
MEAN-WHILE, YOU'VE GOT JUST WHAT IT TAKES.
I DO?
REMEMBER HOW YOU TORE US A NEW ONE BACK AT THAT PARTY FOR OUR RECOVERY?
OUR VILLAGE IS GOING THROUGH TOUGH TIMES, BUT WE'RE HOLDING A BIG OLD BANQUET IN THEIR HONOR?
O-ONLY 'COS I COULDN'T TOTALLY TRUST YOU GUYS AT THAT POINT!

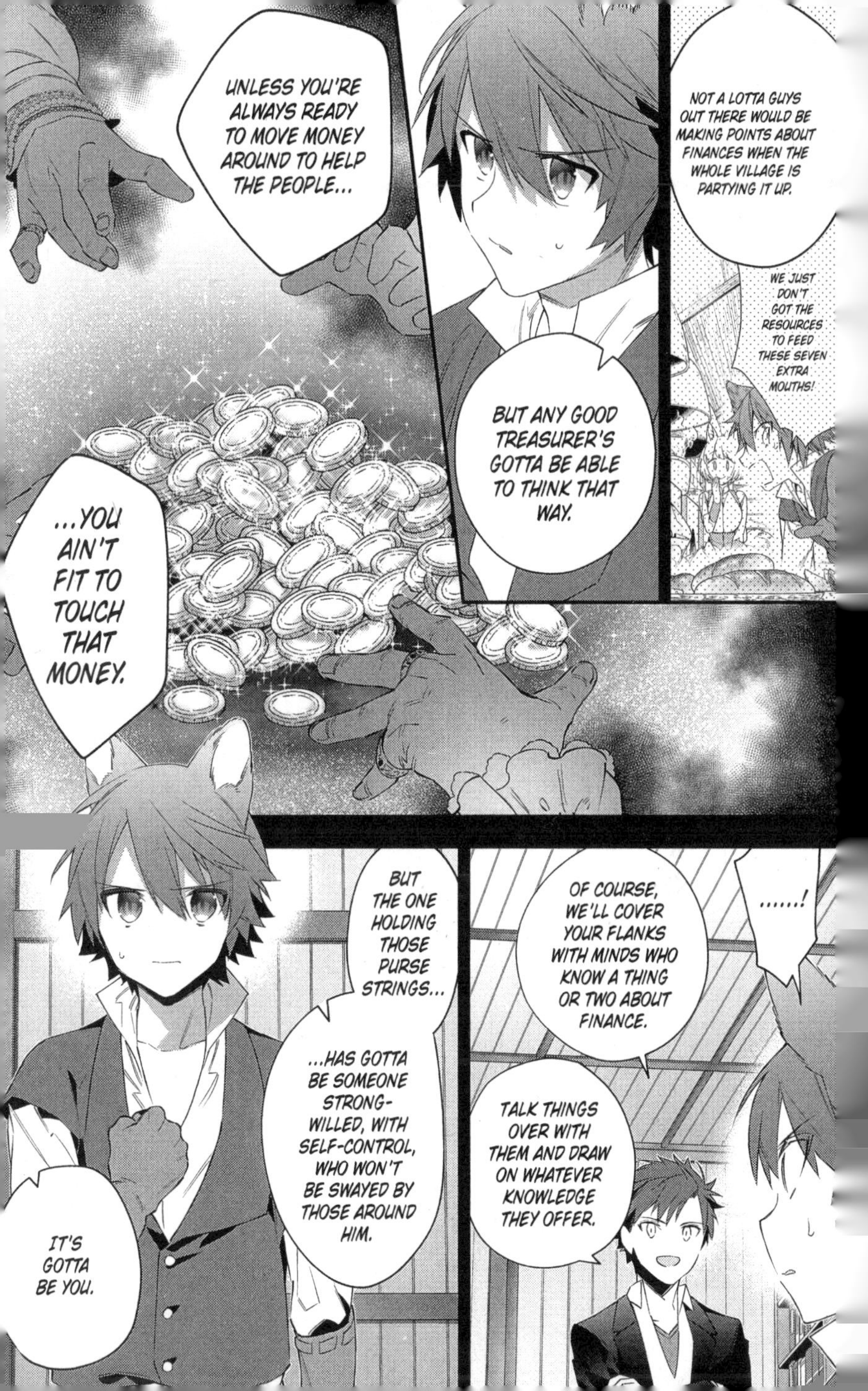
NOT A LOTTA GUYS OUT THERE WOULD BE MAKING POINTS ABOUT FINANCES WHEN THE WHOLE VILLAGE IS PARTYING IT UP.
WE JUST DON'T GOT THE RESOURCES TO FEED THESE SEVEN EXTRA MOUTHS!
BUT ANY GOOD TREASURER'S GOTTA BE ABLE TO THINK THAT WAY.
UNLESS YOU'RE ALWAYS READY TO MOVE MONEY AROUND TO HELP THE PEOPLE...
...YOU AIN'T FIT TO TOUCH THAT MONEY.
......!
OF COURSE, WE'LL COVER YOUR FLANKS WITH MINDS WHO KNOW A THING OR TWO ABOUT FINANCE.
TALK THINGS OVER WITH THEM AND DRAW ON WHATEVER KNOWLEDGE THEY OFFER.
BUT THE ONE HOLDING THOSE PURSE STRINGS...
...HAS GOTTA BE SOMEONE STRONG-WILLED, WITH SELF-CONTROL, WHO WON'T BE SWAYED BY THOSE AROUND HIM.
IT'S GOTTA BE YOU.

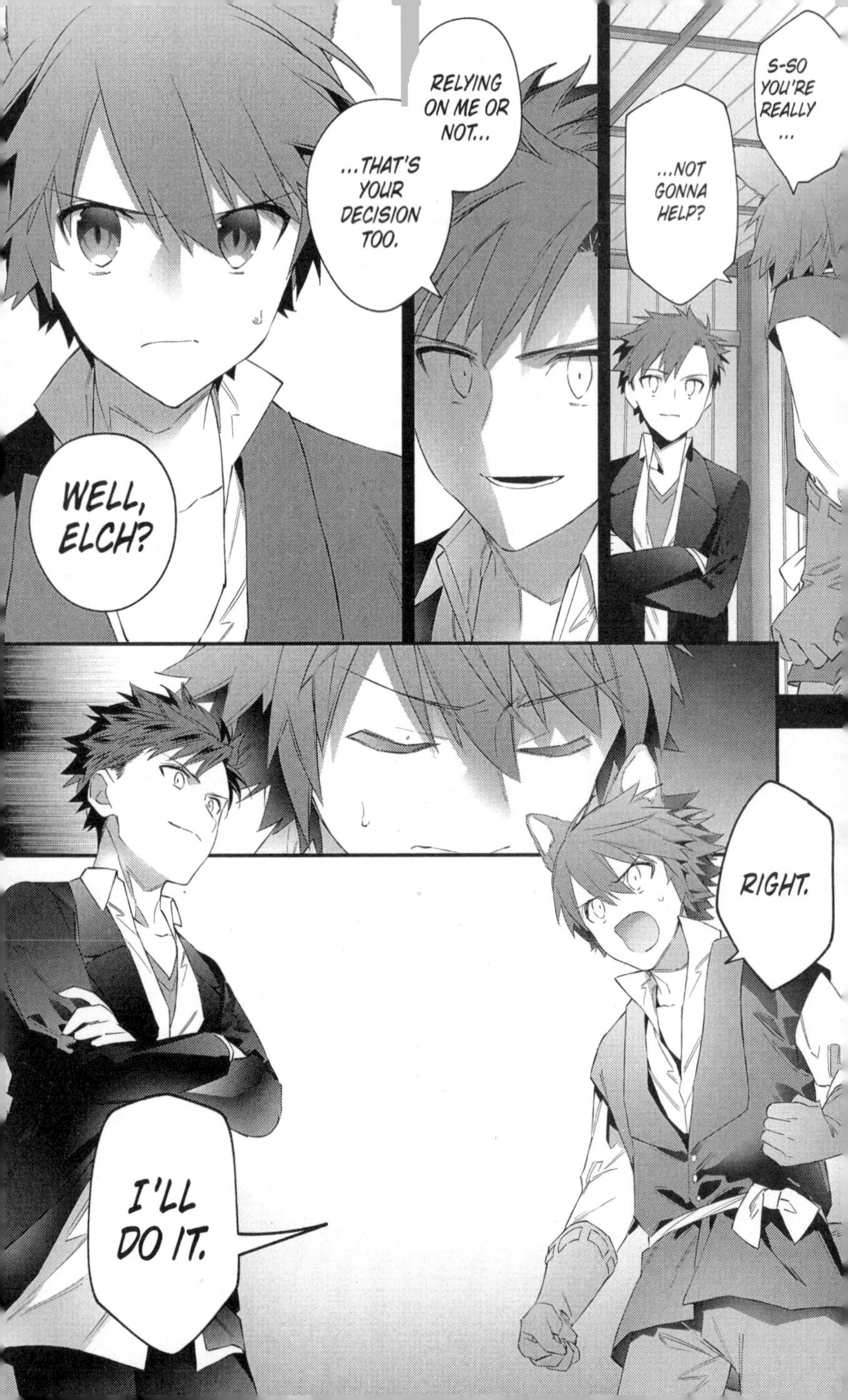
S-SO YOU'RE REALLY ...
...NOT GONNA HELP?
RELYING ON ME OR NOT...
...THAT'S YOUR DECISION TOO.
WELL, ELCH?
RIGHT.
I'LL DO IT.

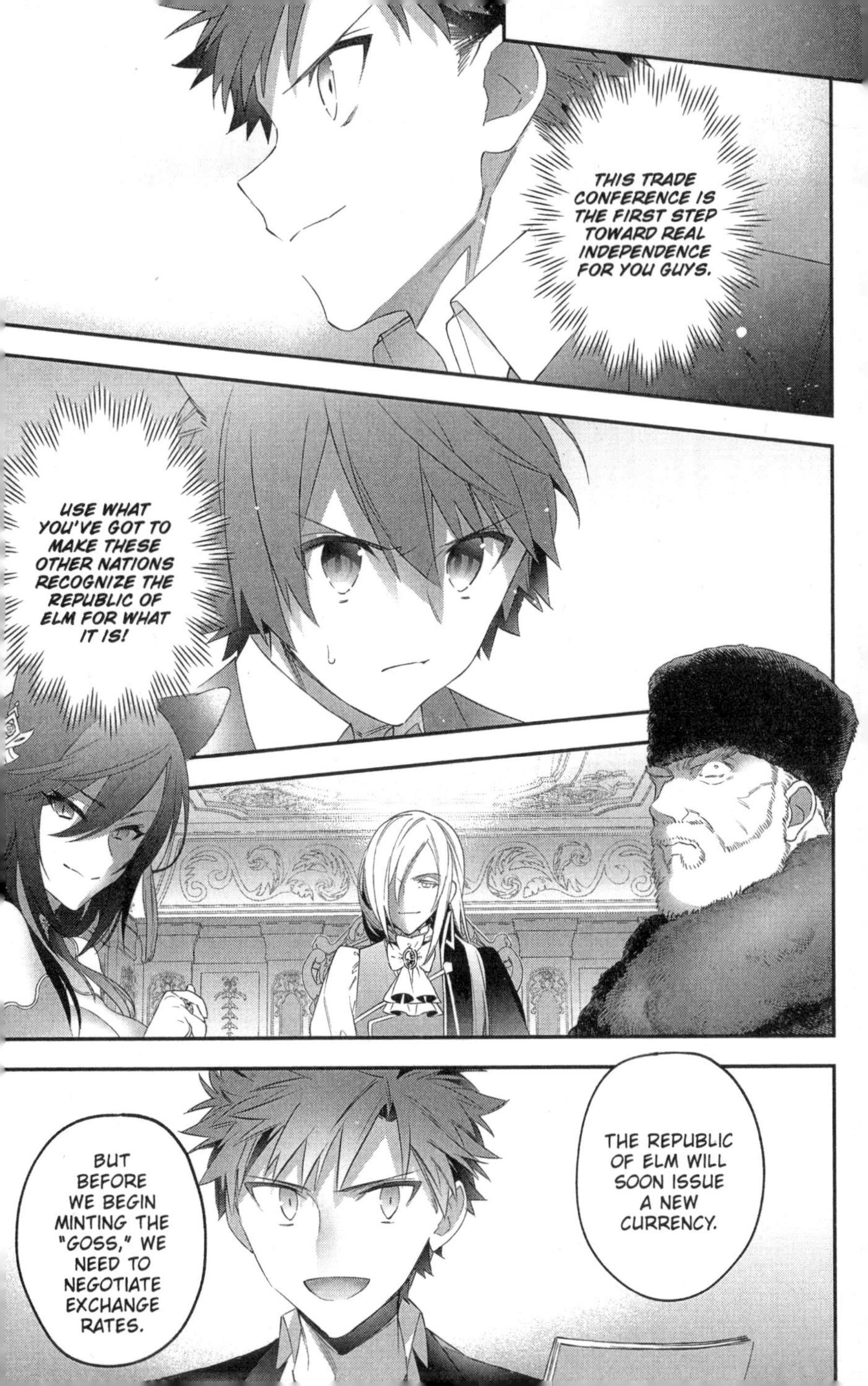
THIS TRADE CONFERENCE IS THE FIRST STEP TOWARD REAL INDEPENDENCE FOR YOU GUYS.
USE WHAT YOU'VE GOT TO MAKE THESE OTHER NATIONS RECOGNIZE THE REPUBLIC OF ELM FOR WHAT IT IS!
THE REPUBLIC OF ELM WILL SOON ISSUE A NEW CURRENCY.
BUT BEFORE WE BEGIN MINTING THE "GOSS," WE NEED TO NEGOTIATE EXCHANGE RATES.

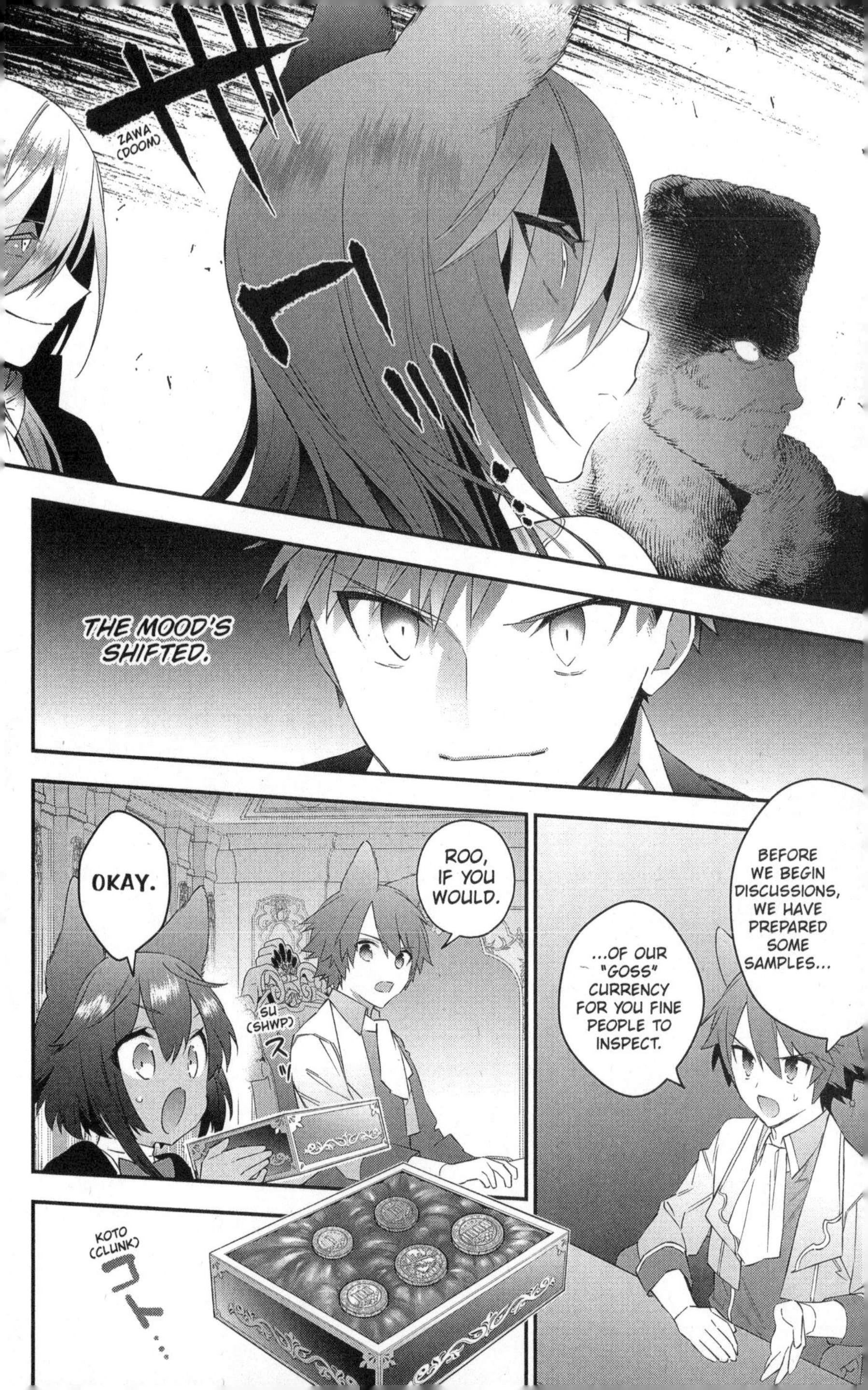
ZAWA (DOOM)
THE MOOD'S SHIFTED.
BEFORE WE BEGIN DISCUSSIONS, WE HAVE PREPARED SOME SAMPLES...
...OF OUR "GOSS" CURRENCY FOR YOU FINE PEOPLE TO INSPECT.
ROO, IF YOU WOULD.
OKAY.
SU (SHWP)
ス
KOTO (CLUNK)
コト...

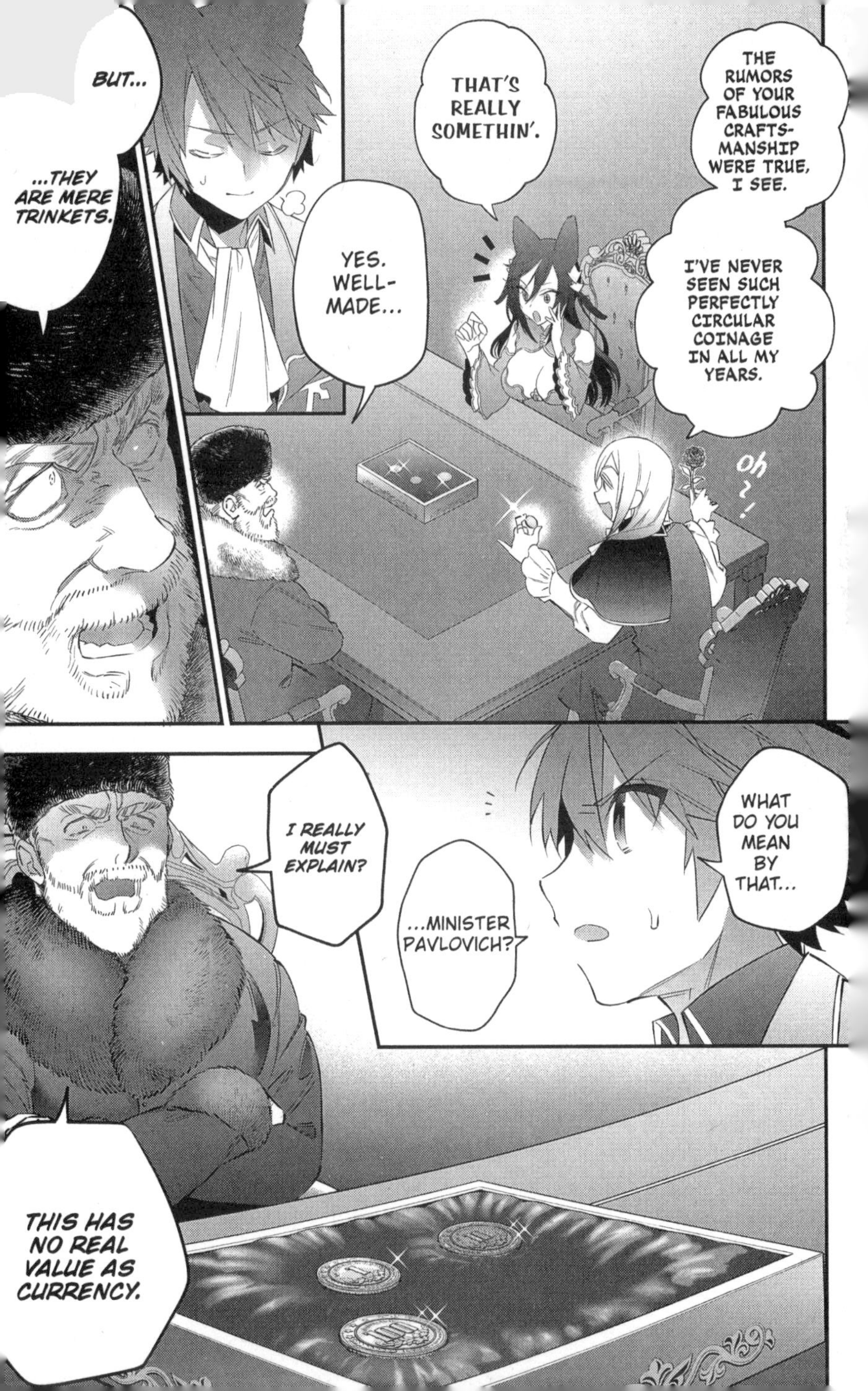
THE RUMORS OF YOUR FABULOUS CRAFTS-MANSHIP WERE TRUE, I SEE.
I'VE NEVER SEEN SUCH PERFECTLY CIRCULAR COINAGE IN ALL MY YEARS.
THAT'S REALLY SOMETHIN'.
Oh?!
YES. WELL-MADE...
BUT...
...THEY ARE MERE TRINKETS.
WHAT DO YOU MEAN BY THAT...
...MINISTER PAVLOVICH?
I REALLY MUST EXPLAIN?
THIS HAS NO REAL VALUE AS CURRENCY.

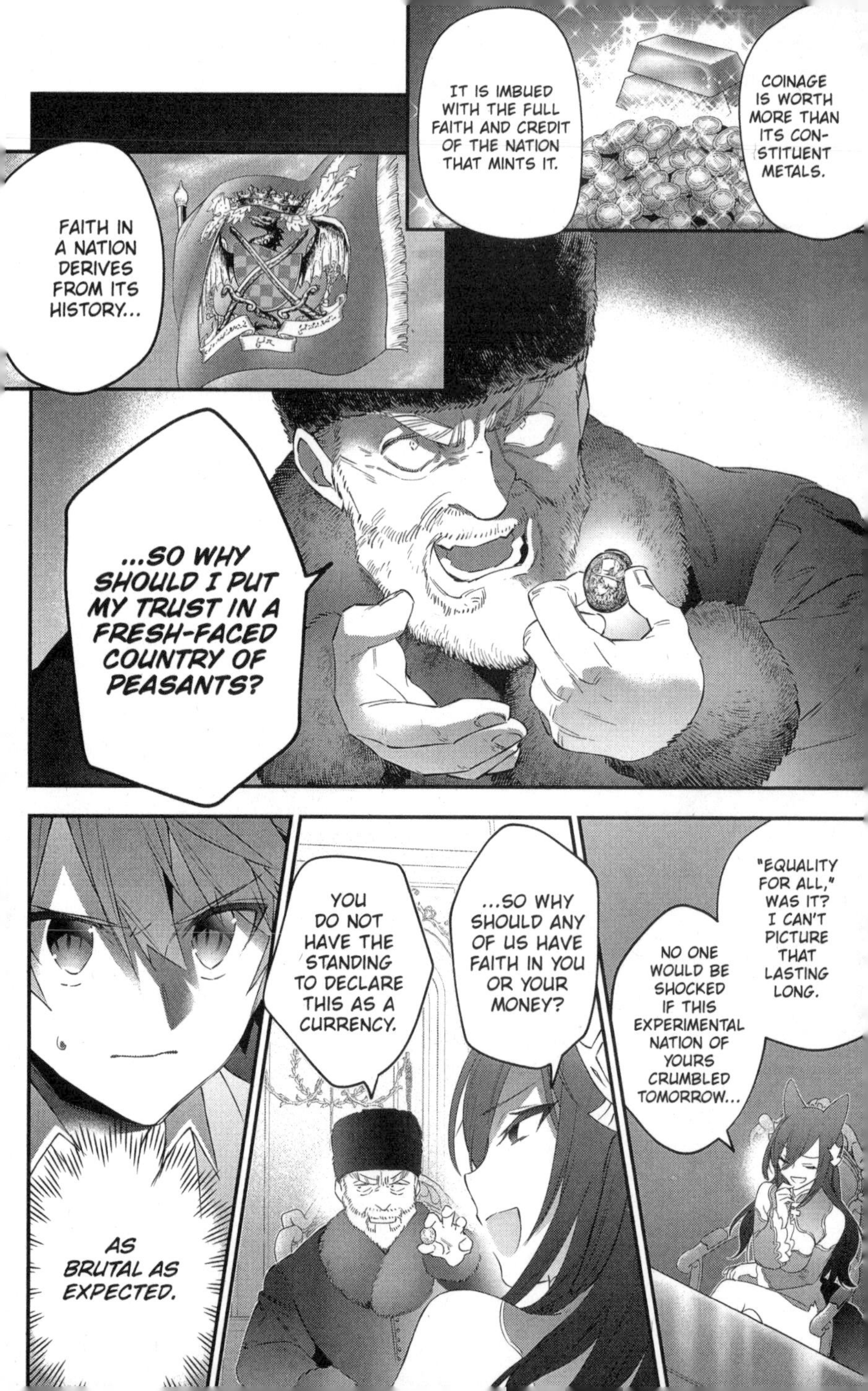
COINAGE IS WORTH MORE THAN ITS CON-STITUENT METALS.
IT IS IMBUED WITH THE FULL FAITH AND CREDIT OF THE NATION THAT MINTS IT.
FAITH IN A NATION DERIVES FROM ITS HISTORY...
...SO WHY SHOULD I PUT MY TRUST IN A FRESH-FACED COUNTRY OF PEASANTS?
"EQUALITY FOR ALL," WAS IT? I CAN'T PICTURE THAT LASTING LONG.
NO ONE WOULD BE SHOCKED IF THIS EXPERIMENTAL NATION OF YOURS CRUMBLED TOMORROW...
...SO WHY SHOULD ANY OF US HAVE FAITH IN YOU OR YOUR MONEY?
YOU DO NOT HAVE THE STANDING TO DECLARE THIS AS A CURRENCY.
AS BRUTAL AS EXPECTED.

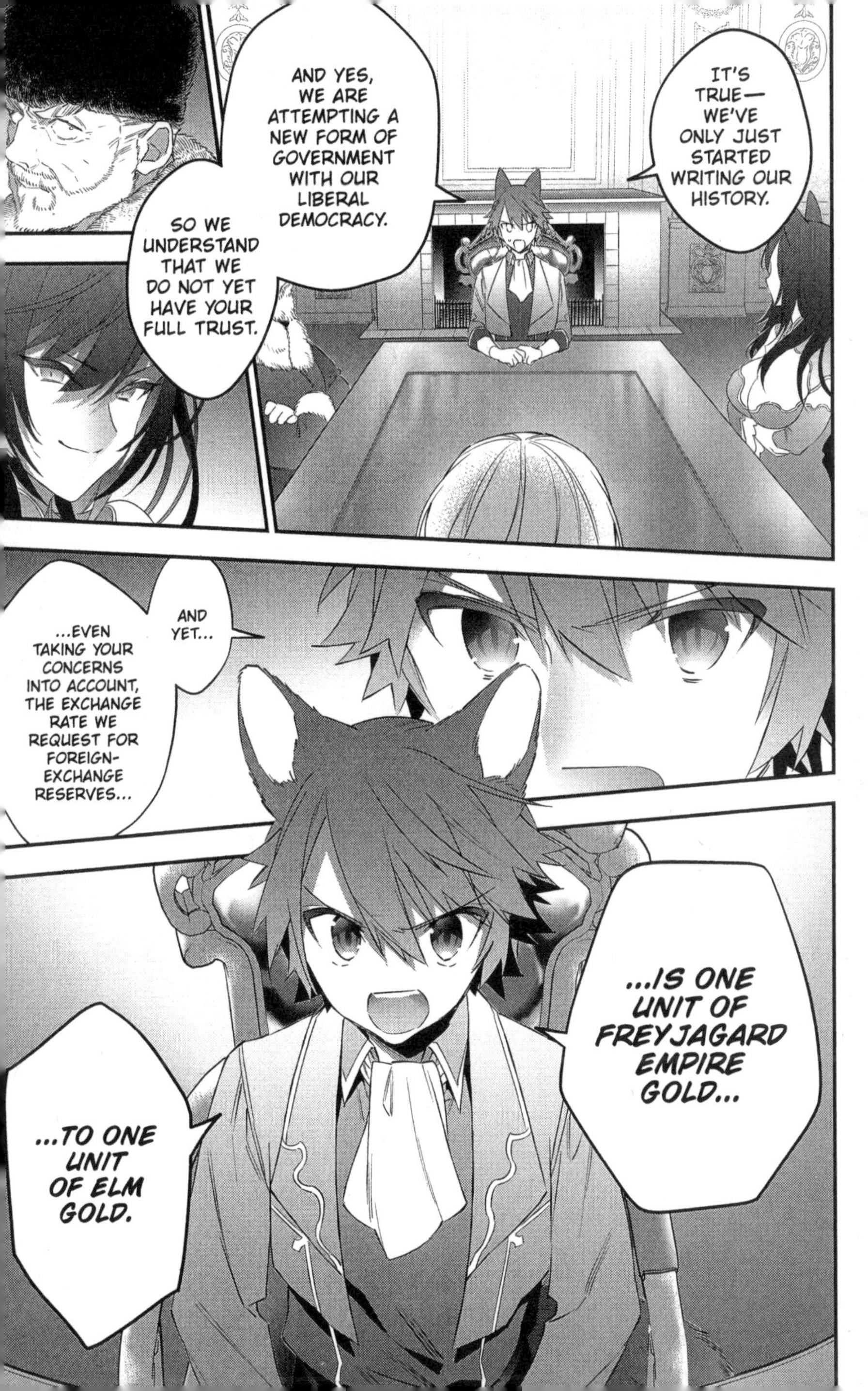
IT'S TRUE—WE'VE ONLY JUST STARTED WRITING OUR HISTORY.
AND YES, WE ARE ATTEMPTING A NEW FORM OF GOVERNMENT WITH OUR LIBERAL DEMOCRACY.
SO WE UNDERSTAND THAT WE DO NOT YET HAVE YOUR FULL TRUST.
AND YET...
...EVEN TAKING YOUR CONCERNS INTO ACCOUNT, THE EXCHANGE RATE WE REQUEST FOR FOREIGN-EXCHANGE RESERVES...
...IS ONE UNIT OF FREYJAGARD EMPIRE GOLD...
...TO ONE UNIT OF ELM GOLD.

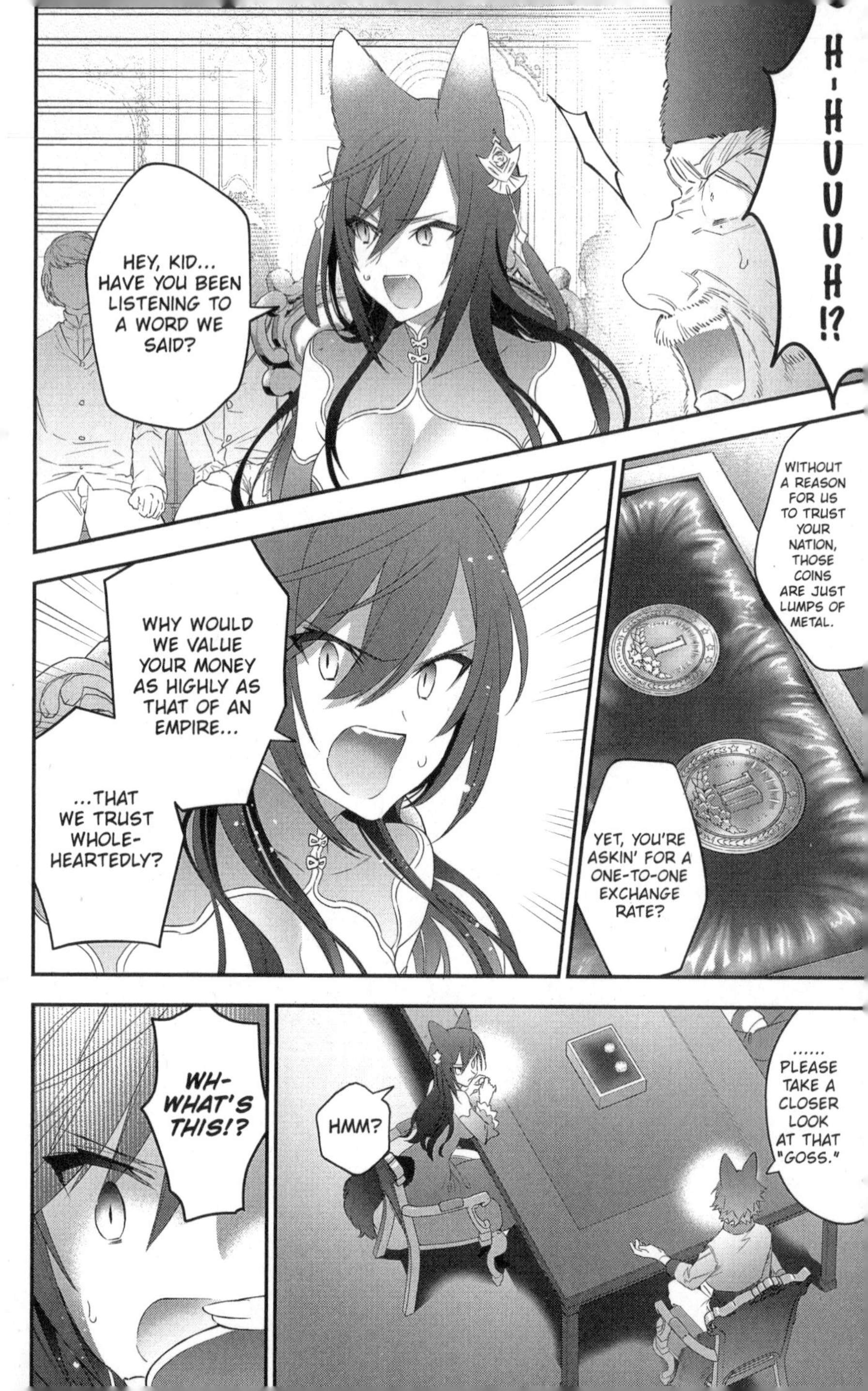
H-HUUUUH!?
HEY, KID... HAVE YOU BEEN LISTENING TO A WORD WE SAID?
WITHOUT A REASON FOR US TO TRUST YOUR NATION, THOSE COINS ARE JUST LUMPS OF METAL.
YET, YOU'RE ASKIN' FOR A ONE-TO-ONE EXCHANGE RATE?
WHY WOULD WE VALUE YOUR MONEY AS HIGHLY AS THAT OF AN EMPIRE...
...THAT WE TRUST WHOLE-HEARTEDLY?
......PLEASE TAKE A CLOSER LOOK AT THAT "GOSS."
HMM?
WH-WHAT'S THIS!?

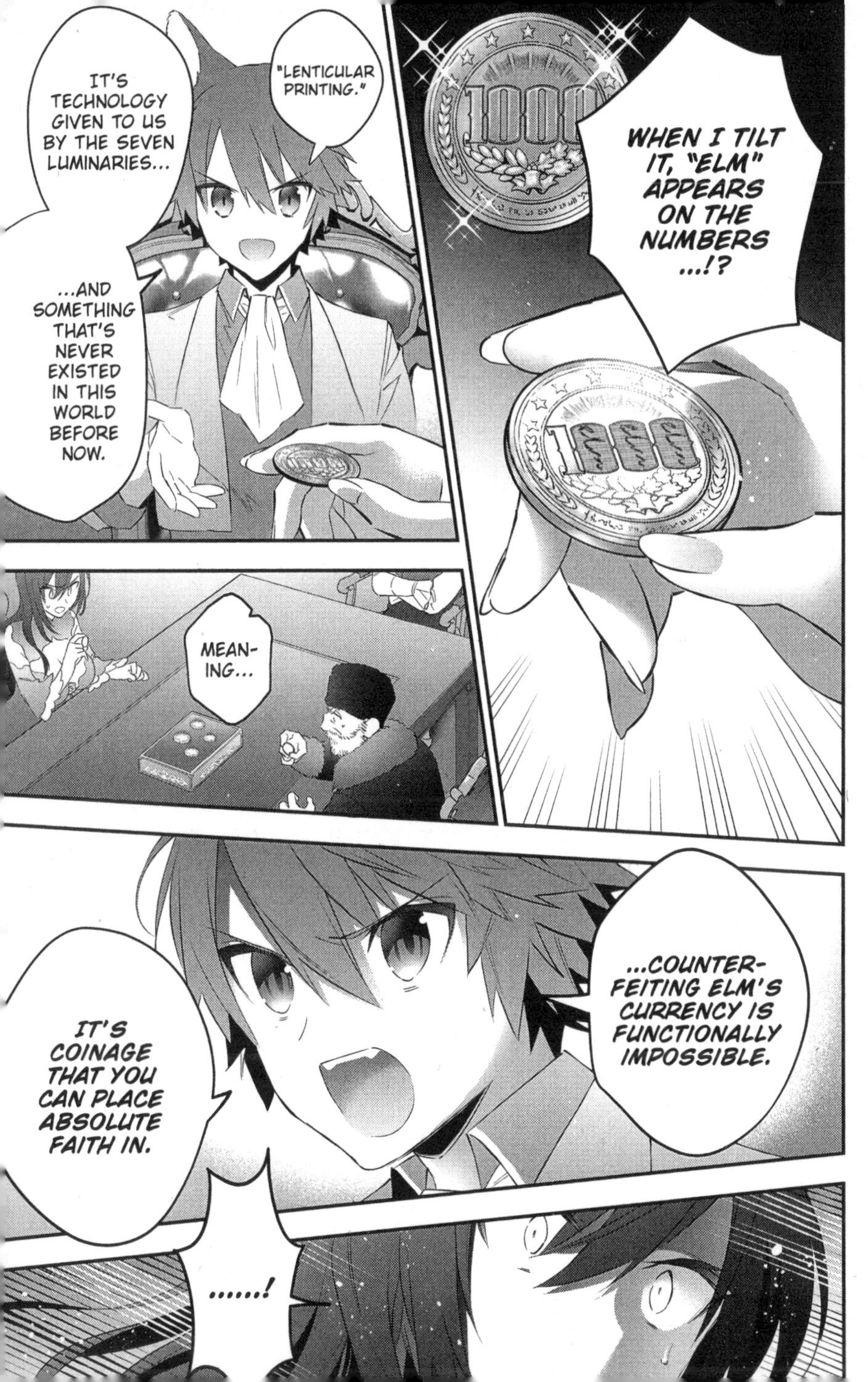
WHEN I TILT IT, "ELM" APPEARS ON THE NUMBERS ...!?
"LENTICULAR PRINTING."
IT'S TECHNOLOGY GIVEN TO US BY THE SEVEN LUMINARIES...
...AND SOMETHING THAT'S NEVER EXISTED IN THIS WORLD BEFORE NOW.
MEAN-ING...
...COUNTER-FEITING ELM'S CURRENCY IS FUNCTIONALLY IMPOSSIBLE.
IT'S COINAGE THAT YOU CAN PLACE ABSOLUTE FAITH IN.
......!

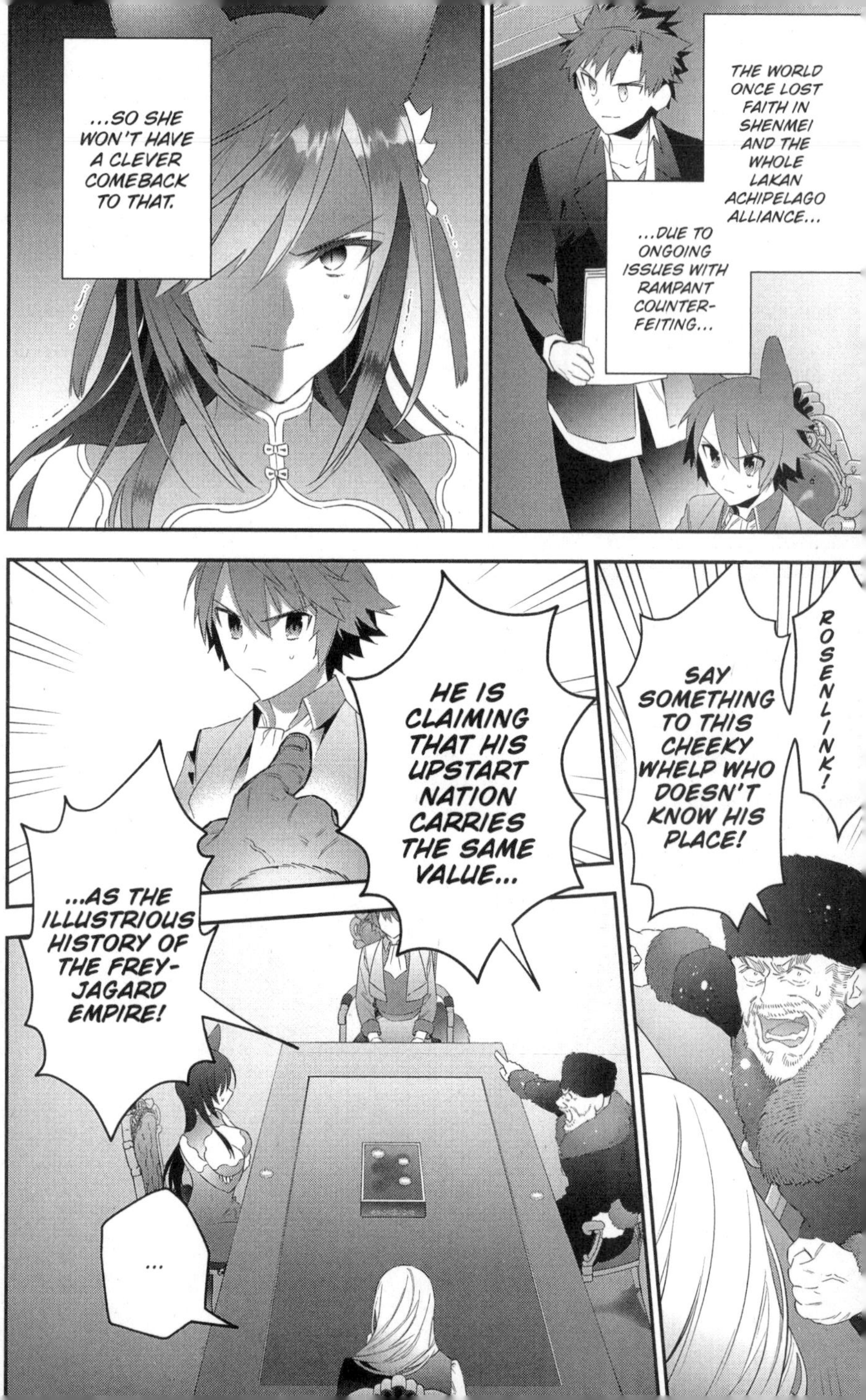
THE WORLD ONCE LOST FAITH IN SHENMEI AND THE WHOLE LAKAN ACHIPELAGO ALLIANCE...
...DUE TO ONGOING ISSUES WITH RAMPANT COUNTER-FEITING...
...SO SHE WON'T HAVE A CLEVER COMEBACK TO THAT.
ROSENLINK!
SAY SOMETHING TO THIS CHEEKY WHELP WHO DOESN'T KNOW HIS PLACE!
HE IS CLAIMING THAT HIS UPSTART NATION CARRIES THE SAME VALUE...
...AS THE ILLUSTRIOUS HISTORY OF THE FREY-JAGARD EMPIRE!
...

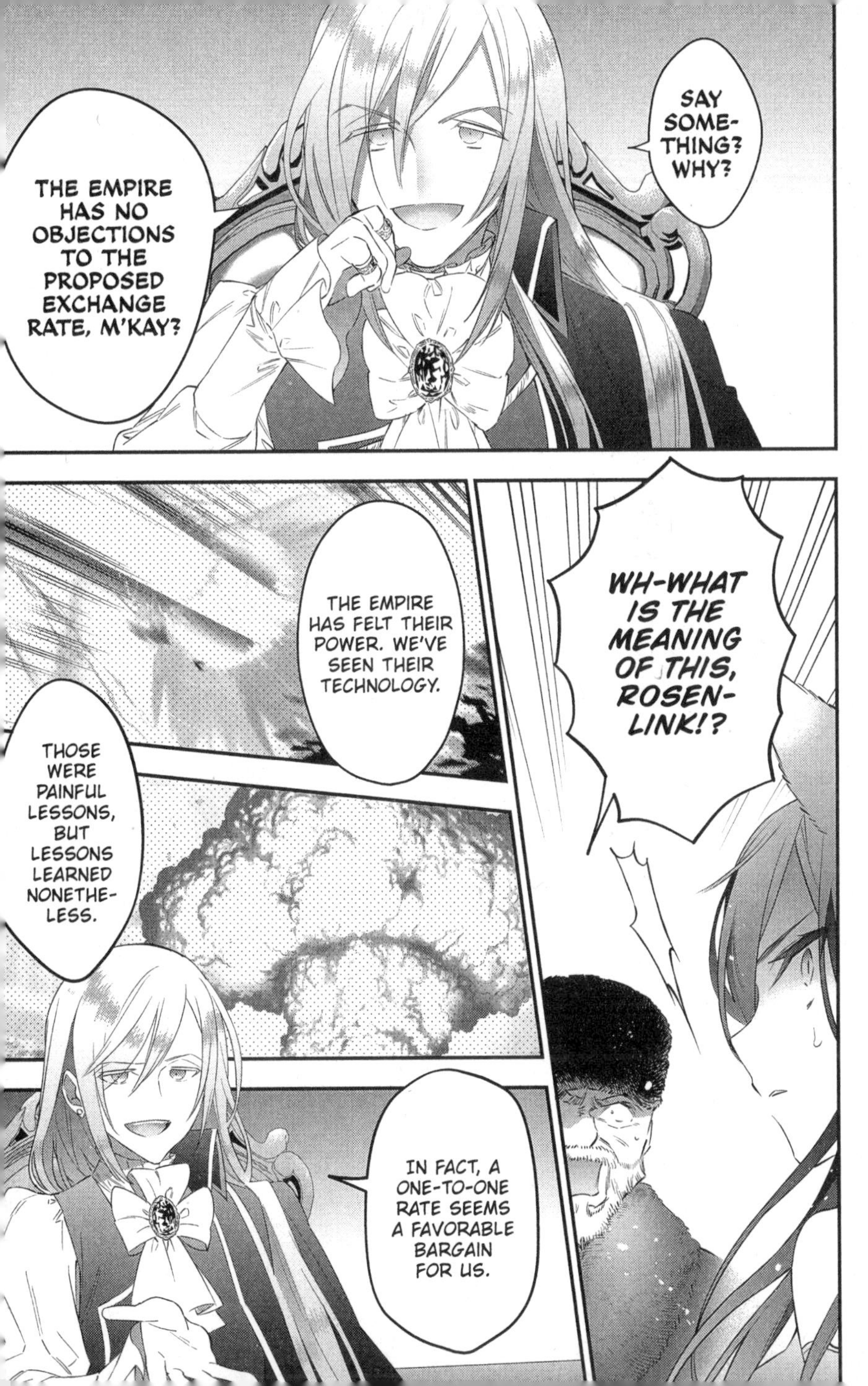
SAY SOME-THING? WHY?
THE EMPIRE HAS NO OBJECTIONS TO THE PROPOSED EXCHANGE RATE, M'KAY?
WH-WHAT IS THE MEANING OF THIS, ROSEN-LINK!?
THE EMPIRE HAS FELT THEIR POWER. WE'VE SEEN THEIR TECHNOLOGY.
THOSE WERE PAINFUL LESSONS, BUT LESSONS LEARNED NONETHE-LESS.
IN FACT, A ONE-TO-ONE RATE SEEMS A FAVORABLE BARGAIN FOR US.

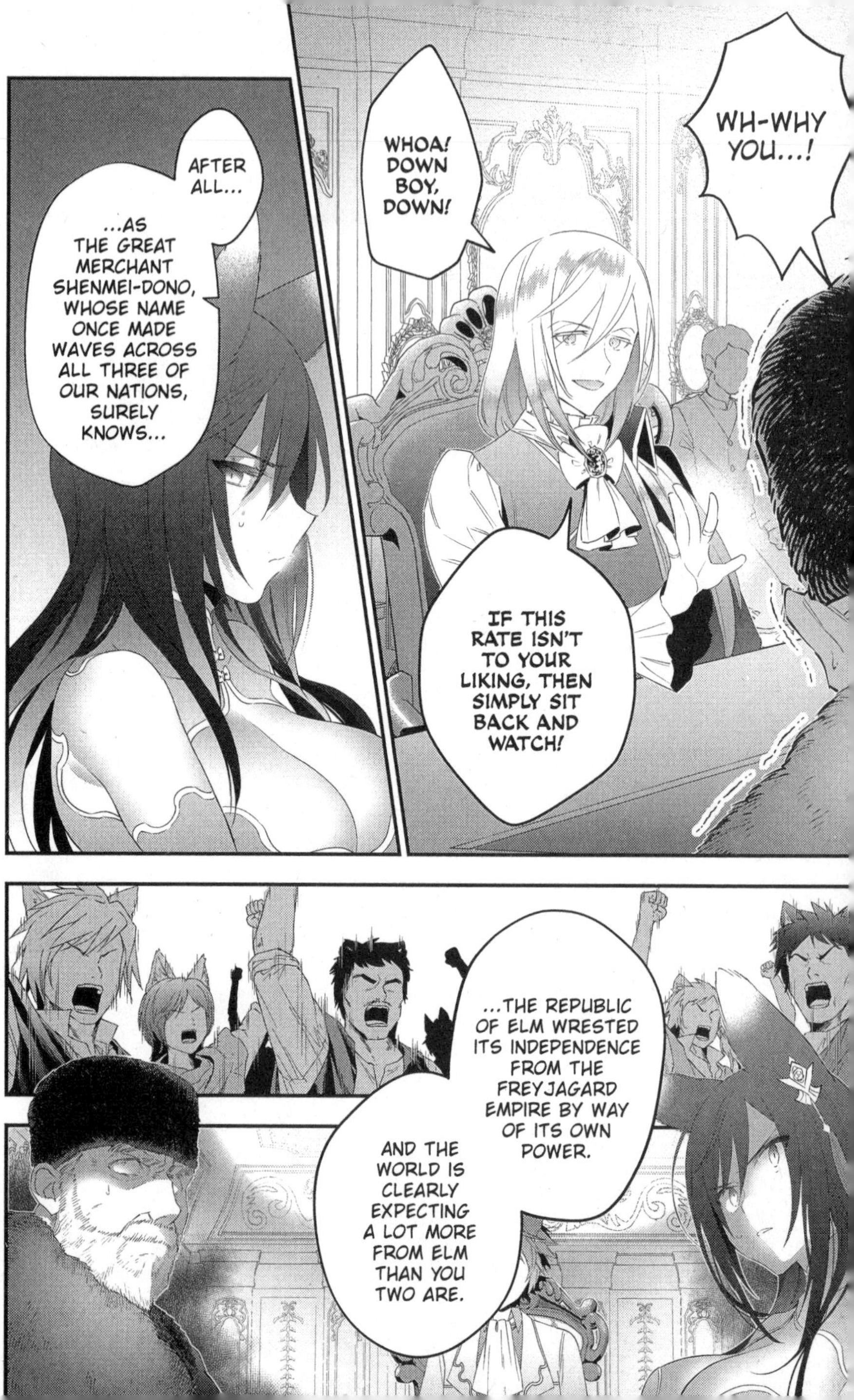
WH-WHY YOU...!
WHOA! DOWN BOY, DOWN!
IF THIS RATE ISN'T TO YOUR LIKING, THEN SIMPLY SIT BACK AND WATCH!
AFTER ALL...
...AS THE GREAT MERCHANT SHENMEI-DONO, WHOSE NAME ONCE MADE WAVES ACROSS ALL THREE OF OUR NATIONS, SURELY KNOWS...
...THE REPUBLIC OF ELM WRESTED ITS INDEPENDENCE FROM THE FREYJAGARD EMPIRE BY WAY OF ITS OWN POWER.
AND THE WORLD IS CLEARLY EXPECTING A LOT MORE FROM ELM THAN YOU TWO ARE.

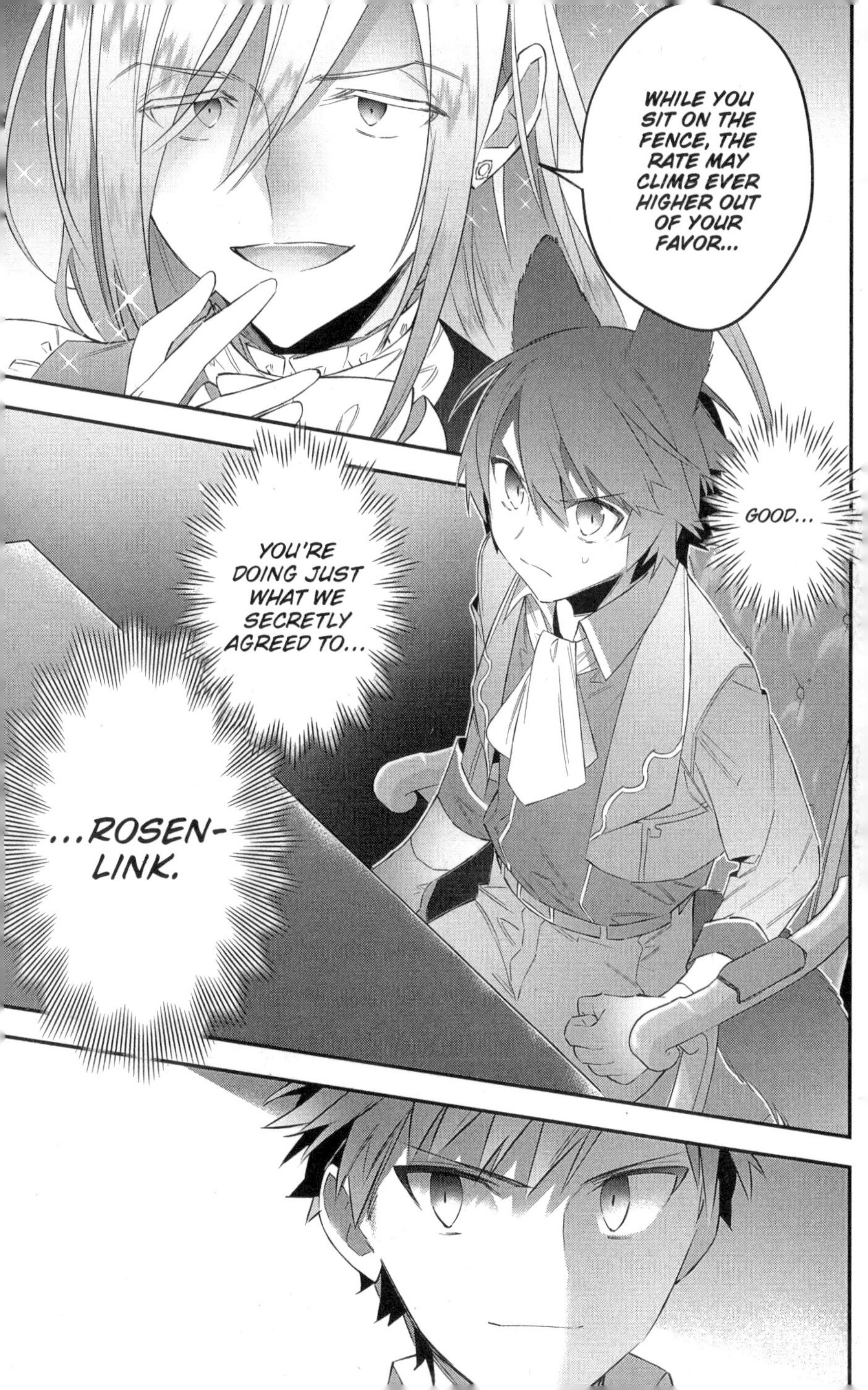
WHILE YOU SIT ON THE FENCE, THE RATE MAY CLIMB EVER HIGHER OUT OF YOUR FAVOR...
GOOD...
YOU'RE DOING JUST WHAT WE SECRETLY AGREED TO...
...ROSEN-LINK.

CHARACTER FILE 26

Heinrich von Rosenlink

Director of the empire's mint and a member of the Bluebloods.

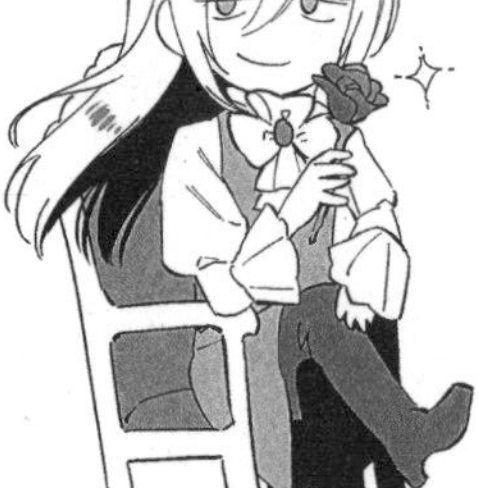

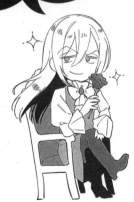

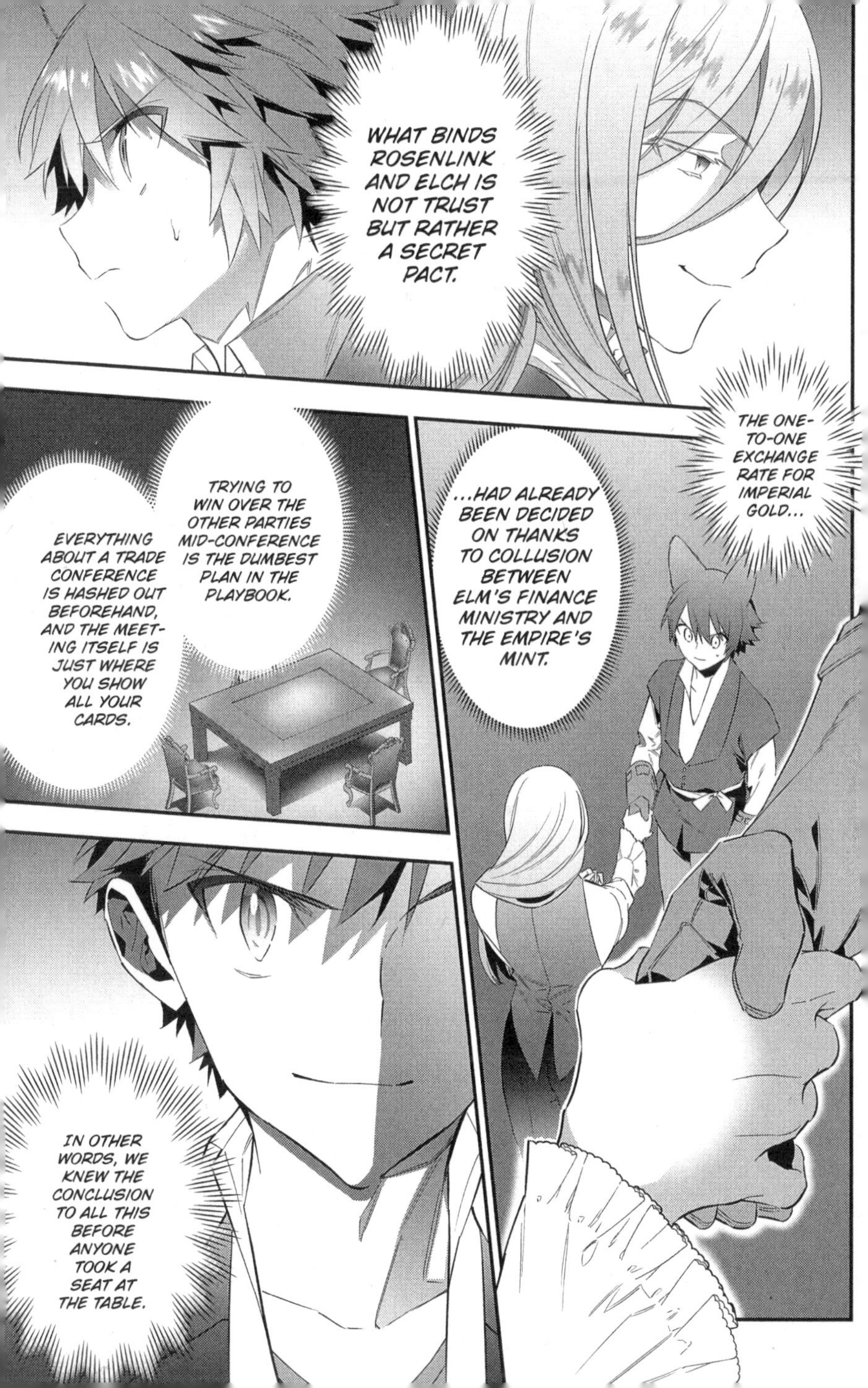
WHAT BINDS ROSENLINK AND ELCH IS NOT TRUST BUT RATHER A SECRET PACT.
THE ONE-TO-ONE EXCHANGE RATE FOR IMPERIAL GOLD...
...HAD ALREADY BEEN DECIDED ON THANKS TO COLLUSION BETWEEN ELM'S FINANCE MINISTRY AND THE EMPIRE'S MINT.
TRYING TO WIN OVER THE OTHER PARTIES MID-CONFERENCE IS THE DUMBEST PLAN IN THE PLAYBOOK.
EVERYTHING ABOUT A TRADE CONFERENCE IS HASHED OUT BEFOREHAND, AND THE MEETING ITSELF IS JUST WHERE YOU SHOW ALL YOUR CARDS.
IN OTHER WORDS, WE KNEW THE CONCLUSION TO ALL THIS BEFORE ANYONE TOOK A SEAT AT THE TABLE.

CHAPTER 54: OPPORTUNITY AND CRISIS

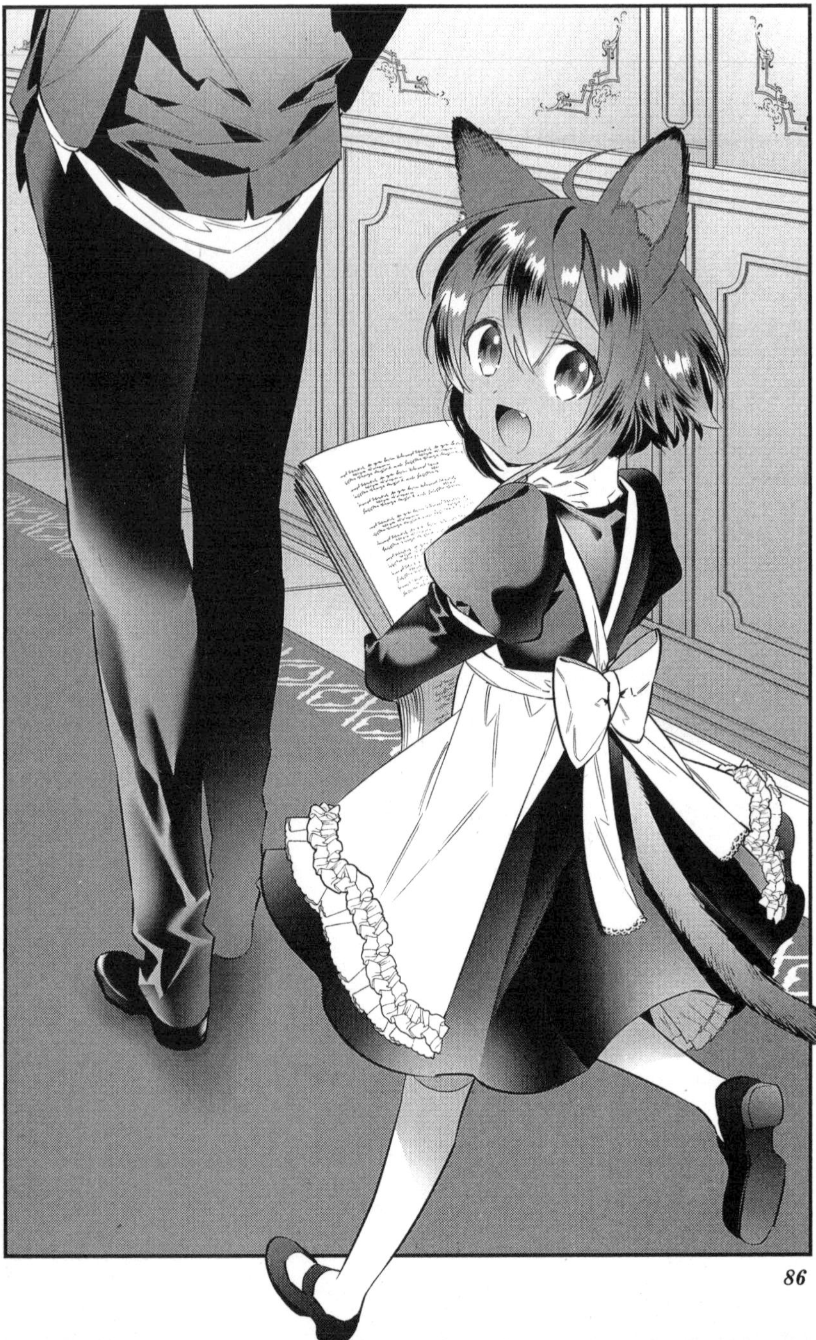

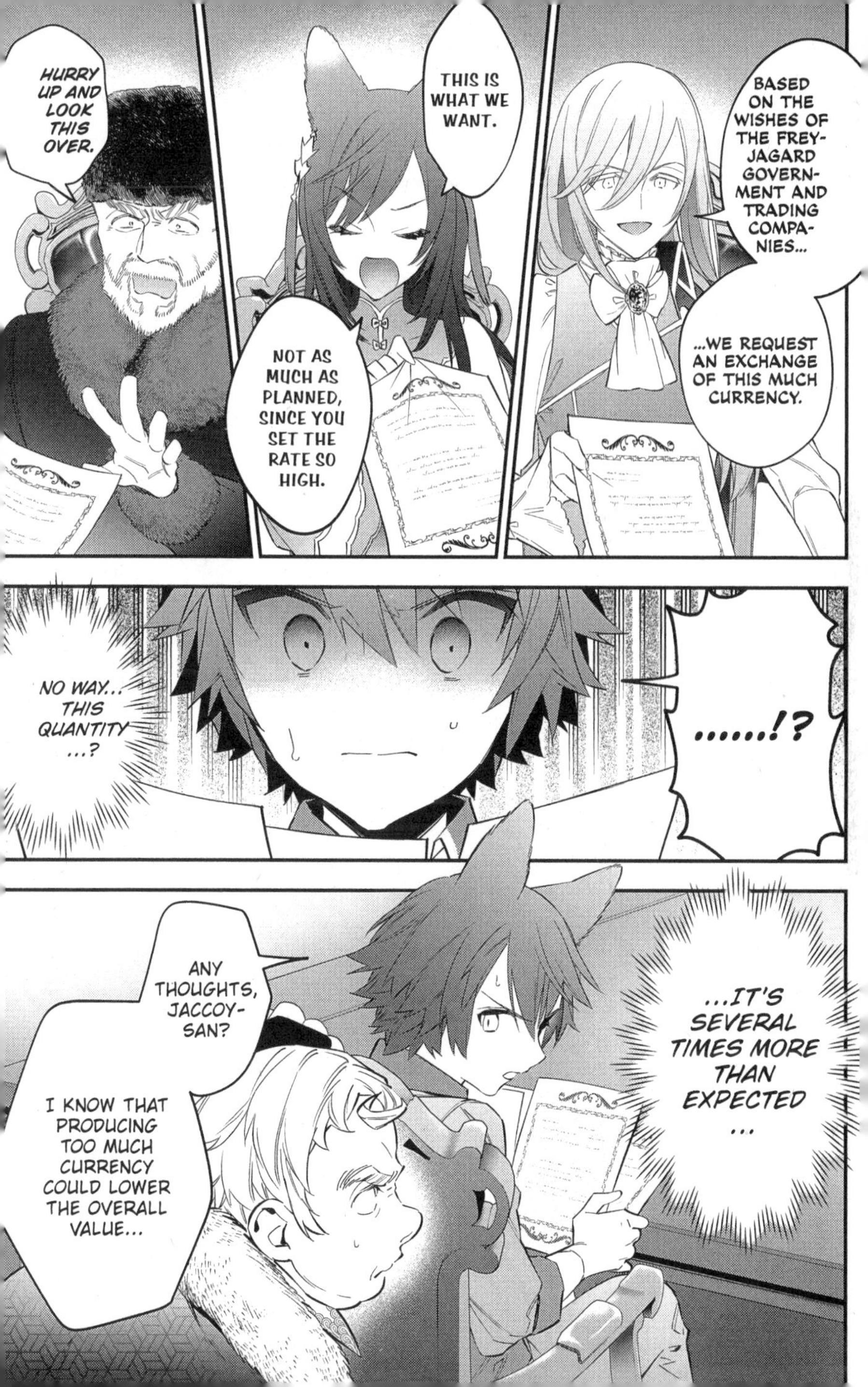
BASED ON THE WISHES OF THE FREY-JAGARD GOVERNMENT AND TRADING COMPANIES...
...WE REQUEST AN EXCHANGE OF THIS MUCH CURRENCY.
THIS IS WHAT WE WANT.
NOT AS MUCH AS PLANNED, SINCE YOU SET THE RATE SO HIGH.
HURRY UP AND LOOK THIS OVER.
......!?
NO WAY... THIS QUANTITY...?
...IT'S SEVERAL TIMES MORE THAN EXPECTED...
ANY THOUGHTS, JACCOY-SAN?
I KNOW THAT PRODUCING TOO MUCH CURRENCY COULD LOWER THE OVERALL VALUE...

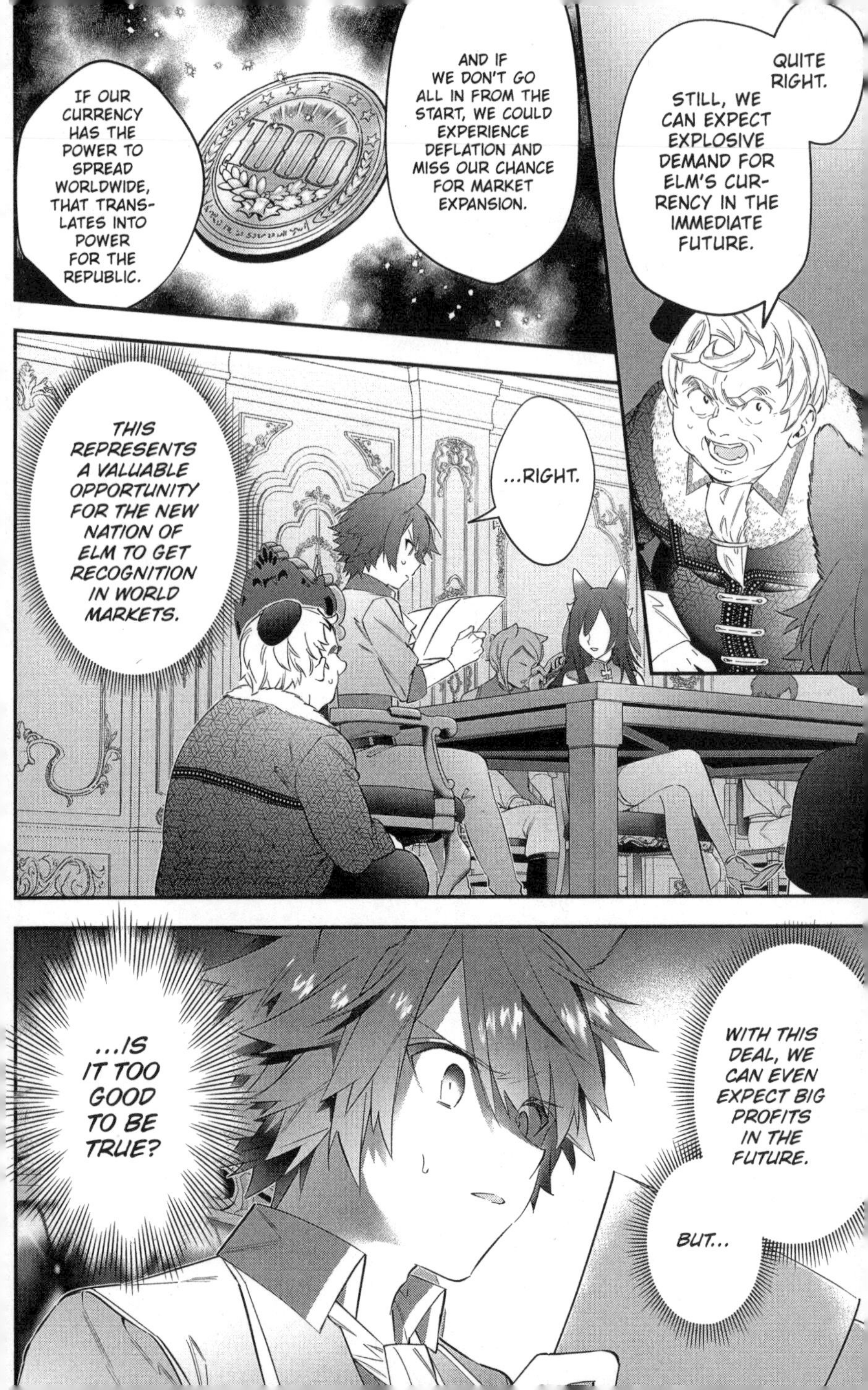
QUITE RIGHT.
STILL, WE CAN EXPECT EXPLOSIVE DEMAND FOR ELM'S CURRENCY IN THE IMMEDIATE FUTURE.
AND IF WE DON'T GO ALL IN FROM THE START, WE COULD EXPERIENCE DEFLATION AND MISS OUR CHANCE FOR MARKET EXPANSION.
IF OUR CURRENCY HAS THE POWER TO SPREAD WORLDWIDE, THAT TRANSLATES INTO POWER FOR THE REPUBLIC.
...RIGHT.
THIS REPRESENTS A VALUABLE OPPORTUNITY FOR THE NEW NATION OF ELM TO GET RECOGNITION IN WORLD MARKETS.
WITH THIS DEAL, WE CAN EVEN EXPECT BIG PROFITS IN THE FUTURE.
BUT...
...IS IT TOO GOOD TO BE TRUE?

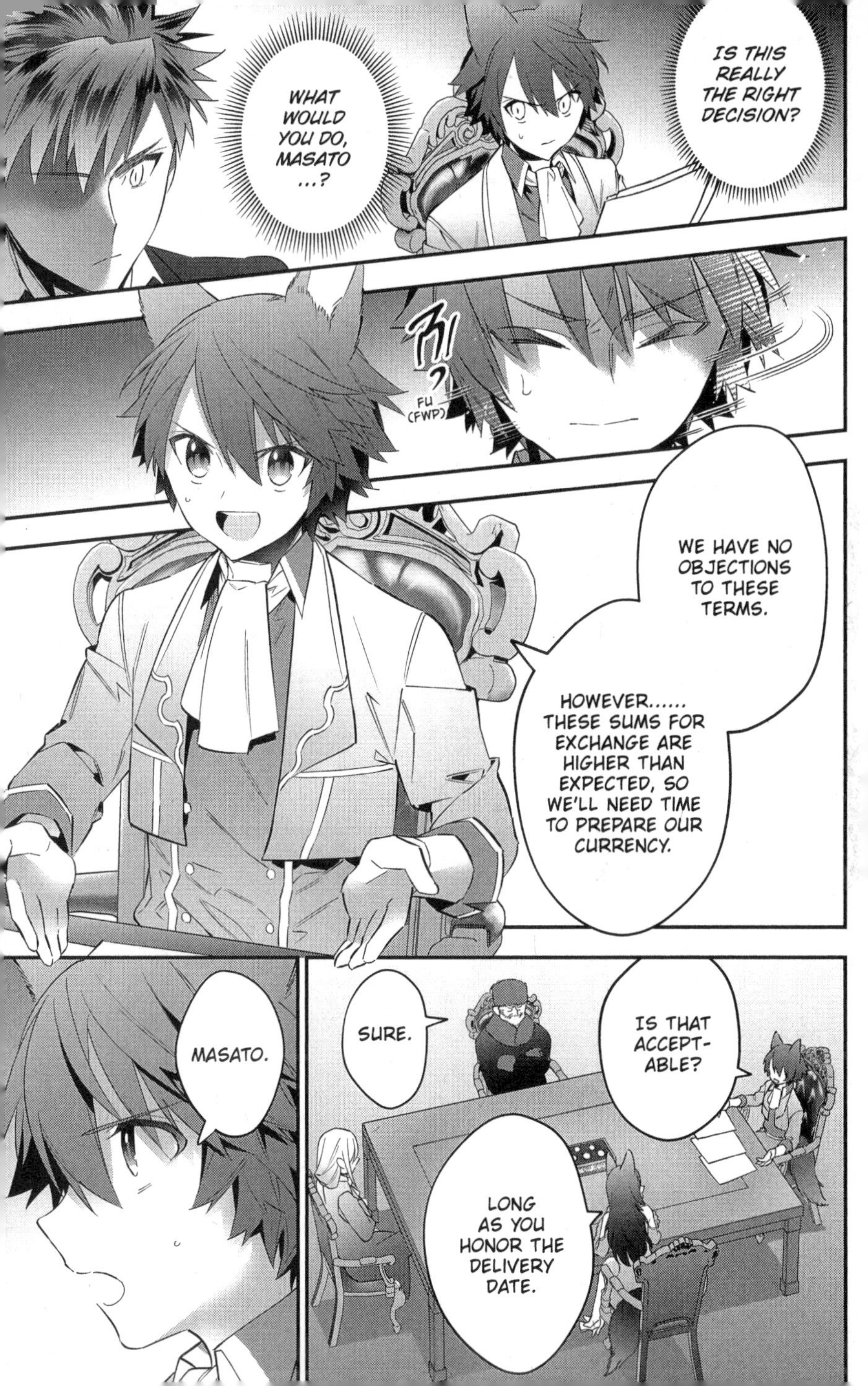
IS THIS REALLY THE RIGHT DECISION?
WHAT WOULD YOU DO, MASATO ...?
FU (FWP)
WE HAVE NO OBJECTIONS TO THESE TERMS.
HOWEVER...... THESE SUMS FOR EXCHANGE ARE HIGHER THAN EXPECTED, SO WE'LL NEED TIME TO PREPARE OUR CURRENCY.
IS THAT ACCEPT-ABLE?
SURE.
LONG AS YOU HONOR THE DELIVERY DATE.
MASATO.

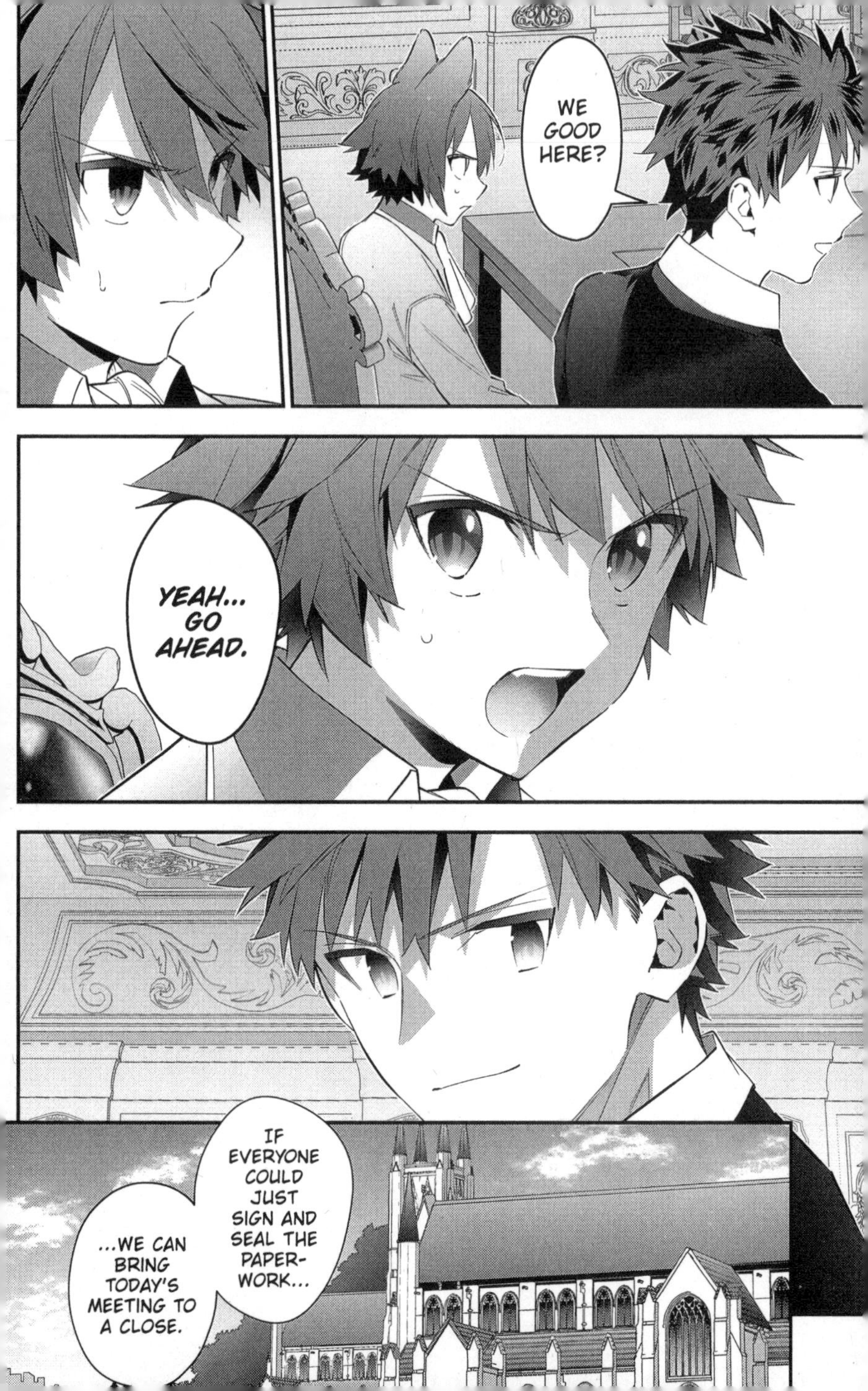
WE GOOD HERE?
YEAH... GO AHEAD.
IF EVERYONE COULD JUST SIGN AND SEAL THE PAPER-WORK...
...WE CAN BRING TODAY'S MEETING TO A CLOSE.

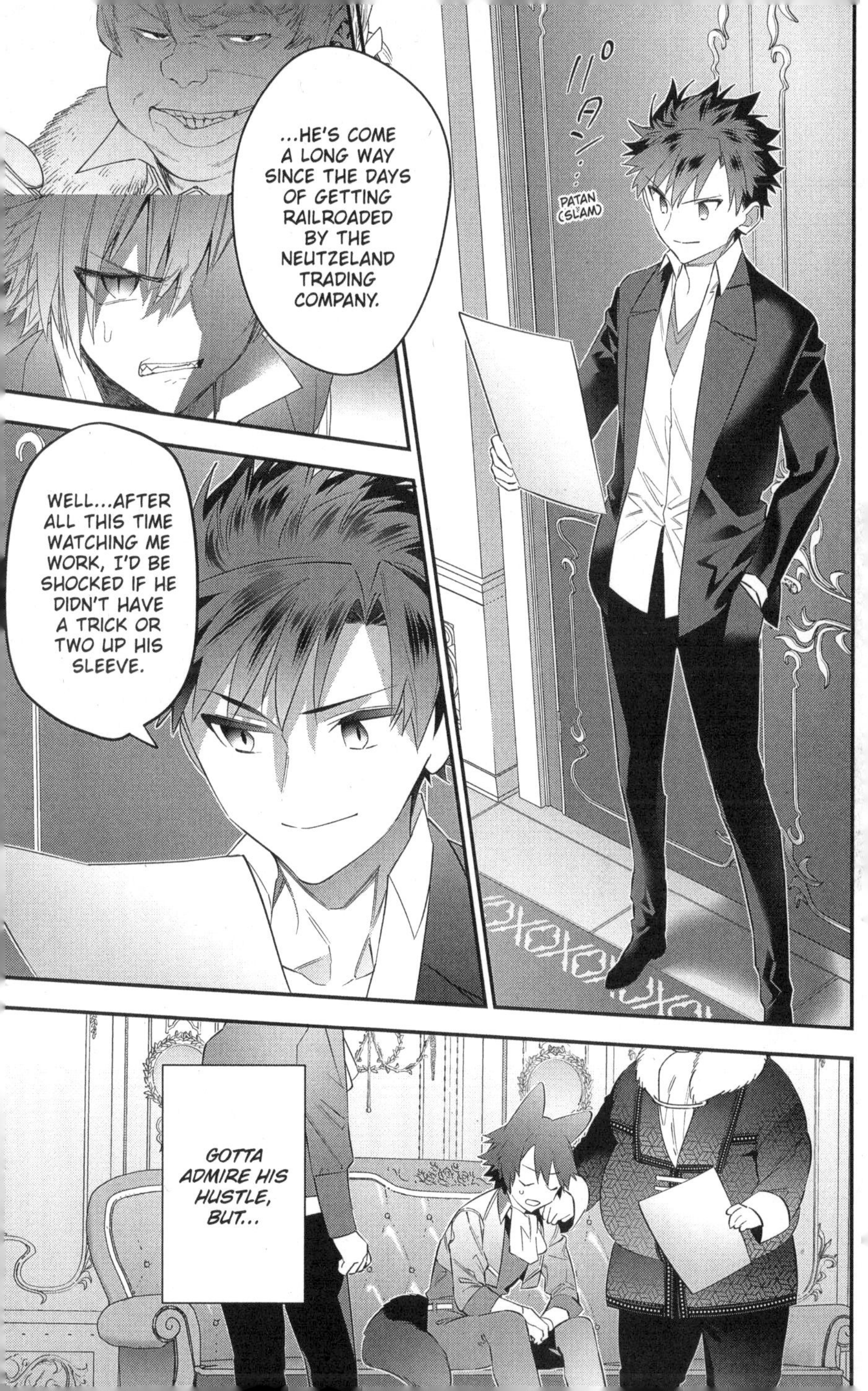

パタン…
PATAN (SLAM)
...HE'S COME A LONG WAY SINCE THE DAYS OF GETTING RAILROADED BY THE NEUTZELAND TRADING COMPANY.
WELL...AFTER ALL THIS TIME WATCHING ME WORK, I'D BE SHOCKED IF HE DIDN'T HAVE A TRICK OR TWO UP HIS SLEEVE.
GOTTA ADMIRE HIS HUSTLE, BUT...

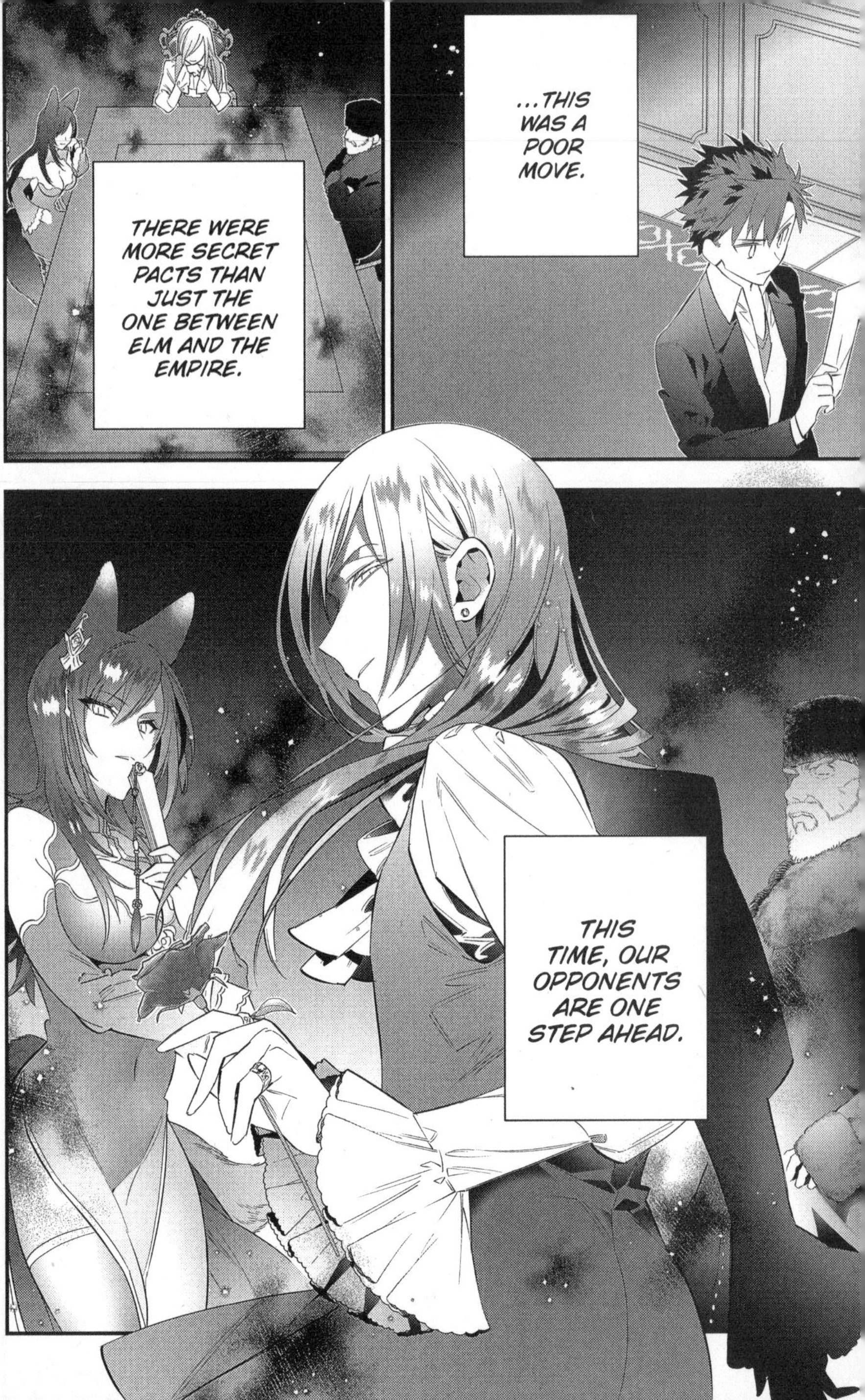
...THIS WAS A POOR MOVE.
THERE WERE MORE SECRET PACTS THAN JUST THE ONE BETWEEN ELM AND THE EMPIRE.
THIS TIME, OUR OPPONENTS ARE ONE STEP AHEAD.

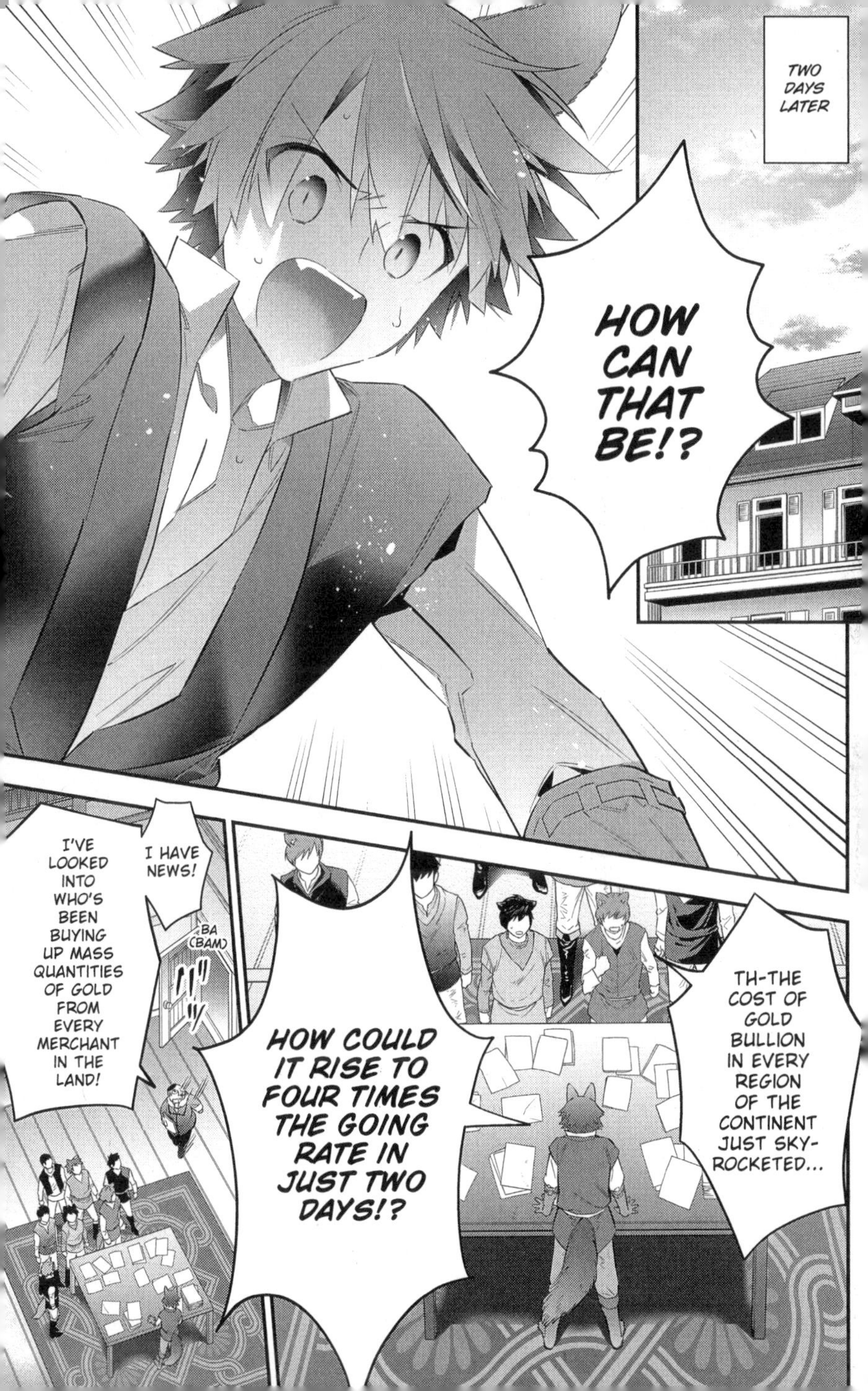
TWO DAYS LATER
HOW CAN THAT BE!?
TH-THE COST OF GOLD BULLION IN EVERY REGION OF THE CONTINENT JUST SKY-ROCKETED...
HOW COULD IT RISE TO FOUR TIMES THE GOING RATE IN JUST TWO DAYS!?
I HAVE NEWS!
BA (BAM)
I'VE LOOKED INTO WHO'S BEEN BUYING UP MASS QUANTITIES OF GOLD FROM EVERY MERCHANT IN THE LAND!

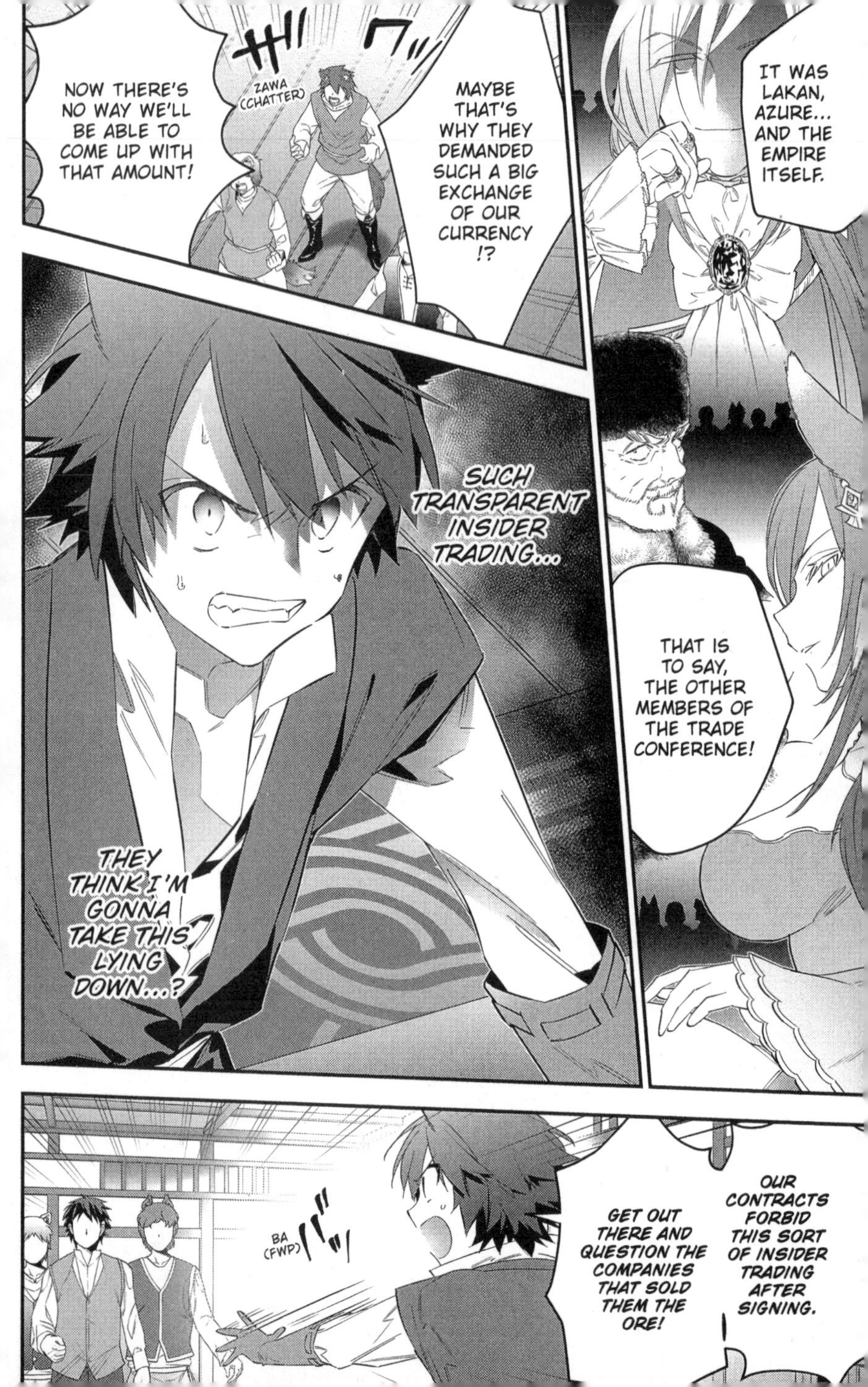
IT WAS LAKAN, AZURE... AND THE EMPIRE ITSELF.
THAT IS TO SAY, THE OTHER MEMBERS OF THE TRADE CONFERENCE!
MAYBE THAT'S WHY THEY DEMANDED SUCH A BIG EXCHANGE OF OUR CURRENCY !?
ZAWA (CHATTER)
NOW THERE'S NO WAY WE'LL BE ABLE TO COME UP WITH THAT AMOUNT!
SUCH TRANSPARENT INSIDER TRADING...
THEY THINK I'M GONNA TAKE THIS LYING DOWN...?
OUR CONTRACTS FORBID THIS SORT OF INSIDER TRADING AFTER SIGNING.
GET OUT THERE AND QUESTION THE COMPANIES THAT SOLD THEM THE ORE!
BA (FWP)

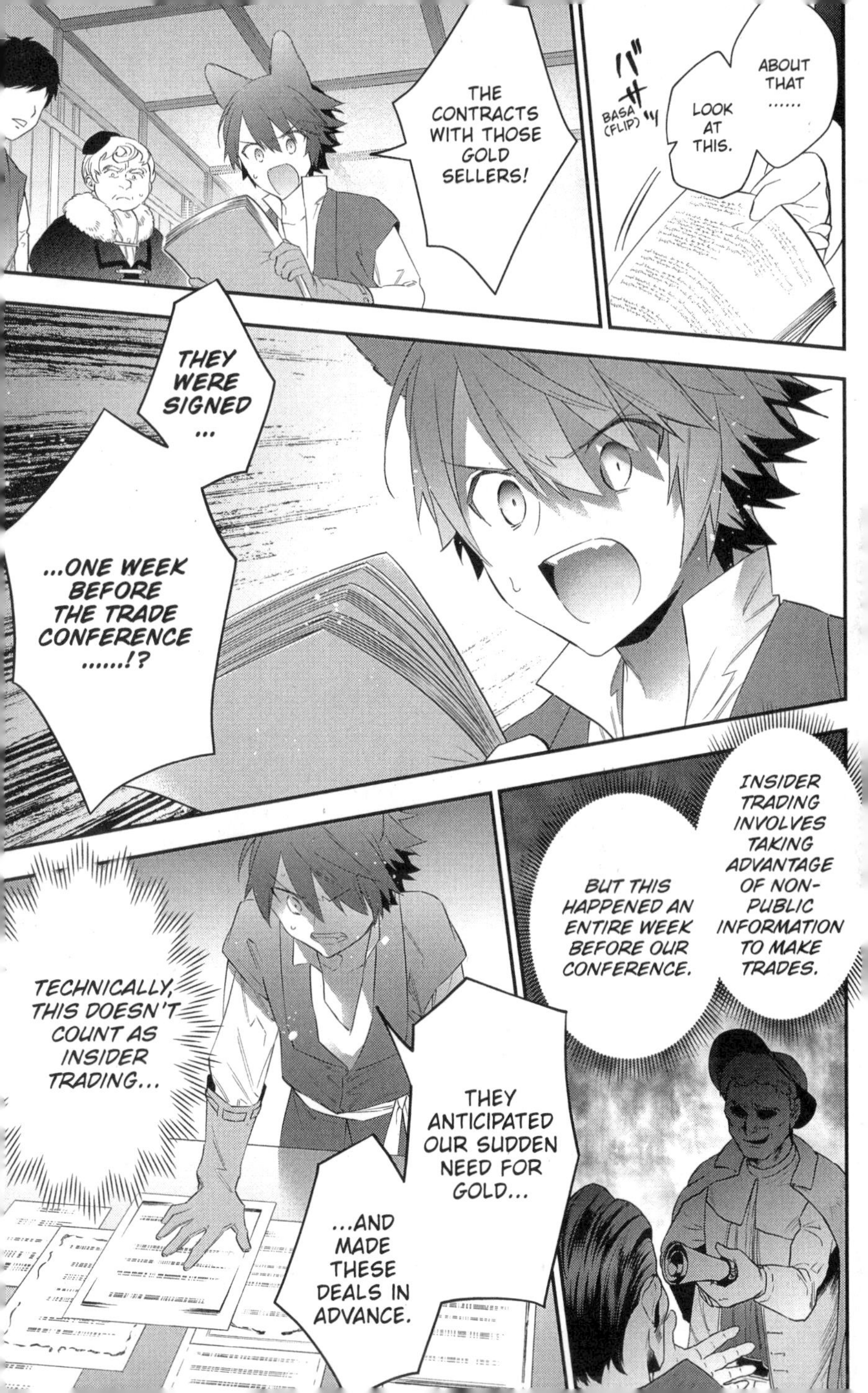
ABOUT THAT ......
LOOK AT THIS.
バサッ
BASA (FLIP)
THE CONTRACTS WITH THOSE GOLD SELLERS!
THEY WERE SIGNED ...
...ONE WEEK BEFORE THE TRADE CONFERENCE ......!?
INSIDER TRADING INVOLVES TAKING ADVANTAGE OF NON-PUBLIC INFORMATION TO MAKE TRADES.
BUT THIS HAPPENED AN ENTIRE WEEK BEFORE OUR CONFERENCE.
TECHNICALLY, THIS DOESN'T COUNT AS INSIDER TRADING...
THEY ANTICIPATED OUR SUDDEN NEED FOR GOLD...
...AND MADE THESE DEALS IN ADVANCE.

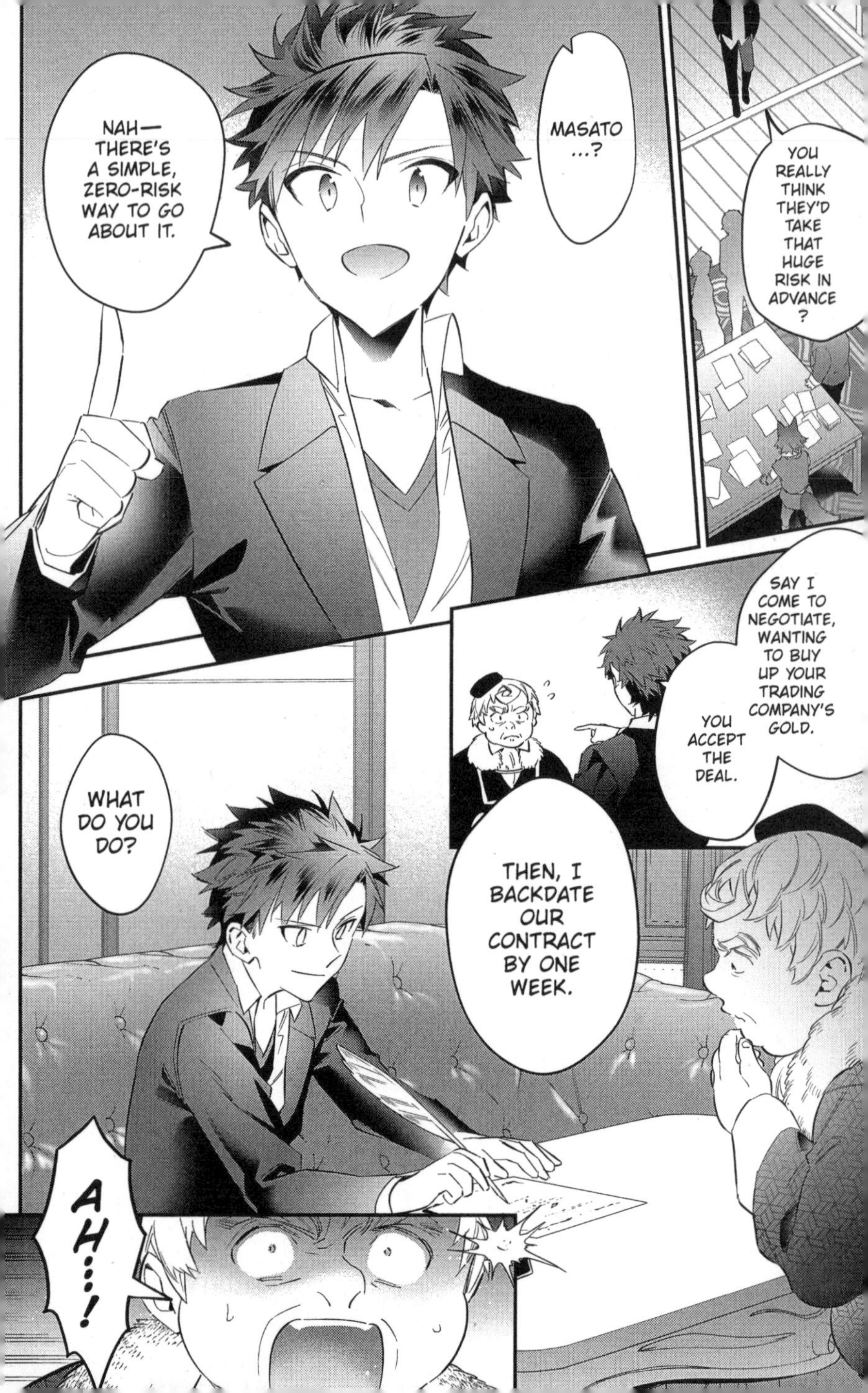
YOU REALLY THINK THEY'D TAKE THAT HUGE RISK IN ADVANCE?
MASATO...?
NAH— THERE'S A SIMPLE, ZERO-RISK WAY TO GO ABOUT IT.
SAY I COME TO NEGOTIATE, WANTING TO BUY UP YOUR TRADING COMPANY'S GOLD.
YOU ACCEPT THE DEAL.
WHAT DO YOU DO?
THEN, I BACKDATE OUR CONTRACT BY ONE WEEK.
AH...!

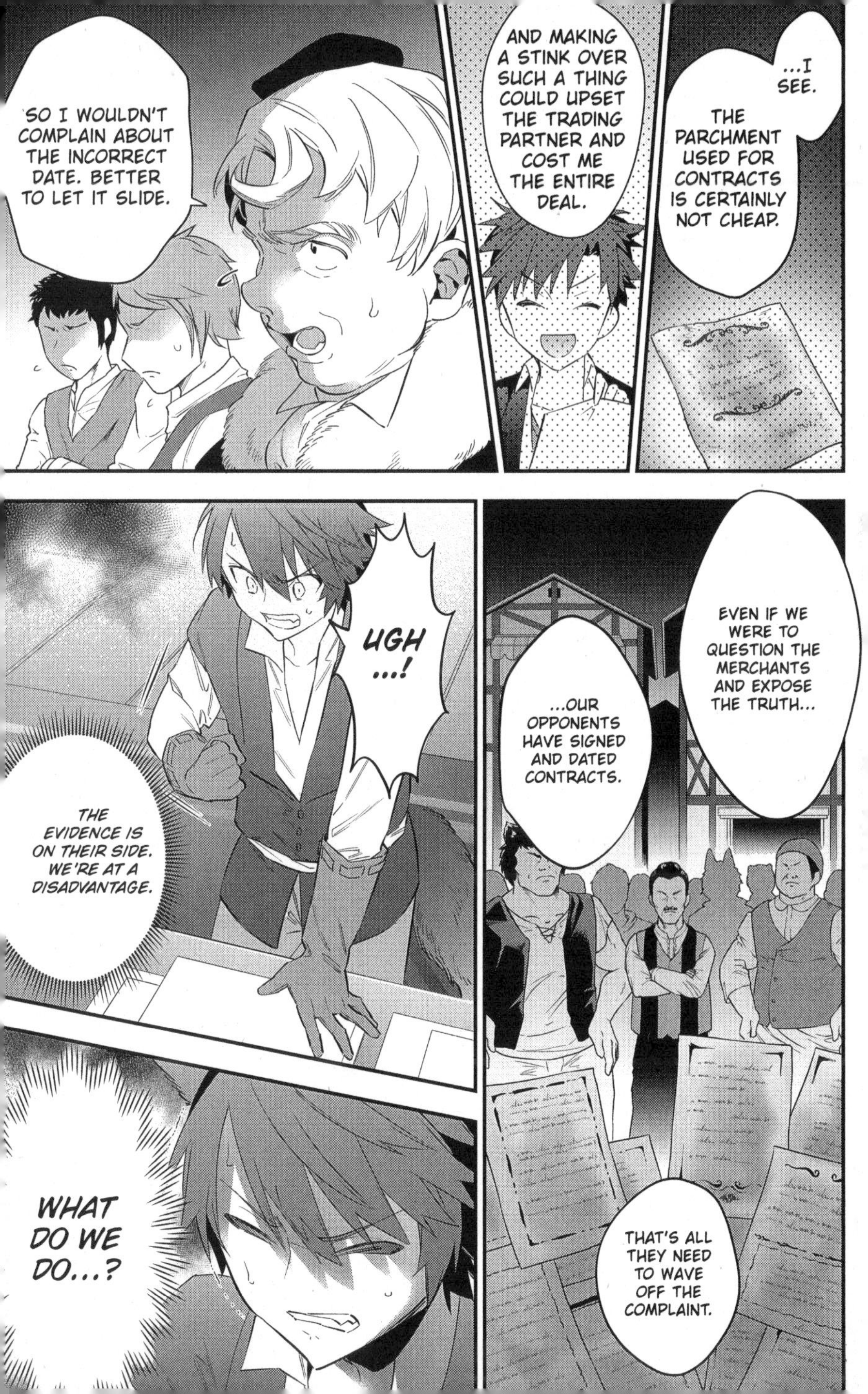
...I SEE.
THE PARCHMENT USED FOR CONTRACTS IS CERTAINLY NOT CHEAP.
AND MAKING A STINK OVER SUCH A THING COULD UPSET THE TRADING PARTNER AND COST ME THE ENTIRE DEAL.
SO I WOULDN'T COMPLAIN ABOUT THE INCORRECT DATE. BETTER TO LET IT SLIDE.
EVEN IF WE WERE TO QUESTION THE MERCHANTS AND EXPOSE THE TRUTH...
...OUR OPPONENTS HAVE SIGNED AND DATED CONTRACTS.
THAT'S ALL THEY NEED TO WAVE OFF THE COMPLAINT.
UGH ...!
THE EVIDENCE IS ON THEIR SIDE. WE'RE AT A DISADVANTAGE.
WHAT DO WE DO...?

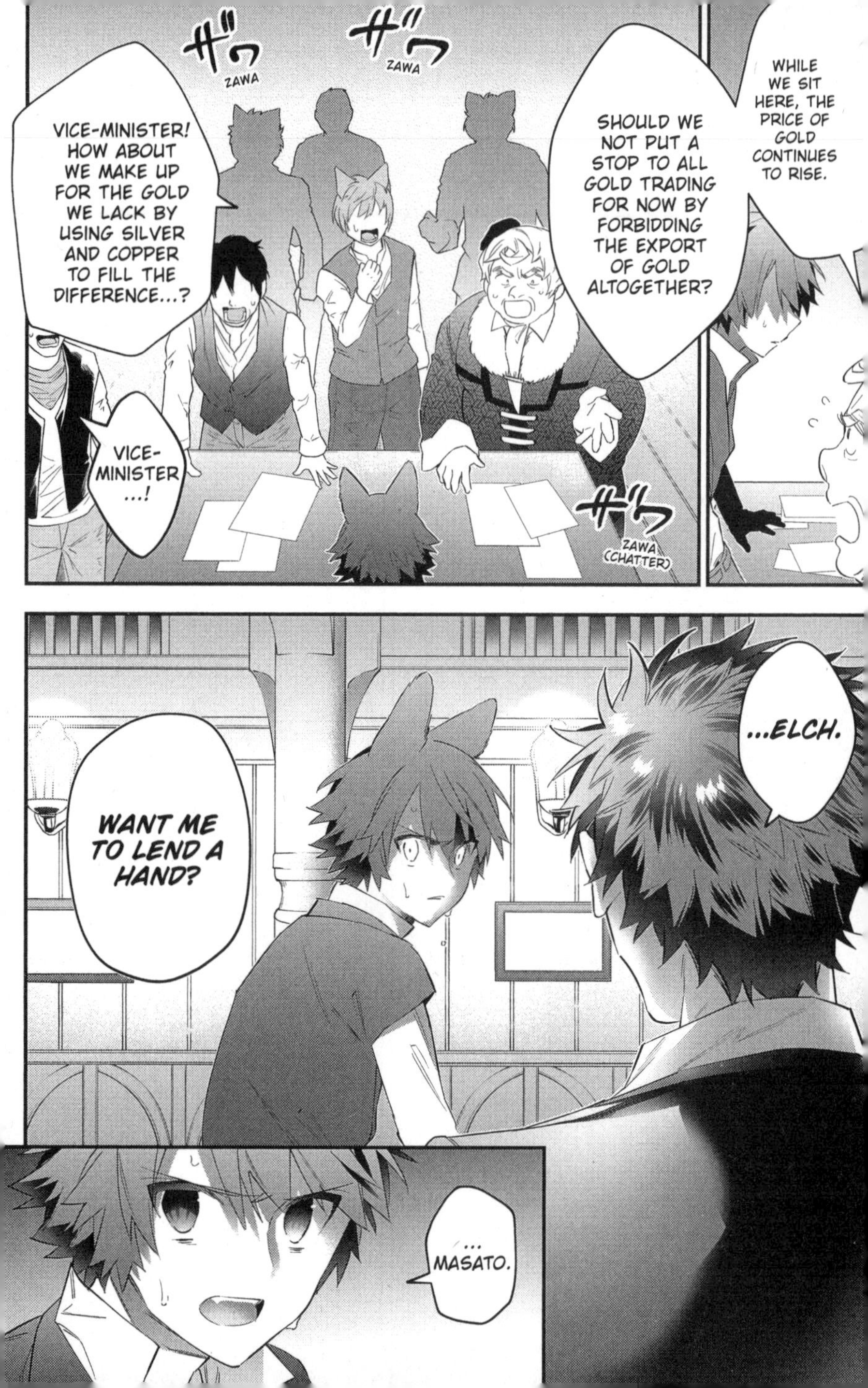
WHILE WE SIT HERE, THE PRICE OF GOLD CONTINUES TO RISE.
ザワ
ZAWA
ザワ
ZAWA
SHOULD WE NOT PUT A STOP TO ALL GOLD TRADING FOR NOW BY FORBIDDING THE EXPORT OF GOLD ALTOGETHER?
VICE-MINISTER! HOW ABOUT WE MAKE UP FOR THE GOLD WE LACK BY USING SILVER AND COPPER TO FILL THE DIFFERENCE...?
VICE-MINISTER...!
ザワ
ZAWA (CHATTER)
...ELCH.
WANT ME TO LEND A HAND?
... MASATO.

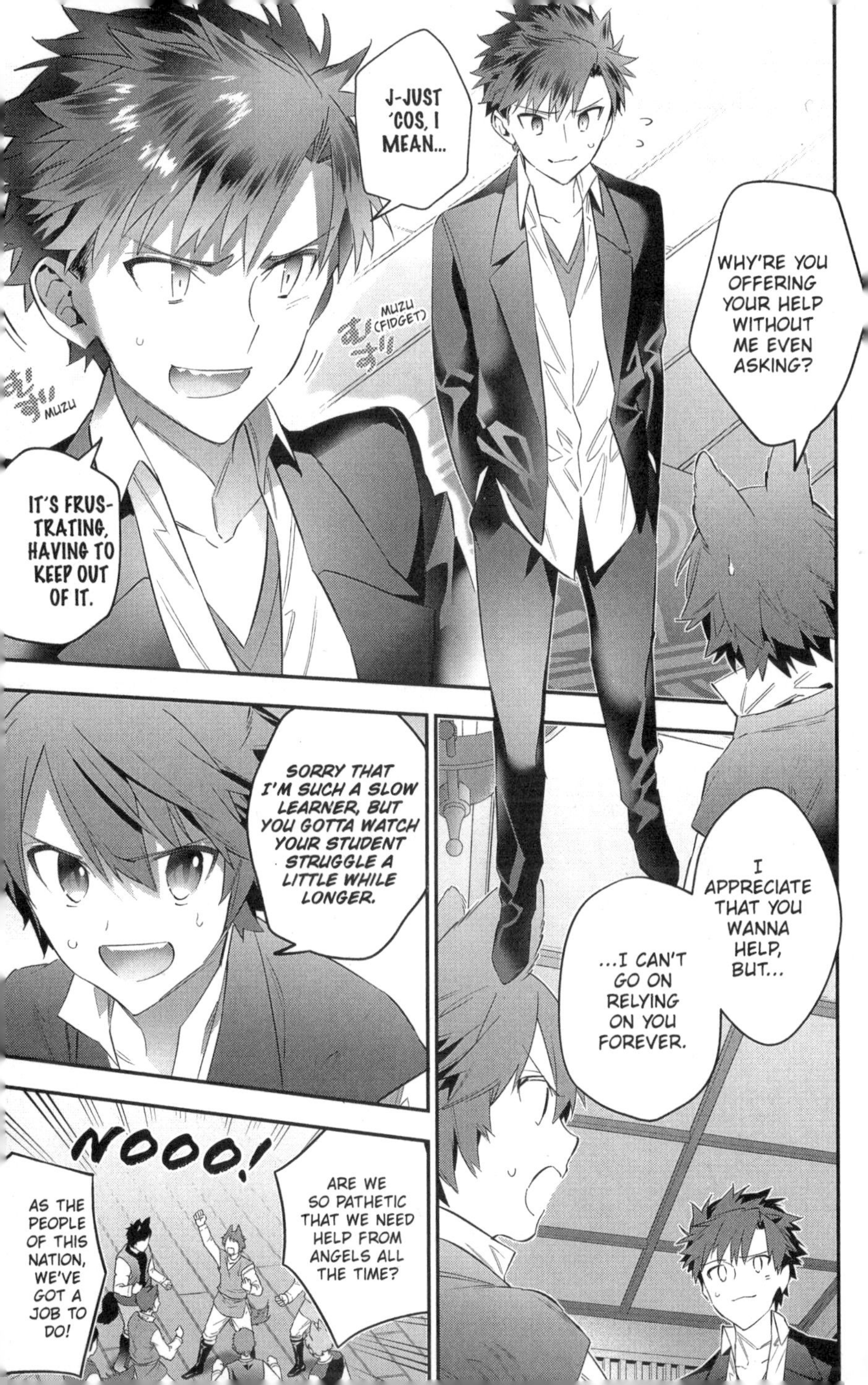

WHY'RE YOU OFFERING YOUR HELP WITHOUT ME EVEN ASKING?
J-JUST 'COS, I MEAN...
MUZU (FIDGET)
MUZU
IT'S FRUSTRATING, HAVING TO KEEP OUT OF IT.
I APPRECIATE THAT YOU WANNA HELP, BUT...
...I CAN'T GO ON RELYING ON YOU FOREVER.
SORRY THAT I'M SUCH A SLOW LEARNER, BUT YOU GOTTA WATCH YOUR STUDENT STRUGGLE A LITTLE WHILE LONGER.
NOOO!
ARE WE SO PATHETIC THAT WE NEED HELP FROM ANGELS ALL THE TIME?
AS THE PEOPLE OF THIS NATION, WE'VE GOT A JOB TO DO!

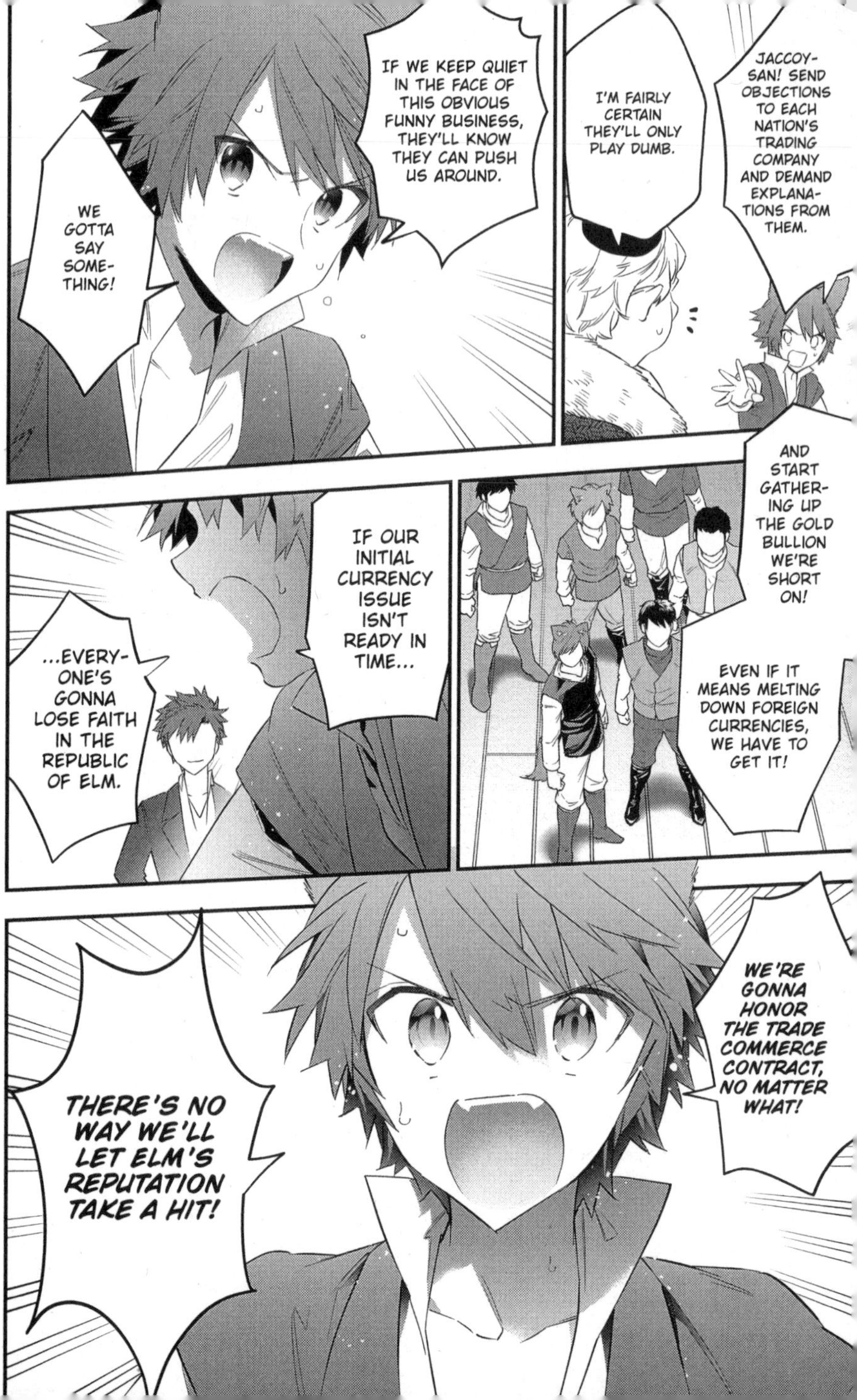
JACCOY-SAN! SEND OBJECTIONS TO EACH NATION'S TRADING COMPANY AND DEMAND EXPLANATIONS FROM THEM.
I'M FAIRLY CERTAIN THEY'LL ONLY PLAY DUMB.
IF WE KEEP QUIET IN THE FACE OF THIS OBVIOUS FUNNY BUSINESS, THEY'LL KNOW THEY CAN PUSH US AROUND.
WE GOTTA SAY SOMETHING!
AND START GATHERING UP THE GOLD BULLION WE'RE SHORT ON!
EVEN IF IT MEANS MELTING DOWN FOREIGN CURRENCIES, WE HAVE TO GET IT!
IF OUR INITIAL CURRENCY ISSUE ISN'T READY IN TIME...
...EVERYONE'S GONNA LOSE FAITH IN THE REPUBLIC OF ELM.
WE'RE GONNA HONOR THE TRADE COMMERCE CONTRACT, NO MATTER WHAT!
THERE'S NO WAY WE'LL LET ELM'S REPUTATION TAKE A HIT!

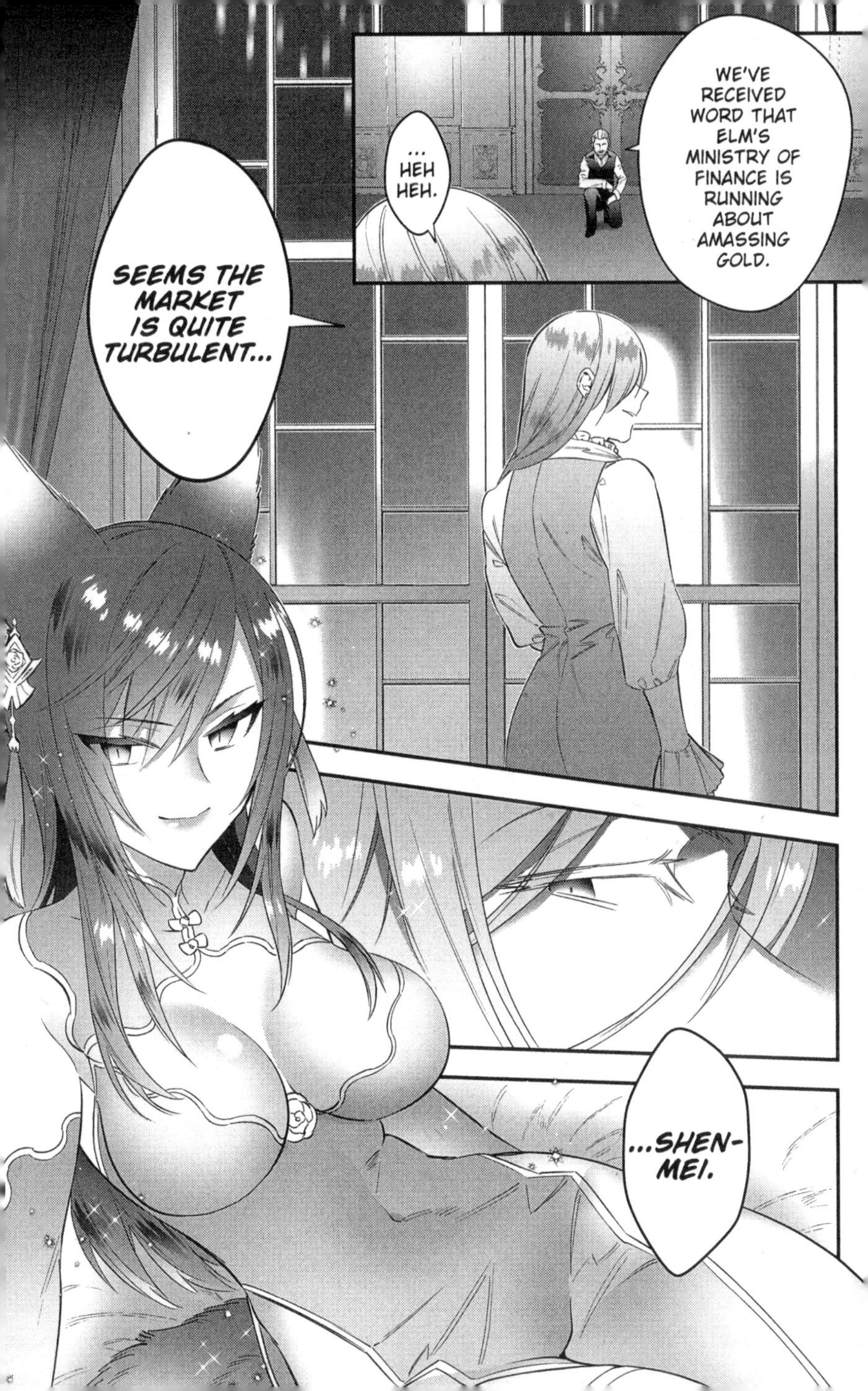
WE'VE RECEIVED WORD THAT ELM'S MINISTRY OF FINANCE IS RUNNING ABOUT AMASSING GOLD.
...HEH HEH.
SEEMS THE MARKET IS QUITE TURBULENT...
...SHEN-MEI.

CHARACTER FILE 27

Shenmei Li

Vice-chief of the Lakan Archipelago
Alliance and a merchant who
single-handedly built a great fortune.

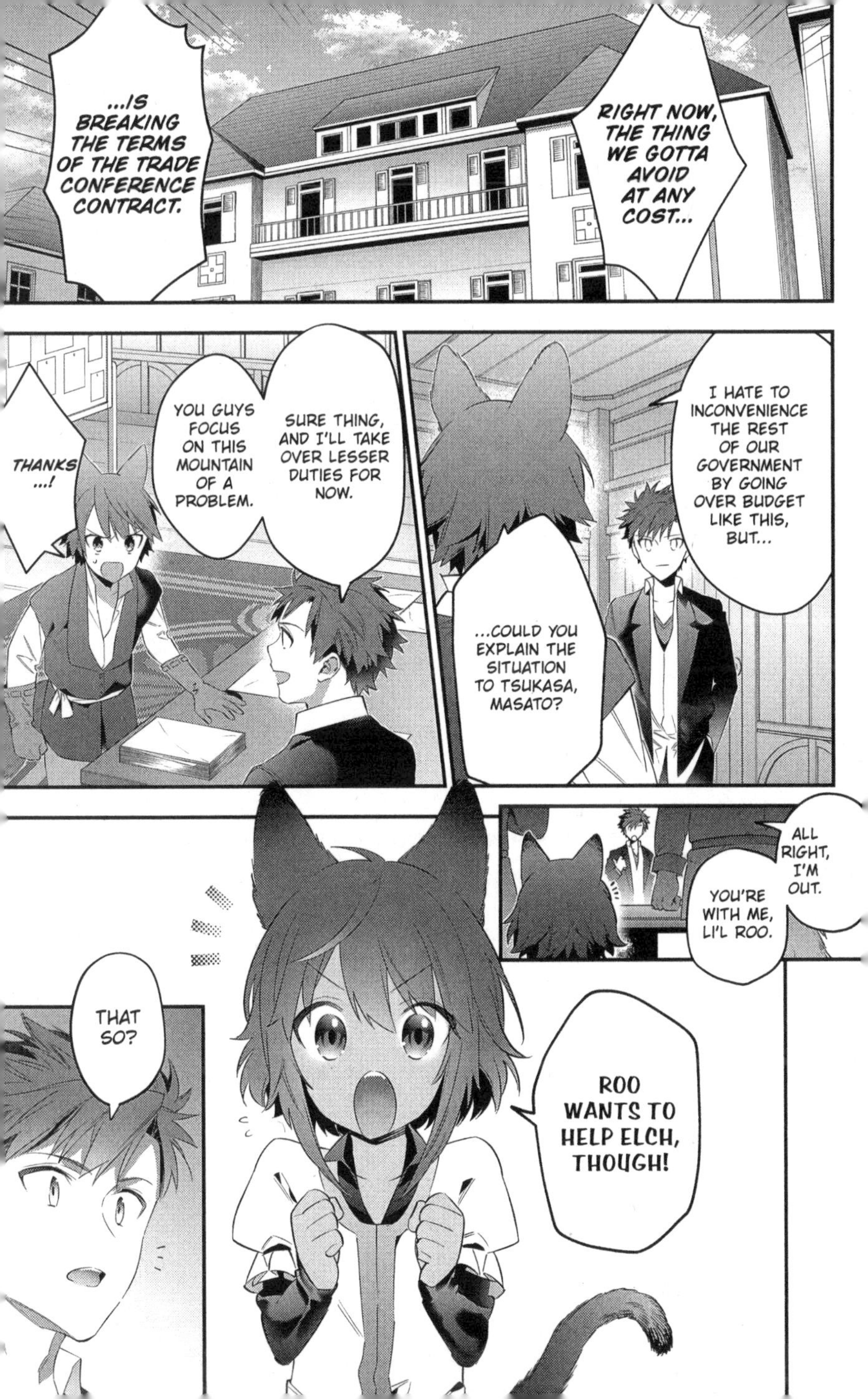
RIGHT NOW, THE THING WE GOTTA AVOID AT ANY COST...
...IS BREAKING THE TERMS OF THE TRADE CONFERENCE CONTRACT.
I HATE TO INCONVENIENCE THE REST OF OUR GOVERNMENT BY GOING OVER BUDGET LIKE THIS, BUT...
...COULD YOU EXPLAIN THE SITUATION TO TSUKASA, MASATO?
SURE THING, AND I'LL TAKE OVER LESSER DUTIES FOR NOW.
YOU GUYS FOCUS ON THIS MOUNTAIN OF A PROBLEM.
THANKS...!
ALL RIGHT, I'M OUT.
YOU'RE WITH ME, LI'L ROO.
ROO WANTS TO HELP ELCH, THOUGH!
THAT SO?

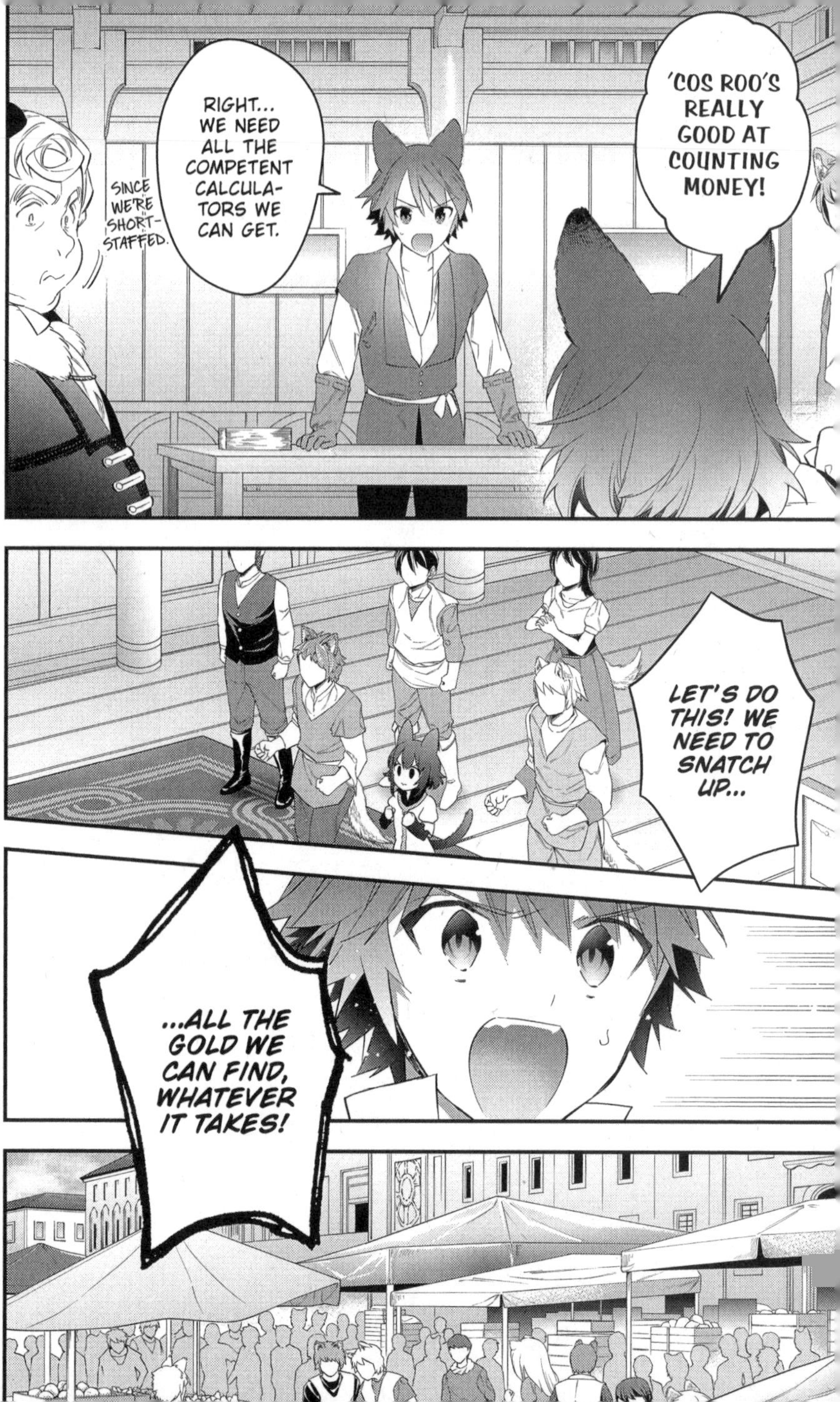
'COS ROO'S REALLY GOOD AT COUNTING MONEY!
RIGHT... WE NEED ALL THE COMPETENT CALCULA-TORS WE CAN GET.
SINCE WE'RE SHORT-STAFFED.
LET'S DO THIS! WE NEED TO SNATCH UP...
...ALL THE GOLD WE CAN FIND, WHATEVER IT TAKES!

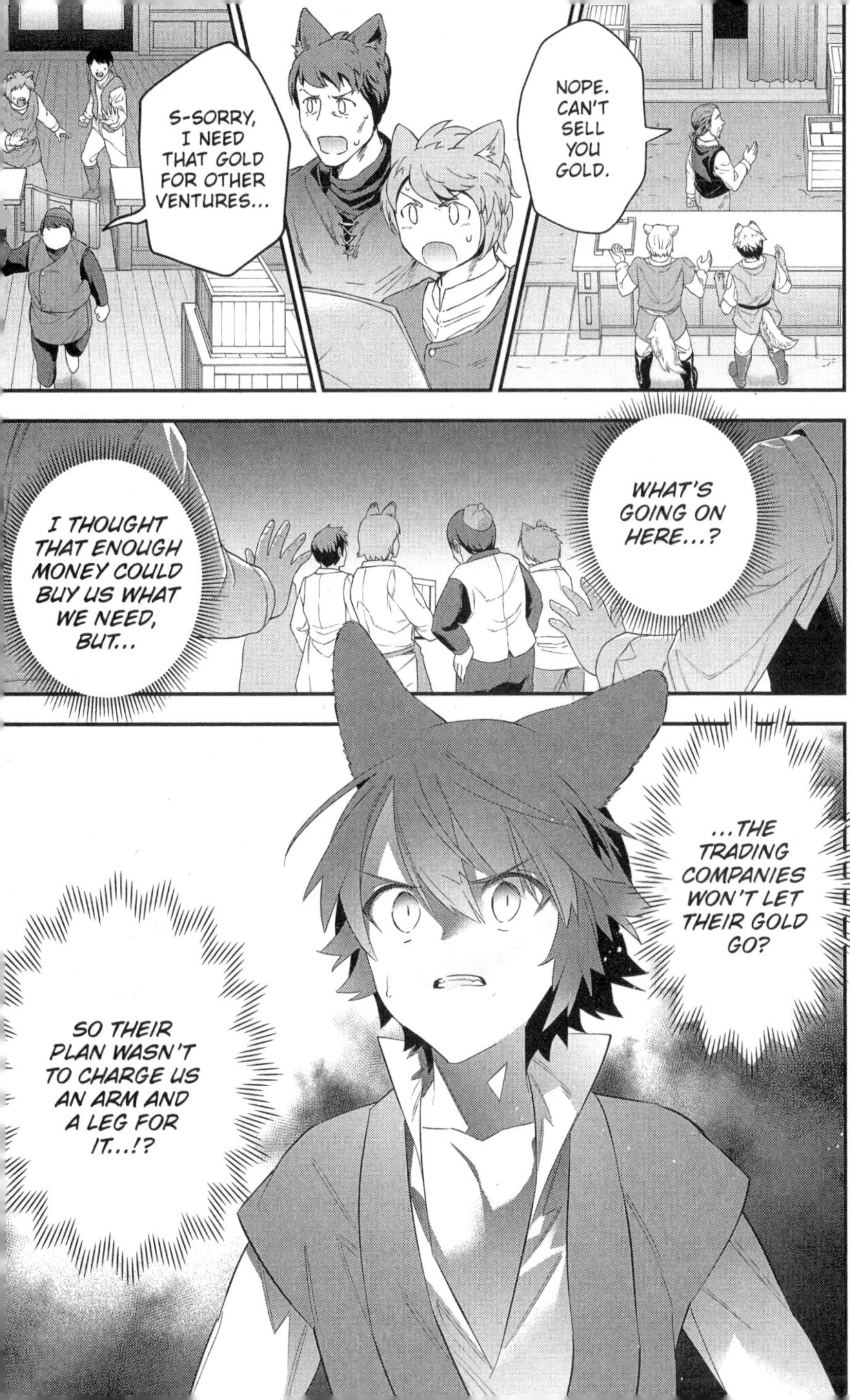
NOPE. CAN'T SELL YOU GOLD.
S-SORRY, I NEED THAT GOLD FOR OTHER VENTURES...
WHAT'S GOING ON HERE...?
I THOUGHT THAT ENOUGH MONEY COULD BUY US WHAT WE NEED, BUT...
...THE TRADING COMPANIES WON'T LET THEIR GOLD GO?
SO THEIR PLAN WASN'T TO CHARGE US AN ARM AND A LEG FOR IT...!?

CHAPTER 55: **TRIPARTITE PLOT**

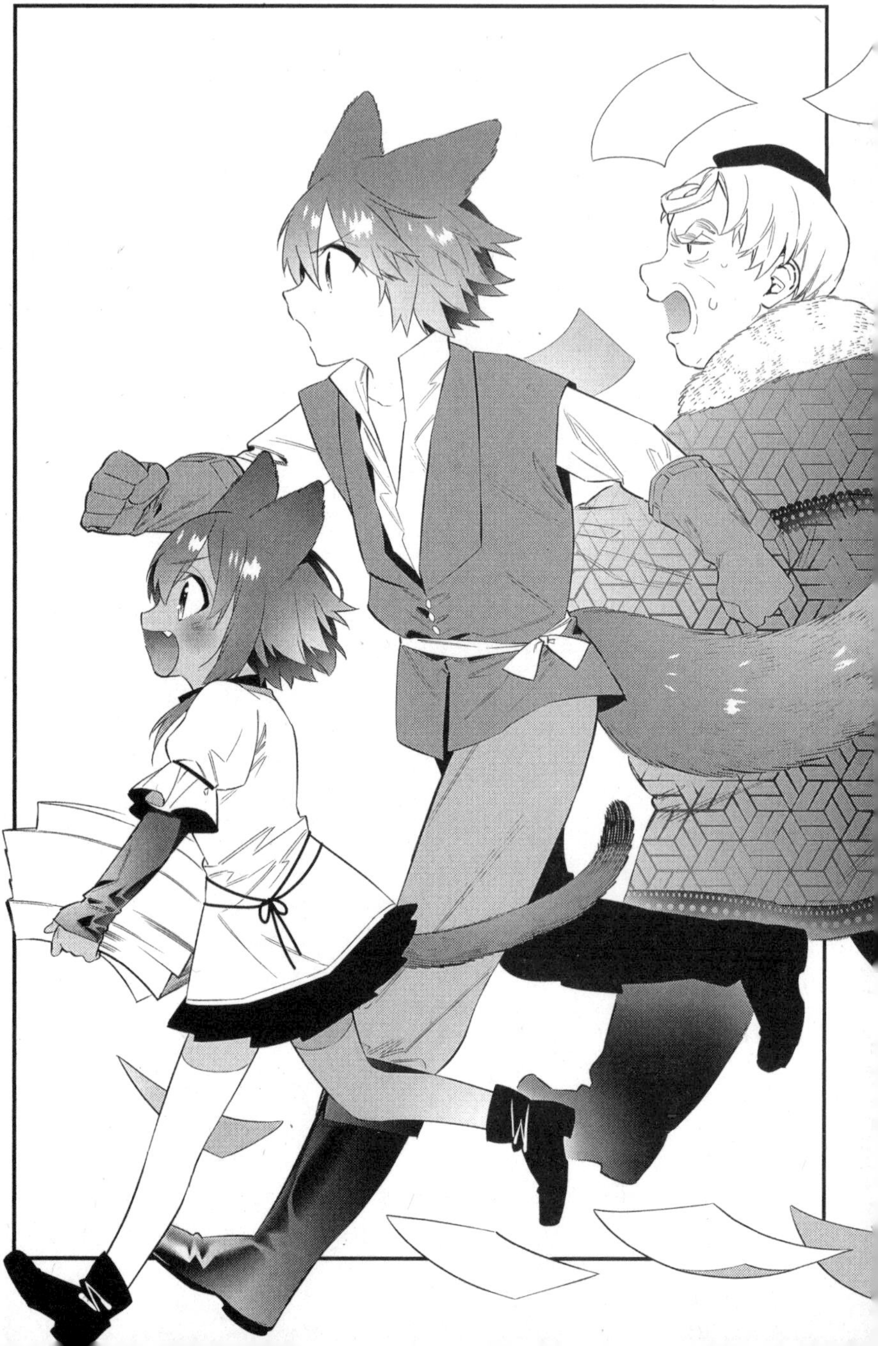

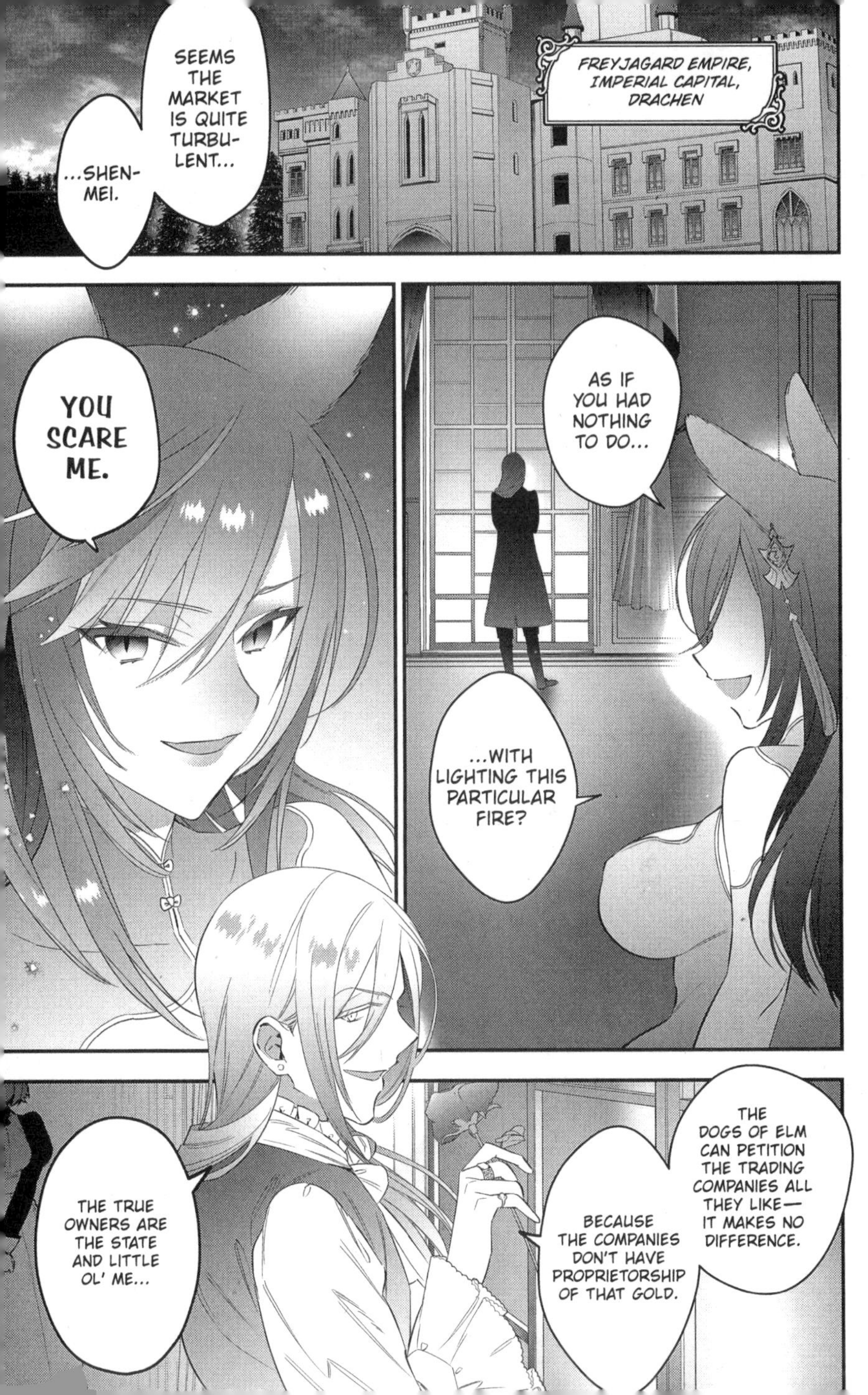
FREYJAGARD EMPIRE, IMPERIAL CAPITAL, DRACHEN
SEEMS THE MARKET IS QUITE TURBULENT...
...SHEN-MEI.
AS IF YOU HAD NOTHING TO DO...
...WITH LIGHTING THIS PARTICULAR FIRE?
YOU SCARE ME.
THE DOGS OF ELM CAN PETITION THE TRADING COMPANIES ALL THEY LIKE—IT MAKES NO DIFFERENCE.
BECAUSE THE COMPANIES DON'T HAVE PROPRIETORSHIP OF THAT GOLD.
THE TRUE OWNERS ARE THE STATE AND LITTLE OL' ME...

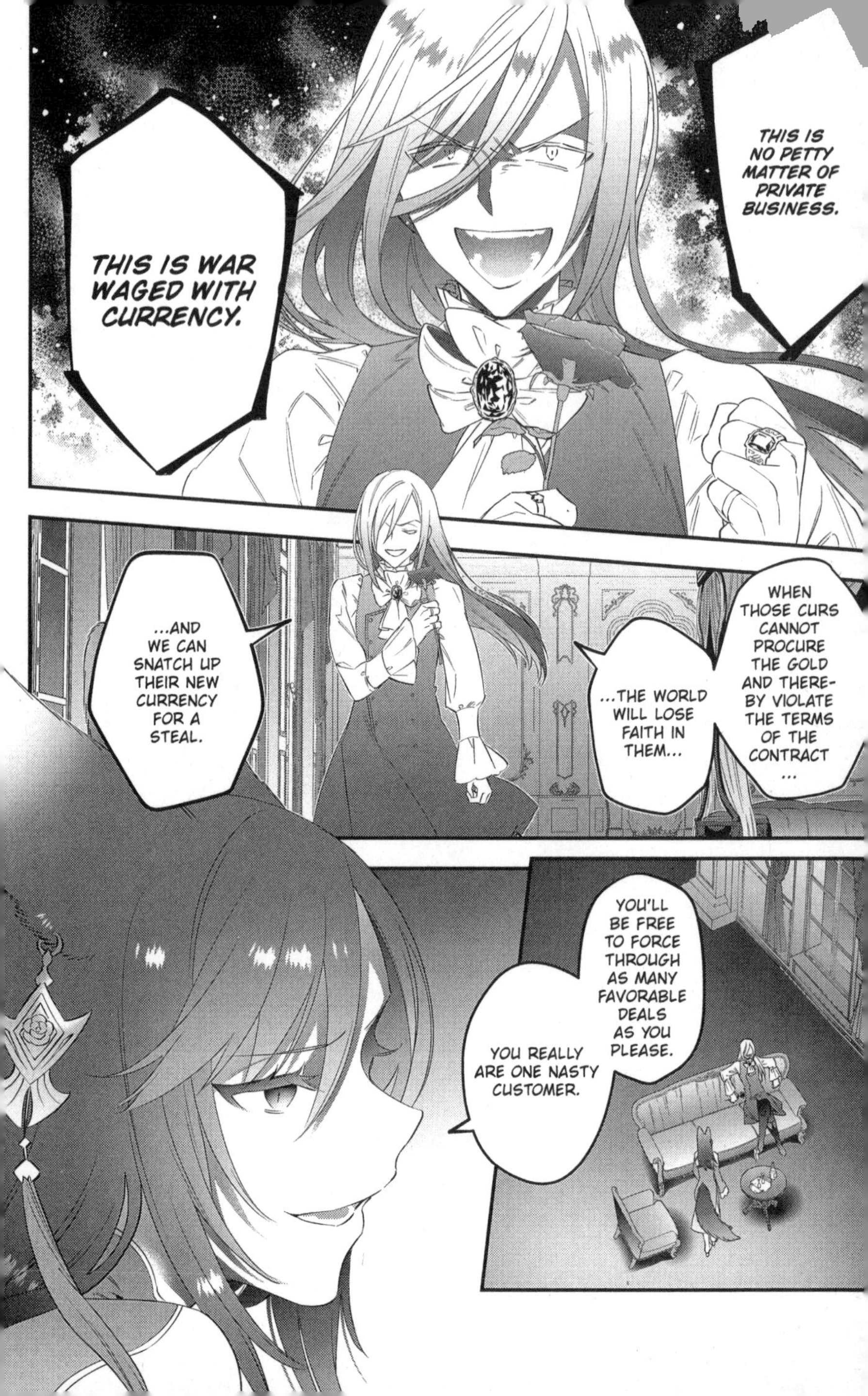

THIS IS NO PETTY MATTER OF PRIVATE BUSINESS.
THIS IS WAR WAGED WITH CURRENCY.
WHEN THOSE CURS CANNOT PROCURE THE GOLD AND THEREBY VIOLATE THE TERMS OF THE CONTRACT...
...THE WORLD WILL LOSE FAITH IN THEM...
...AND WE CAN SNATCH UP THEIR NEW CURRENCY FOR A STEAL.
YOU'LL BE FREE TO FORCE THROUGH AS MANY FAVORABLE DEALS AS YOU PLEASE.
YOU REALLY ARE ONE NASTY CUSTOMER.

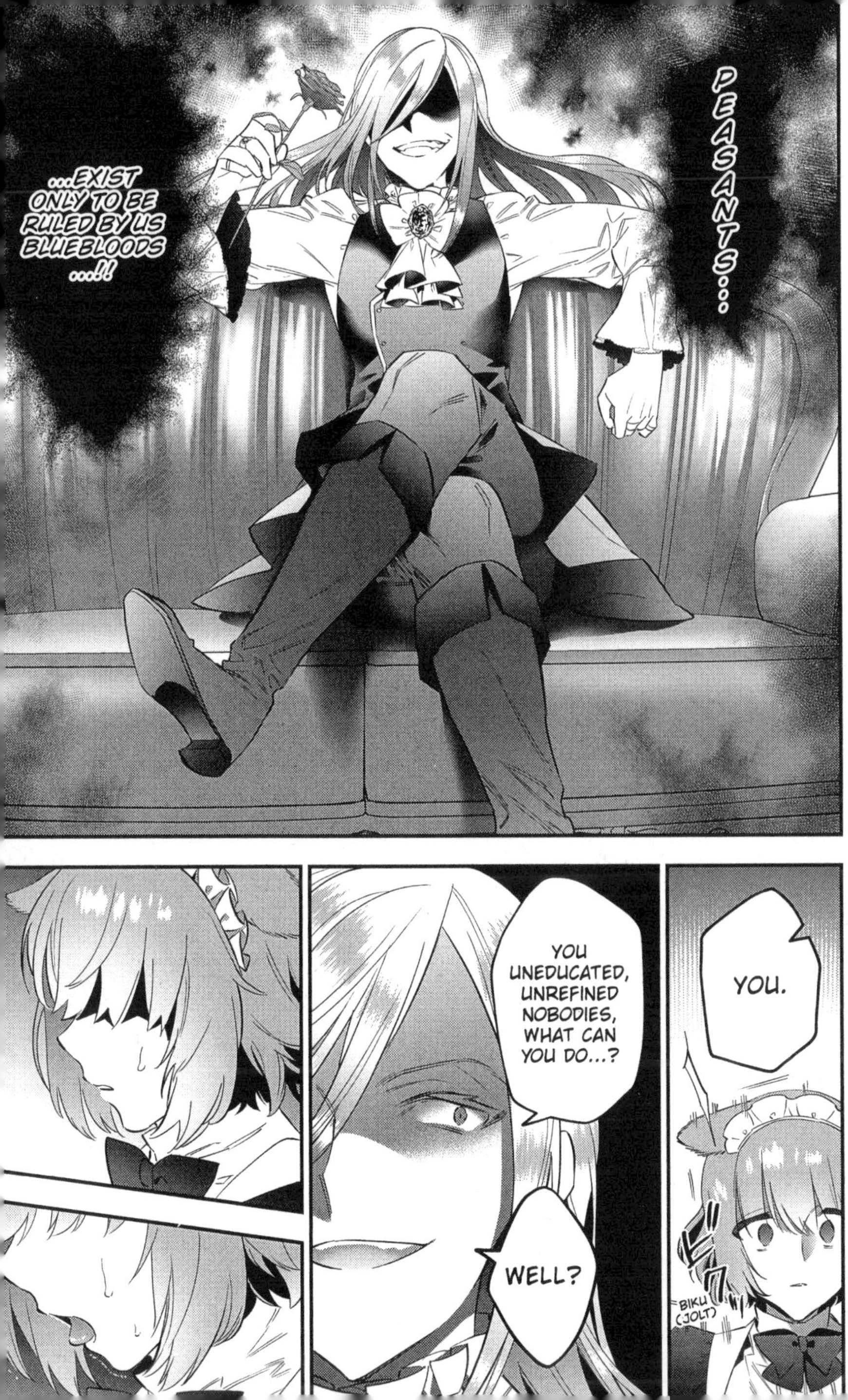
PEASANTS...
...EXIST ONLY TO BE RULED BY US BLUEBLOODS ...!!
YOU.
BIKU (:JOLT)
YOU UNEDUCATED, UNREFINED NOBODIES, WHAT CAN YOU DO...?
WELL?

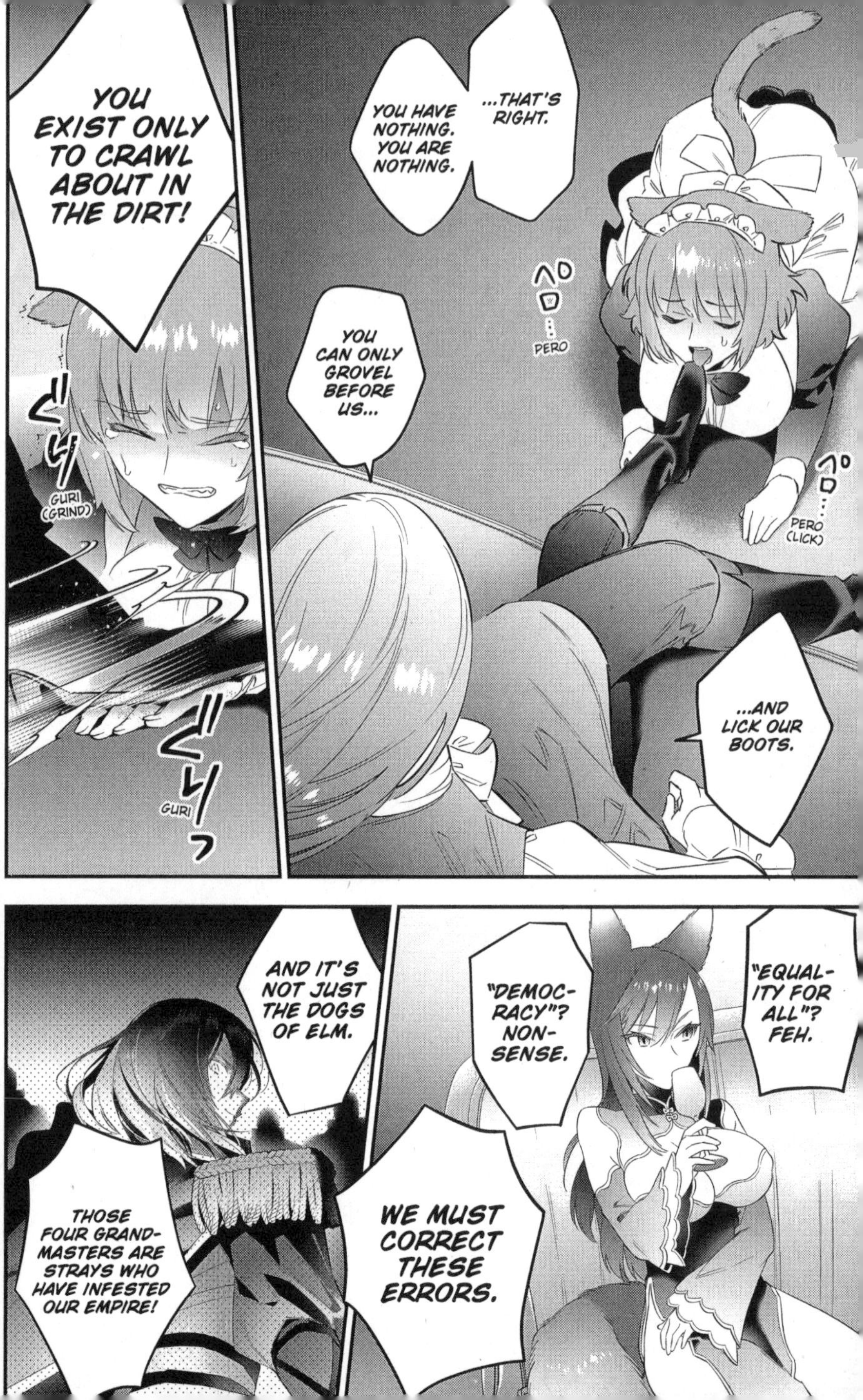
...THAT'S RIGHT.
YOU HAVE NOTHING. YOU ARE NOTHING.
ペロ…
PERO
ペロ…
PERO (LICK)
YOU CAN ONLY GROVEL BEFORE US...
...AND LICK OUR BOOTS.
YOU EXIST ONLY TO CRAWL ABOUT IN THE DIRT!
ぐり
GURI (GRIND)
ぐりっ
GURI
"EQUALITY FOR ALL"? FEH.
"DEMOCRACY"? NONSENSE.
WE MUST CORRECT THESE ERRORS.
AND IT'S NOT JUST THE DOGS OF ELM.
THOSE FOUR GRANDMASTERS ARE STRAYS WHO HAVE INFESTED OUR EMPIRE!

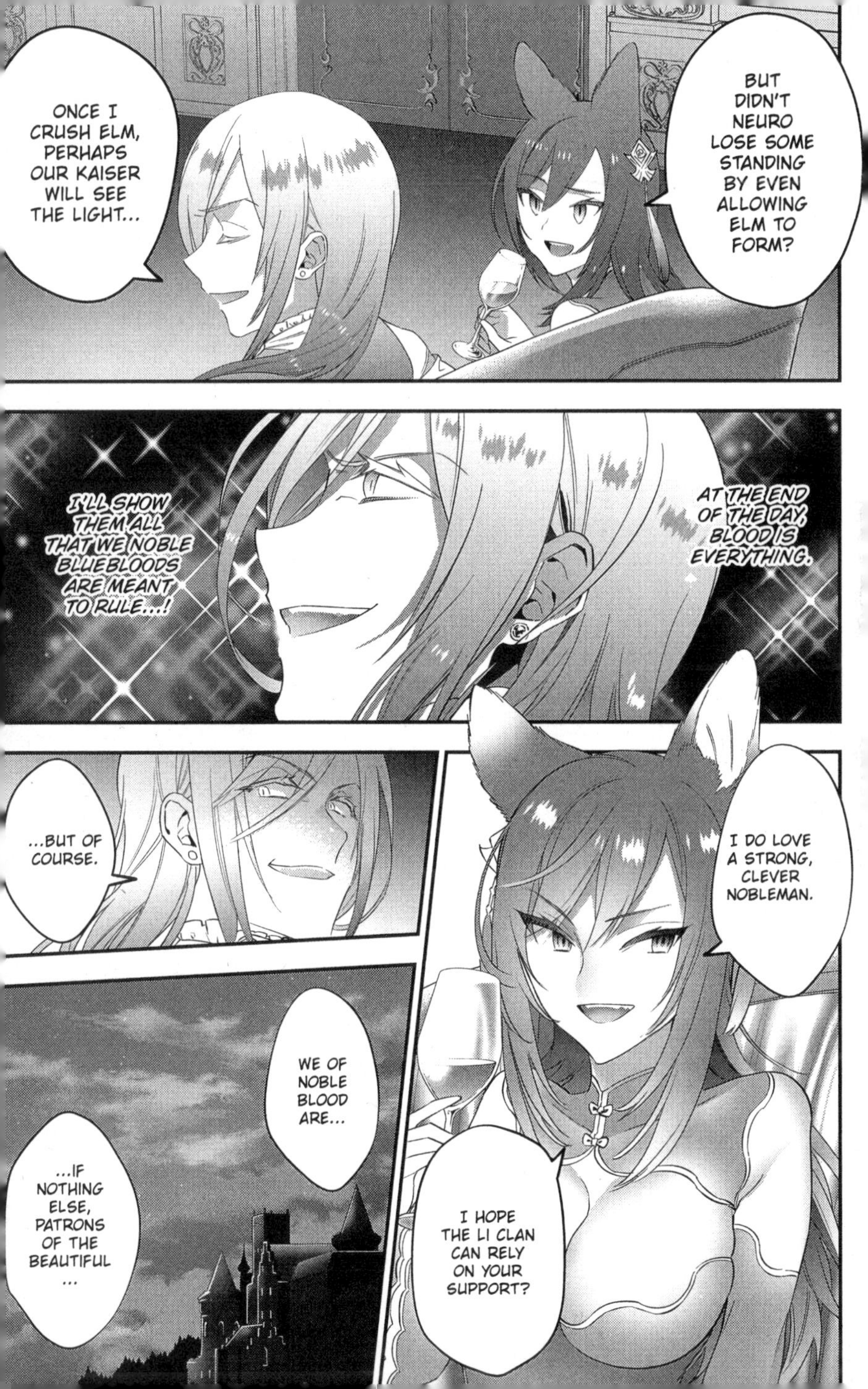
BUT DIDN'T NEURO LOSE SOME STANDING BY EVEN ALLOWING ELM TO FORM?
ONCE I CRUSH ELM, PERHAPS OUR KAISER WILL SEE THE LIGHT...
AT THE END OF THE DAY, BLOOD IS EVERYTHING.
I'LL SHOW THEM ALL THAT WE NOBLE BLUEBLOODS ARE MEANT TO RULE...!
I DO LOVE A STRONG, CLEVER NOBLEMAN.
I HOPE THE LI CLAN CAN RELY ON YOUR SUPPORT?
...BUT OF COURSE.
WE OF NOBLE BLOOD ARE...
...IF NOTHING ELSE, PATRONS OF THE BEAUTIFUL...

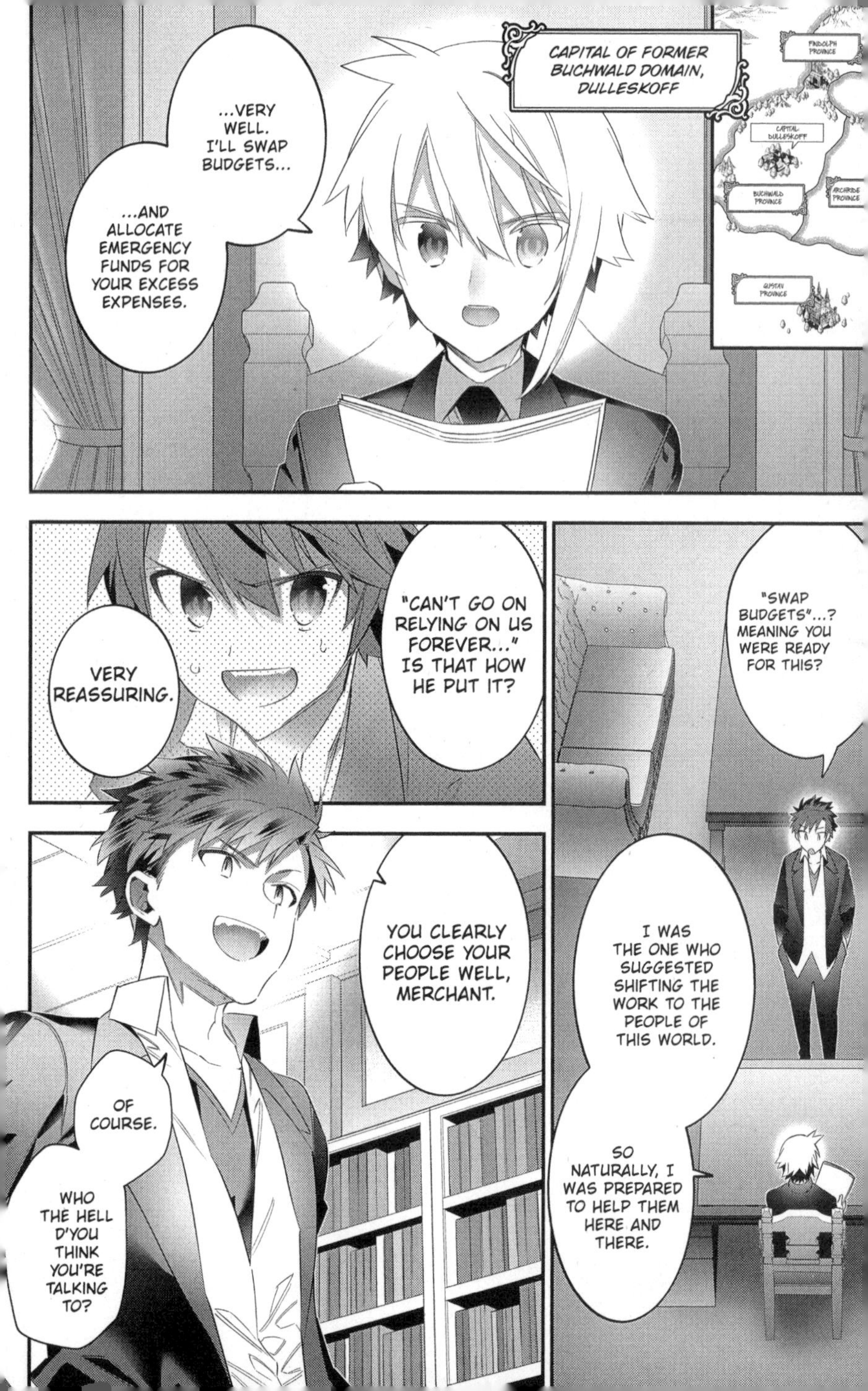
CAPITAL OF FORMER BUCHWALD DOMAIN, DULLESKOFF
FINDOLPH PROVINCE
CAPITAL DULLESKOFF
ARCHRIDE PROVINCE
BUCHWALD PROVINCE
GUSTAV PROVINCE
...VERY WELL. I'LL SWAP BUDGETS...
...AND ALLOCATE EMERGENCY FUNDS FOR YOUR EXCESS EXPENSES.
"SWAP BUDGETS"...? MEANING YOU WERE READY FOR THIS?
I WAS THE ONE WHO SUGGESTED SHIFTING THE WORK TO THE PEOPLE OF THIS WORLD.
SO NATURALLY, I WAS PREPARED TO HELP THEM HERE AND THERE.
"CAN'T GO ON RELYING ON US FOREVER..." IS THAT HOW HE PUT IT?
VERY REASSURING.
YOU CLEARLY CHOOSE YOUR PEOPLE WELL, MERCHANT.
OF COURSE.
WHO THE HELL D'YOU THINK YOU'RE TALKING TO?

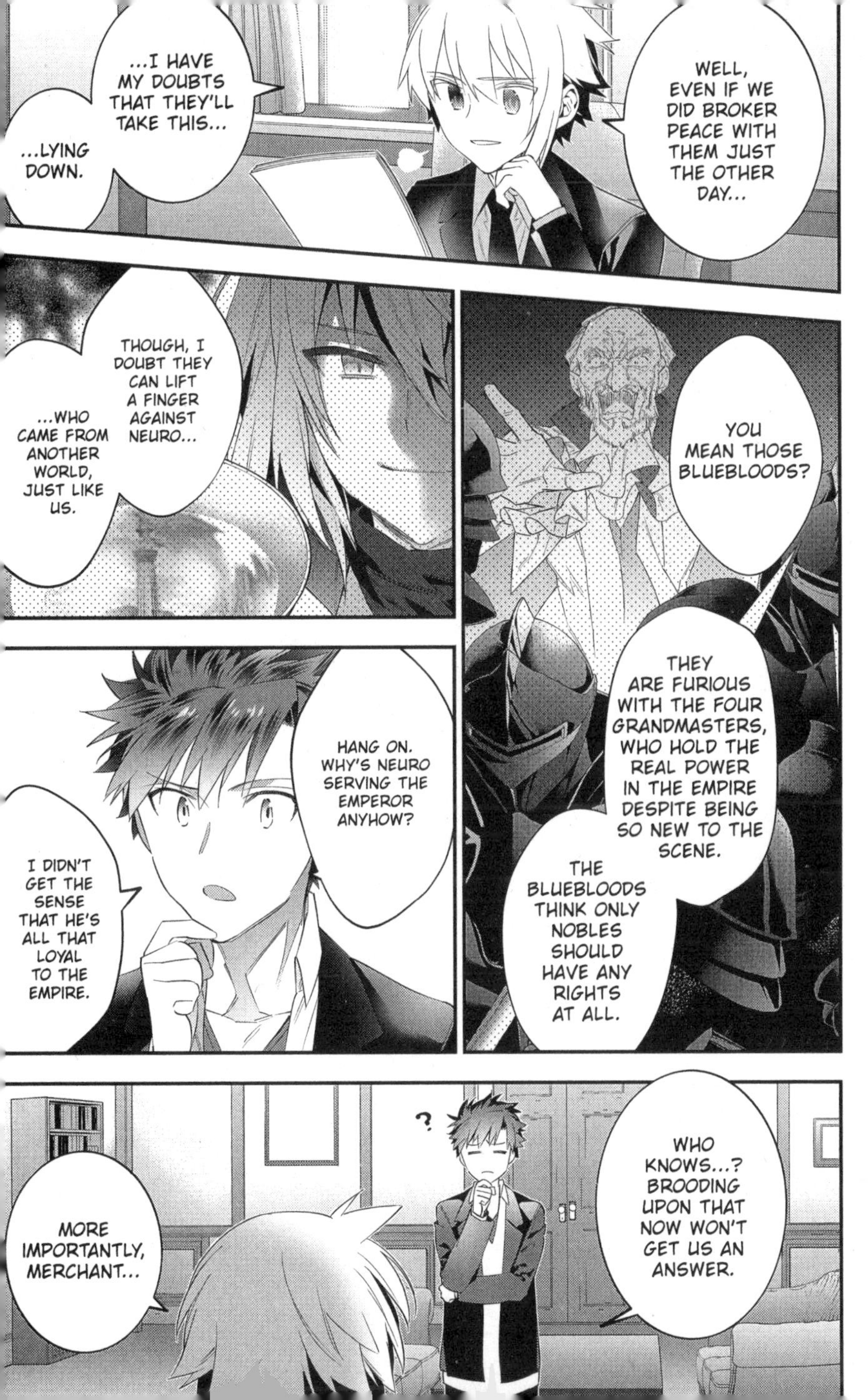
WELL, EVEN IF WE DID BROKER PEACE WITH THEM JUST THE OTHER DAY...
...I HAVE MY DOUBTS THAT THEY'LL TAKE THIS...
...LYING DOWN.
YOU MEAN THOSE BLUEBLOODS?
THEY ARE FURIOUS WITH THE FOUR GRANDMASTERS, WHO HOLD THE REAL POWER IN THE EMPIRE DESPITE BEING SO NEW TO THE SCENE.
THE BLUEBLOODS THINK ONLY NOBLES SHOULD HAVE ANY RIGHTS AT ALL.
THOUGH, I DOUBT THEY CAN LIFT A FINGER AGAINST NEURO...
...WHO CAME FROM ANOTHER WORLD, JUST LIKE US.
HANG ON. WHY'S NEURO SERVING THE EMPEROR ANYHOW?
I DIDN'T GET THE SENSE THAT HE'S ALL THAT LOYAL TO THE EMPIRE.
WHO KNOWS...? BROODING UPON THAT NOW WON'T GET US AN ANSWER.
?
MORE IMPORTANTLY, MERCHANT...

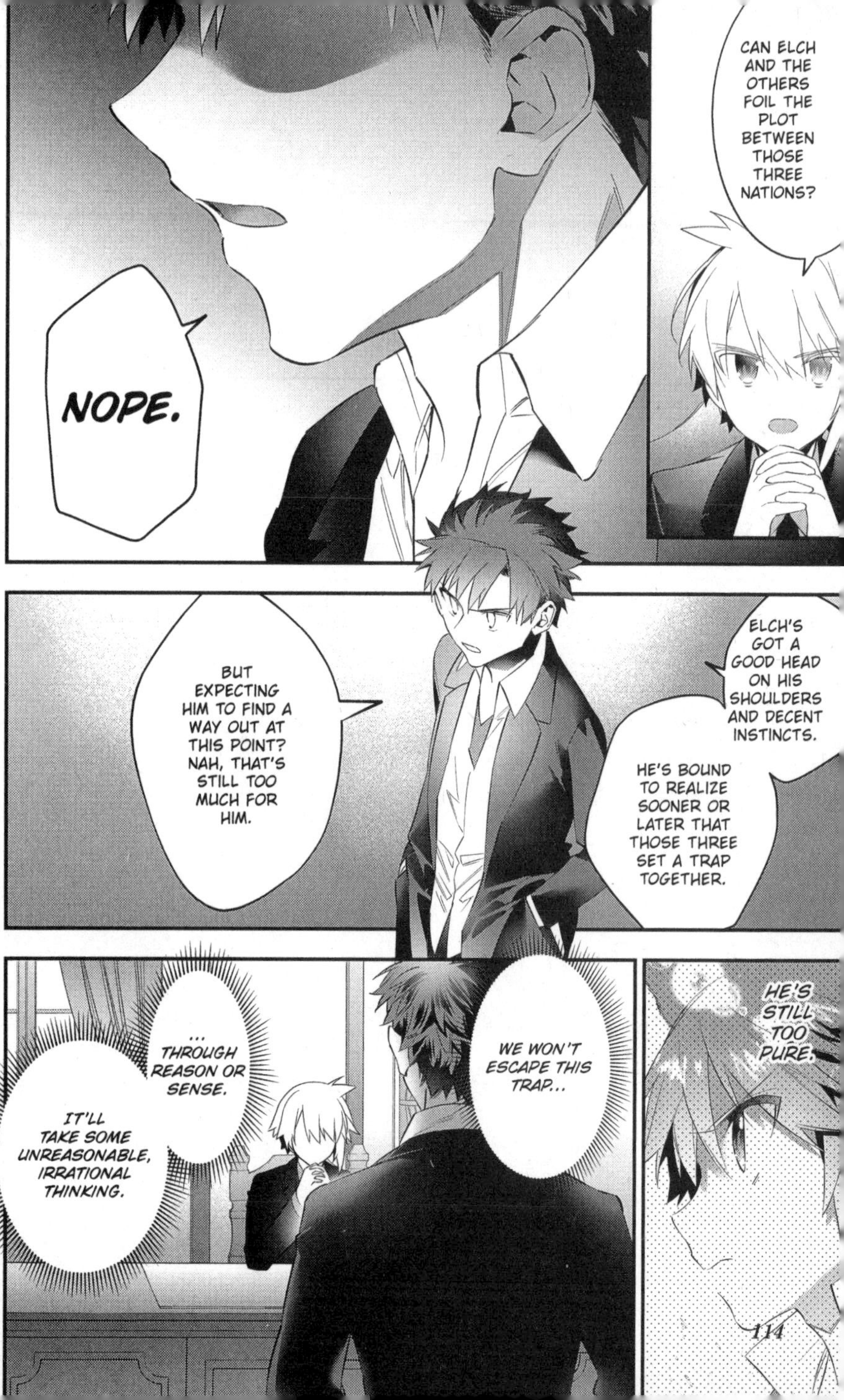
CAN ELCH AND THE OTHERS FOIL THE PLOT BETWEEN THOSE THREE NATIONS?
NOPE.
ELCH'S GOT A GOOD HEAD ON HIS SHOULDERS AND DECENT INSTINCTS.
HE'S BOUND TO REALIZE SOONER OR LATER THAT THOSE THREE SET A TRAP TOGETHER.
BUT EXPECTING HIM TO FIND A WAY OUT AT THIS POINT? NAH, THAT'S STILL TOO MUCH FOR HIM.
HE'S STILL TOO PURE.
WE WON'T ESCAPE THIS TRAP...
...THROUGH REASON OR SENSE.
IT'LL TAKE SOME UNREASONABLE, IRRATIONAL THINKING.

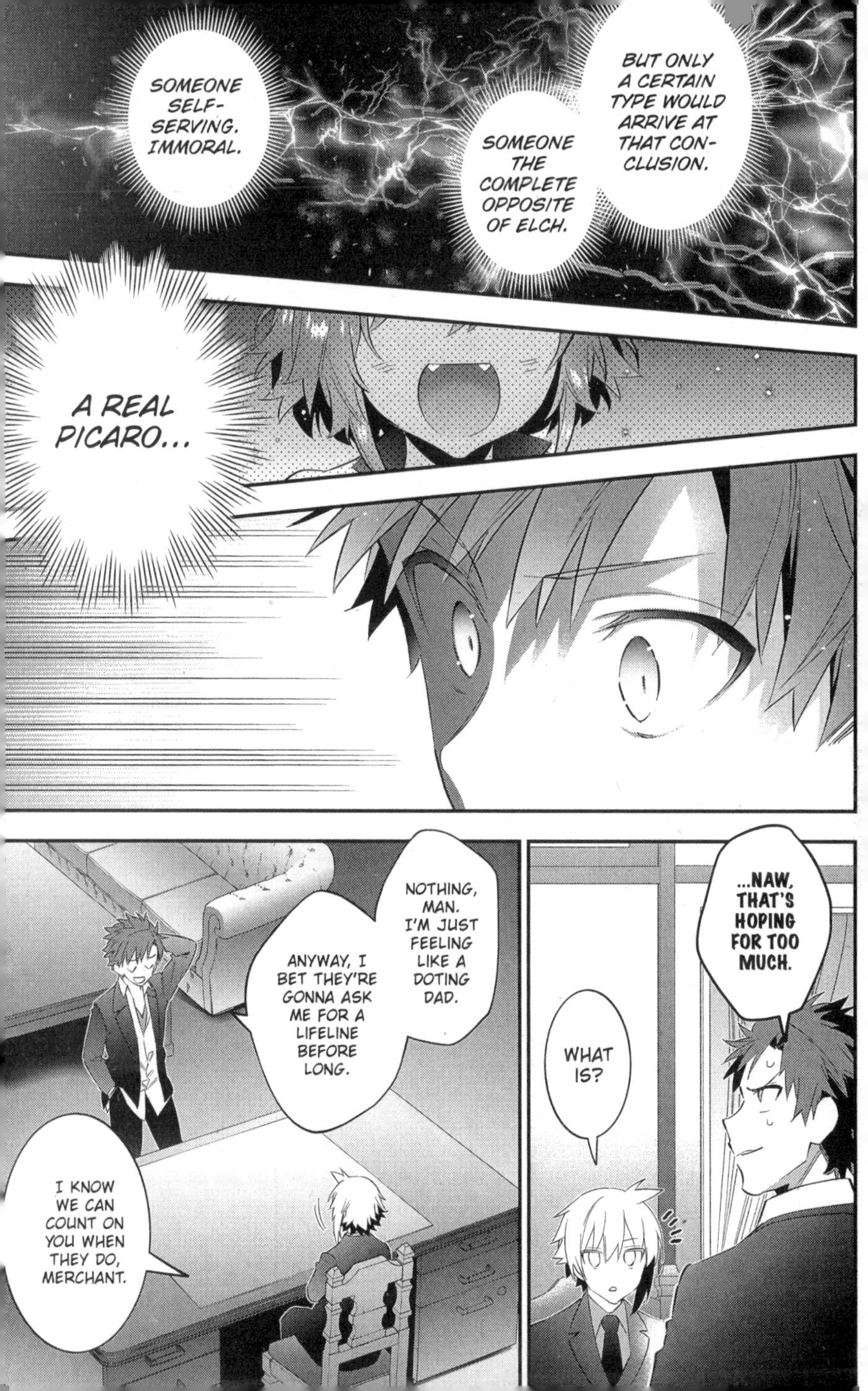
BUT ONLY A CERTAIN TYPE WOULD ARRIVE AT THAT CONCLUSION.
SOMEONE THE COMPLETE OPPOSITE OF ELCH.
SOMEONE SELF-SERVING. IMMORAL.
A REAL PICARO...
...NAW, THAT'S HOPING FOR TOO MUCH.
WHAT IS?
NOTHING, MAN. I'M JUST FEELING LIKE A DOTING DAD.
ANYWAY, I BET THEY'RE GONNA ASK ME FOR A LIFELINE BEFORE LONG.
I KNOW WE CAN COUNT ON YOU WHEN THEY DO, MERCHANT.

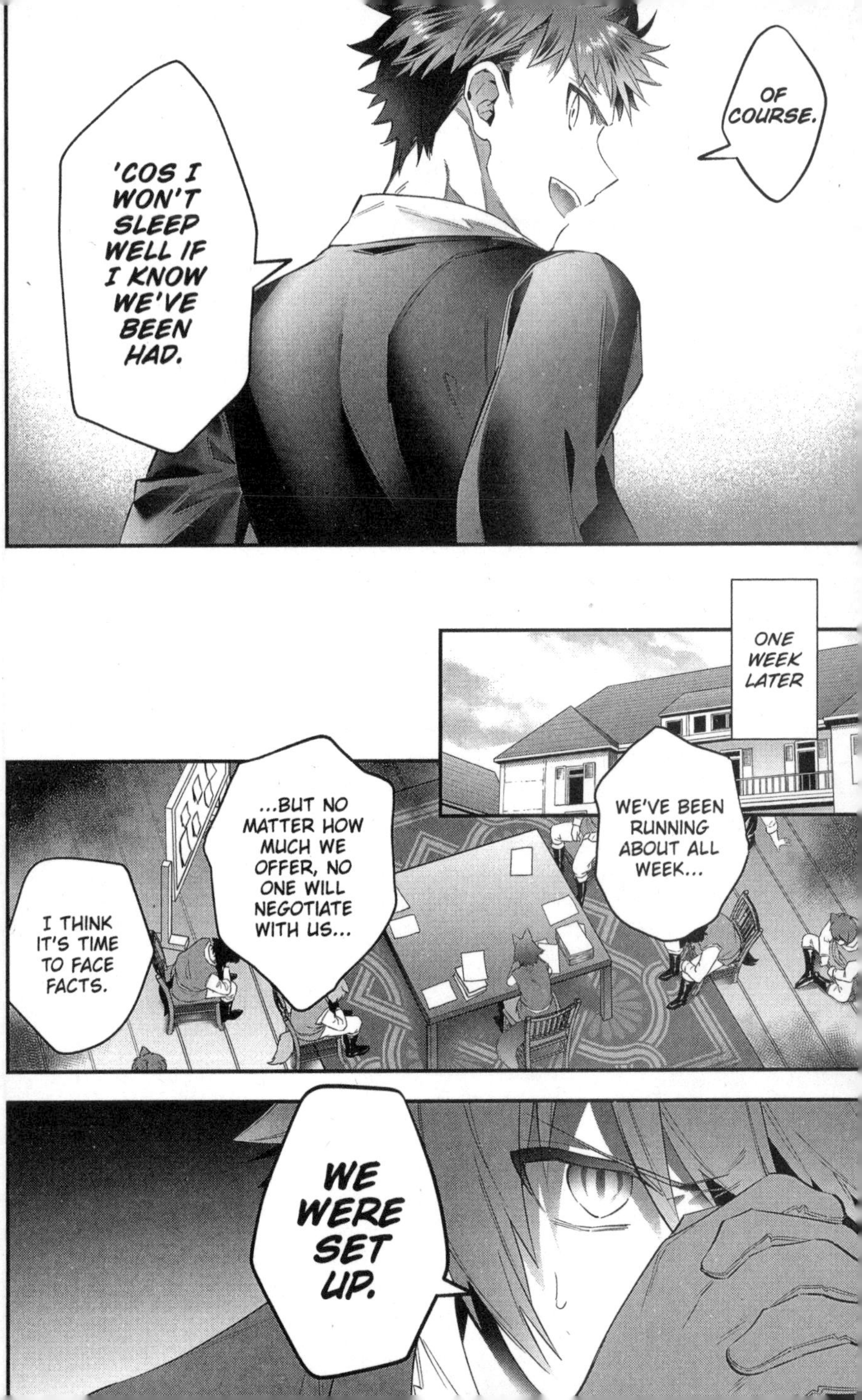
OF COURSE.
'COS I WON'T SLEEP WELL IF I KNOW WE'VE BEEN HAD.
ONE WEEK LATER
WE'VE BEEN RUNNING ABOUT ALL WEEK...
...BUT NO MATTER HOW MUCH WE OFFER, NO ONE WILL NEGOTIATE WITH US...
I THINK IT'S TIME TO FACE FACTS.
WE WERE SET UP.

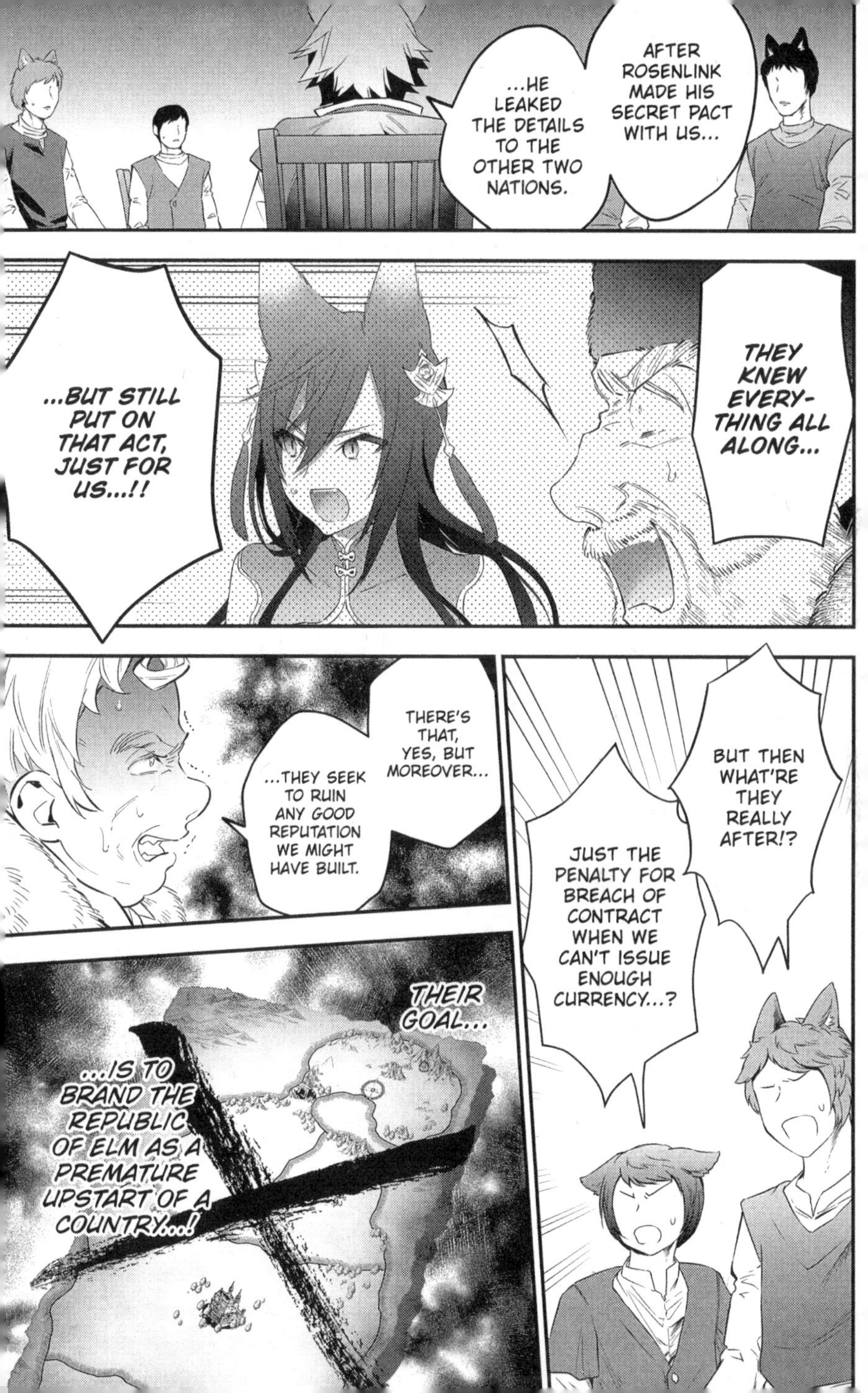
AFTER ROSENLINK MADE HIS SECRET PACT WITH US...
...HE LEAKED THE DETAILS TO THE OTHER TWO NATIONS.
THEY KNEW EVERY-THING ALL ALONG...
...BUT STILL PUT ON THAT ACT, JUST FOR US...!!
BUT THEN WHAT'RE THEY REALLY AFTER!?
JUST THE PENALTY FOR BREACH OF CONTRACT WHEN WE CAN'T ISSUE ENOUGH CURRENCY...?
THERE'S THAT, YES, BUT MOREOVER...
...THEY SEEK TO RUIN ANY GOOD REPUTATION WE MIGHT HAVE BUILT.
THEIR GOAL...
...IS TO BRAND THE REPUBLIC OF ELM AS A PREMATURE UPSTART OF A COUNTRY...!

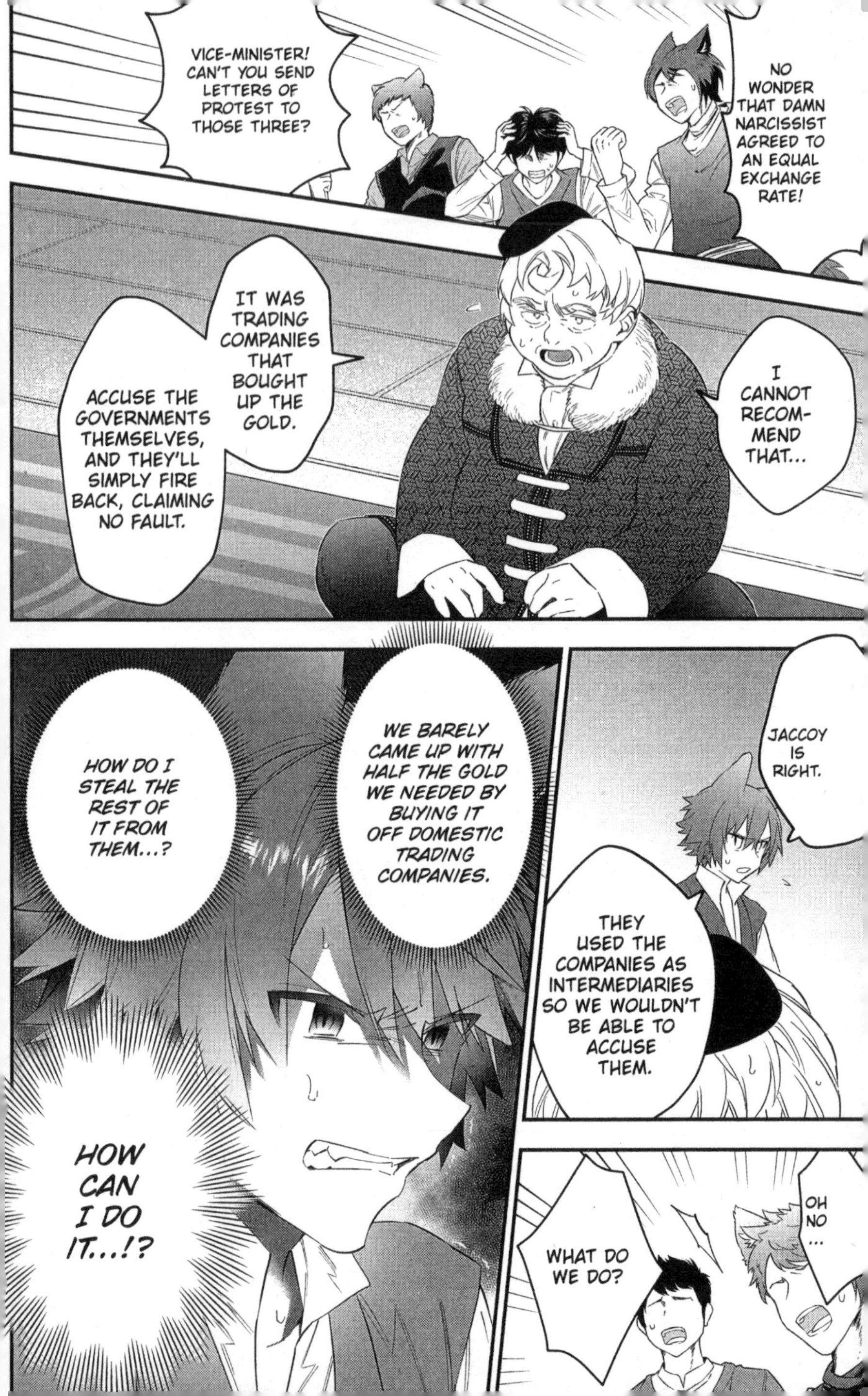
NO WONDER THAT DAMN NARCISSIST AGREED TO AN EQUAL EXCHANGE RATE!
VICE-MINISTER! CAN'T YOU SEND LETTERS OF PROTEST TO THOSE THREE?
I CANNOT RECOMMEND THAT...
IT WAS TRADING COMPANIES THAT BOUGHT UP THE GOLD.
ACCUSE THE GOVERNMENTS THEMSELVES, AND THEY'LL SIMPLY FIRE BACK, CLAIMING NO FAULT.
JACCOY IS RIGHT.
THEY USED THE COMPANIES AS INTERMEDIARIES SO WE WOULDN'T BE ABLE TO ACCUSE THEM.
OH NO ...
WHAT DO WE DO?
WE BARELY CAME UP WITH HALF THE GOLD WE NEEDED BY BUYING IT OFF DOMESTIC TRADING COMPANIES.
HOW DO I STEAL THE REST OF IT FROM THEM...?
HOW CAN I DO IT...!?

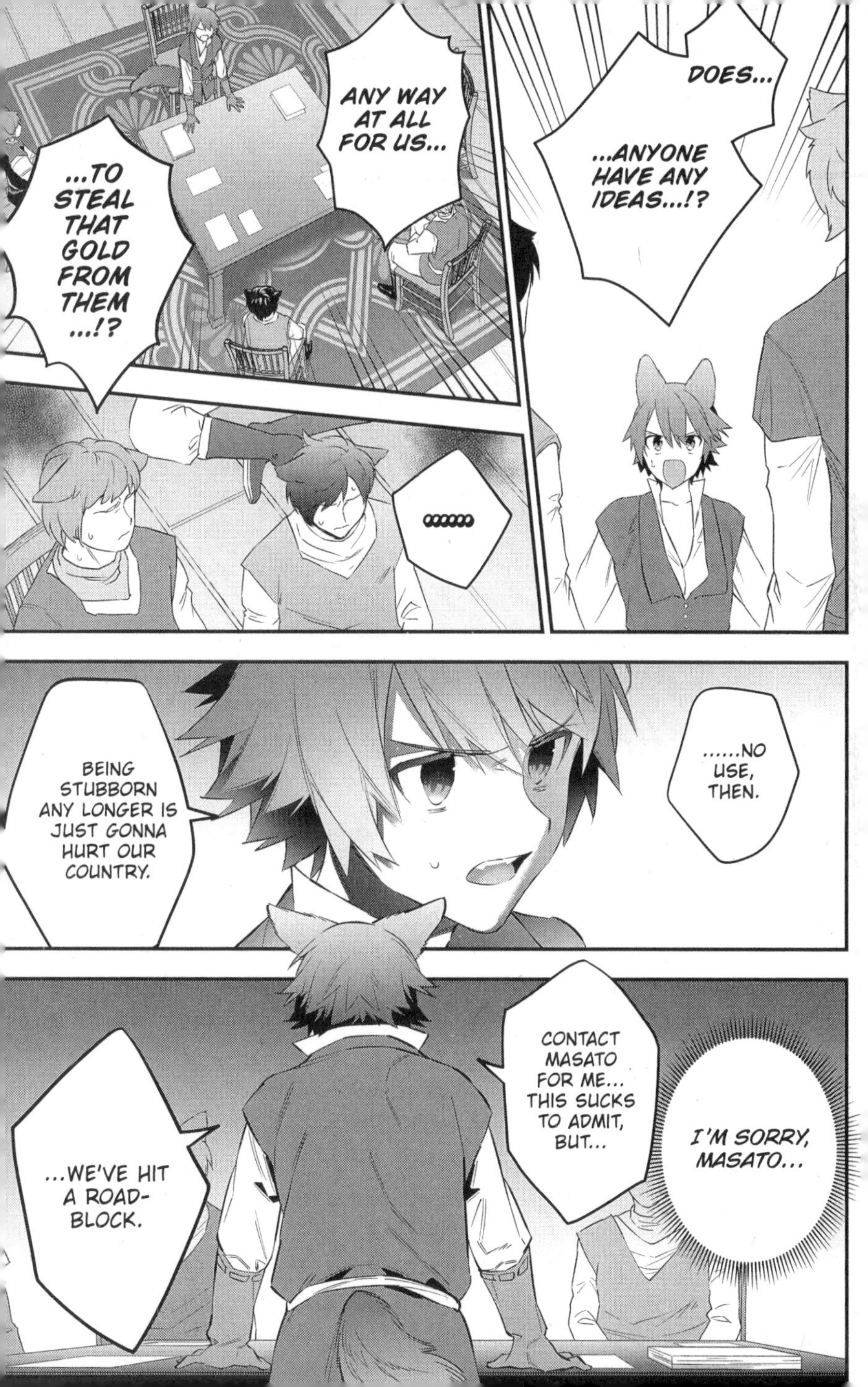
DOES...
...ANYONE HAVE ANY IDEAS...!?
ANY WAY AT ALL FOR US...
...TO STEAL THAT GOLD FROM THEM...!?
......NO USE, THEN.
BEING STUBBORN ANY LONGER IS JUST GONNA HURT OUR COUNTRY.
I'M SORRY, MASATO...
CONTACT MASATO FOR ME... THIS SUCKS TO ADMIT, BUT...
...WE'VE HIT A ROAD-BLOCK.

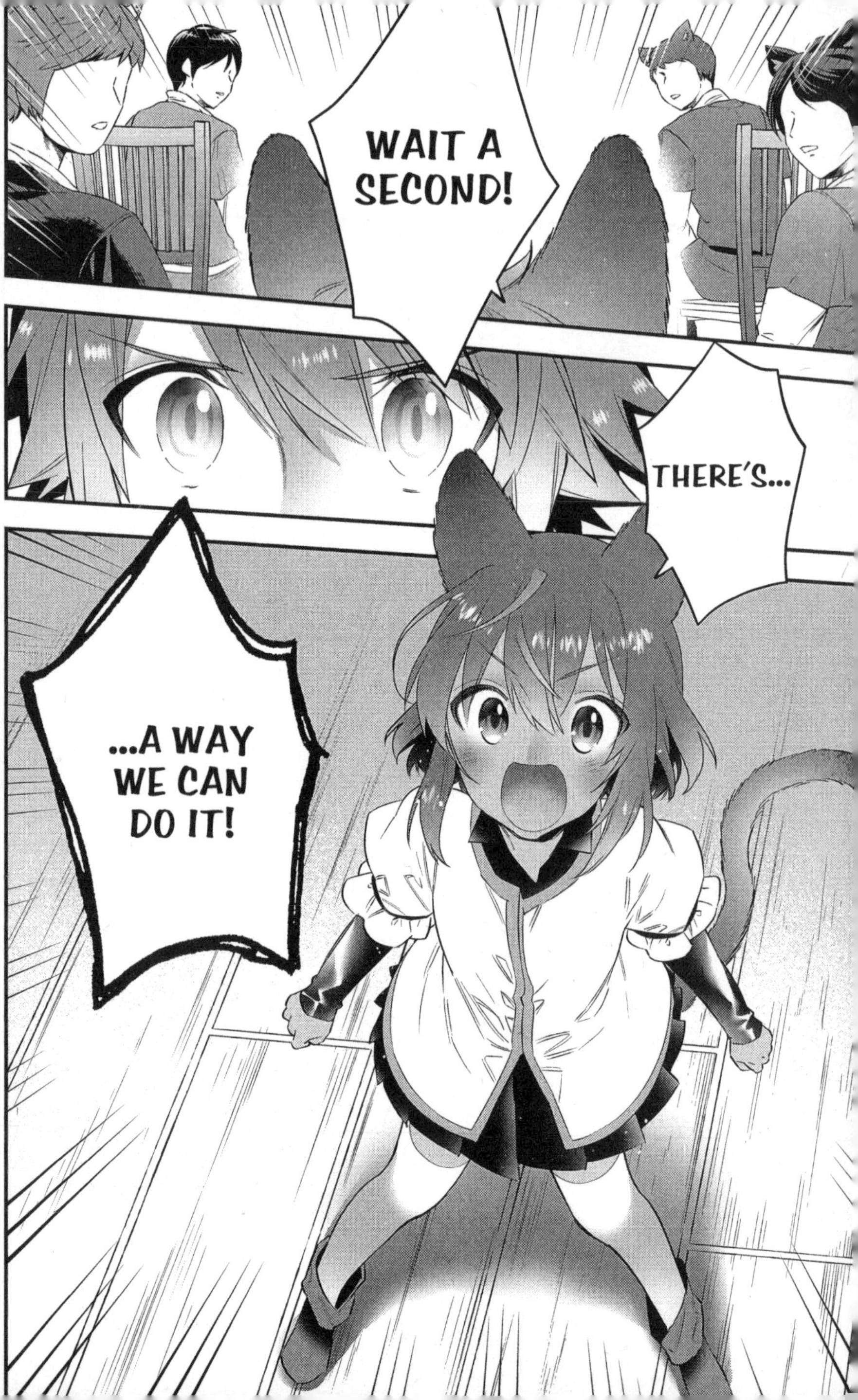
WAIT A SECOND!
THERE'S...
...A WAY WE CAN DO IT!

HIGH SCHOOL
PRODIGIES HAVE
IT EASY EVEN IN
ANOTHER
WORLD!

CHARACTER FILE 28

Sergei Pavlovich

Foreign affairs minister of the
Azure Kingdom, a frigid land
perpetually covered in snow.

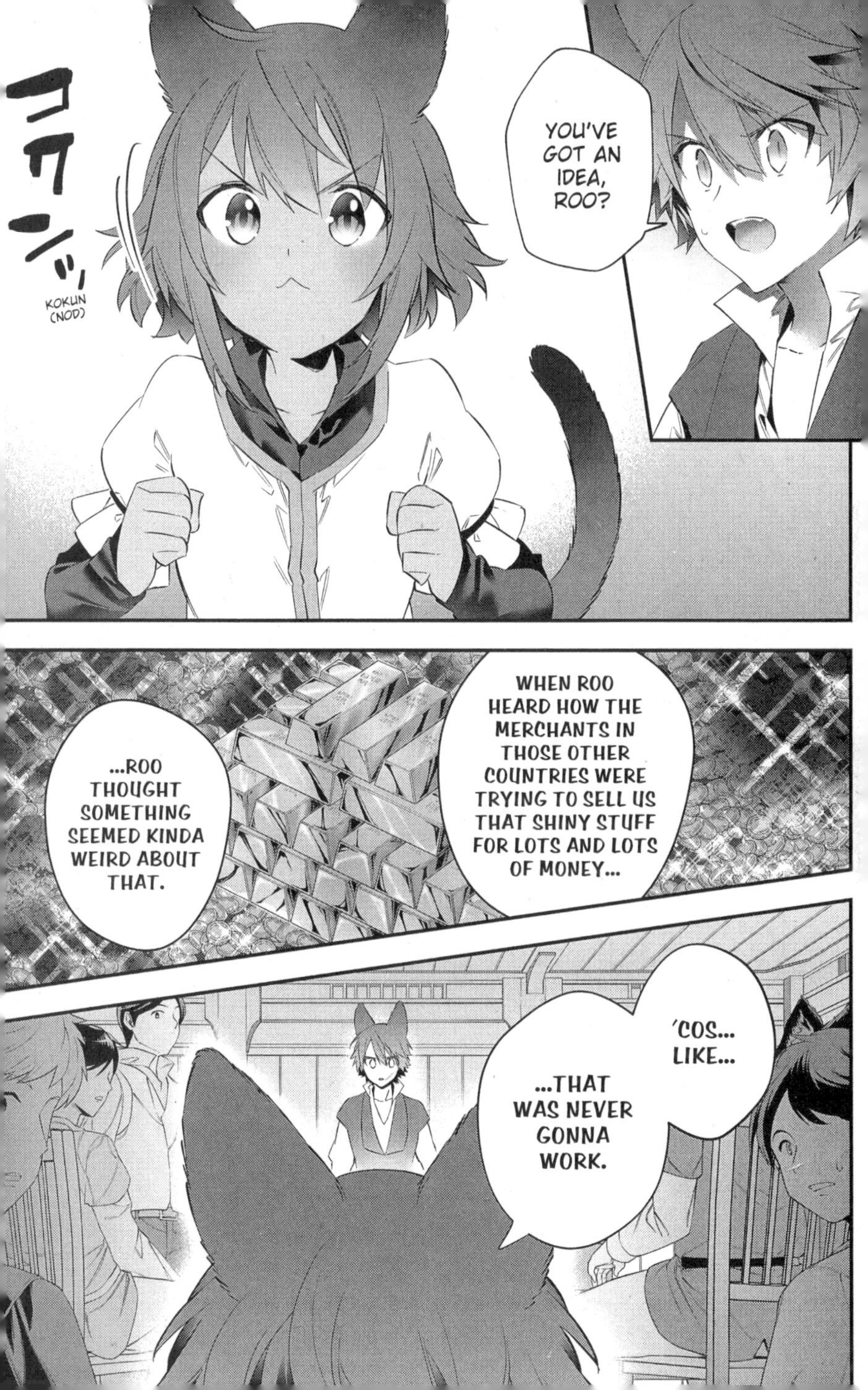
YOU'VE GOT AN IDEA, ROO?
コクンッ
KOKUN (NOD)
WHEN ROO HEARD HOW THE MERCHANTS IN THOSE OTHER COUNTRIES WERE TRYING TO SELL US THAT SHINY STUFF FOR LOTS AND LOTS OF MONEY...
...ROO THOUGHT SOMETHING SEEMED KINDA WEIRD ABOUT THAT.
'COS... LIKE...
...THAT WAS NEVER GONNA WORK.

CHAPTER 56: **CAUSE FOR UNEASE**

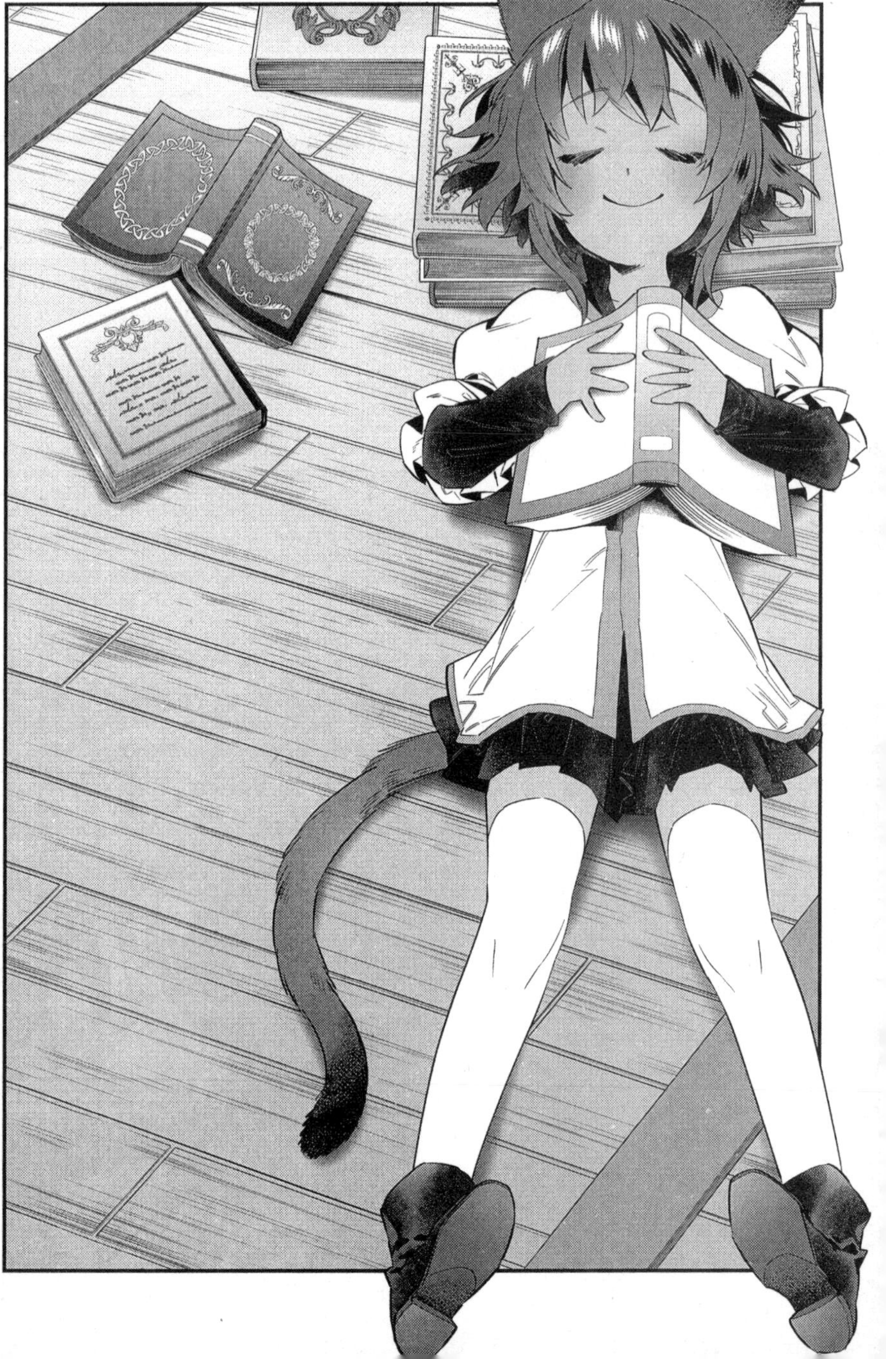

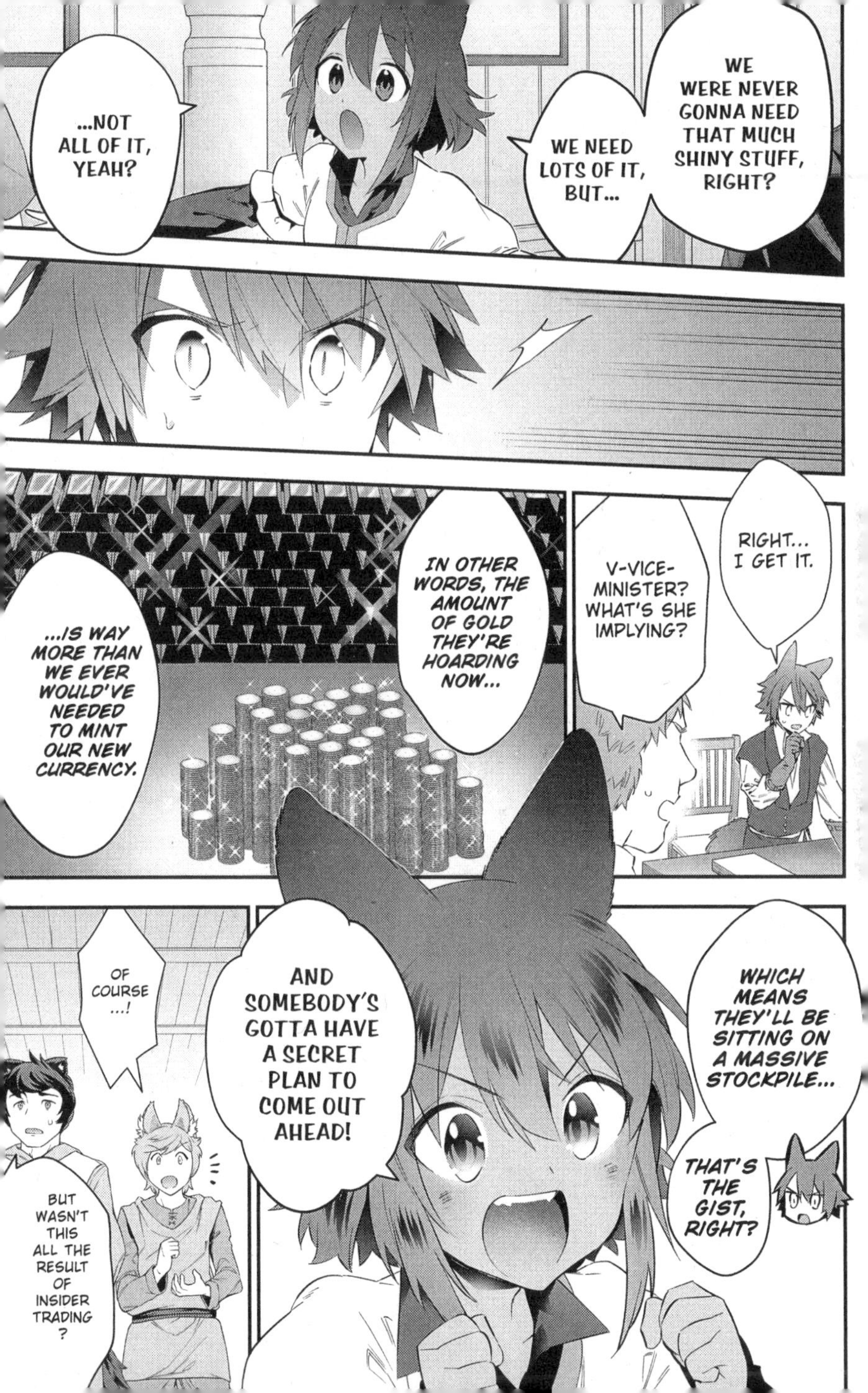
WE WERE NEVER GONNA NEED THAT MUCH SHINY STUFF, RIGHT?
WE NEED LOTS OF IT, BUT...
...NOT ALL OF IT, YEAH?
RIGHT... I GET IT.
V-VICE-MINISTER? WHAT'S SHE IMPLYING?
IN OTHER WORDS, THE AMOUNT OF GOLD THEY'RE HOARDING NOW...
...IS WAY MORE THAN WE EVER WOULD'VE NEEDED TO MINT OUR NEW CURRENCY.
WHICH MEANS THEY'LL BE SITTING ON A MASSIVE STOCKPILE...
THAT'S THE GIST, RIGHT?
AND SOMEBODY'S GOTTA HAVE A SECRET PLAN TO COME OUT AHEAD!
OF COURSE...!
BUT WASN'T THIS ALL THE RESULT OF INSIDER TRADING?

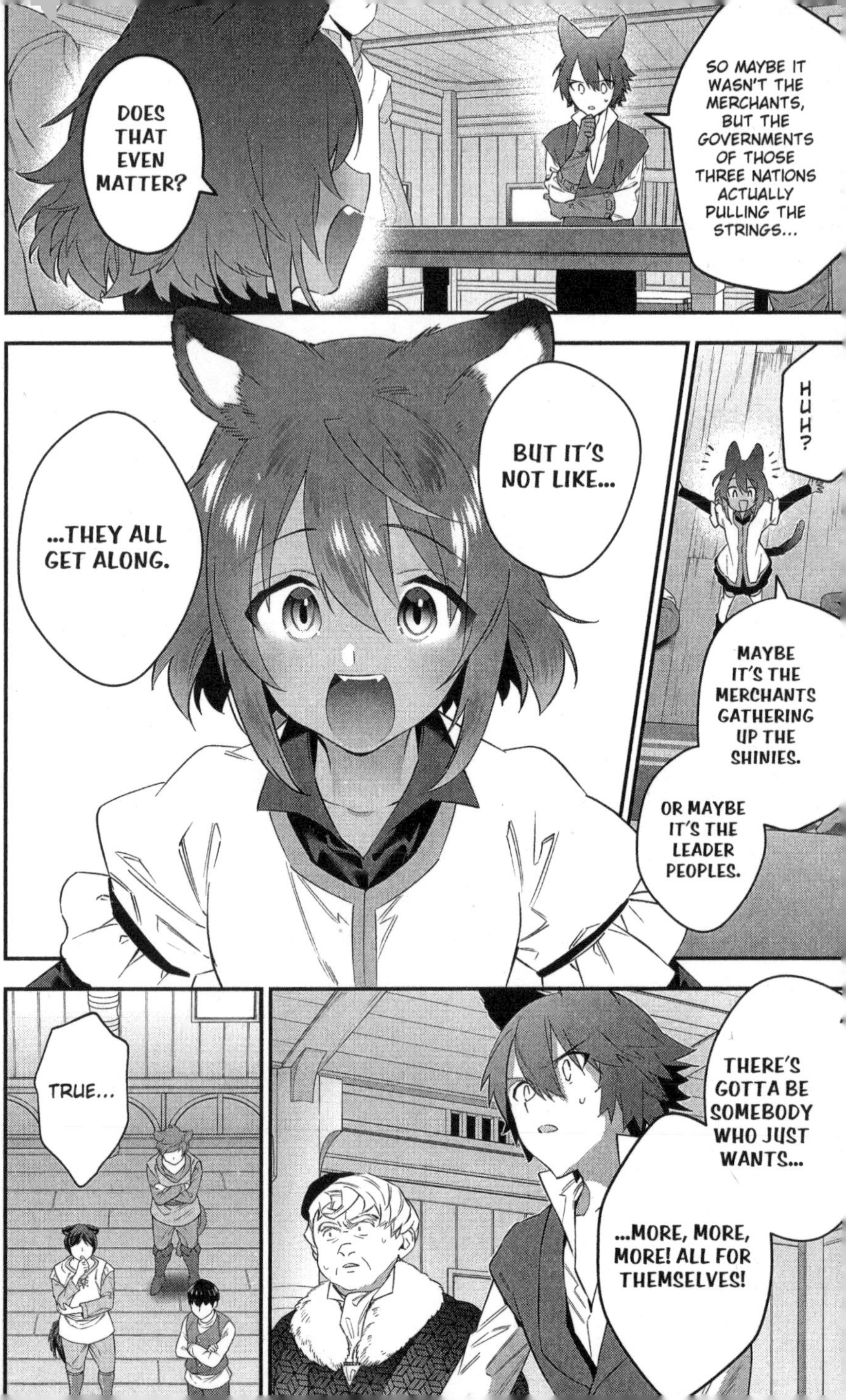
SO MAYBE IT WASN'T THE MERCHANTS, BUT THE GOVERNMENTS OF THOSE THREE NATIONS ACTUALLY PULLING THE STRINGS...
DOES THAT EVEN MATTER?
HUH?
MAYBE IT'S THE MERCHANTS GATHERING UP THE SHINIES.
OR MAYBE IT'S THE LEADER PEOPLES.
BUT IT'S NOT LIKE...
...THEY ALL GET ALONG.
THERE'S GOTTA BE SOMEBODY WHO JUST WANTS...
...MORE, MORE, MORE! ALL FOR THEMSELVES!
TRUE...

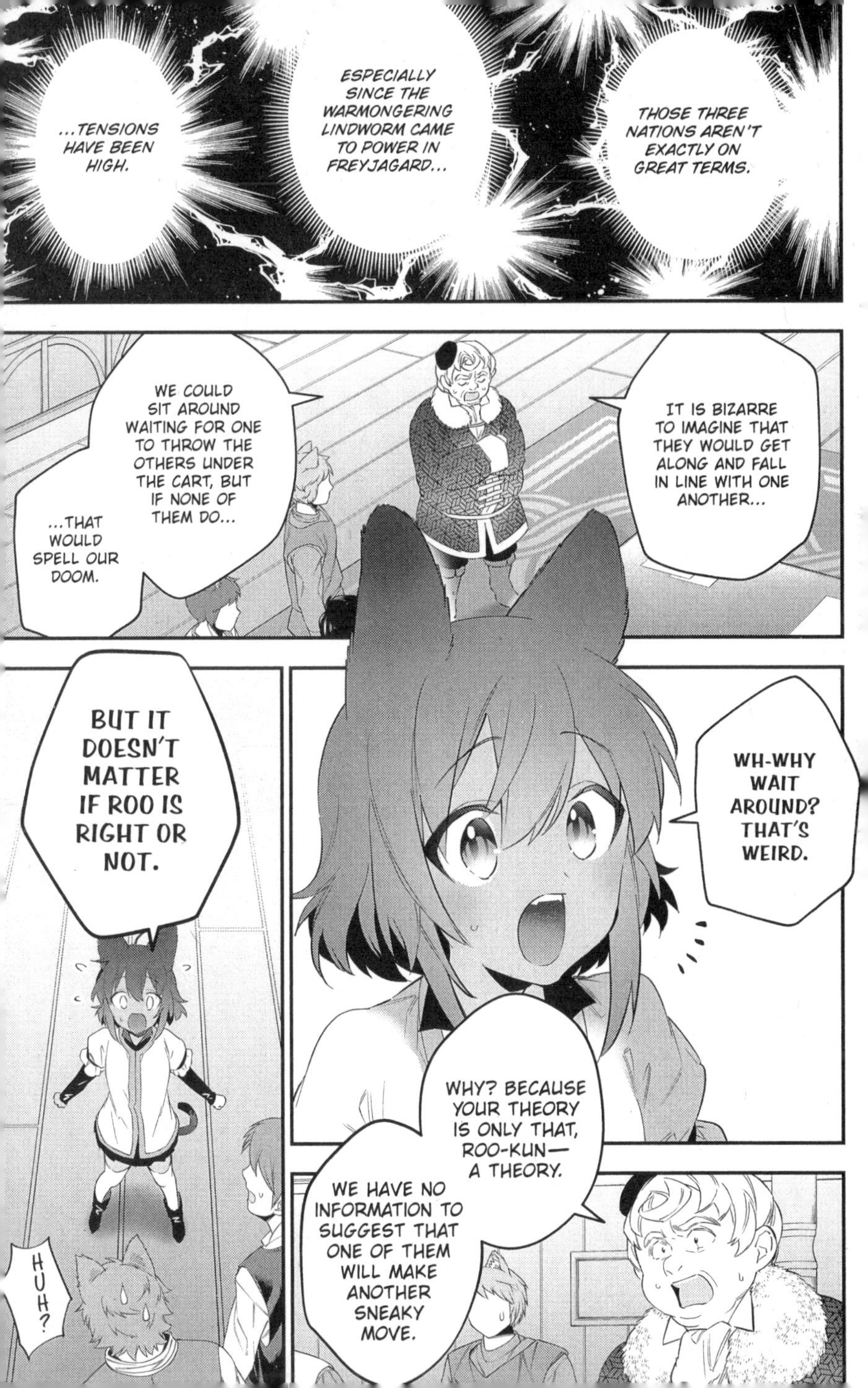
THOSE THREE NATIONS AREN'T EXACTLY ON GREAT TERMS.
ESPECIALLY SINCE THE WARMONGERING LINDWORM CAME TO POWER IN FREYJAGARD...
...TENSIONS HAVE BEEN HIGH.
IT IS BIZARRE TO IMAGINE THAT THEY WOULD GET ALONG AND FALL IN LINE WITH ONE ANOTHER...
WE COULD SIT AROUND WAITING FOR ONE TO THROW THE OTHERS UNDER THE CART, BUT IF NONE OF THEM DO...
...THAT WOULD SPELL OUR DOOM.
WH-WHY WAIT AROUND? THAT'S WEIRD.
WHY? BECAUSE YOUR THEORY IS ONLY THAT, ROO-KUN—A THEORY.
WE HAVE NO INFORMATION TO SUGGEST THAT ONE OF THEM WILL MAKE ANOTHER SNEAKY MOVE.
BUT IT DOESN'T MATTER IF ROO IS RIGHT OR NOT.
HUH?

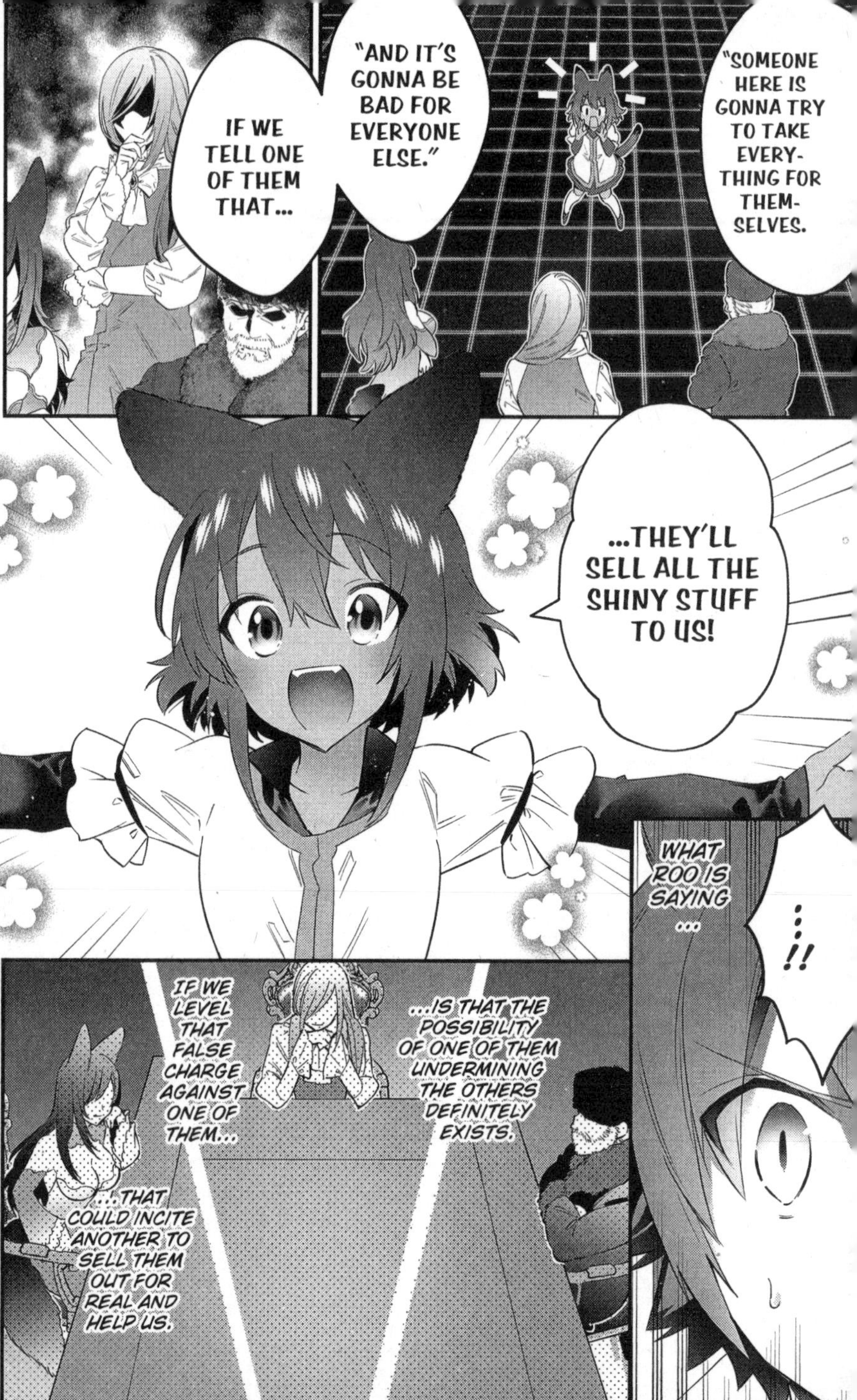
"SOMEONE HERE IS GONNA TRY TO TAKE EVERY-THING FOR THEM-SELVES.
"AND IT'S GONNA BE BAD FOR EVERYONE ELSE."
IF WE TELL ONE OF THEM THAT...
...THEY'LL SELL ALL THE SHINY STUFF TO US!
...!!
WHAT ROO IS SAYING...
...IS THAT THE POSSIBILITY OF ONE OF THEM UNDERMINING THE OTHERS DEFINITELY EXISTS.
IF WE LEVEL THAT FALSE CHARGE AGAINST ONE OF THEM...
...THAT COULD INCITE ANOTHER TO SELL THEM OUT FOR REAL AND HELP US.

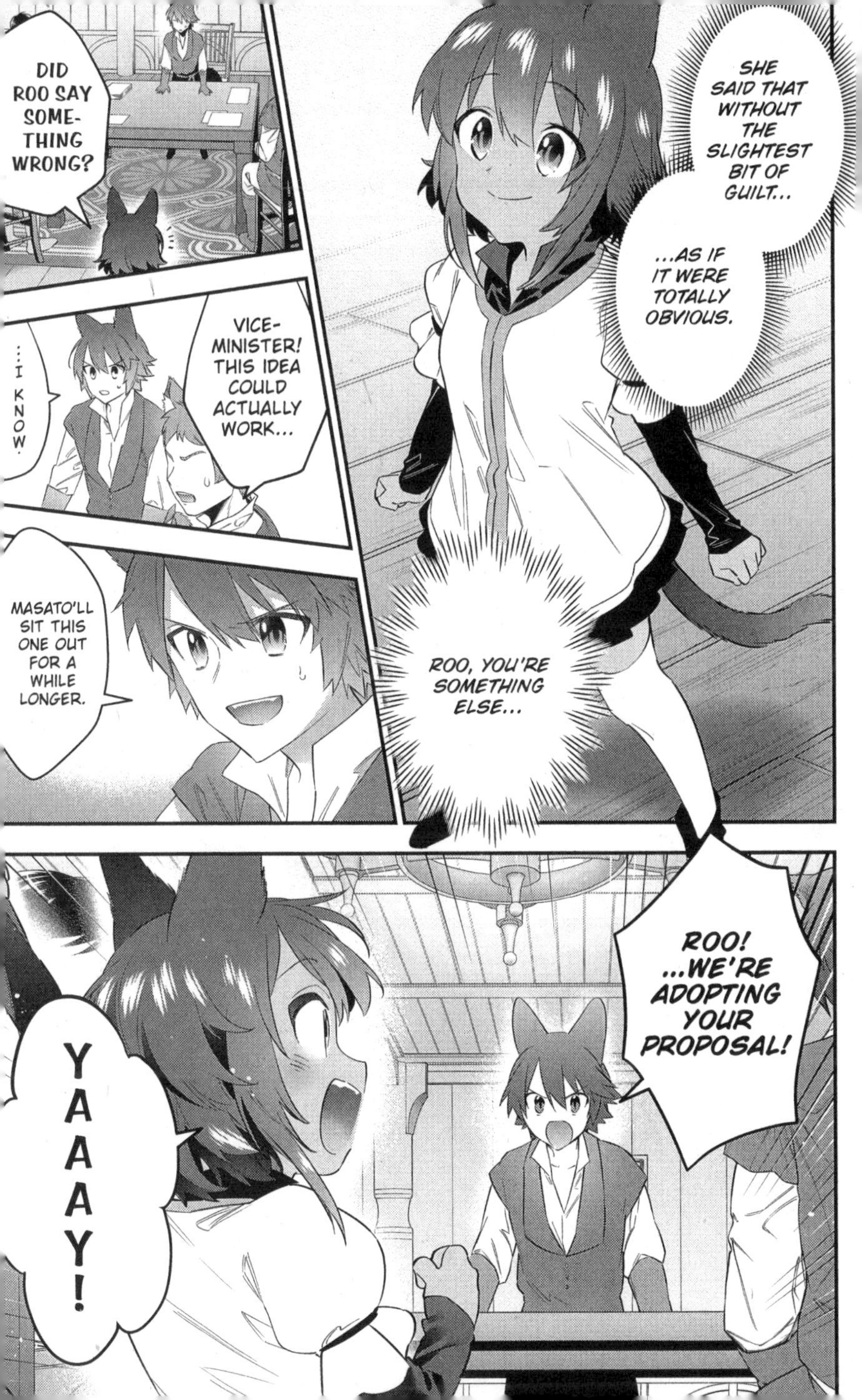
SHE SAID THAT WITHOUT THE SLIGHTEST BIT OF GUILT...
...AS IF IT WERE TOTALLY OBVIOUS.
ROO, YOU'RE SOMETHING ELSE...
DID ROO SAY SOME-THING WRONG?
VICE-MINISTER! THIS IDEA COULD ACTUALLY WORK...
...I KNOW.
MASATO'LL SIT THIS ONE OUT FOR A WHILE LONGER.
ROO! ...WE'RE ADOPTING YOUR PROPOSAL!
YAAAAY!

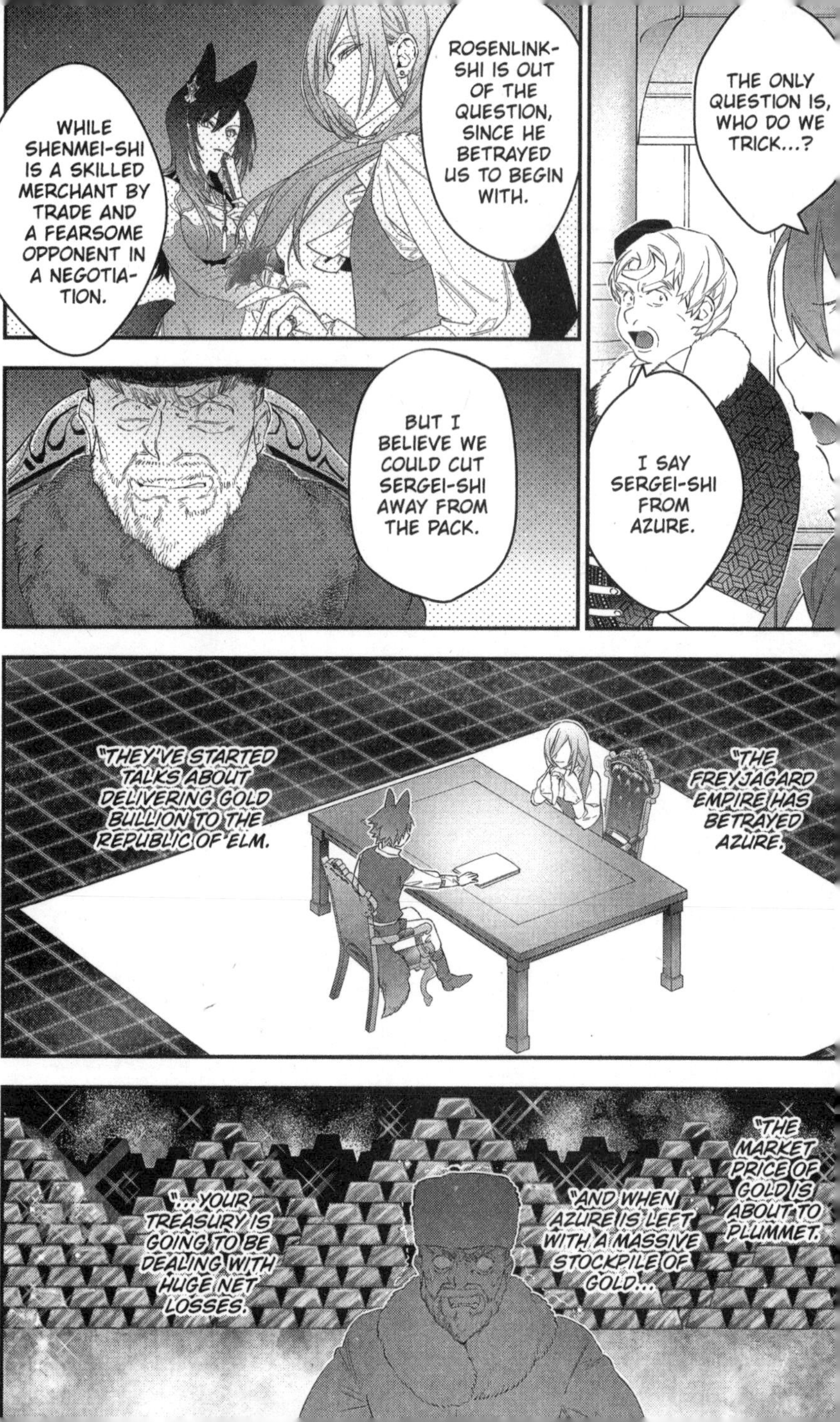
THE ONLY QUESTION IS, WHO DO WE TRICK...?
I SAY SERGEI-SHI FROM AZURE.
ROSENLINK-SHI IS OUT OF THE QUESTION, SINCE HE BETRAYED US TO BEGIN WITH.
WHILE SHENMEI-SHI IS A SKILLED MERCHANT BY TRADE AND A FEARSOME OPPONENT IN A NEGOTIATION.
BUT I BELIEVE WE COULD CUT SERGEI-SHI AWAY FROM THE PACK.
"THE FREYJAGARD EMPIRE HAS BETRAYED AZURE.
"THEY'VE STARTED TALKS ABOUT DELIVERING GOLD BULLION TO THE REPUBLIC OF ELM.
"THE MARKET PRICE OF GOLD IS ABOUT TO PLUMMET.
"AND WHEN AZURE IS LEFT WITH A MASSIVE STOCKPILE OF GOLD...
"...YOUR TREASURY IS GOING TO BE DEALING WITH HUGE NET LOSSES.

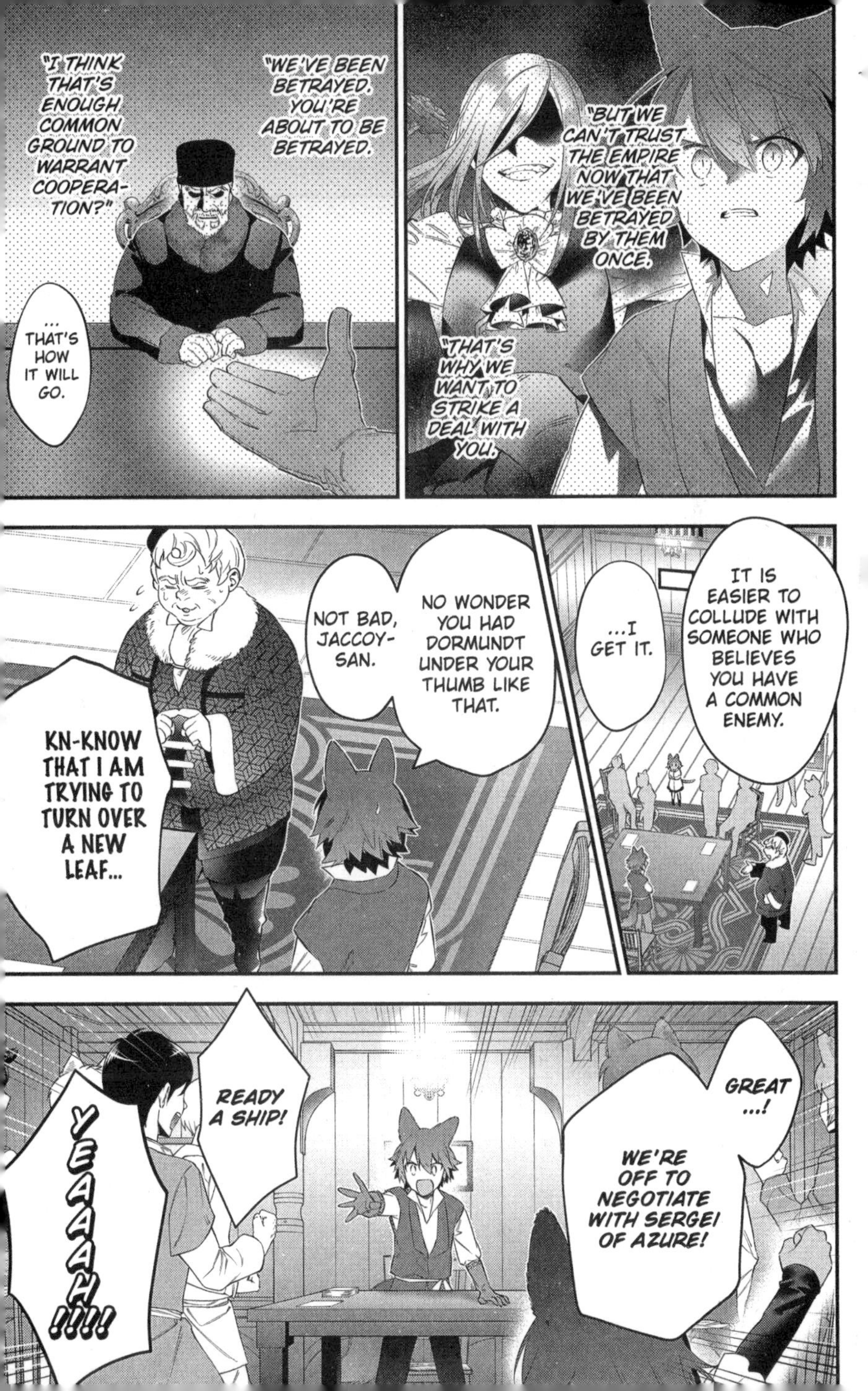
"BUT WE CAN'T TRUST THE EMPIRE NOW THAT WE'VE BEEN BETRAYED BY THEM ONCE.
"THAT'S WHY WE WANT TO STRIKE A DEAL WITH YOU.
"WE'VE BEEN BETRAYED. YOU'RE ABOUT TO BE BETRAYED.
"I THINK THAT'S ENOUGH COMMON GROUND TO WARRANT COOPERA-TION?"
...THAT'S HOW IT WILL GO.
IT IS EASIER TO COLLUDE WITH SOMEONE WHO BELIEVES YOU HAVE A COMMON ENEMY.
...I GET IT.
NO WONDER YOU HAD DORMUNDT UNDER YOUR THUMB LIKE THAT.
NOT BAD, JACCOY-SAN.
KN-KNOW THAT I AM TRYING TO TURN OVER A NEW LEAF...
GREAT ...!
WE'RE OFF TO NEGOTIATE WITH SERGEI OF AZURE!
READY A SHIP!
YEAAAAH!!!!

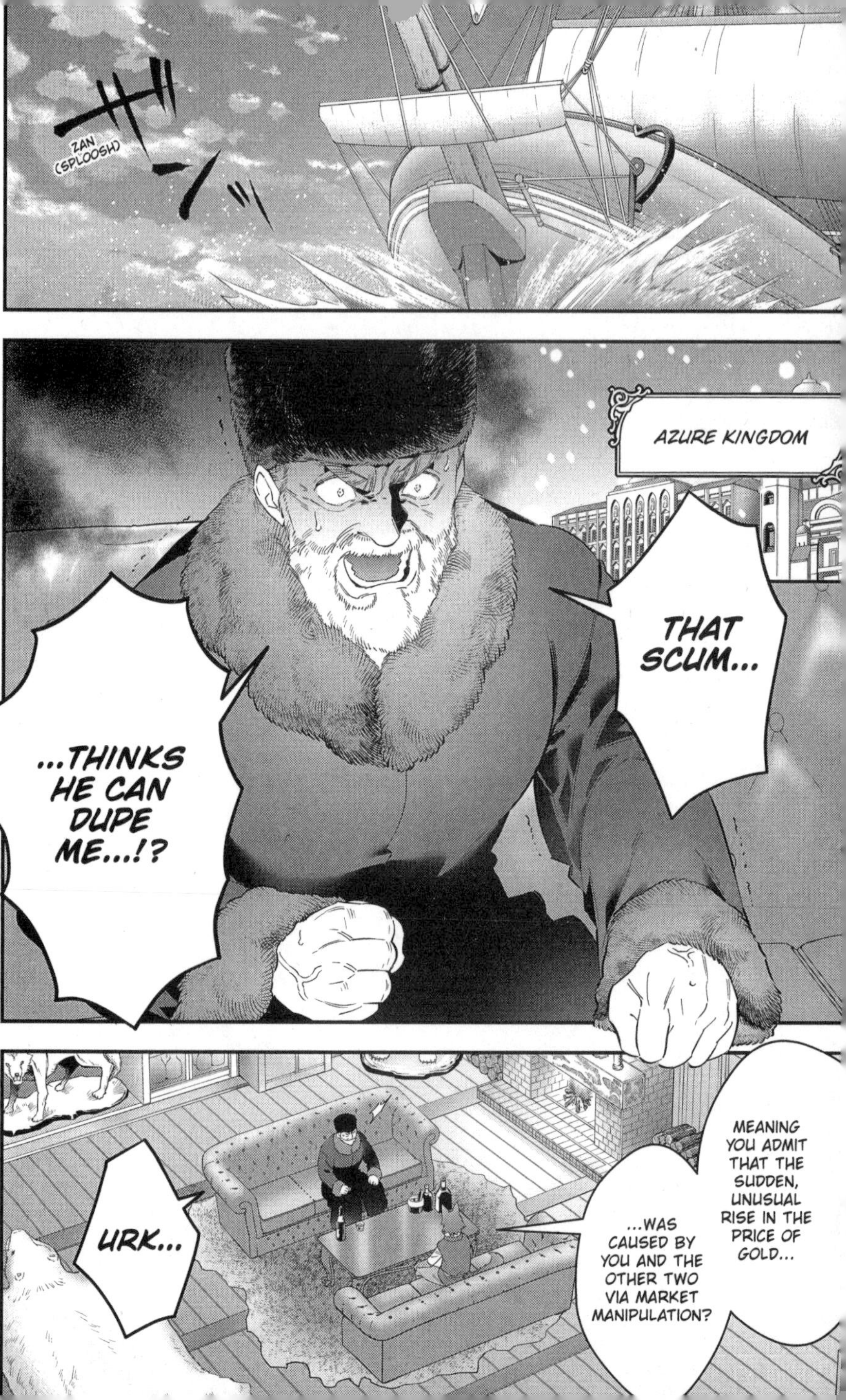
ZAN
(SPLOOSH)
AZURE KINGDOM
THAT SCUM...
...THINKS HE CAN DUPE ME...!?
MEANING YOU ADMIT THAT THE SUDDEN, UNUSUAL RISE IN THE PRICE OF GOLD...
...WAS CAUSED BY YOU AND THE OTHER TWO VIA MARKET MANIPULATION?
URK...

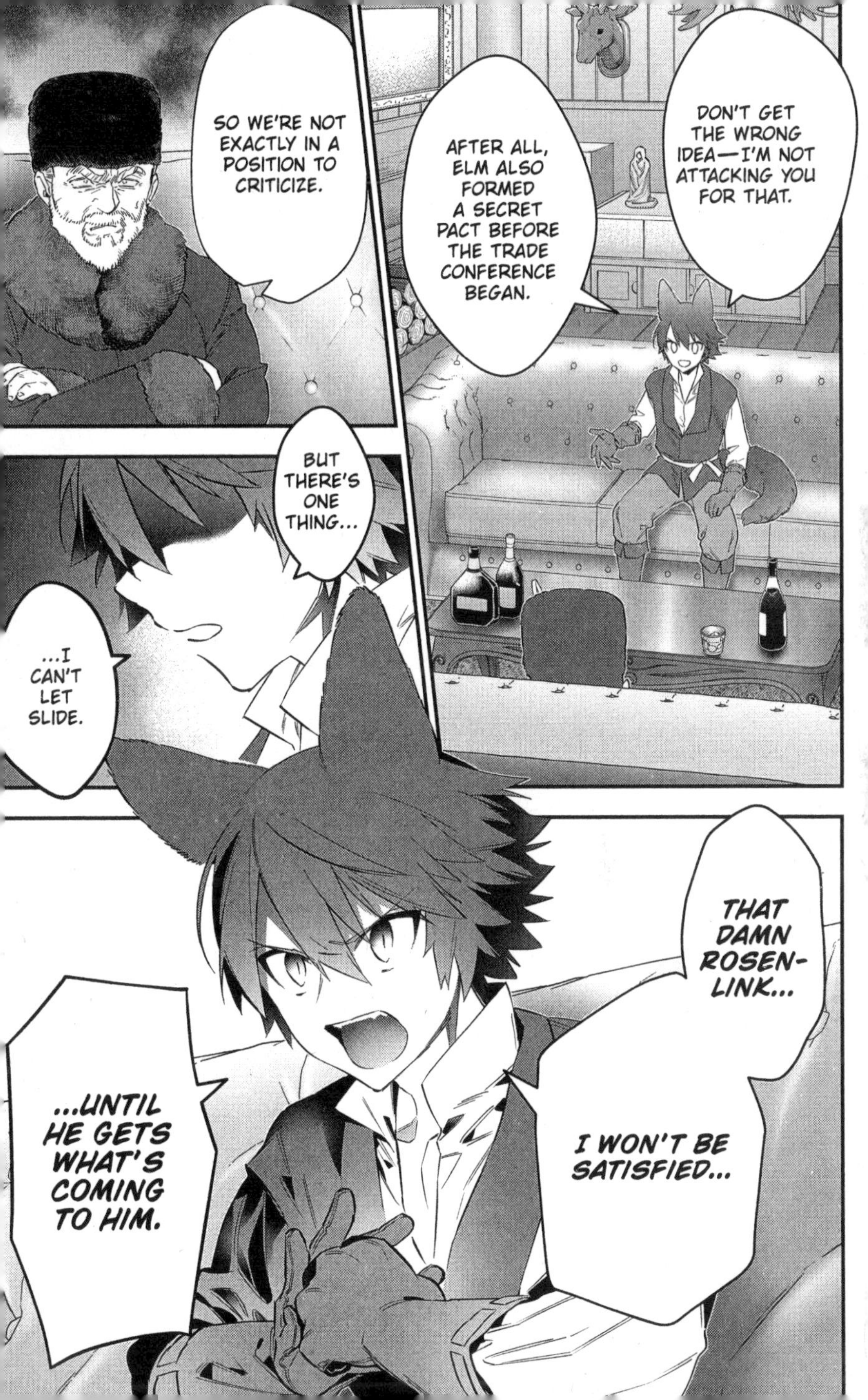
DON'T GET THE WRONG IDEA—I'M NOT ATTACKING YOU FOR THAT.
AFTER ALL, ELM ALSO FORMED A SECRET PACT BEFORE THE TRADE CONFERENCE BEGAN.
SO WE'RE NOT EXACTLY IN A POSITION TO CRITICIZE.
BUT THERE'S ONE THING...
...I CAN'T LET SLIDE.
THAT DAMN ROSEN-LINK...
I WON'T BE SATISFIED...
...UNTIL HE GETS WHAT'S COMING TO HIM.

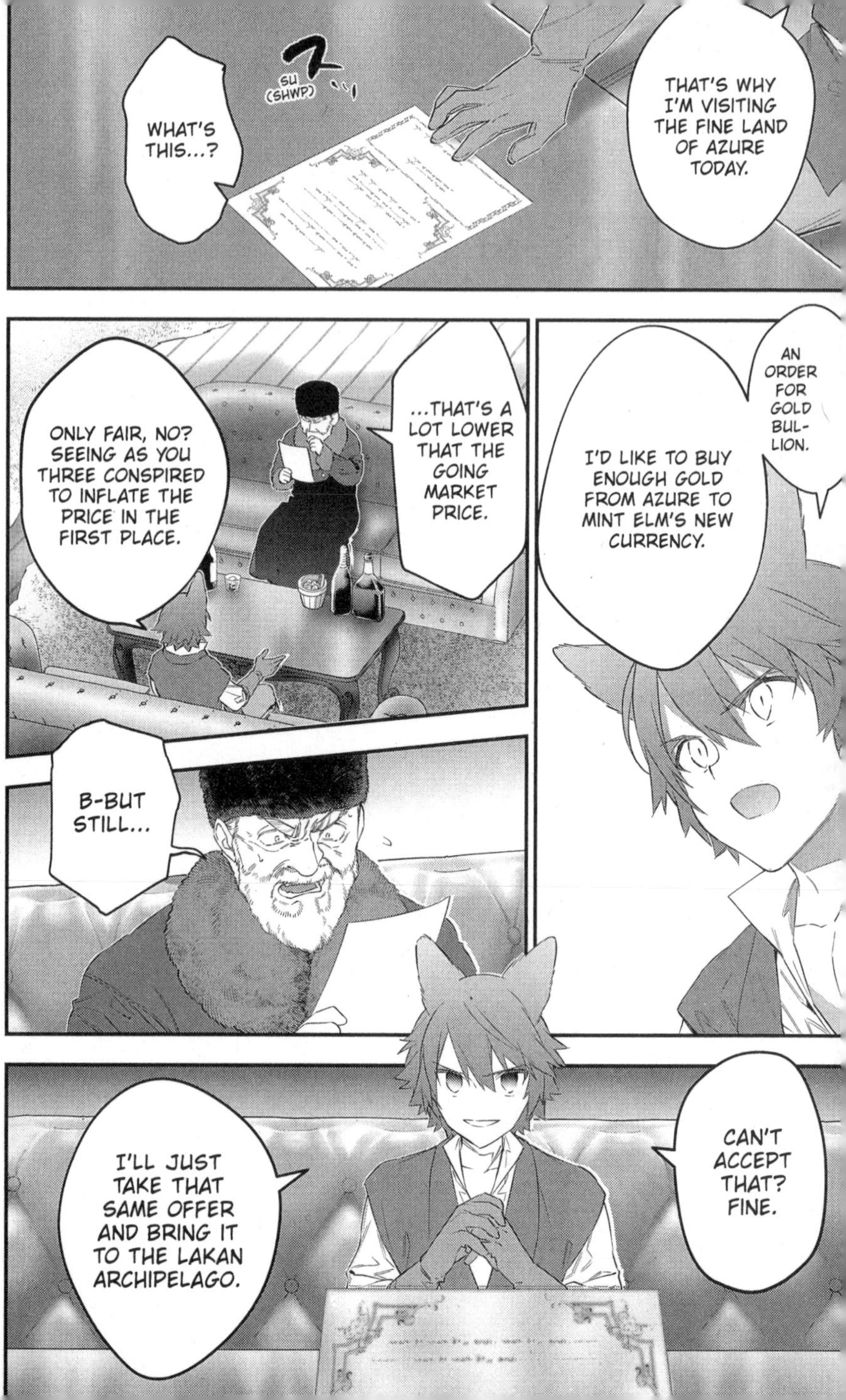
THAT'S WHY I'M VISITING THE FINE LAND OF AZURE TODAY.
SU (SHWP)
WHAT'S THIS...?
AN ORDER FOR GOLD BUL-LION.
I'D LIKE TO BUY ENOUGH GOLD FROM AZURE TO MINT ELM'S NEW CURRENCY.
...THAT'S A LOT LOWER THAT THE GOING MARKET PRICE.
ONLY FAIR, NO? SEEING AS YOU THREE CONSPIRED TO INFLATE THE PRICE IN THE FIRST PLACE.
B-BUT STILL...
CAN'T ACCEPT THAT? FINE.
I'LL JUST TAKE THAT SAME OFFER AND BRING IT TO THE LAKAN ARCHIPELAGO.

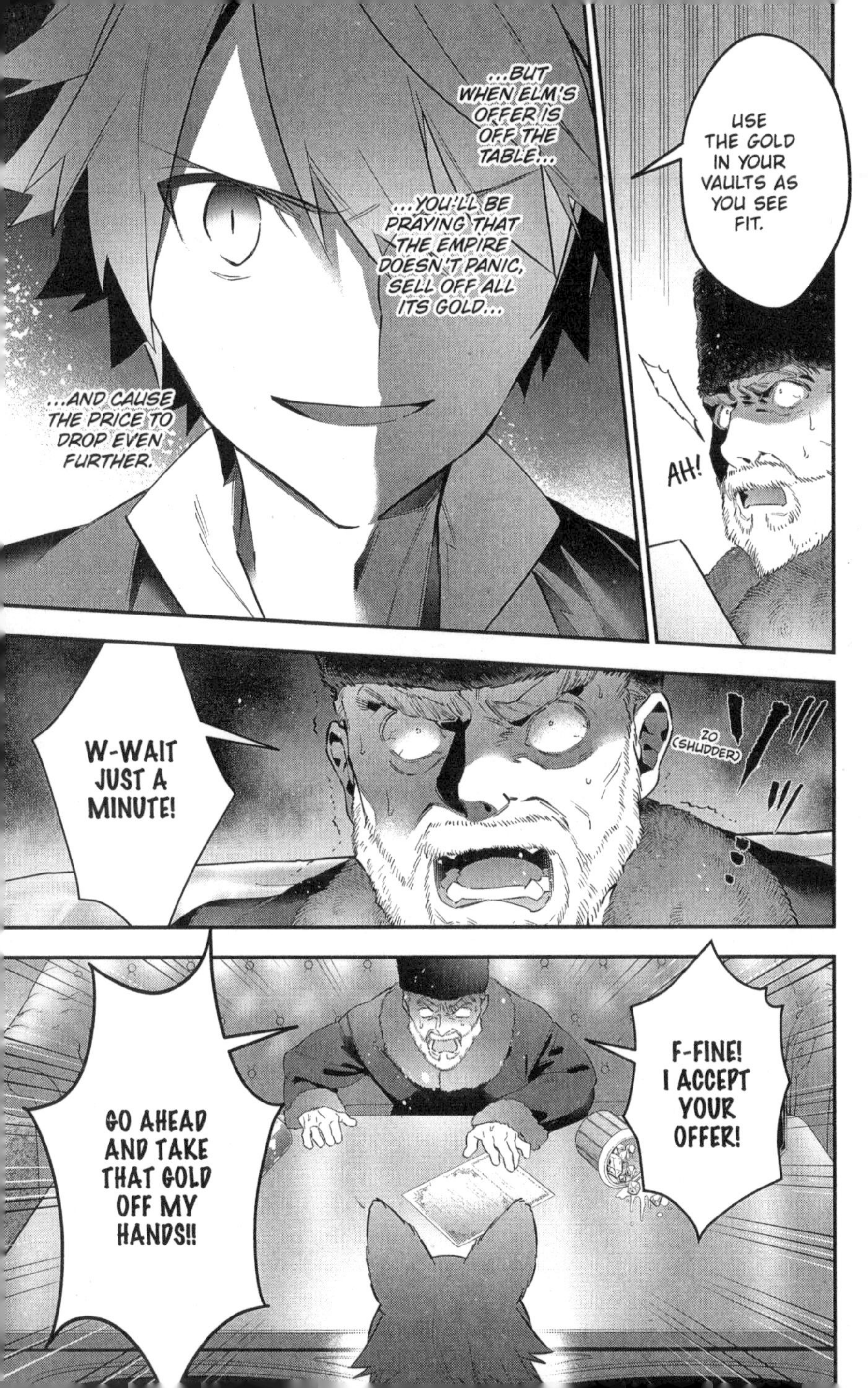
USE THE GOLD IN YOUR VAULTS AS YOU SEE FIT.
AH!
...BUT WHEN ELM'S OFFER IS OFF THE TABLE...
...YOU'LL BE PRAYING THAT THE EMPIRE DOESN'T PANIC, SELL OFF ALL ITS GOLD...
...AND CAUSE THE PRICE TO DROP EVEN FURTHER.
ZO (SHUDDER)
W-WAIT JUST A MINUTE!
F-FINE! I ACCEPT YOUR OFFER!
GO AHEAD AND TAKE THAT GOLD OFF MY HANDS!!

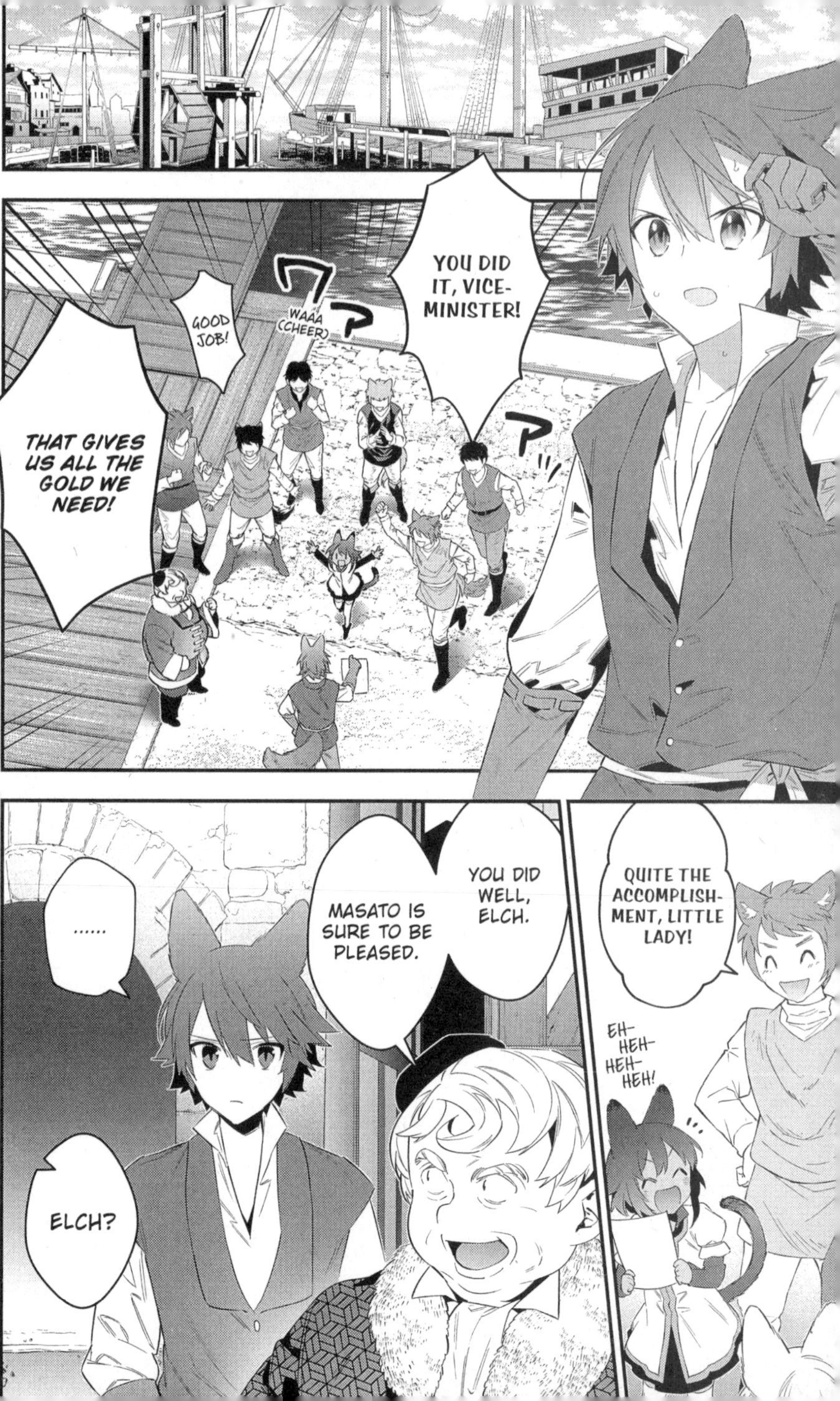
YOU DID IT, VICE-MINISTER!
WAAA (CHEER)
GOOD JOB!
THAT GIVES US ALL THE GOLD WE NEED!
QUITE THE ACCOMPLISHMENT, LITTLE LADY!
EH-HEH-HEH-HEH!
YOU DID WELL, ELCH.
MASATO IS SURE TO BE PLEASED.
......
ELCH?

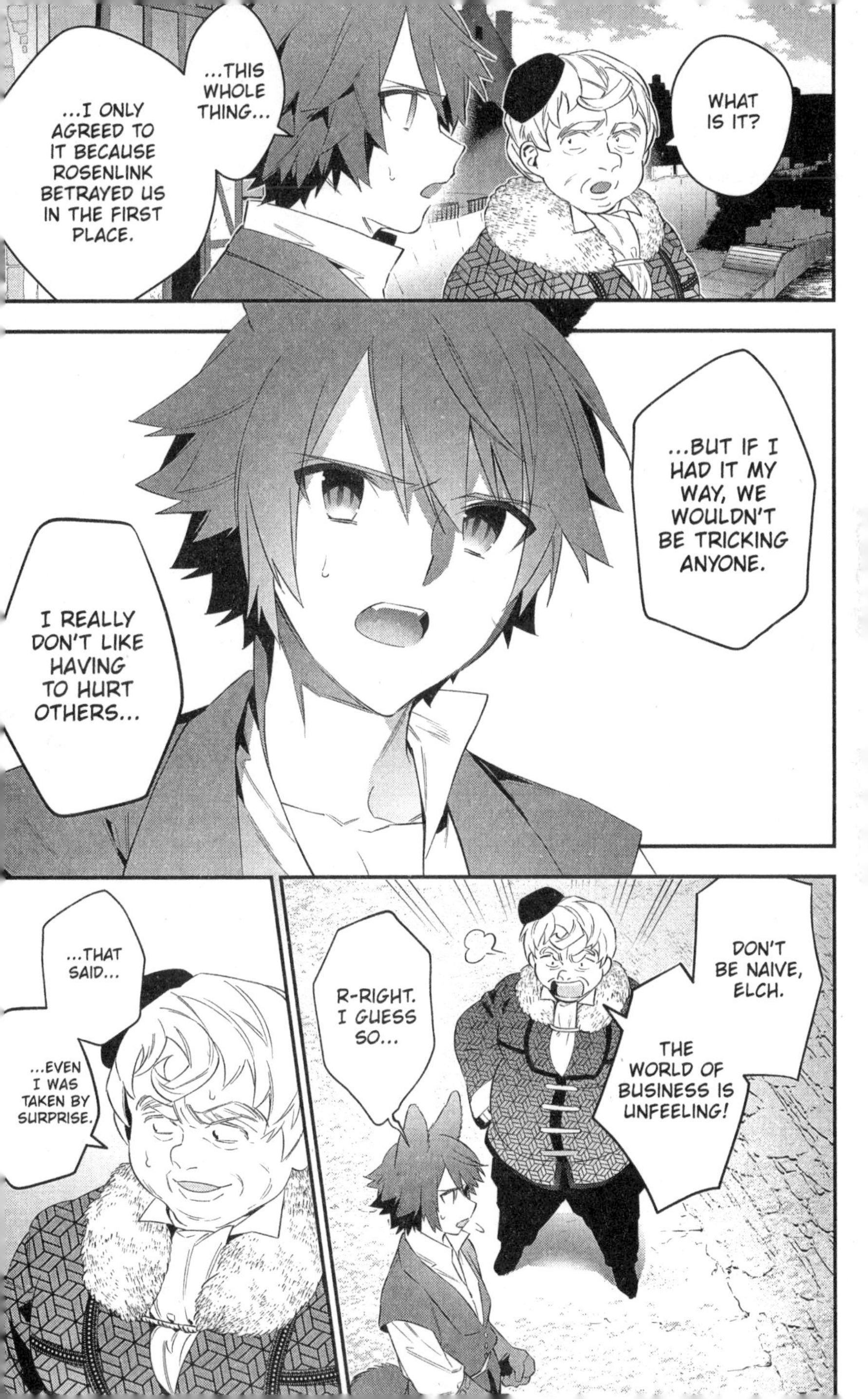
WHAT IS IT?
...THIS WHOLE THING...
...I ONLY AGREED TO IT BECAUSE ROSENLINK BETRAYED US IN THE FIRST PLACE.
...BUT IF I HAD IT MY WAY, WE WOULDN'T BE TRICKING ANYONE.
I REALLY DON'T LIKE HAVING TO HURT OTHERS...
DON'T BE NAIVE, ELCH.
THE WORLD OF BUSINESS IS UNFEELING!
R-RIGHT. I GUESS SO...
...THAT SAID...
...EVEN I WAS TAKEN BY SURPRISE.

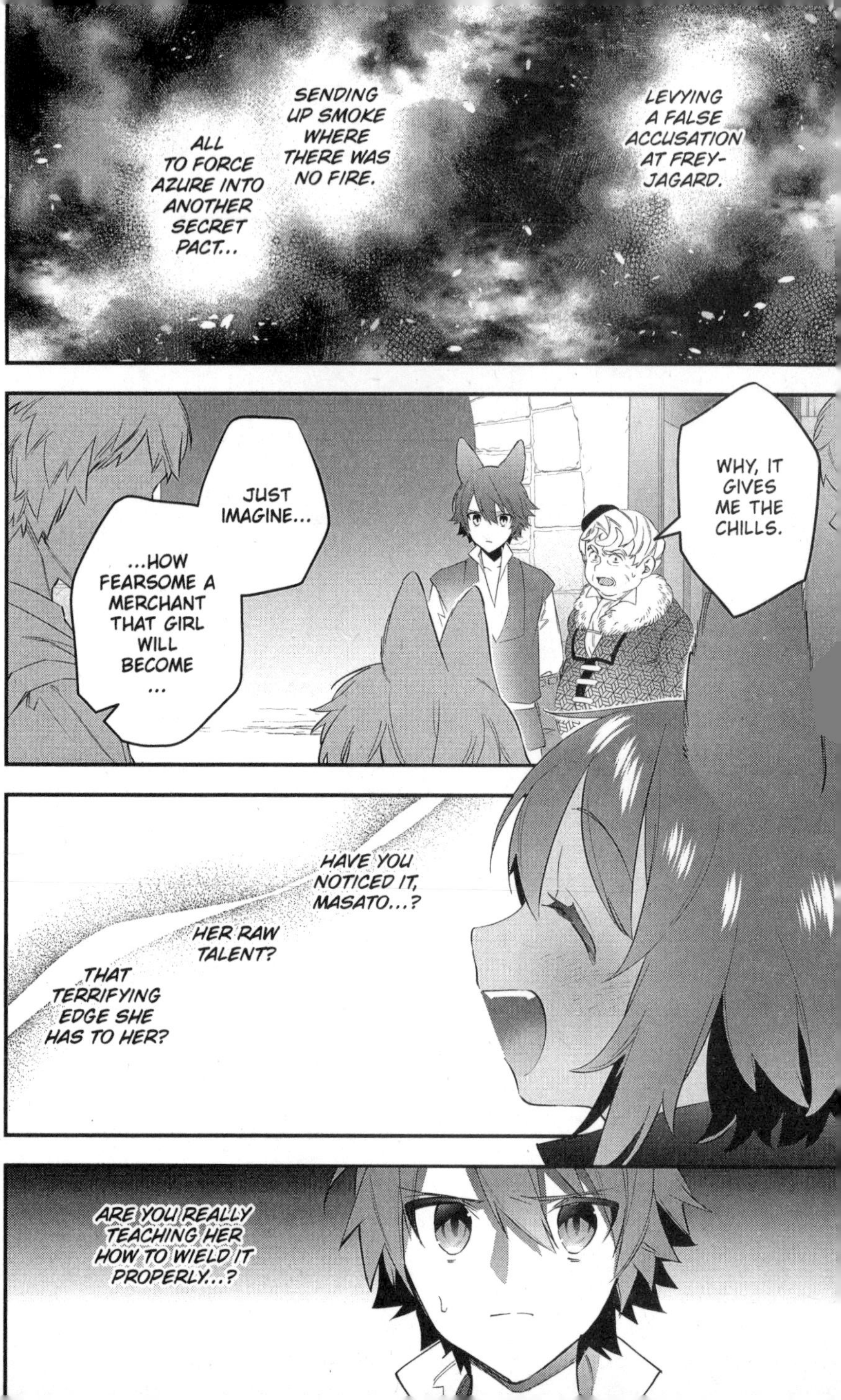
LEVYING A FALSE ACCUSATION AT FREY-JAGARD.
SENDING UP SMOKE WHERE THERE WAS NO FIRE.
ALL TO FORCE AZURE INTO ANOTHER SECRET PACT...
WHY, IT GIVES ME THE CHILLS.
JUST IMAGINE...
...HOW FEARSOME A MERCHANT THAT GIRL WILL BECOME...
HAVE YOU NOTICED IT, MASATO...?
HER RAW TALENT?
THAT TERRIFYING EDGE SHE HAS TO HER?
ARE YOU REALLY TEACHING HER HOW TO WIELD IT PROPERLY...?

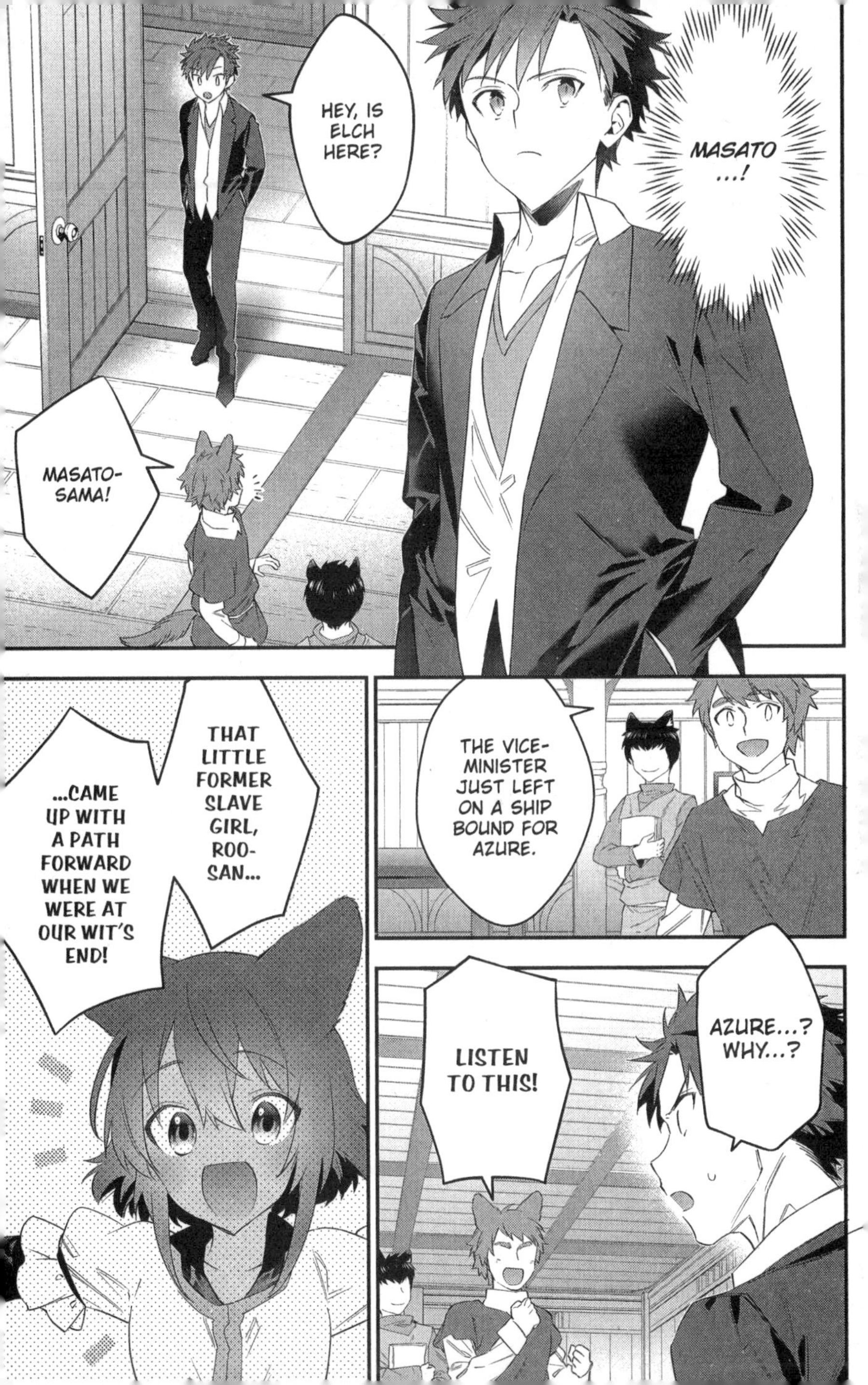
MASATO...!
HEY, IS ELCH HERE?
MASATO-SAMA!
THE VICE-MINISTER JUST LEFT ON A SHIP BOUND FOR AZURE.
AZURE...? WHY...?
LISTEN TO THIS!
THAT LITTLE FORMER SLAVE GIRL, ROO-SAN...
...CAME UP WITH A PATH FORWARD WHEN WE WERE AT OUR WIT'S END!

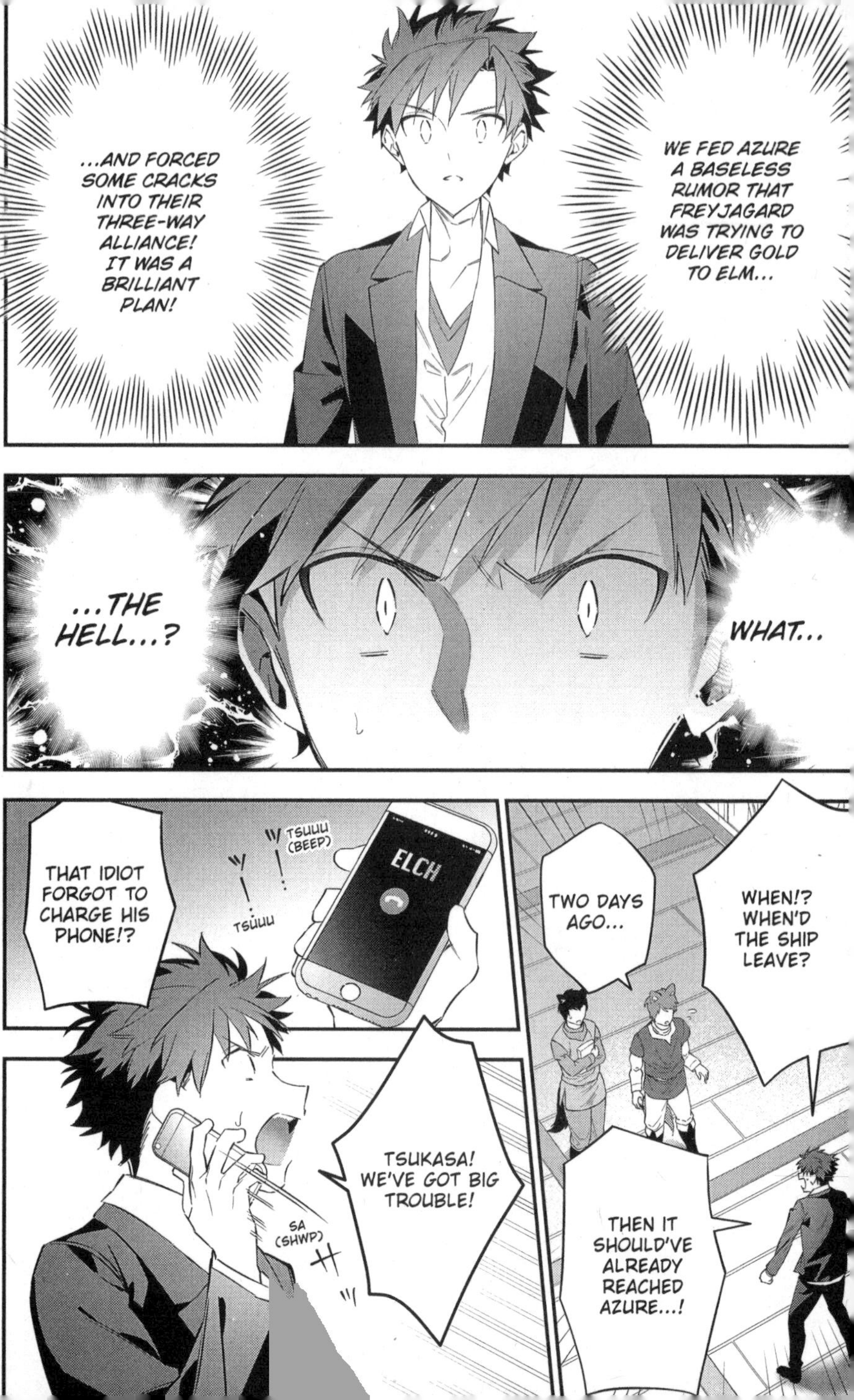
WE FED AZURE A BASELESS RUMOR THAT FREYJAGARD WAS TRYING TO DELIVER GOLD TO ELM...
...AND FORCED SOME CRACKS INTO THEIR THREE-WAY ALLIANCE! IT WAS A BRILLIANT PLAN!
WHAT...
...THE HELL...?
WHEN!? WHEN'D THE SHIP LEAVE?
TWO DAYS AGO...
THEN IT SHOULD'VE ALREADY REACHED AZURE...!
TSUUU (BEEP)
ELCH
TSUUU
THAT IDIOT FORGOT TO CHARGE HIS PHONE!?
TSUKASA! WE'VE GOT BIG TROUBLE!
SA (SHWP)

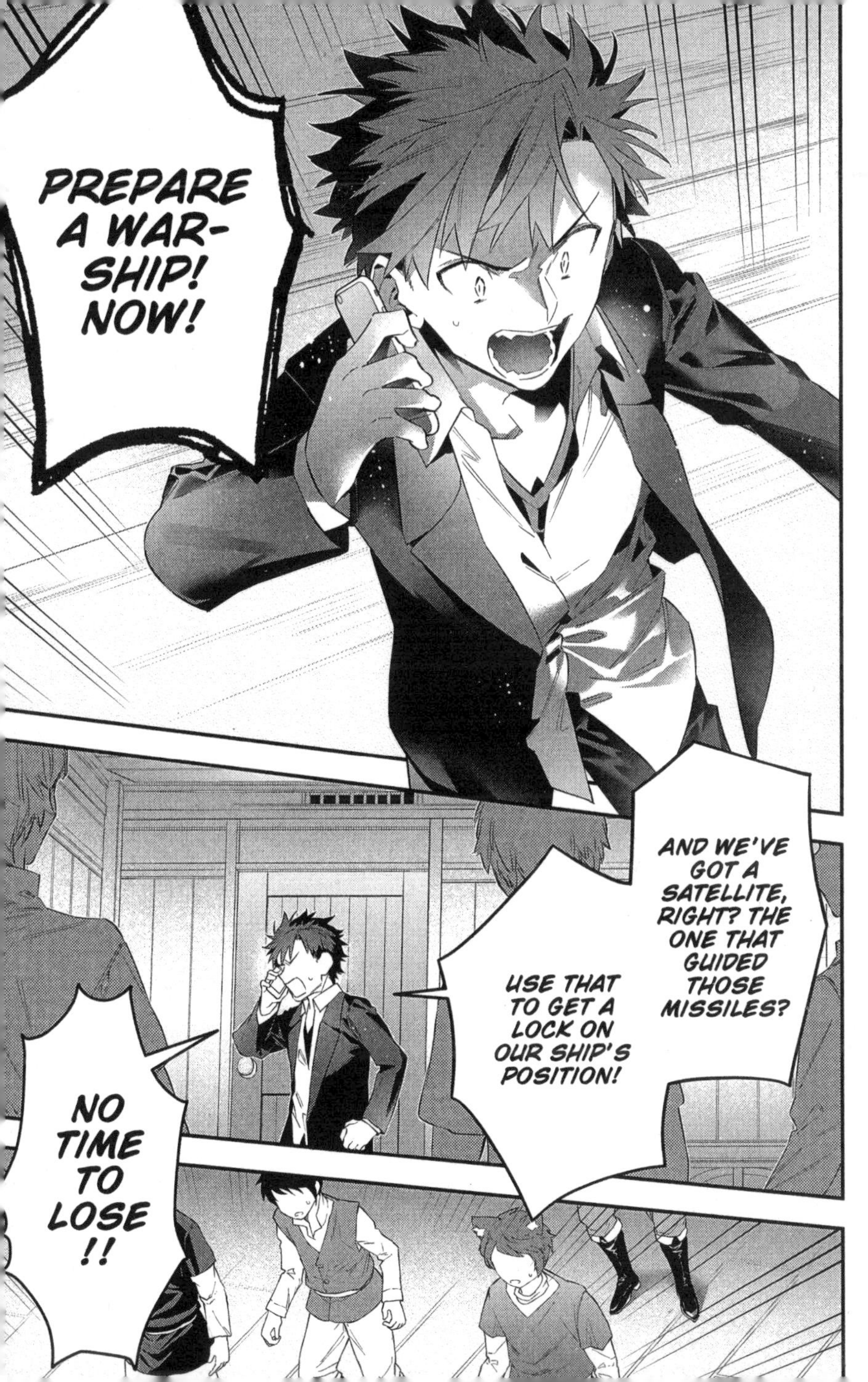
PREPARE A WAR-SHIP! NOW!
AND WE'VE GOT A SATELLITE, RIGHT? THE ONE THAT GUIDED THOSE MISSILES?
USE THAT TO GET A LOCK ON OUR SHIP'S POSITION!
NO TIME TO LOSE !!

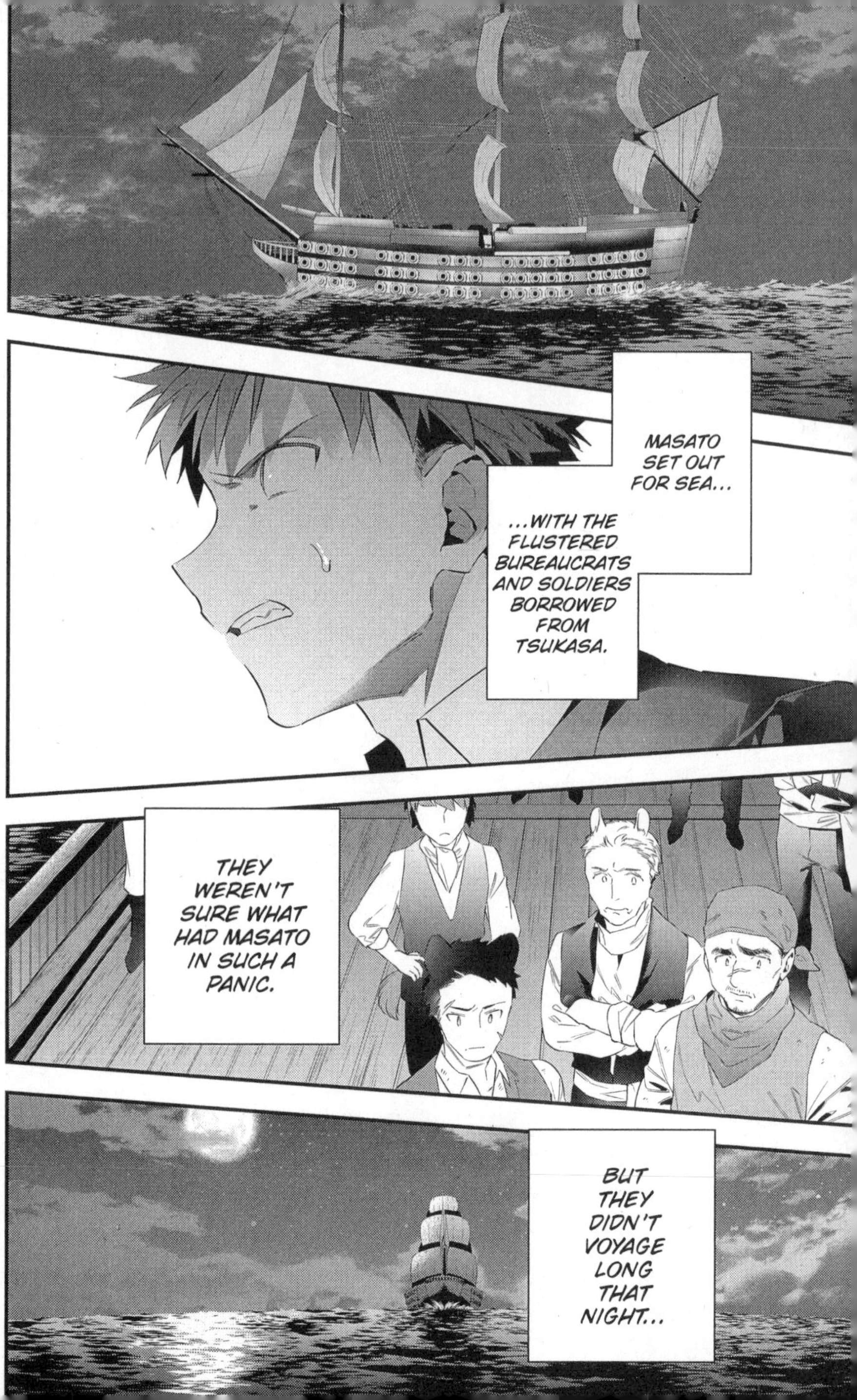
MASATO SET OUT FOR SEA...
...WITH THE FLUSTERED BUREAUCRATS AND SOLDIERS BORROWED FROM TSUKASA.
THEY WEREN'T SURE WHAT HAD MASATO IN SUCH A PANIC.
BUT THEY DIDN'T VOYAGE LONG THAT NIGHT...

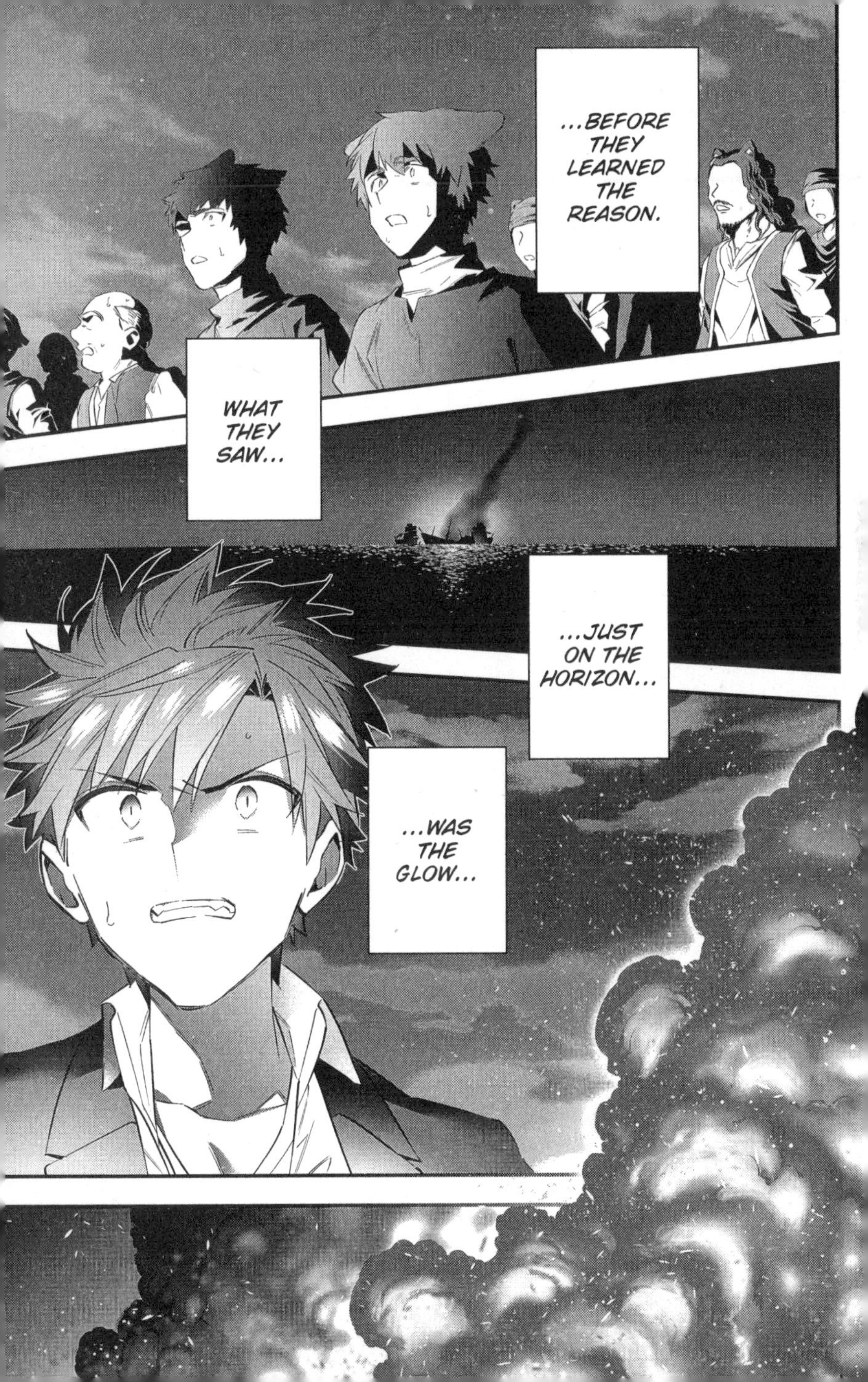
...BEFORE THEY LEARNED THE REASON.
WHAT THEY SAW...
...JUST ON THE HORIZON...
...WAS THE GLOW...

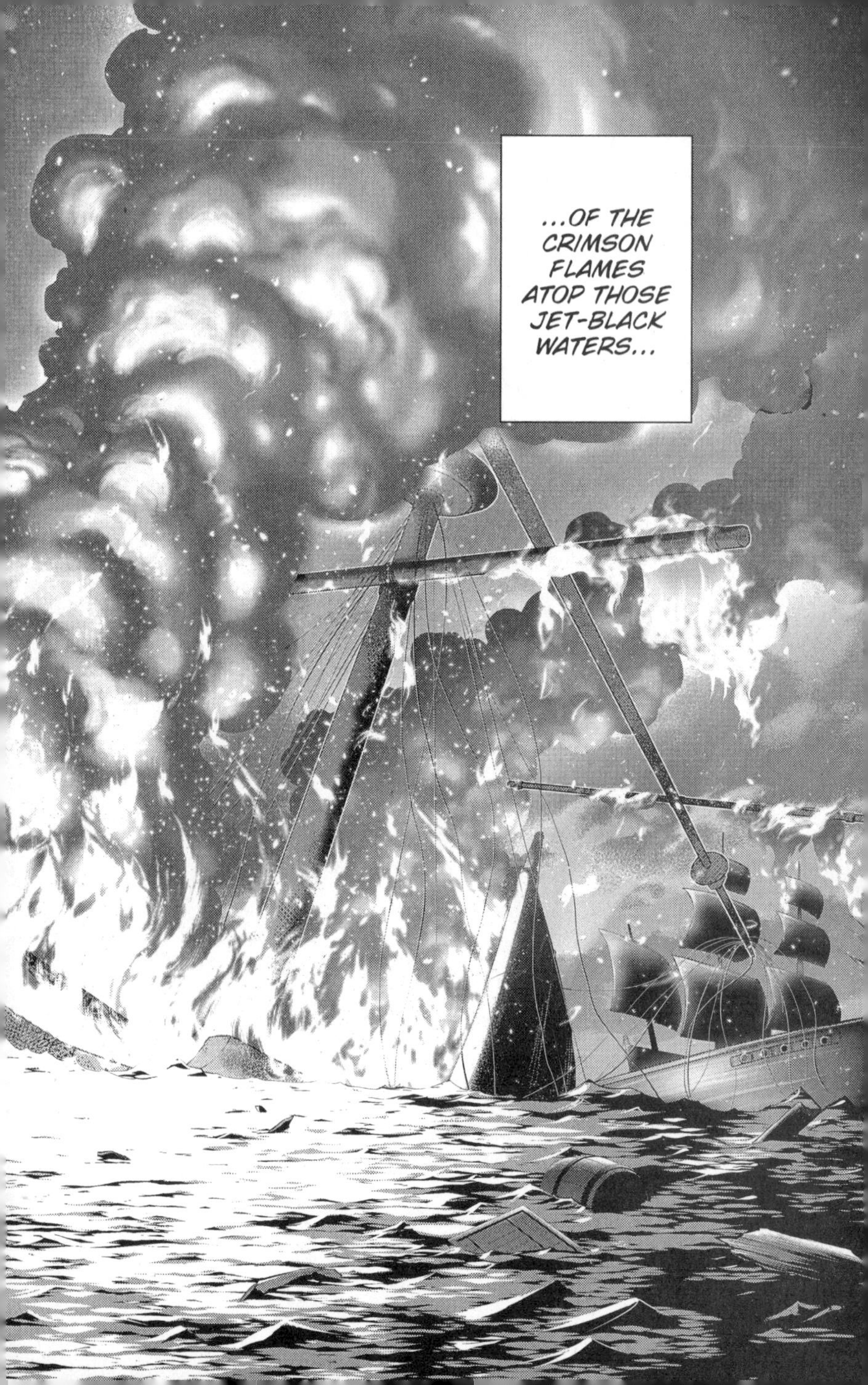
...OF THE CRIMSON FLAMES ATOP THOSE JET-BLACK WATERS...

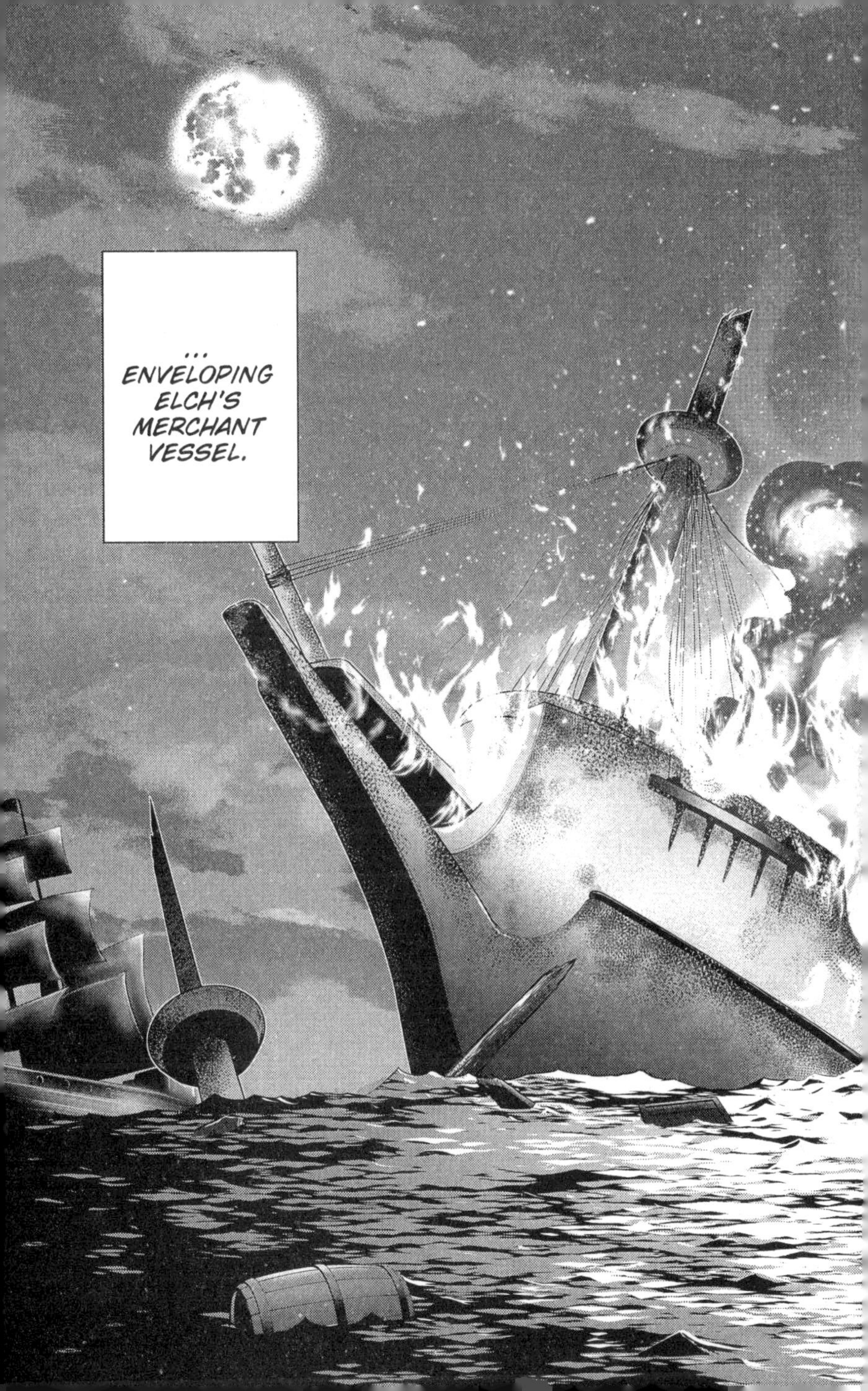
... ENVELOPING ELCH'S MERCHANT VESSEL.

CHARACTER FILE 29

Jaccoy

Once monopolized Dormundt's markets as the head of the Neutzeland Trading Company. Masato crushed his enterprise in a single week, so nowadays he's using his knowledge to support the Republic of Elm.

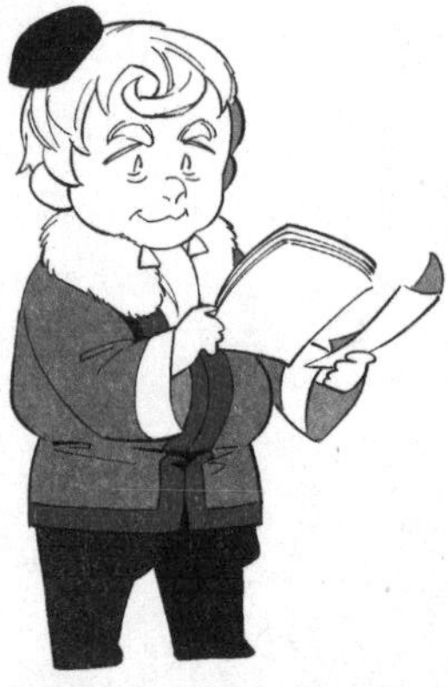

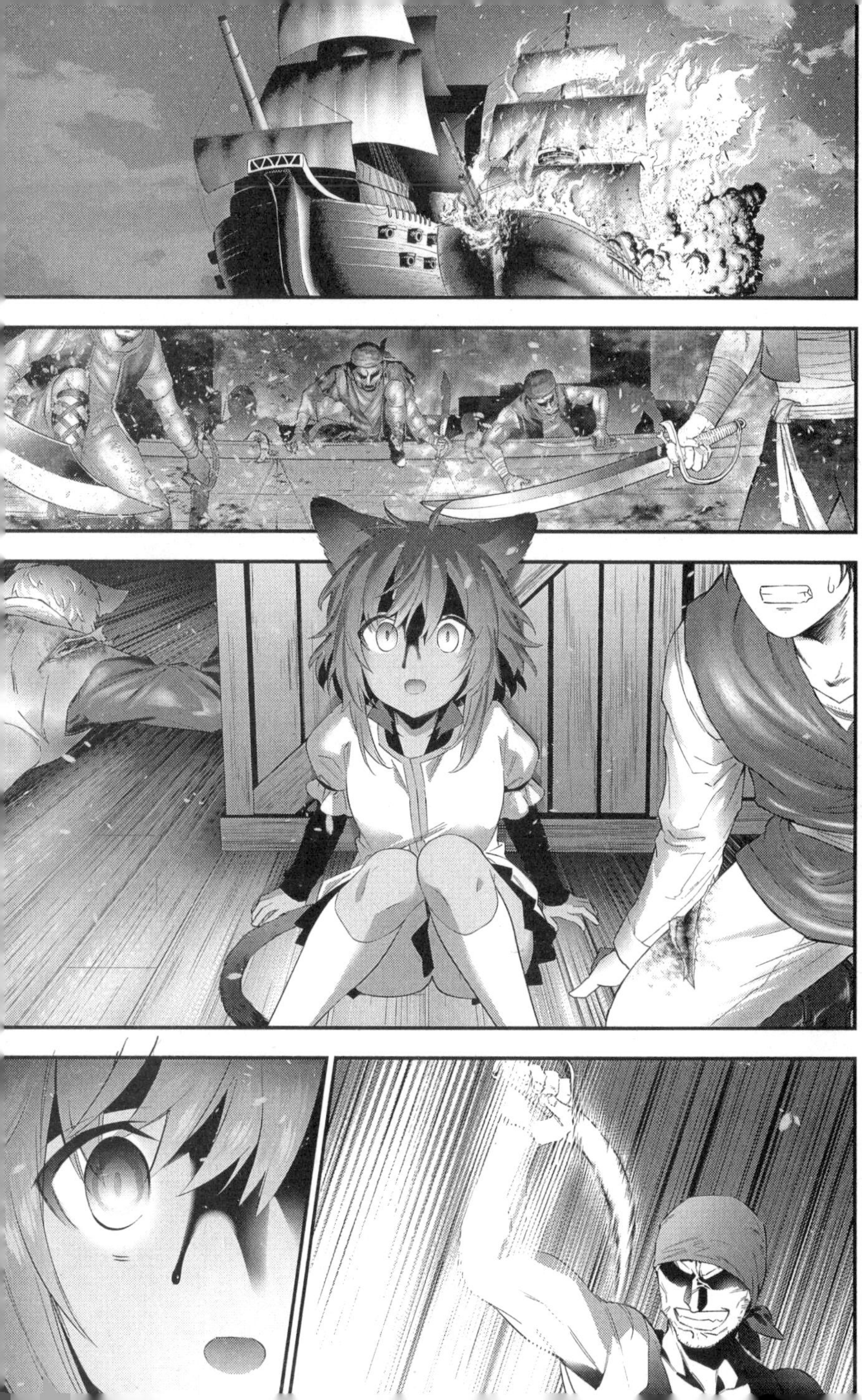

CHAPTER 57: FIRST FAILURE

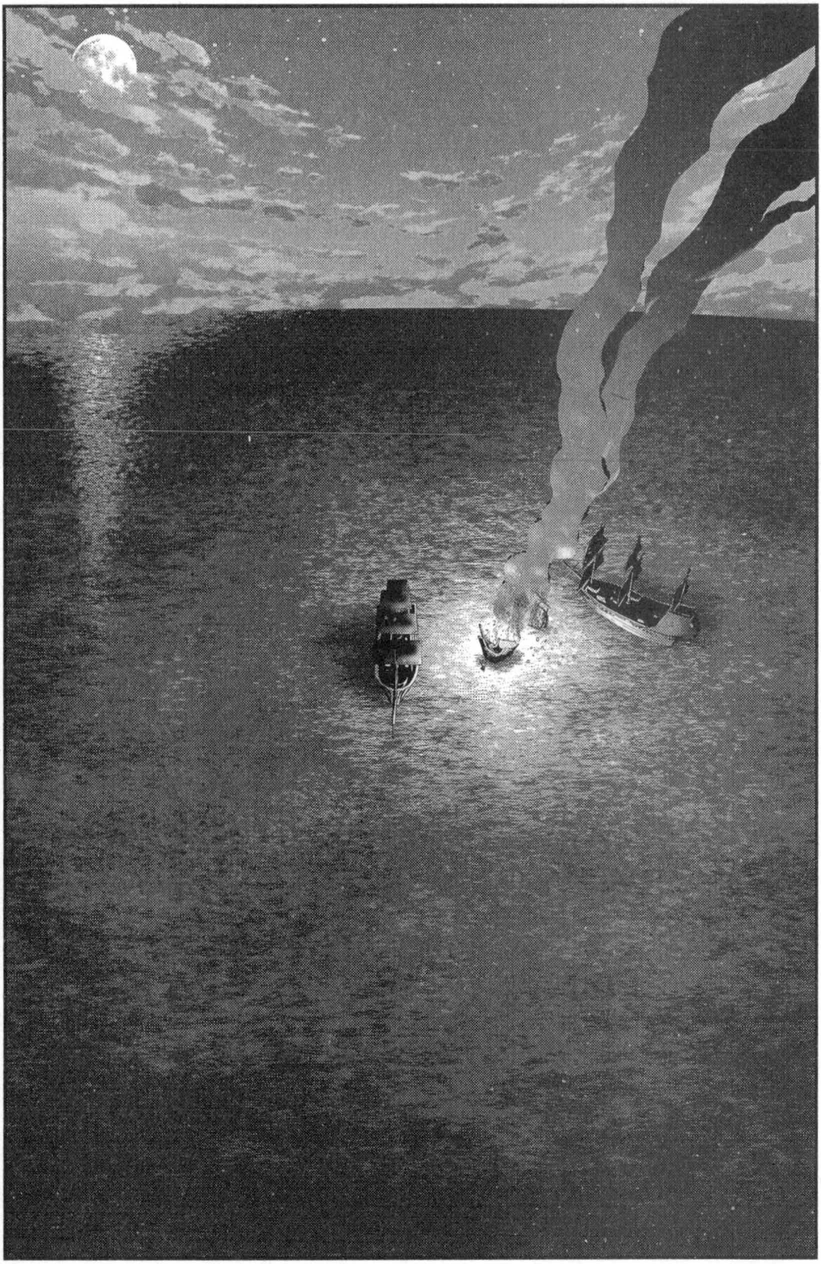

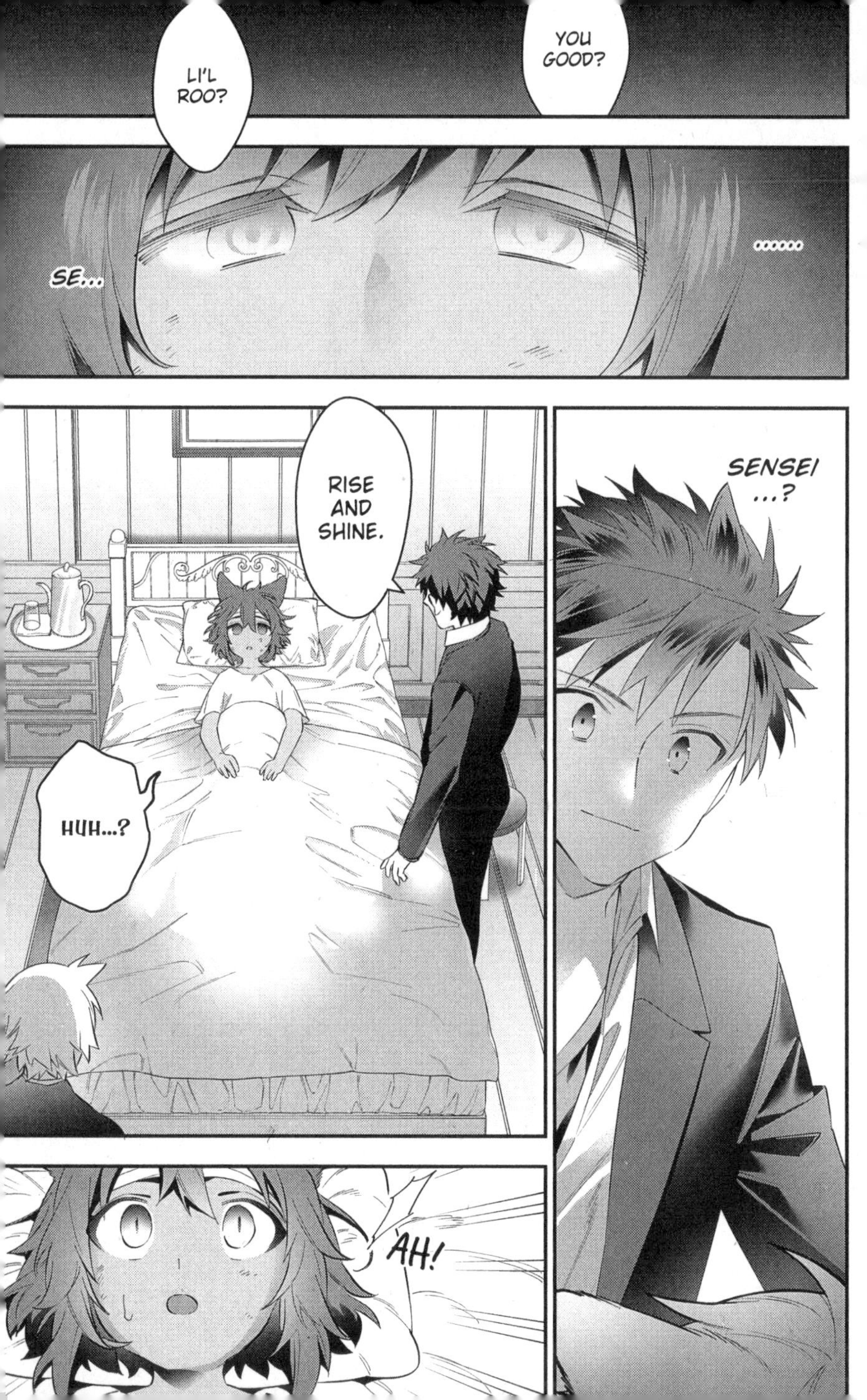
YOU GOOD?
LI'L ROO?
......
SE...
SENSEI ...?
RISE AND SHINE.
HUH...?
AH!

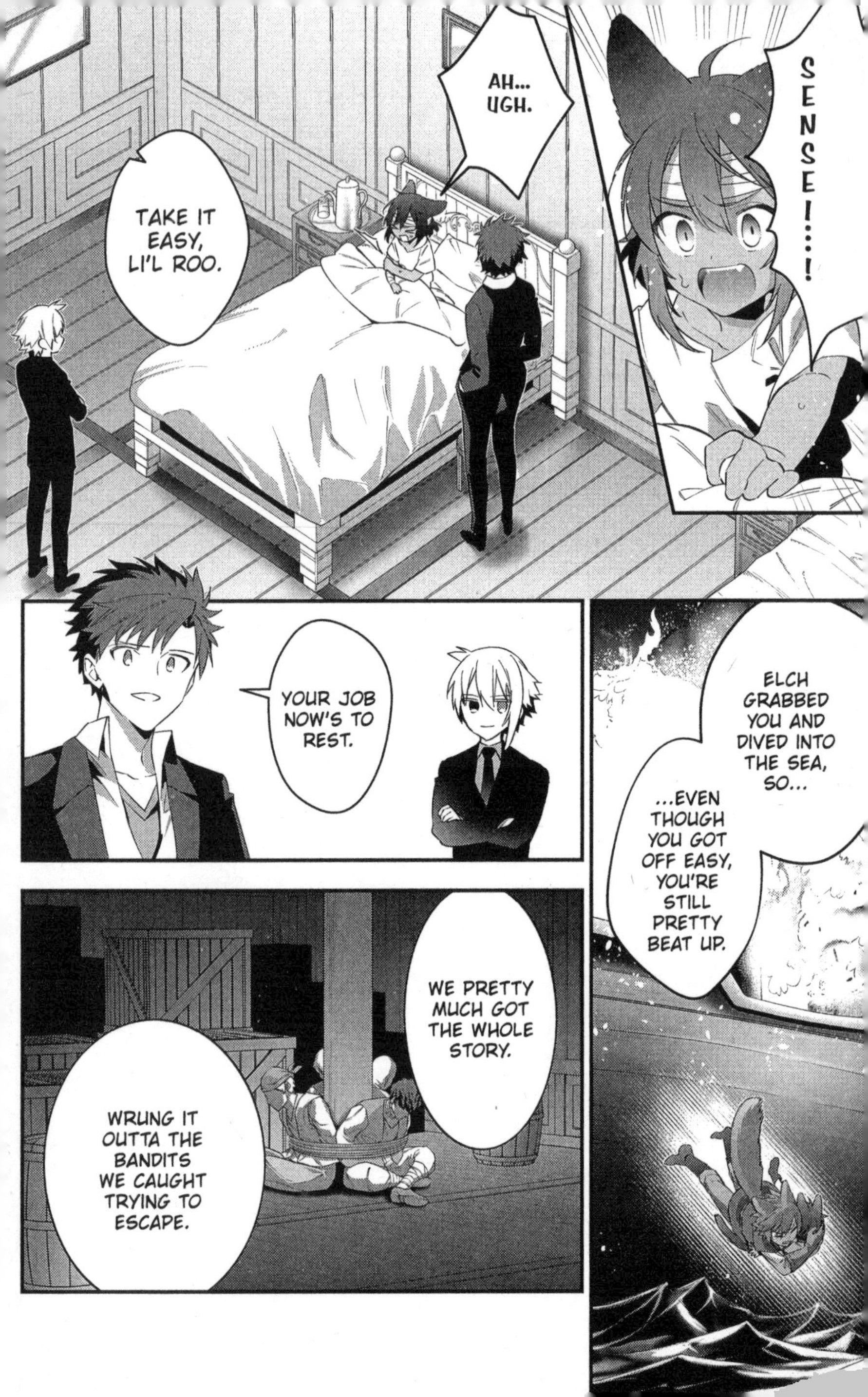
SENSE!...!
AH... UGH.
TAKE IT EASY, LI'L ROO.
ELCH GRABBED YOU AND DIVED INTO THE SEA, SO...
...EVEN THOUGH YOU GOT OFF EASY, YOU'RE STILL PRETTY BEAT UP.
YOUR JOB NOW'S TO REST.
WE PRETTY MUCH GOT THE WHOLE STORY.
WRUNG IT OUTTA THE BANDITS WE CAUGHT TRYING TO ESCAPE.

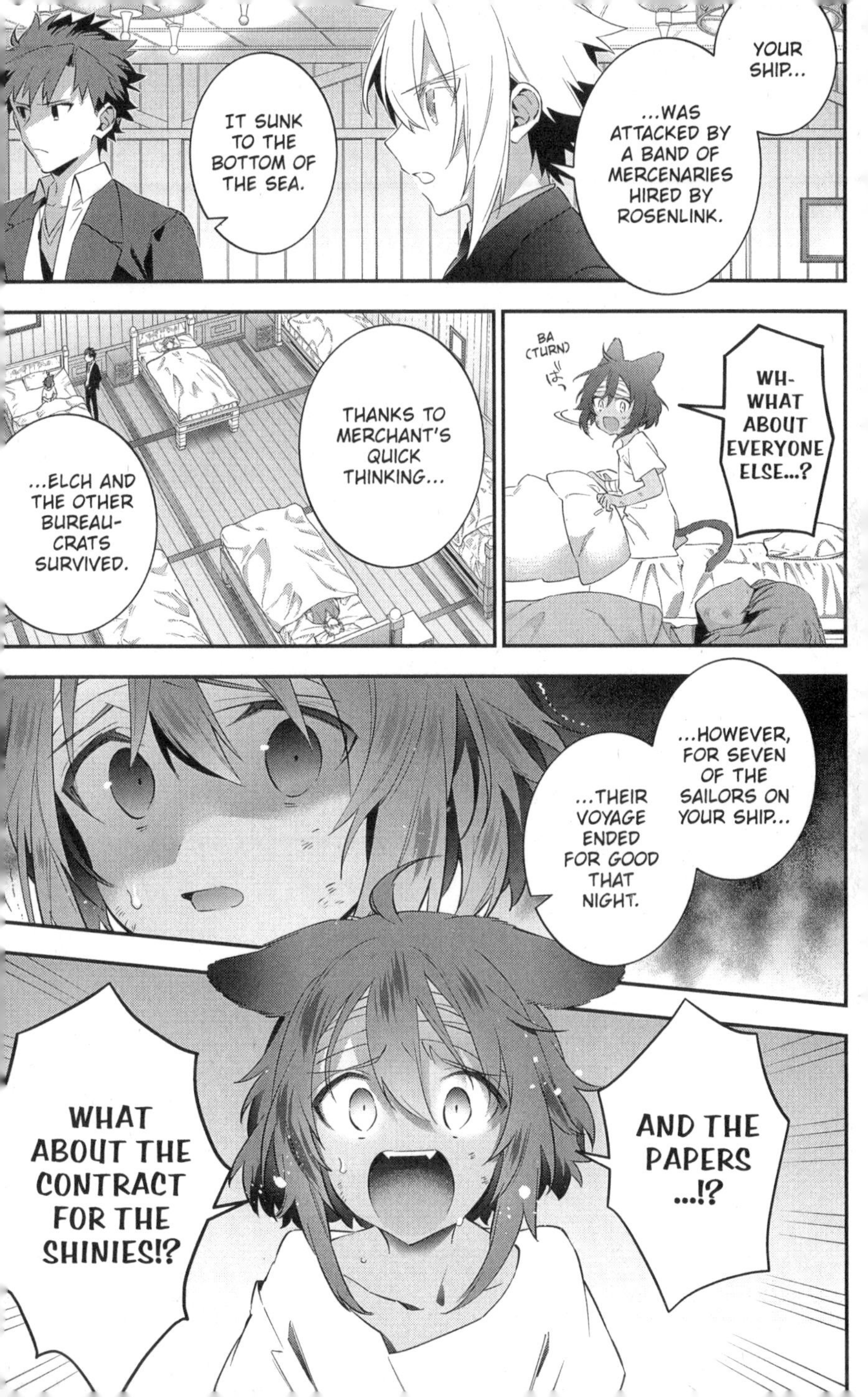
YOUR SHIP...
...WAS ATTACKED BY A BAND OF MERCENARIES HIRED BY ROSENLINK.
IT SUNK TO THE BOTTOM OF THE SEA.
BA (TURN)
ぱっ
WH- WHAT ABOUT EVERYONE ELSE...?
THANKS TO MERCHANT'S QUICK THINKING...
...ELCH AND THE OTHER BUREAU-CRATS SURVIVED.
...HOWEVER, FOR SEVEN OF THE SAILORS ON YOUR SHIP...
...THEIR VOYAGE ENDED FOR GOOD THAT NIGHT.
AND THE PAPERS ...!?
WHAT ABOUT THE CONTRACT FOR THE SHINIES!?

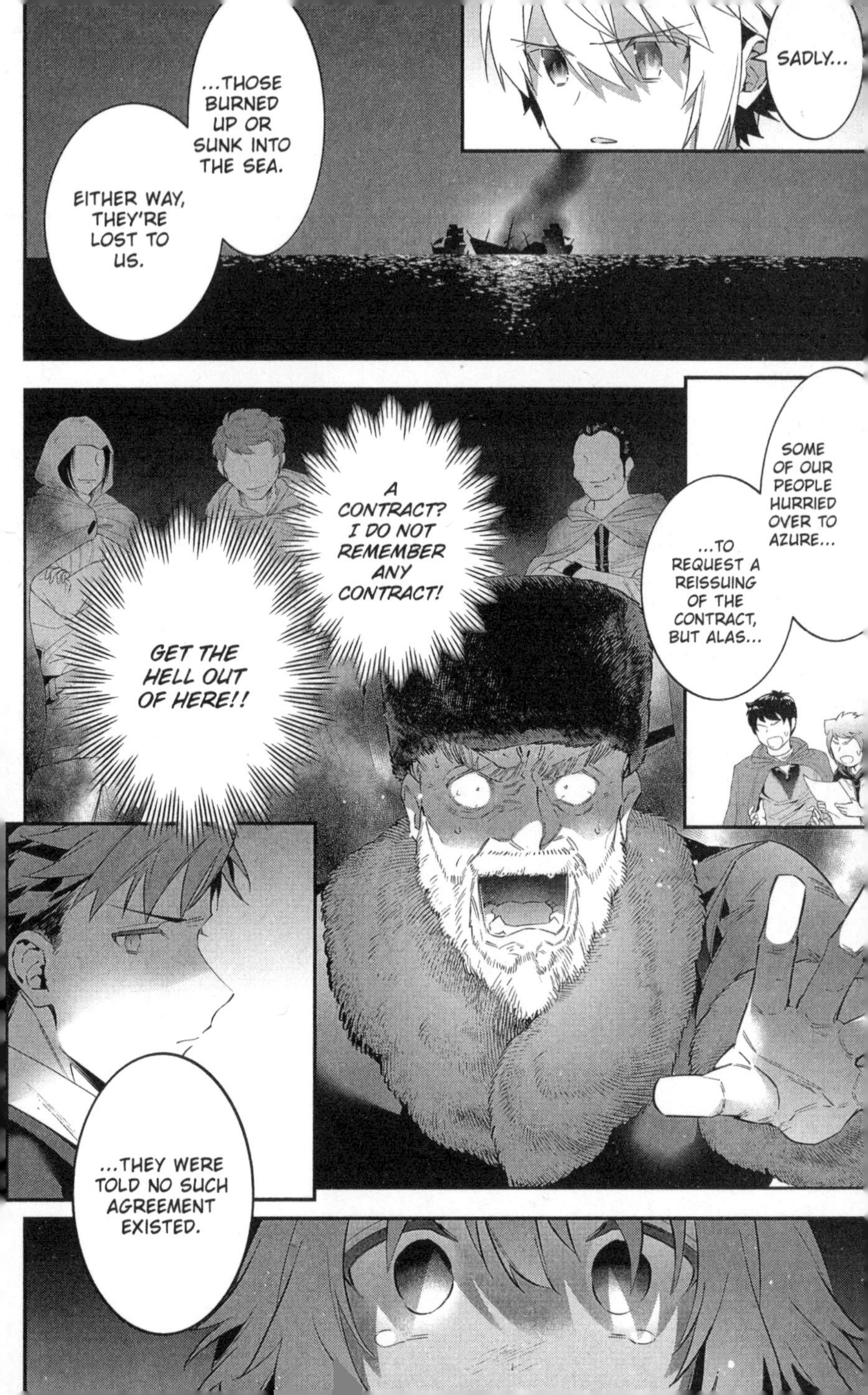
SADLY...
...THOSE BURNED UP OR SUNK INTO THE SEA.
EITHER WAY, THEY'RE LOST TO US.
SOME OF OUR PEOPLE HURRIED OVER TO AZURE...
...TO REQUEST A REISSUING OF THE CONTRACT, BUT ALAS...
A CONTRACT? I DO NOT REMEMBER ANY CONTRACT!
GET THE HELL OUT OF HERE!!
...THEY WERE TOLD NO SUCH AGREEMENT EXISTED.

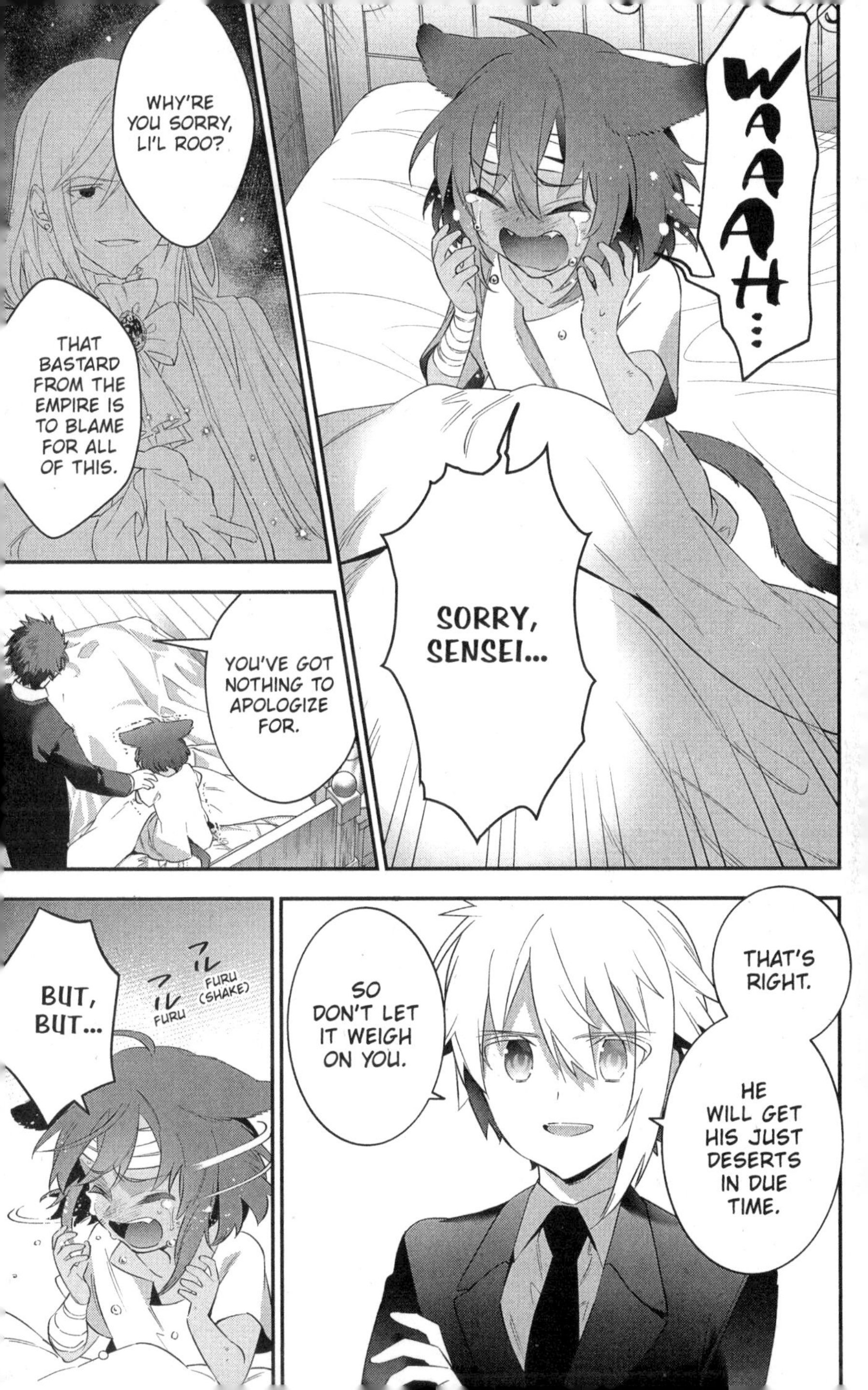
WAAAH...
SORRY, SENSEI...
WHY'RE YOU SORRY, LI'L ROO?
THAT BASTARD FROM THE EMPIRE IS TO BLAME FOR ALL OF THIS.
YOU'VE GOT NOTHING TO APOLOGIZE FOR.
THAT'S RIGHT.
HE WILL GET HIS JUST DESERTS IN DUE TIME.
SO DON'T LET IT WEIGH ON YOU.
BUT, BUT...
フル FURU (SHAKE)
フル FURU

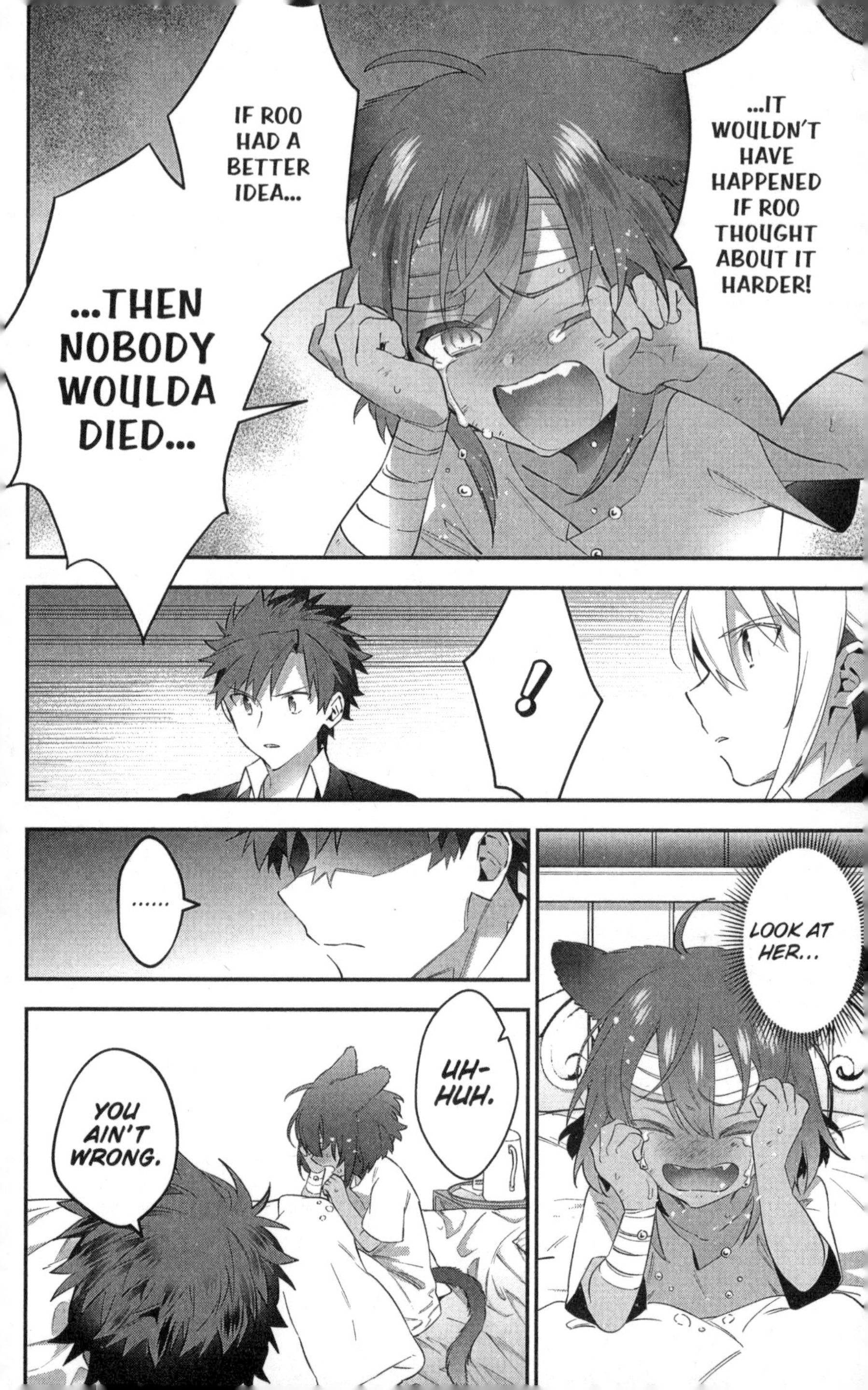
...IT WOULDN'T HAVE HAPPENED IF ROO THOUGHT ABOUT IT HARDER!
IF ROO HAD A BETTER IDEA...
...THEN NOBODY WOULDA DIED...
!
LOOK AT HER...
......
UH-HUH.
YOU AIN'T WRONG.

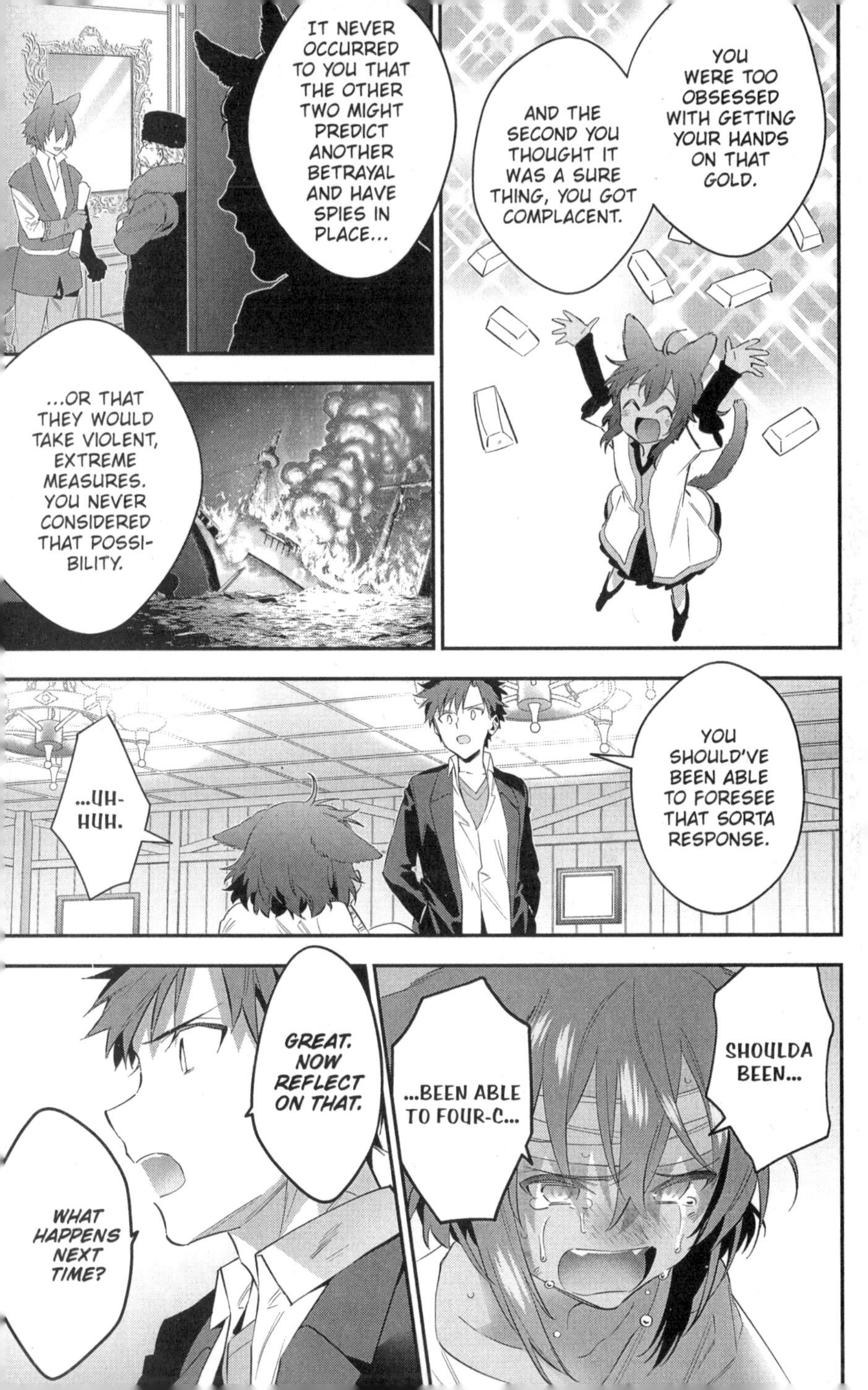
YOU WERE TOO OBSESSED WITH GETTING YOUR HANDS ON THAT GOLD.
AND THE SECOND YOU THOUGHT IT WAS A SURE THING, YOU GOT COMPLACENT.
IT NEVER OCCURRED TO YOU THAT THE OTHER TWO MIGHT PREDICT ANOTHER BETRAYAL AND HAVE SPIES IN PLACE...
...OR THAT THEY WOULD TAKE VIOLENT, EXTREME MEASURES. YOU NEVER CONSIDERED THAT POSSI-BILITY.
YOU SHOULD'VE BEEN ABLE TO FORESEE THAT SORTA RESPONSE.
...UH-HUH.
SHOULDA BEEN...
...BEEN ABLE TO FOUR-C...
GREAT. NOW REFLECT ON THAT.
WHAT HAPPENS NEXT TIME?

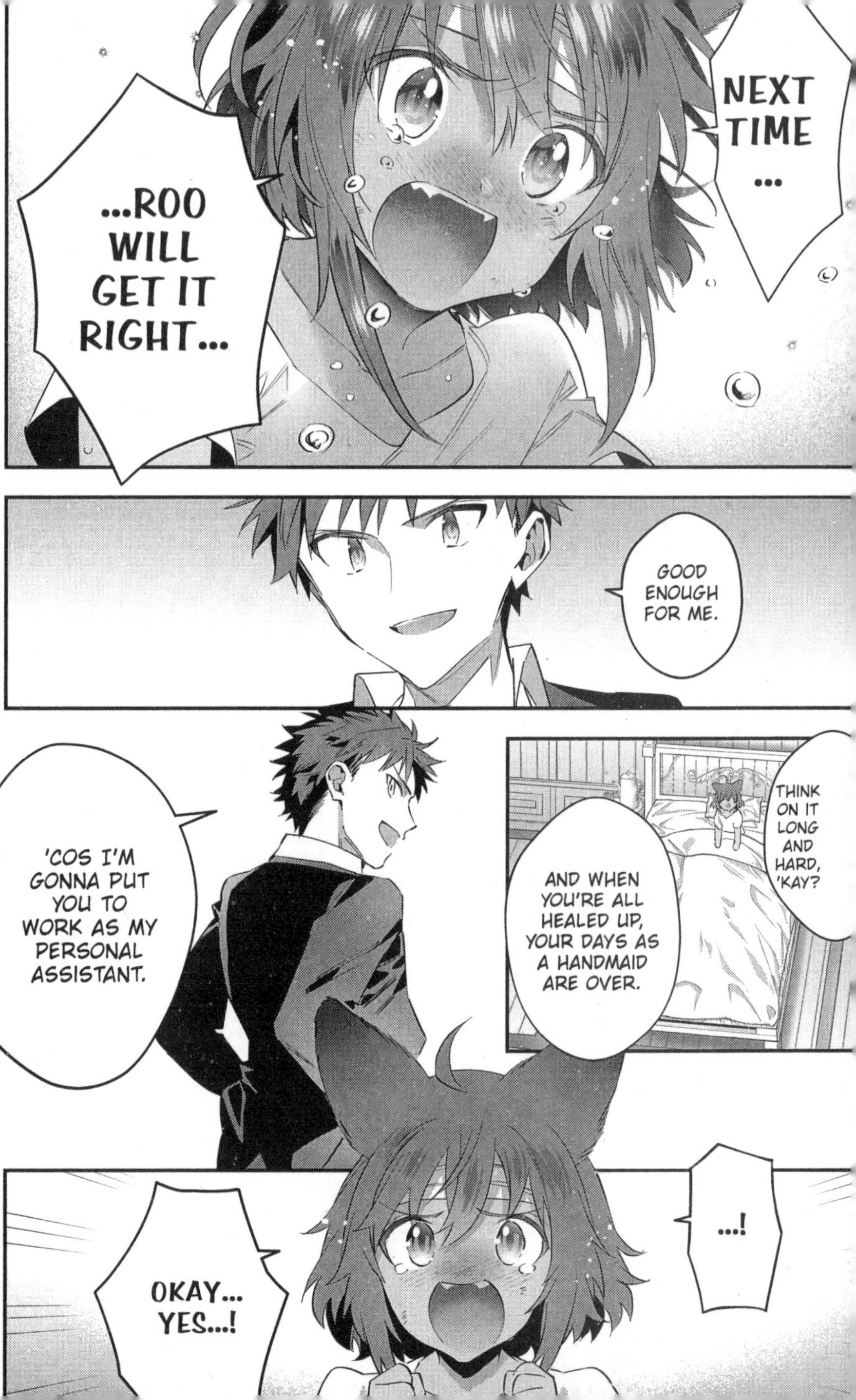
NEXT TIME ...
...ROO WILL GET IT RIGHT...
GOOD ENOUGH FOR ME.
THINK ON IT LONG AND HARD, 'KAY?
AND WHEN YOU'RE ALL HEALED UP, YOUR DAYS AS A HANDMAID ARE OVER.
'COS I'M GONNA PUT YOU TO WORK AS MY PERSONAL ASSISTANT.
...!
OKAY... YES...!

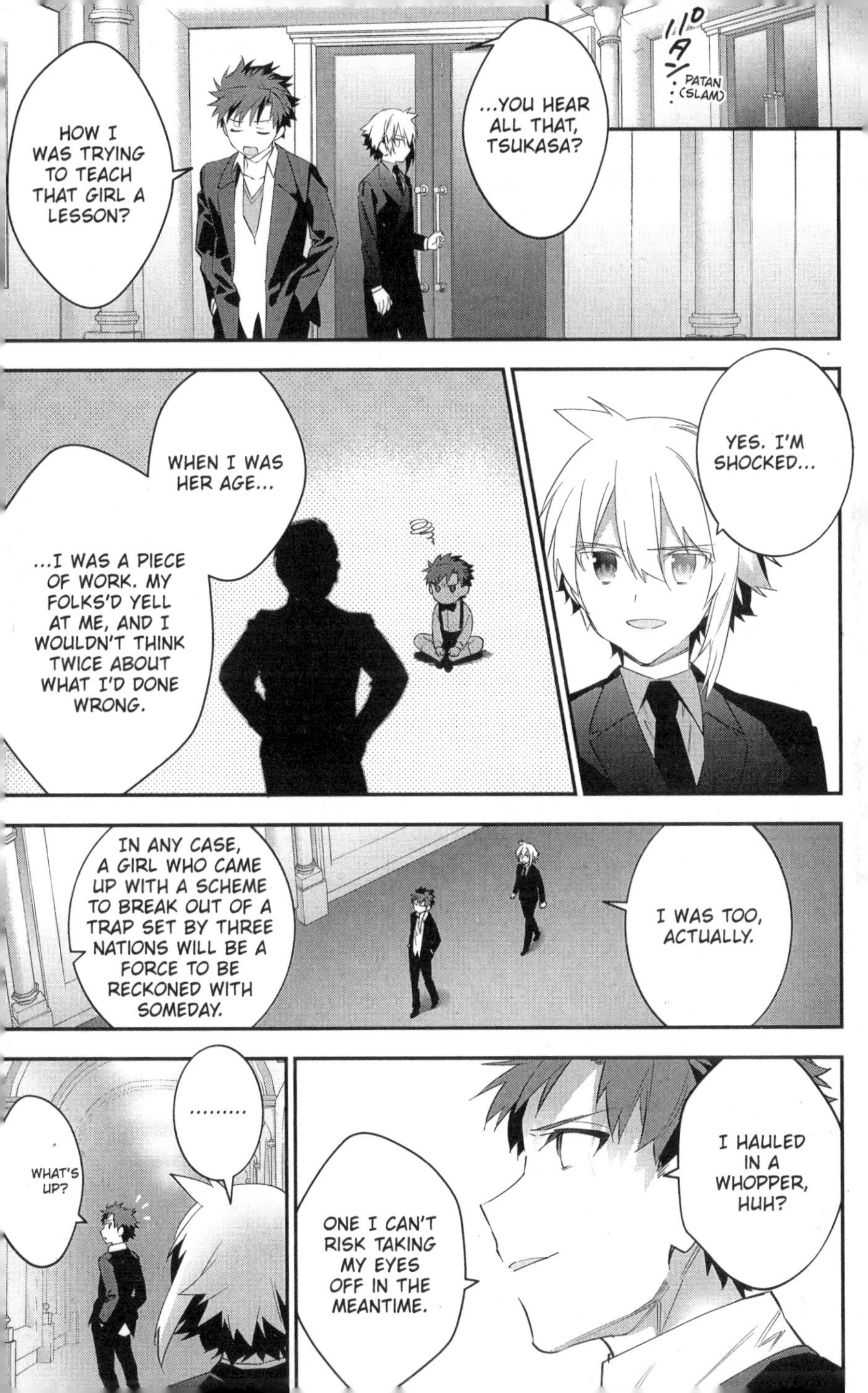

PATAN (SLAM)
...YOU HEAR ALL THAT, TSUKASA?
HOW I WAS TRYING TO TEACH THAT GIRL A LESSON?
YES. I'M SHOCKED...
WHEN I WAS HER AGE...
...I WAS A PIECE OF WORK. MY FOLKS'D YELL AT ME, AND I WOULDN'T THINK TWICE ABOUT WHAT I'D DONE WRONG.
I WAS TOO, ACTUALLY.
IN ANY CASE, A GIRL WHO CAME UP WITH A SCHEME TO BREAK OUT OF A TRAP SET BY THREE NATIONS WILL BE A FORCE TO BE RECKONED WITH SOMEDAY.
I HAULED IN A WHOPPER, HUH?
ONE I CAN'T RISK TAKING MY EYES OFF IN THE MEANTIME.
....
WHAT'S UP?

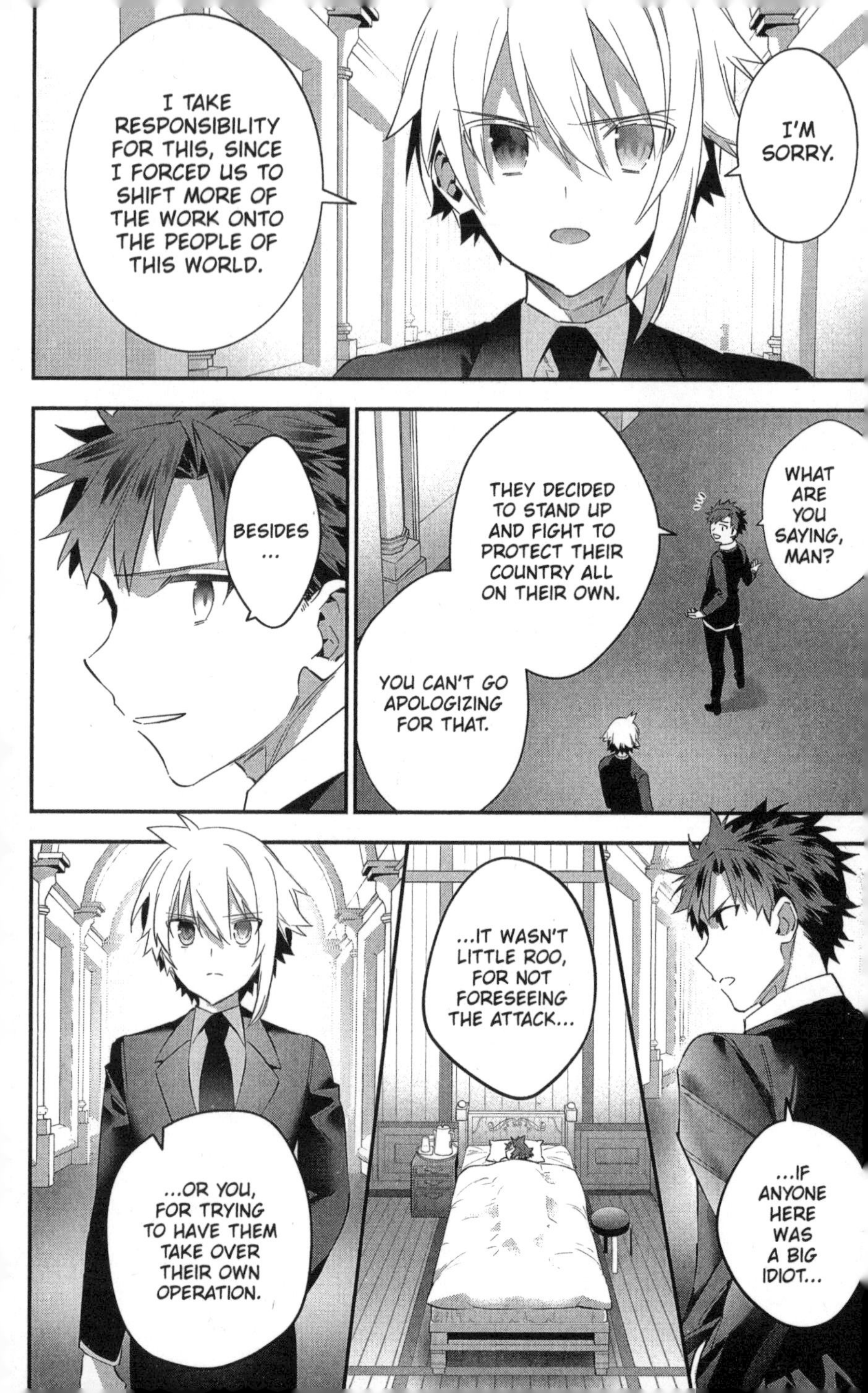
I'M SORRY.
I TAKE RESPONSIBILITY FOR THIS, SINCE I FORCED US TO SHIFT MORE OF THE WORK ONTO THE PEOPLE OF THIS WORLD.
WHAT ARE YOU SAYING, MAN?
THEY DECIDED TO STAND UP AND FIGHT TO PROTECT THEIR COUNTRY ALL ON THEIR OWN.
YOU CAN'T GO APOLOGIZING FOR THAT.
BESIDES...
...IF ANYONE HERE WAS A BIG IDIOT...
...IT WASN'T LITTLE ROO, FOR NOT FORESEEING THE ATTACK...
...OR YOU, FOR TRYING TO HAVE THEM TAKE OVER THEIR OWN OPERATION.

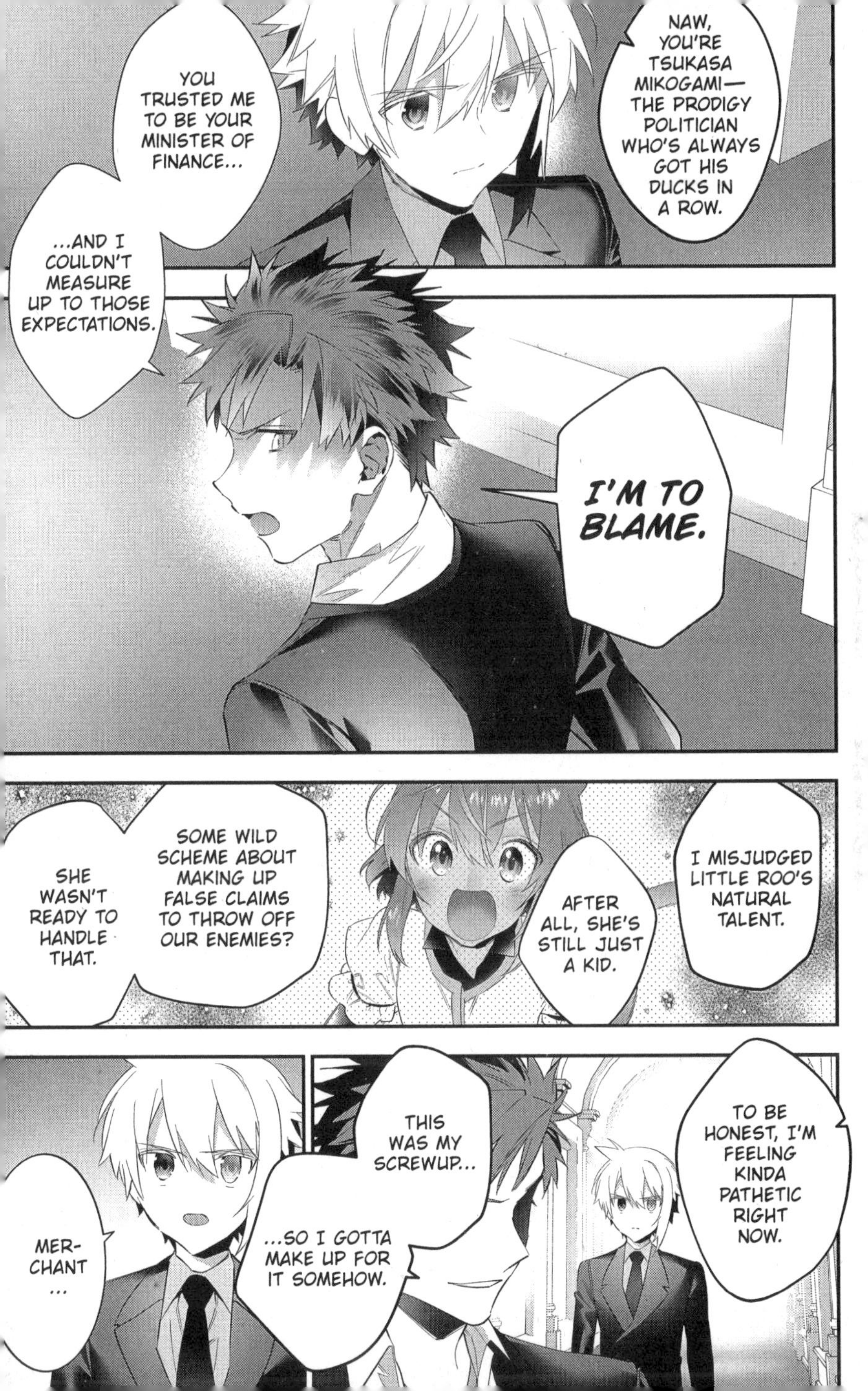
NAW, YOU'RE TSUKASA MIKOGAMI—THE PRODIGY POLITICIAN WHO'S ALWAYS GOT HIS DUCKS IN A ROW.
YOU TRUSTED ME TO BE YOUR MINISTER OF FINANCE...
...AND I COULDN'T MEASURE UP TO THOSE EXPECTATIONS.
I'M TO BLAME.
I MISJUDGED LITTLE ROO'S NATURAL TALENT.
AFTER ALL, SHE'S STILL JUST A KID.
SOME WILD SCHEME ABOUT MAKING UP FALSE CLAIMS TO THROW OFF OUR ENEMIES?
SHE WASN'T READY TO HANDLE THAT.
TO BE HONEST, I'M FEELING KINDA PATHETIC RIGHT NOW.
THIS WAS MY SCREWUP...
...SO I GOTTA MAKE UP FOR IT SOMEHOW.
MER-CHANT...

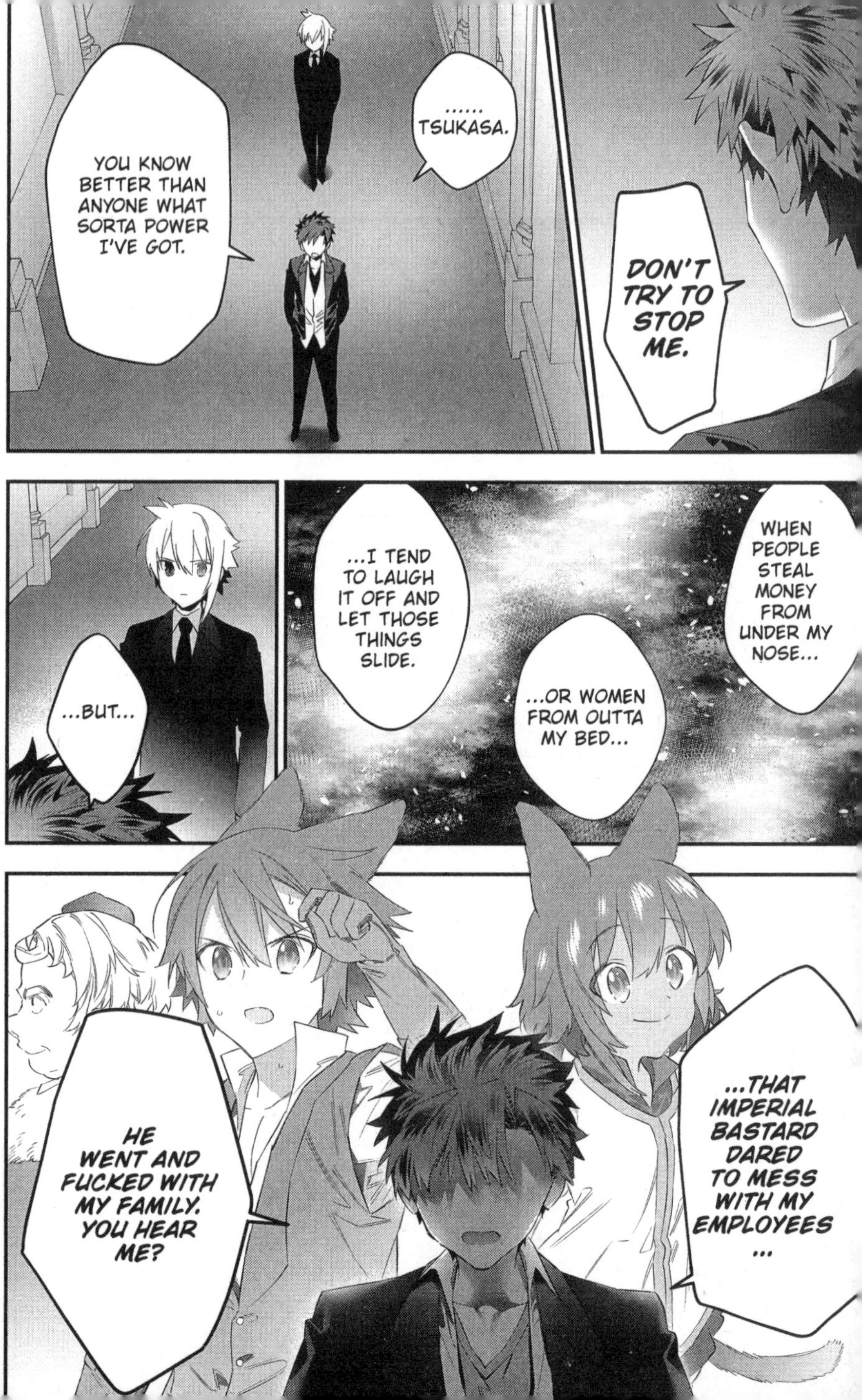
DON'T TRY TO STOP ME.
......TSUKASA.
YOU KNOW BETTER THAN ANYONE WHAT SORTA POWER I'VE GOT.
WHEN PEOPLE STEAL MONEY FROM UNDER MY NOSE...
...OR WOMEN FROM OUTTA MY BED...
...I TEND TO LAUGH IT OFF AND LET THOSE THINGS SLIDE.
...BUT...
...THAT IMPERIAL BASTARD DARED TO MESS WITH MY EMPLOYEES...
HE WENT AND FUCKED WITH MY FAMILY. YOU HEAR ME?

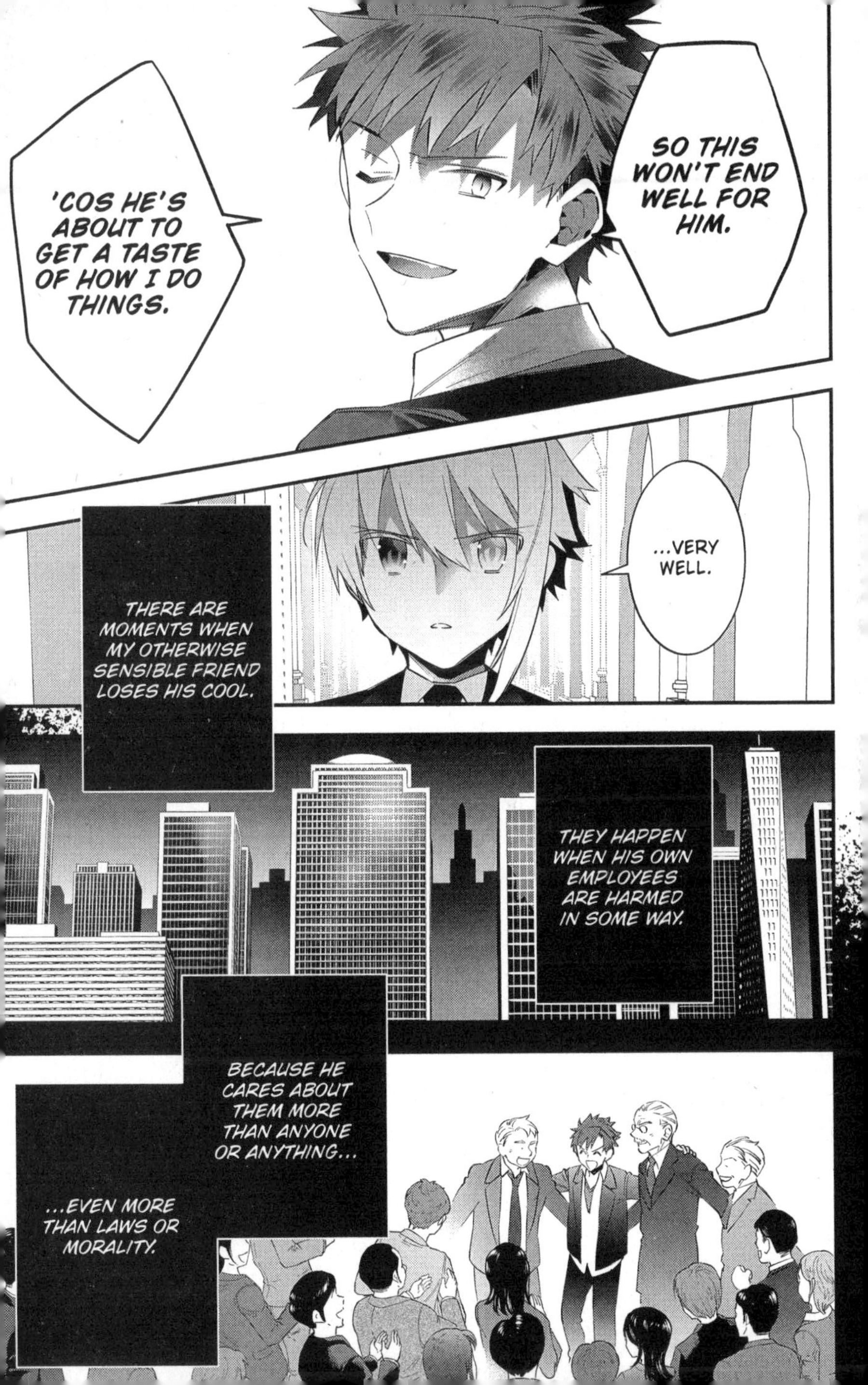
SO THIS WON'T END WELL FOR HIM.
'COS HE'S ABOUT TO GET A TASTE OF HOW I DO THINGS.
...VERY WELL.
THERE ARE MOMENTS WHEN MY OTHERWISE SENSIBLE FRIEND LOSES HIS COOL.
THEY HAPPEN WHEN HIS OWN EMPLOYEES ARE HARMED IN SOME WAY.
BECAUSE HE CARES ABOUT THEM MORE THAN ANYONE OR ANYTHING...
...EVEN MORE THAN LAWS OR MORALITY.

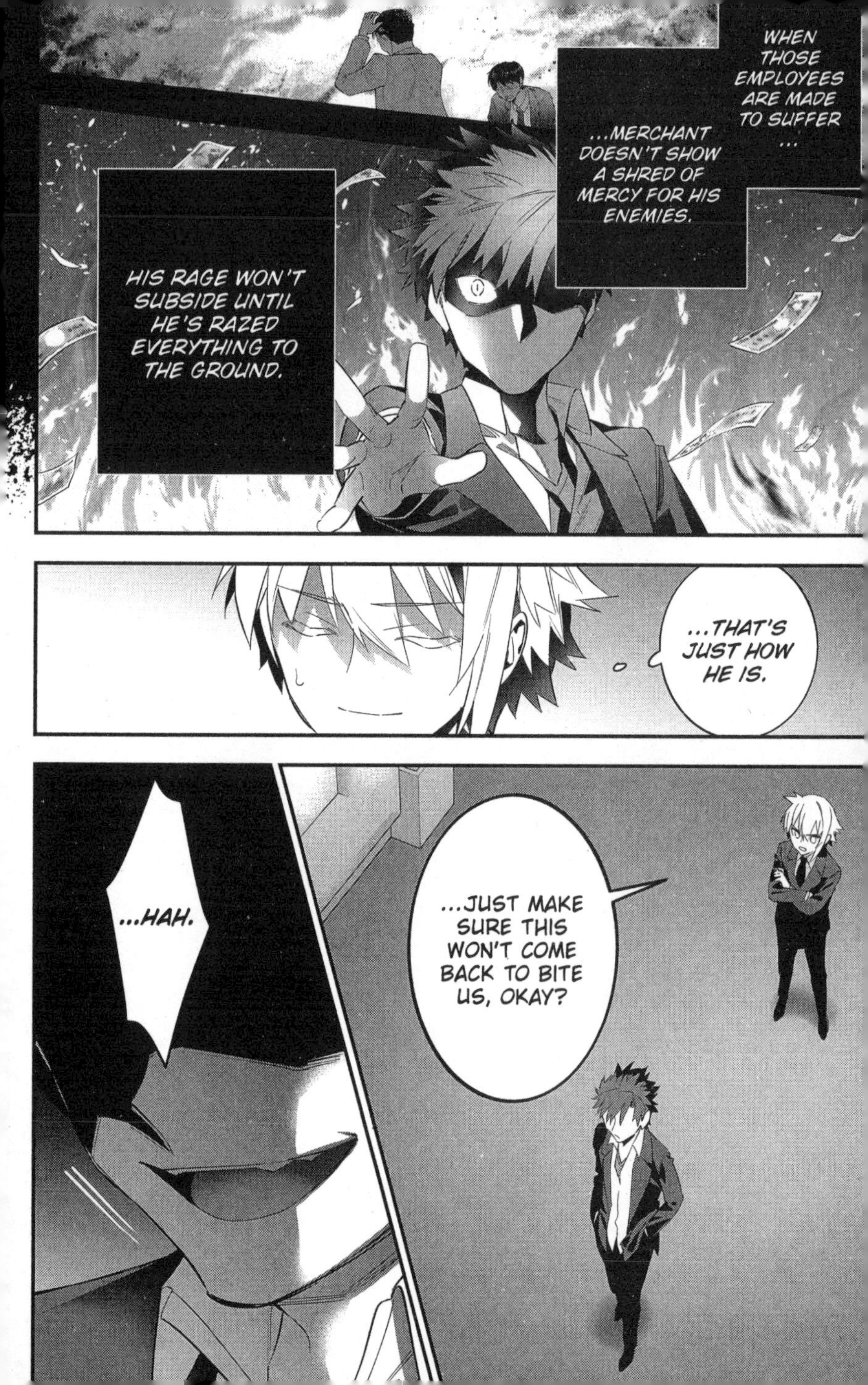
WHEN THOSE EMPLOYEES ARE MADE TO SUFFER...
...MERCHANT DOESN'T SHOW A SHRED OF MERCY FOR HIS ENEMIES.
HIS RAGE WON'T SUBSIDE UNTIL HE'S RAZED EVERYTHING TO THE GROUND.
...THAT'S JUST HOW HE IS.
...JUST MAKE SURE THIS WON'T COME BACK TO BITE US, OKAY?
...HAH.

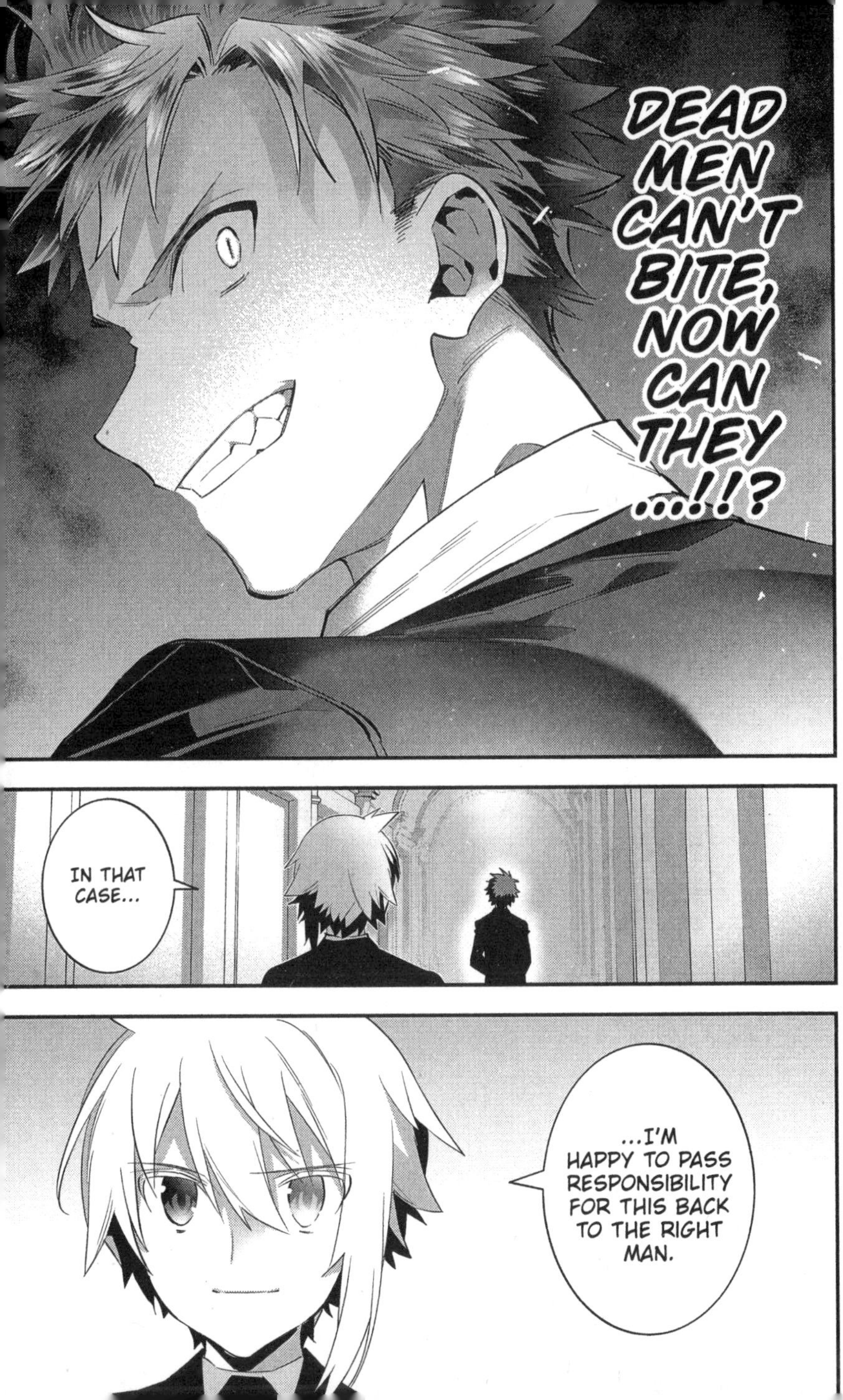
DEAD MEN CAN'T BITE, NOW CAN THEY ...!!?
IN THAT CASE...
...I'M HAPPY TO PASS RESPONSIBILITY FOR THIS BACK TO THE RIGHT MAN.

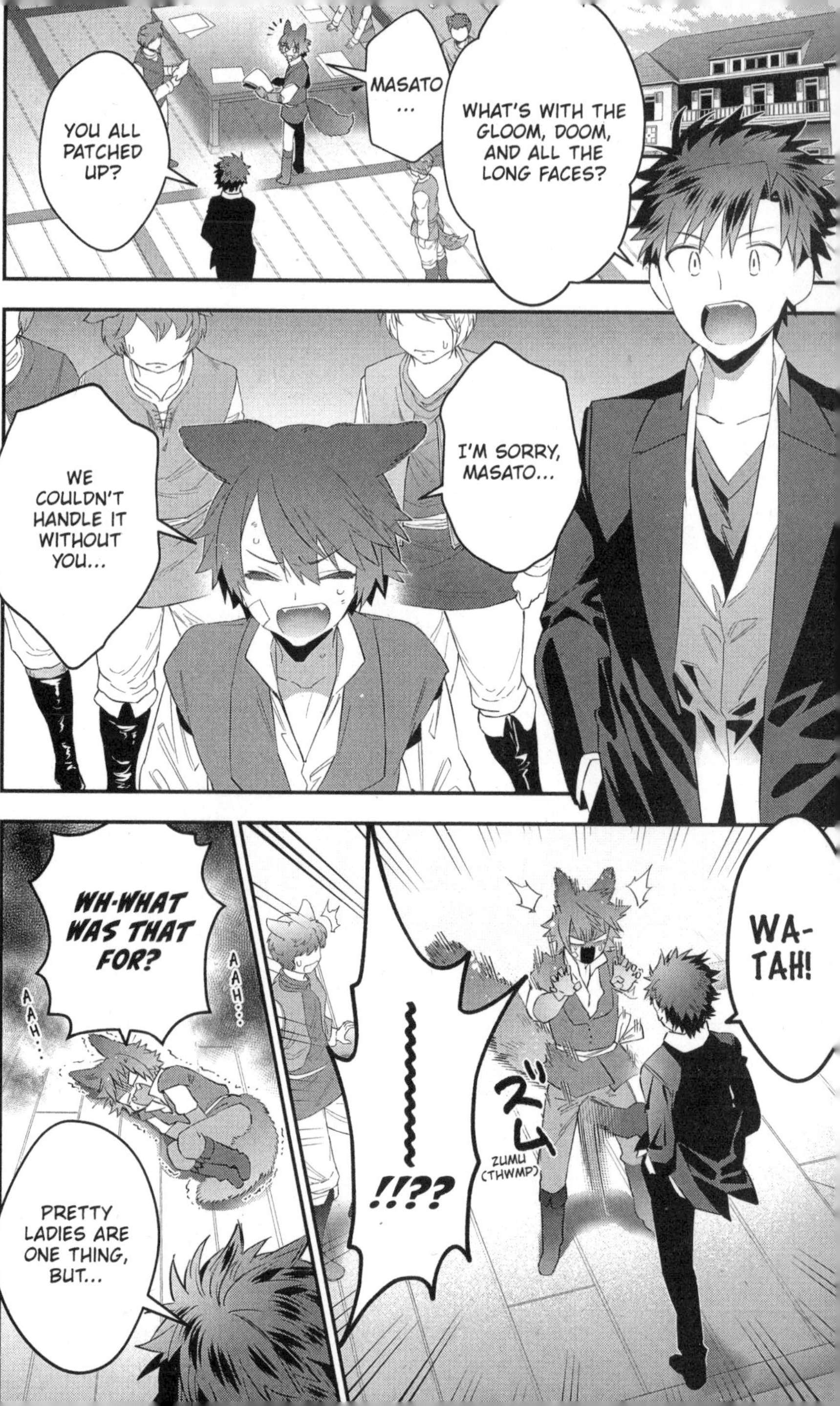
WHAT'S WITH THE GLOOM, DOOM, AND ALL THE LONG FACES?
MASATO...
YOU ALL PATCHED UP?
I'M SORRY, MASATO...
WE COULDN'T HANDLE IT WITHOUT YOU...
WA-TAH!
~~~~!!??
ズム
ZUMU (THWMP)
WH-WHAT WAS THAT FOR?
AAH...
AAH...
PRETTY LADIES ARE ONE THING, BUT...
~~~~

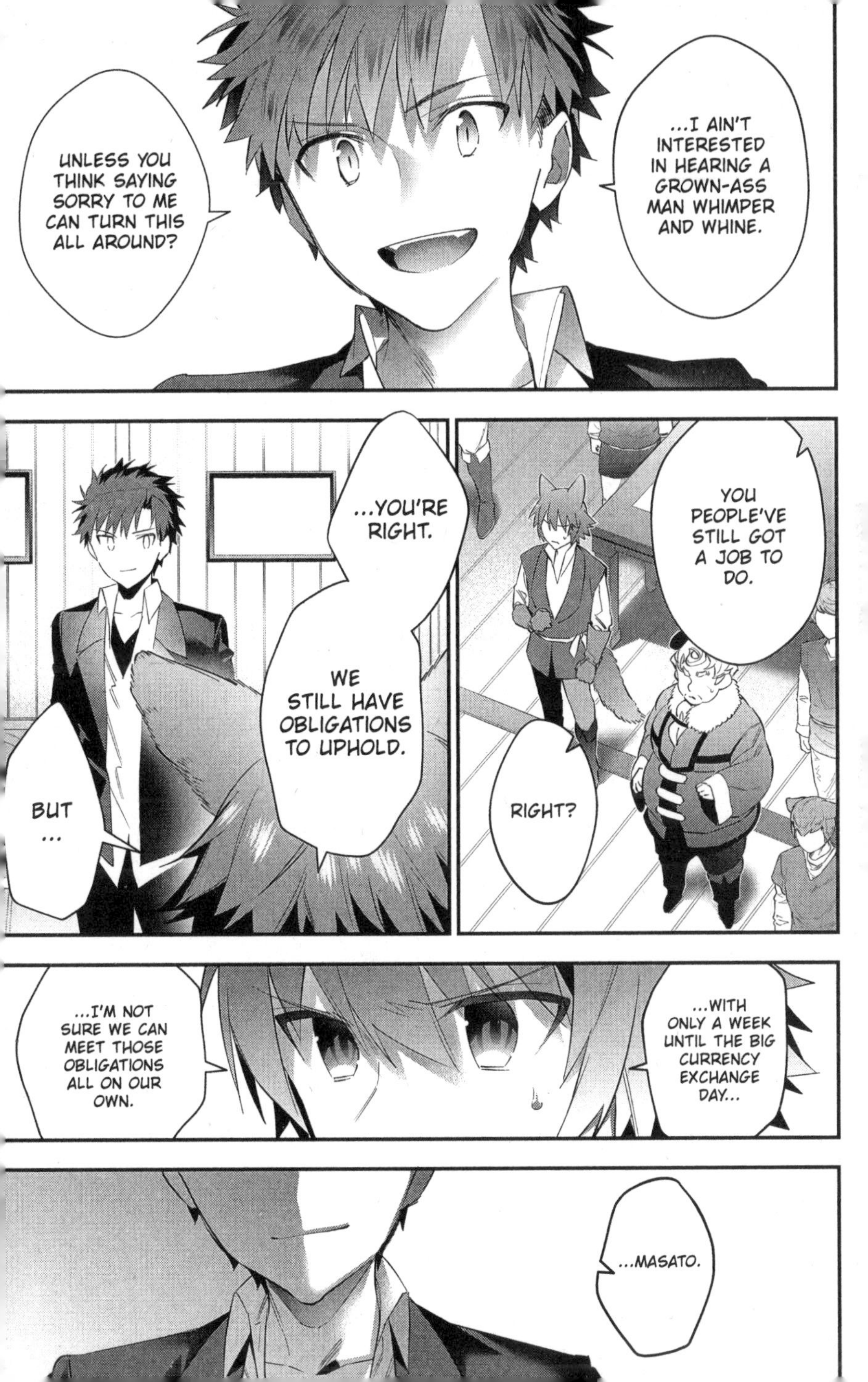
...I AIN'T INTERESTED IN HEARING A GROWN-ASS MAN WHIMPER AND WHINE.
UNLESS YOU THINK SAYING SORRY TO ME CAN TURN THIS ALL AROUND?
YOU PEOPLE'VE STILL GOT A JOB TO DO.
RIGHT?
...YOU'RE RIGHT.
WE STILL HAVE OBLIGATIONS TO UPHOLD.
BUT ...
...WITH ONLY A WEEK UNTIL THE BIG CURRENCY EXCHANGE DAY...
...I'M NOT SURE WE CAN MEET THOSE OBLIGATIONS ALL ON OUR OWN.
...MASATO.

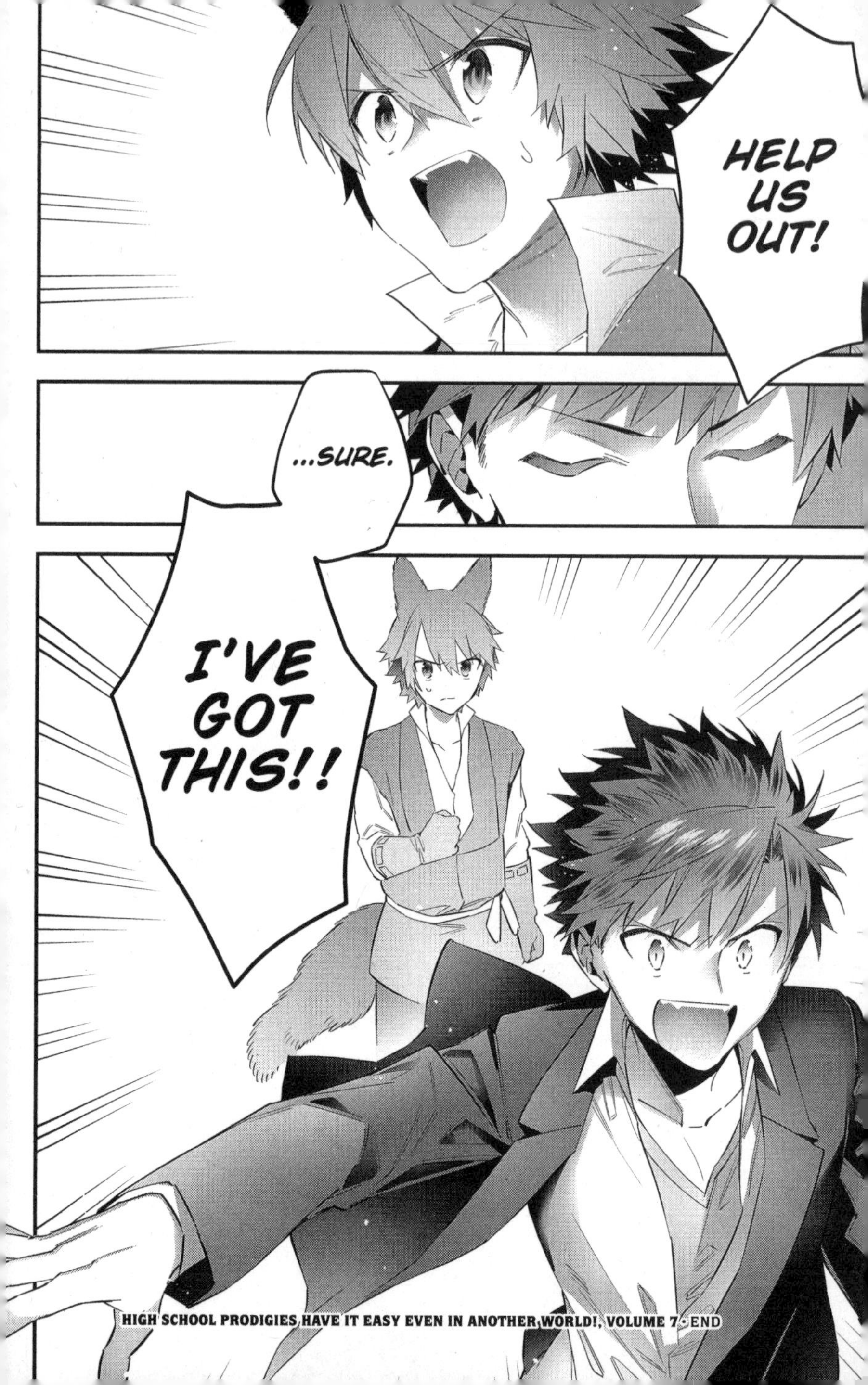
HELP US OUT!
...SURE.
I'VE GOT THIS!!
HIGH SCHOOL PRODIGIES HAVE IT EASY EVEN IN ANOTHER WORLD!, VOLUME 7 • END

TRANSLATION NOTES

COMMON HONORIFICS

no honorific: Indicates familiarity or closeness; if used without permission or reason, addressing someone in this manner would constitute an insult.

-san: The Japanese equivalent of Mr./Mrs./Miss. If a situation calls for politeness, this is the fail-safe honorific.

-sama: Conveys great respect; may also indicate that the social status of the speaker is lower than that of the addressee.

-kun: Used most often when referring to boys, this indicates affection or familiarity. Occasionally used by older men among their peers, but it may also be used by anyone referring to a person of lower standing.

-sensei: A respectful term for teachers, artists, or high-level professionals.

-dono: A respectful term typically equated with "lord" or "master," this honorific has an archaic spin to it when used in colloquial parlance.

-shi: A respectful term for those of higher status, particularly those who the speaker is not personally acquainted with. More formal than *-san* but not as formal as *-sama*.

Page 3
Shinobu's offer of a **"massage that'll give a bountiful bosom"** refers to the Japanese old wives' tale that touching breasts will cause them to grow. There is no evidence to support this belief, but it is easy to understand why the idea remains popular among teenagers of both genders.

Page 8
Masato's nickname **Merchant** obviously fits his chosen profession, but it's also a play on words: *shounin* is both an alternate reading of the kanji for Masato and how the Japanese word for "merchant" is pronounced.

URK...

PURU
(SHAKE)
プル

PURU
プル

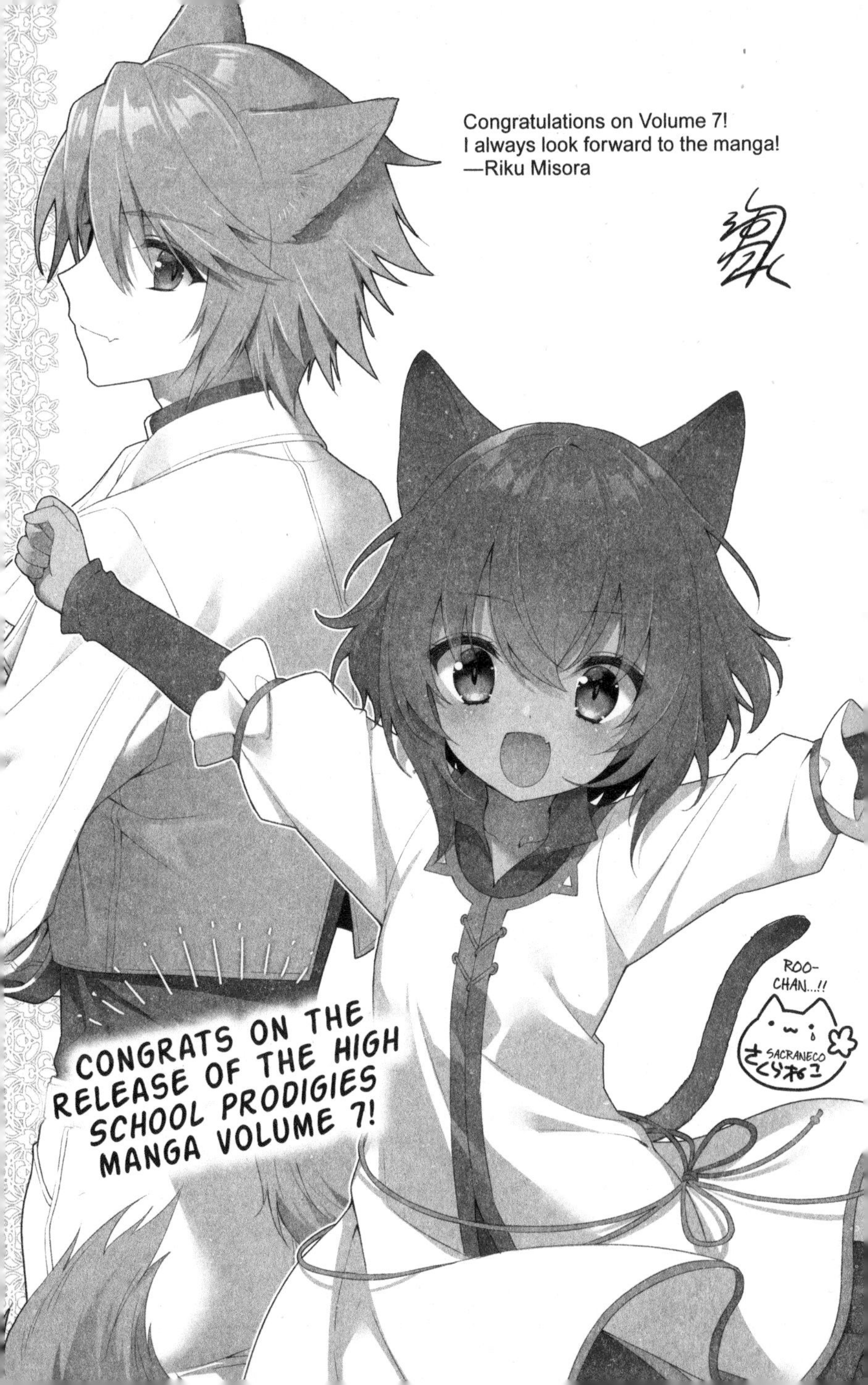
Congratulations on Volume 7!
I always look forward to the manga!
—Riku Misora
CONGRATS ON THE RELEASE OF THE HIGH SCHOOL PRODIGIES MANGA VOLUME 7!
ROO-CHAN...!!
SACRANECO
さくらねこ

HIGH SCHOOL PRODIGIES HAVE IT EASY EVEN IN ANOTHER WORLD!

Special Thanks

ORIGINAL STORY: RIKU MISORA
CHARACTER DESIGNS: SACRANECO
GA BUNKO
YG EDITOR
ASSISTANTS
AND YOU READERS

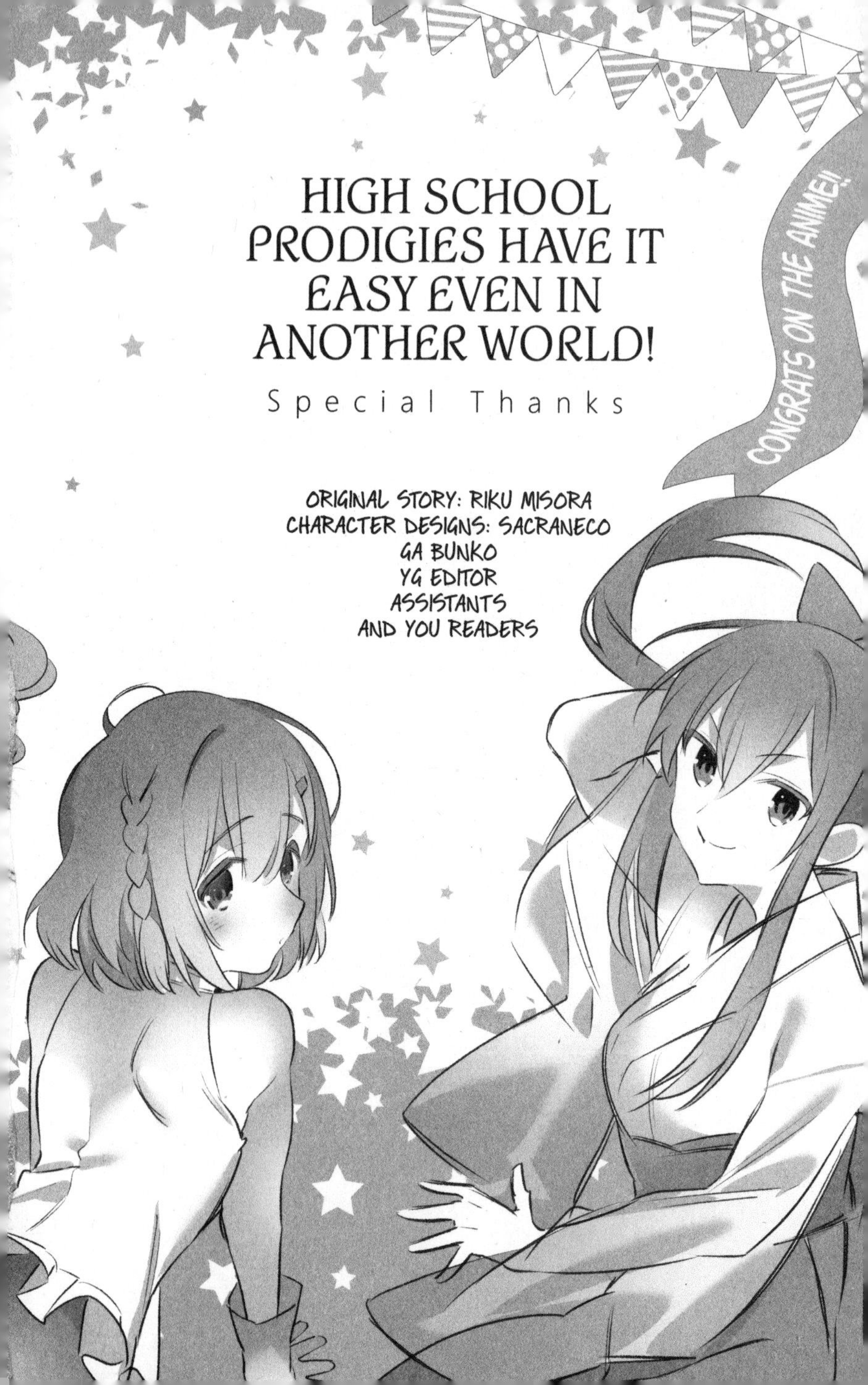
CONGRATS ON THE ANIME!!

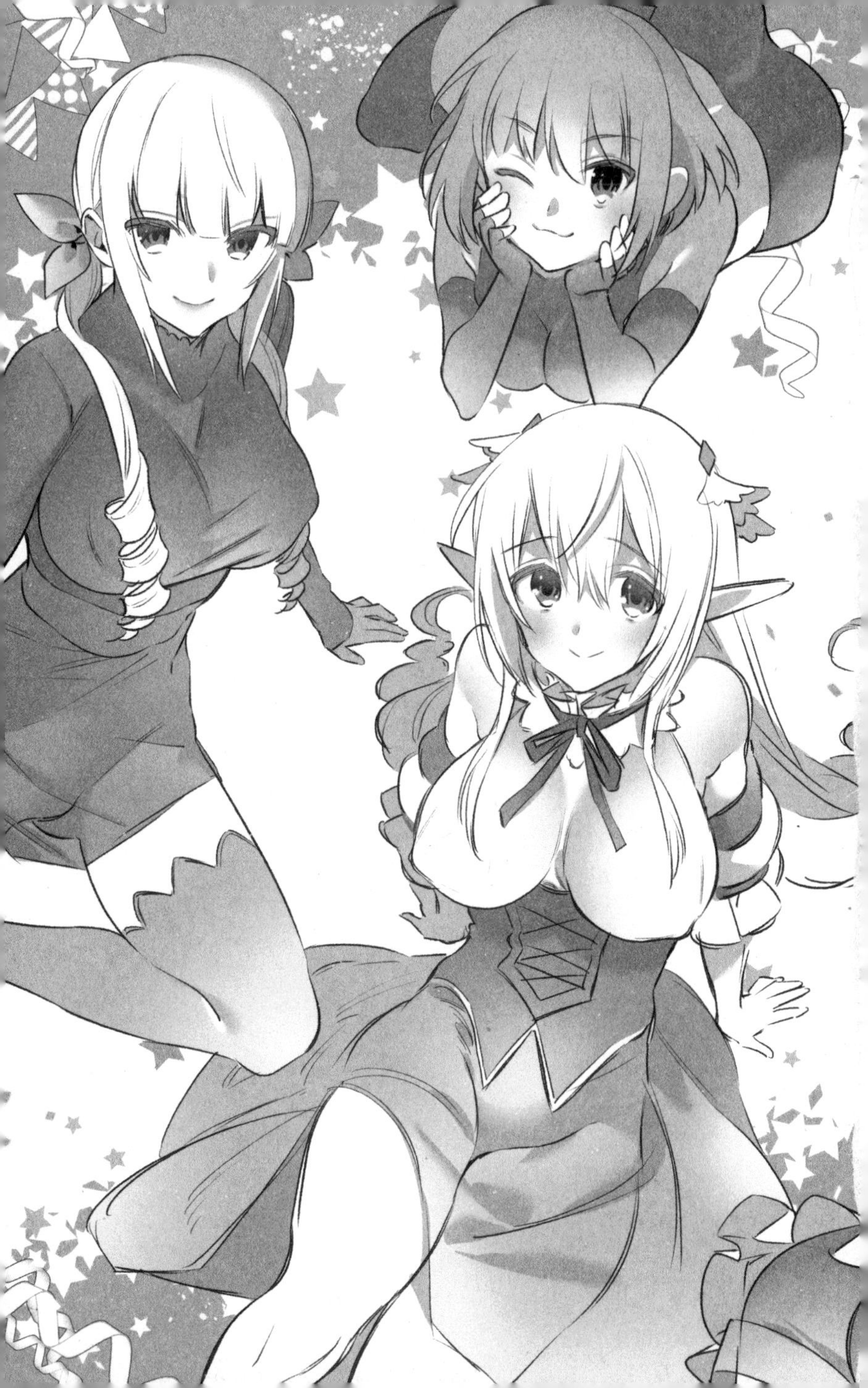

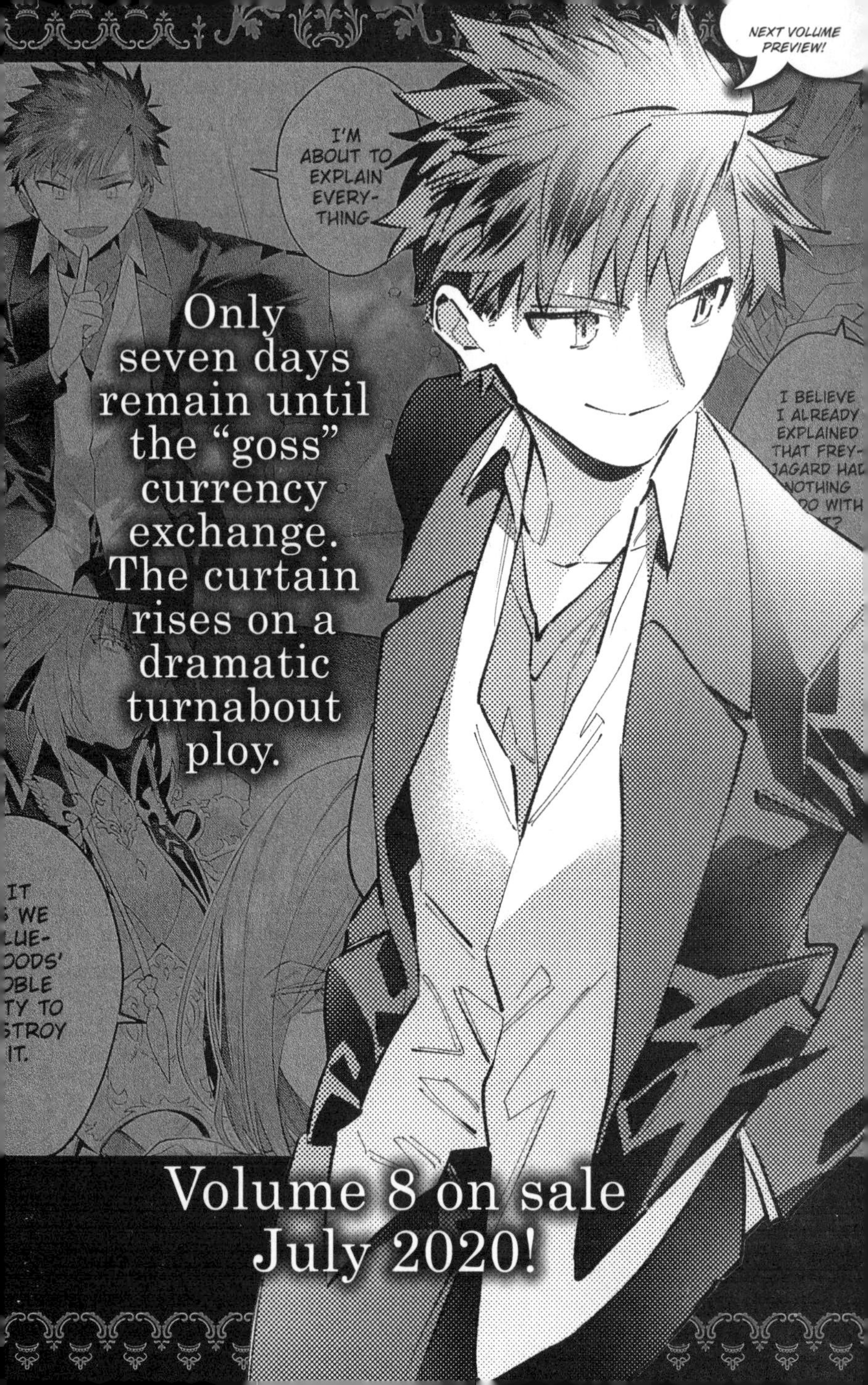
NEXT VOLUME PREVIEW!
I BELIEVE I ALREADY EXPLAINED THAT FREY-JAGARD HAD NOTHING
I'M ABOUT TO EXPLAIN EVERY-THING.
Only seven days remain until the "goss" currency exchange. The curtain rises on a dramatic turnabout ploy.
Volume 8 on sale July 2020!

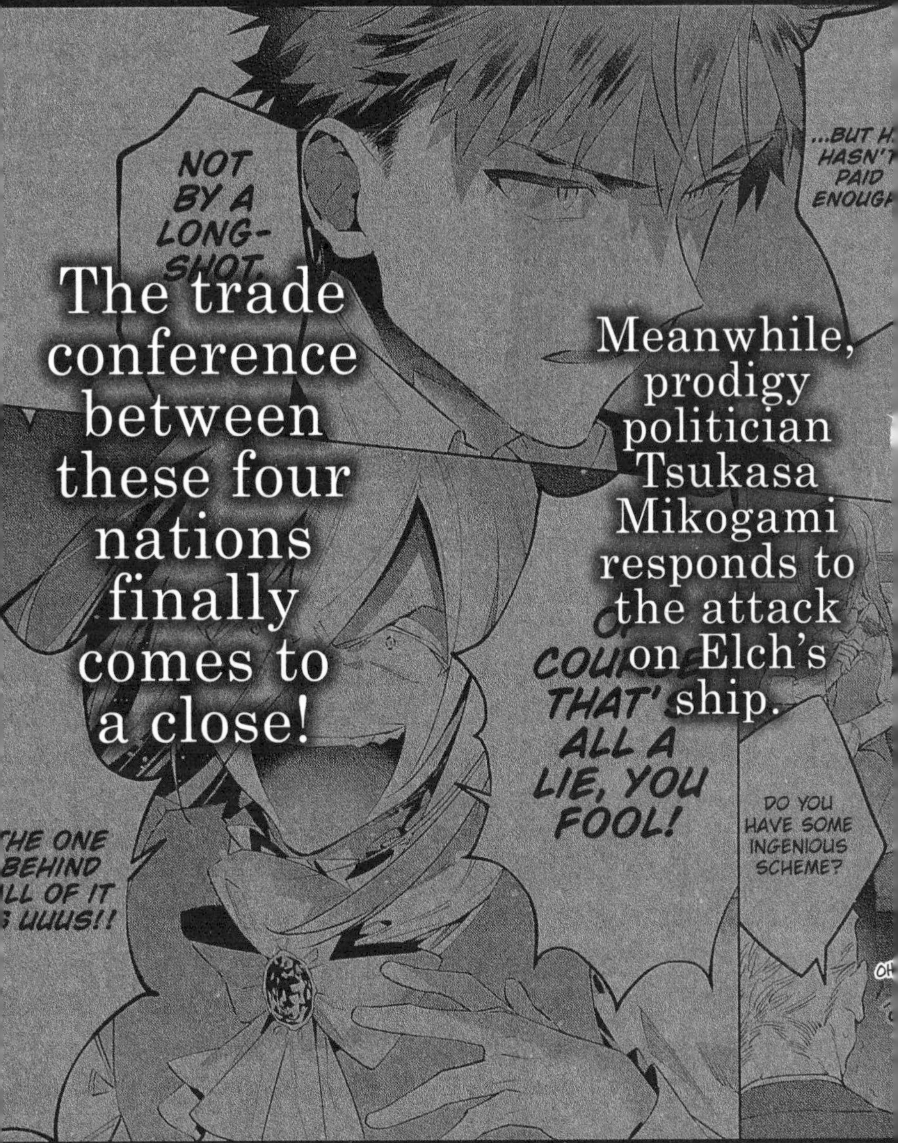

...BUT H HASN'T PAID ENOUG
NOT BY A LONG-SHOT.
DO YOU HAVE SOME INGENIOUS SCHEME?
OH
COU THAT' ALL A LIE, YOU FOOL!
HE ONE BEHIND LL OF IT UUUS!!

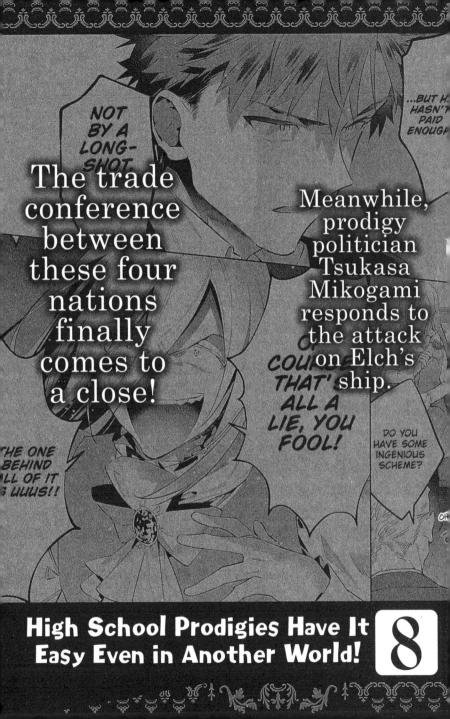

The trade conference between these four nations finally comes to a close!

Meanwhile, prodigy politician Tsukasa Mikogami responds to the attack on Elch's ship.

High School Prodigies Have It Easy Even in Another World! 8

High School Prodigies Have It Easy Even in Another World!

Volume VII

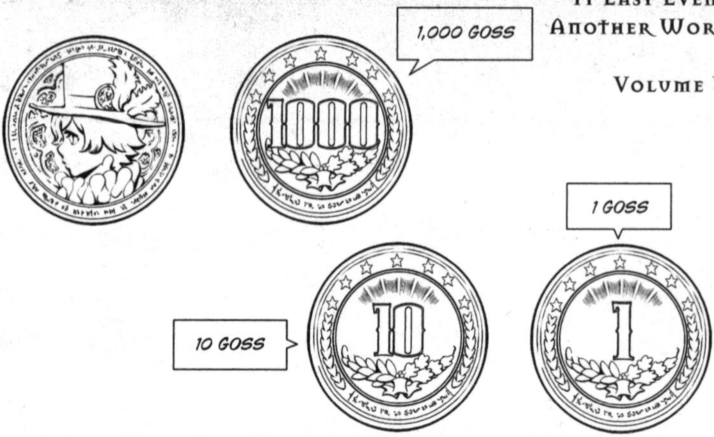

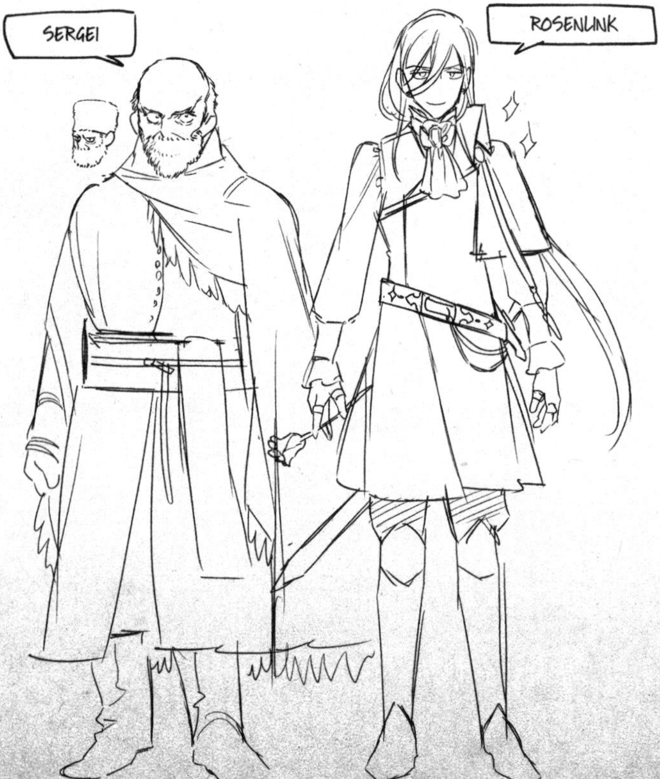

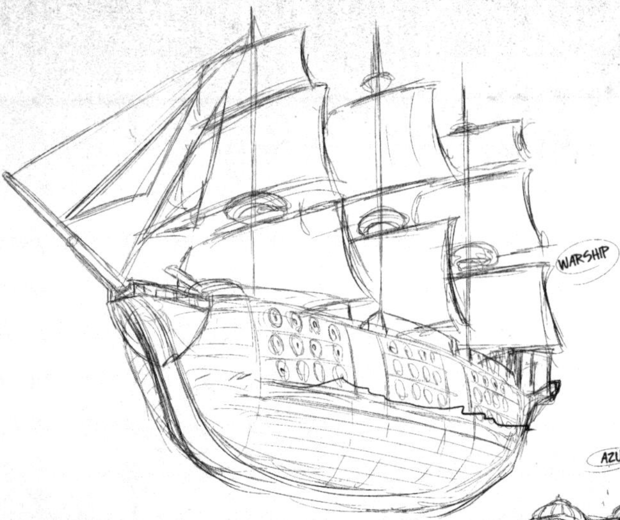
WARSHIP

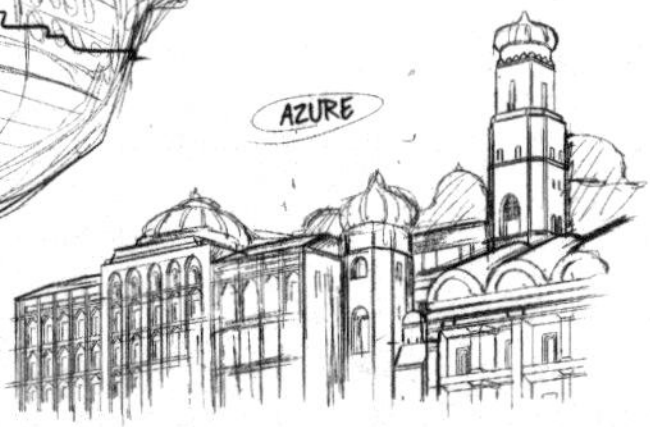
AZURE

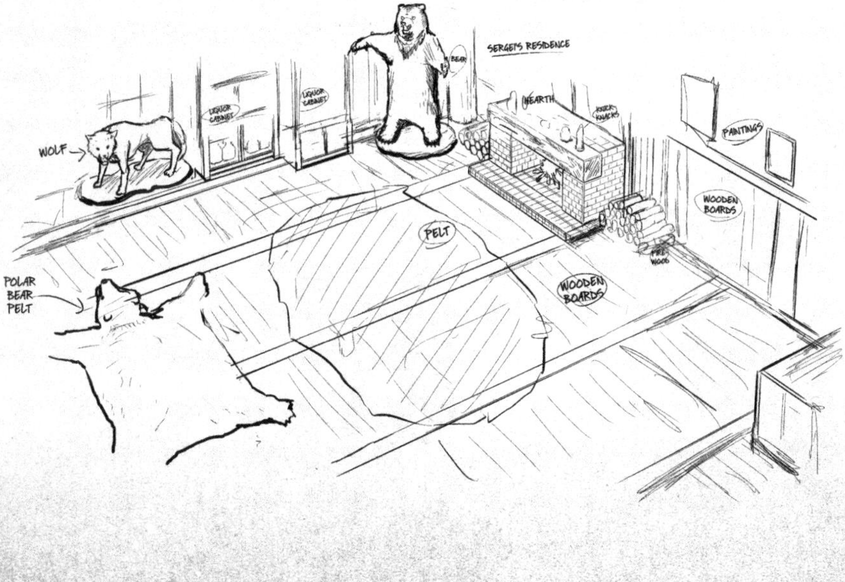
SERGEI'S RESIDENCE
BEAR
LIQUOR CABINET
LIQUOR CABINET
HEARTH
KNICK KNACKS
PAINTINGS
WOLF
WOODEN BOARDS
PELT
FIRE WOOD
POLAR BEAR PELT
WOODEN BOARDS

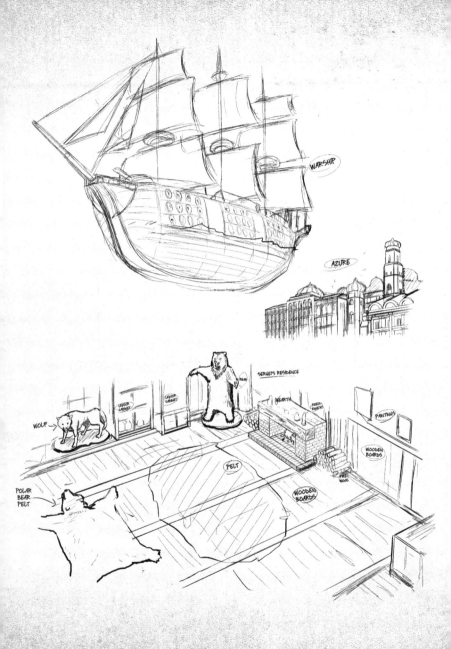

RED IS THE NEW BLACK IN THIS BLOODY, ACTION-PACKED SERIES ABOUT A GROUP OF RIGHTEOUS ASSASSINS!

Teenage country bumpkin Tatsumi dreams of earning enough money for his impoverished village by working in the Capital—but his short-lived plans go awry when he's robbed by a buxom beauty upon arrival! Penniless, Tatsumi is taken in by the lovely Miss Aria, but just when his Capital dreams seem in reach yet again, Miss Aria's mansion is besieged by Night Raid—a team of ruthless assassins who targets high-ranking members of the upper class! As Tatsumi is quick to learn, appearances can be deceiving in the Capital, and this team of assassins just might be... the good guys?!

Akame ga KILL!

FULL SERIES AVAILABLE NOW!

HE DOES NOT LET ANYONE ROLL THE DICE.

A young Priestess joins her first adventuring party, but blind to the dangers, they almost immediately find themselves in trouble. It's Goblin Slayer who comes to their rescue—a man who has dedicated his life to the extermination of all goblins by any means necessary. A dangerous, dirty, and thankless job, but he does it better than anyone. And when rumors of his feats begin to circulate, there's no telling who might be calling next...

Light Novel V. 1-9 Available Now!

Check out the simul-pub manga chapters every month!

Yen Press YEN ON
www.yenpress.com

High School Prodigies Have It Easy Even in Another World! 7

STORY BY **Riku Misora**   ART BY **Kotaro Yamada**

CHARACTER DESIGN BY **Sacraneco**

TRANSLATION: CALEB D. COOK
LETTERING: BRANDON BOVIA

CHOUJIN KOUKOUSEI TACHI WA ISEKAI DEMO YOYU DE IKINUKU YOUDESU! vol. 7
© Riku Misora / SB Creative Corp. Character Design: Sacraneco
© 2019 Kotaro Yamada / SQUARE ENIX CO., LTD.
First published in Japan in 2019 by SQUARE ENIX CO., LTD.
English translation rights arranged with SQUARE ENIX CO., LTD.
and Yen Press, LLC through Tuttle Mori Agency, Inc.

English translation © 2020 by SQUARE ENIX CO., LTD.

Yen Press
150 West 30th Street, 19th Floor
New York, NY 10001

Visit us at yenpress.com

facebook.com/yenpress
twitter.com/yenpress

yenpress.tumblr.com
instagram.com/yenpress

First Yen Press Edition: April 2020

Yen Press is an imprint of Yen Press, LLC.
The Yen Press name and logo are trademarks of Yen Press, LLC.

Library of Congress Control Number: 2018948324

ISBNs: 978-1-9753-0889-6 (paperback)
978-1-9753-0890-2 (ebook)

10 9 8 7 6 5 4 3 2 1

BVG

Printed in the United States of America